Trump IS UNFIT

The Most Unfit Presidential Nominee Ever

LARRY F. MURPHY

CMM Publishing

The opinions expressed in this manuscript are solely the opinions of the author and do not represent the opinions or thoughts of the publisher. The author has represented and warranted full ownership and/or legal right to publish all the materials in this book.

TRUMP IS UNFIT
The Most Unfit Presidential Nominee Ever
All Rights Reserved.
Copyright © 2016 Larry F. Murphy
v1.0

Cover Photo © 2016 thinkstockphotos.com. All rights reserved - used with permission.

This book may not be reproduced, transmitted, or stored in whole or in part by any means, including graphic, electronic, or mechanical without the express written consent of the publisher except in the case of brief quotations embodied in critical articles and reviews.

CMM Publishing

ISBN: 978-0-578-18464-7

PRINTED IN THE UNITED STATES OF AMERICA

FLASH NOTICE!!!

Hillary Rodham Clinton, Democratic Presidential Nominee 2016
The Most Qualified Presidential Nominee in U.S. History

Vs.

Donald John Trump, Republican Presidential Nominee 2016
The Most Unqualified Presidential Nominee in U.S. History

Character, Academies, Experience, and Love for Country and People

VOTE Hillary Rodham Clinton!!!

Table of Contents

Acknowledgements i

Preface iii

1. Arrogant Pride a Major Disqualifier 1
2. Trump's Arrogant Pride Behavior 18
3. Trump Gives New Life to White Supremacists 27
4. God's Truth at Work 49
5. The Truth's Transcending Power 55
6. America's Religious Status 73
7. Understanding Mindsets 85
8. A Fool's Profile and Actions 89
9. Republican Delegate Refuses to Vote for Trump 100
10. Donald Trump's Hero—Saddam Hussein 107
11. U.S. Supreme Court Justice Calls Trump a Fake 131
12. Trump University a Fake/a True Con 144

13. Trump's Income Tax Returns—Bombshells 161

14. Trump verses Truth 191

15. Trump's Call for Violence at Rallies 202

16. Trump the Cult Leader 216

17. Trump's Acceptance Speech Confirms His Hatred..................... 233

18. Minds Resonating with Trump's Ideology 252

19. Trump's Black Soul.. 274

20. Republicans Disavowing or Repudiating Donald Trump............ 293

21. Clinton's E-mail Server Issue Resolved 306

22. Clinton's Benghazi Issue Resolved 314

23. Trump's Audacity to Question Clinton's Faith 329

24. The Ban on Assault Weapons... 334

25. Trump's Idiocy is Endless 348

Author's Closing Comments 373

Acknowledgements

First and foremost, I am profoundly thankful and grateful to God, the Father of our Lord and Savior Jesus Christ for His Holy Spirit who has supplied me abundantly with grace and guided me into unchartered areas of knowledge, wisdom, and understanding to accomplish this project. Secondly, I am profoundly thankful and grateful to my wife Linda for her unconditional love in caring for me, especially, during my time of injury and nursing me back into a healthy condition that now allows me to take care of myself (at least I try to; but I still need her). I also so very thankful and grateful to Linda for sacrificing all the time that I was away from her to work on completing this project; many times it was hard, but she endured and stuck by me.

Thirdly, I am profoundly thankful and grateful to God for Roxie (our dog), who is so loving and caring to us and brings laughter and joy into our home like only Roxie is capable of doing. She is now 11 years old and had 2 operations this year to remove cancer from her inner legs; she's doing just fine and we are so thankful and grateful to God for taking care of her and preserving her for our company and joy. Many or most ever time I've come in from working on this project, Roxie always meets me with excitement and lets me know how pleased she is to see me; and in return, we have our conversations while I rub her and we exchange kisses. She has been and continue to be a very vital part of our lives.

Fourthly, I am profoundly thankful and grateful to the NEWS MEDIA (via TV, radio, newspapers, magazines, web pages and blogs) for providing vitally important information to the general public. These painstaking tasks require a special brand of people with a great degree of dignity, respect, and temperament, especially under adverse conditions when attempting to obtain information from difficult and somewhat disrespectful people having their own personal agendas. Great job to all of you; be encouraged and keep up the good works.

Therefore I personally salute CNN, NPR, MSNBC, CBS, New York Times, Washington Post, local television, local radio, Fox News, Yahoo News, Google News, local newspapers, web sites, Mother Jones and all other sources for providing me such a variety of information to read, examine, evaluate, and compare that assisted in driving my mind into creative thought processing that aided me in the creation and production of this project. With information from these MEDIA sources, along with some information from Wikipedia, and of course, the source of all truth, the Holy Bible, I was able to accomplish this project for the benefit of WE THE PEOPLE.

Fifthly, and finally, I want to acknowledge and thank Outskirts Press for reviewing my work and providing some very important guidance. Through Outskirts Press' guidance I was able to review and submit a final work that should have been submitted in the first place; as a result, I'm thoroughly pleased with my final manuscript and will be extremely cautious in the future before submitting anything prematurely and without due thought; thanks again!

[24] *Now to Him who is able to keep you from stumbling, And to present you faultless Before the presence of His glory with exceeding joy,* [25] *To God our Savior, Who alone is wise, Be glory and majesty, Dominion and power, Both now and forever. Amen. (Jude 24-25)*

Preface

November 8, 2016 Election Day will be one of the most important days in history for most of us, just as it was on November 4, 2008 when WE THE PEOPLE elected Barack Obama as our 44th President of the United States of America, the first (1st) African American to be elected to that office. He was subsequently elected to a second (2nd) term over former Massachusetts Governor Mitt Romney on November 6, 2012, in which Obama received 332 electoral votes, 65,915,776 popular votes, and carried 26 states plus Washington, D.C.

Now, Barack Obama is campaigning for Democratic Presidential Nominee Hillary Rodham Clinton and WE THE PEOPLE have real important reasons to join Obama and his vice president Joe Biden and their families in supporting Hillary Clinton to become the 45th President Elect on November 8, 2016. Just what are these real important reasons that WE THE PEOPLE should support Hillary Clinton; I'm honored, thankful, and exceedingly grateful to present them to America and the rest of the world.

She's of the Christian faith and has strived to manifest the royal law of love as a public servant, which begin in 1973 when she graduated from Yale Law School at age 25, and that very year joined the Children's Defense Fund, and advocacy group for children. She then joined the House Judiciary Committee and worked on the impeachment of

President Nixon. Afterwards she taught law in Arkansas for three (3) years (while running a legal aid clinic) before joining the Rose Law Firm, a prominent corporate firm in Little Rock. Although she has not always drawn a paycheck for her political work, it's very clear from her resume that public service, involving particularly, the welfare of children has been a major focus for her career and outside activities.

As first lady of Arkansas, she was active in several groups involving education, child welfare and poverty. In 1977, President Carter appointed her to the board of directors for the Legal Services Corporation, a federal agency that provided legal aid to the poor. She was co-founder of Arkansas Advocates for Children and Families and she served as president and a member of the group's board of directors until 1984. She also chaired an advisory committee on rural health, served on a task force on infant mortality and chaired an Arkansas education task force. She chaired the Children's Defense Fund board from 1986 through 1992. This work occurred while she was practicing corporate law at the Rose Law Firm.

She also had parental responsibilities. Her daughter Chelsea was born in 1980, after she had been at the law firm for four (4) years. Like many women, her life was a juggling act. She had her family, her full-time job and she had these other activities that really were on the side. Her legal work gave her entree into the corporate world: She served on the boards of Wal-Mart, the yogurt chain TCBY and the French building materials company Lafarge. She became first lady of the White House when her husband (Bill Clinton) was elected president November 3, 1992. He, like Obama was subsequently elected to a second (2nd) term over former Kansas Senator Bob Dole on November 5, 1996, in which Clinton received 379 electoral votes, and 47,401,185 popular votes, and carried 31 states plus Washington, D.C.

Prior to the Bill Clinton administration the U.S. government suffered budget deficits every year from 1970 through 1997. In 1998 the federal government finally recorded a surplus.

It's also very important to note that there were also budget surpluses in 1999, 2000 and in 2001; and that 2001 was the last year the

Clinton administration proposed the budget that incoming President elect George Walker Bush the 43rd President rejected and created a federal debt of 4.9 trillion dollars. Of course, Hillary left the Rose Law Firm and while being first lady was a part of her husband's success as President.

By most accounts, she was one of the more active first ladies in U.S. history. In contrast to some predecessors (Mamie Eisenhower once described her duties as "Ike runs the country. I turn the pork chops"), Clinton became especially involved in public policy. She chaired the White House task force that made an unsuccessful proposal to provide universal health care and she played a key role in creating a children's health care program. Soon after the legislation passed, the New York Times reported, "Participants in the campaign for the health bill both on and off Capitol Hill said the first lady had played a crucial behind-the-scenes role in lining up White House support."

As first lady, she advised her husband on Cabinet appointments and senior White House staff positions; she also was active on welfare reform and foreign policy issues. Her activism was quite unprecedented. It has been said that if she had been given a title that matched her role at the White House it would have been Special Counsel to the President of the U.S. of America.

She served as the 67th United States Secretary of State, under President Barack Obama, from 2009 to 2013, overseeing the department that conducted the foreign policy of the Obama administration. She was preceded in office by Condoleezza Rice, and succeeded by John Kerry.

Hillary Clinton has an amazing 35 years of political experience which she mixed with her duties as a corporate lawyer and as a mother. Her resume and interviews with her biographers show she as having a wide range of political and public service roles for some 35 years plus; a quite impressive resume for the position she's seeking as President of the United States of America. Some believe her to be the most qualified presidential nominee ever; quite a complement and recognition by some experienced and successful politicians.

The next President needs to have a consensus-building mentality, that is, cross the isles and find common ground from which to build the future of our nation; consensus building involves multiple perspectives and opinions from Democrats, Republicans, Liberals and Green Party members; there are some (may be few) godly people in all four (4) parties. He or she needs to be effective and resolute in the decision making process from all levels of his or her administration. A wise President will guide and encourage convergent thinking (the ability to give the "correct" answer to standard questions that do not require significant creativity).

The next President should be able to create collaborative trigger teams (people with the best and brightest skills in our nation, crossing party lines, to lead some dramatic trigger teams to solve the huge problems we're facing with jobs, energy, and social issues, including, but not limited to, racism. As such, he or she should have the ability to encourage dynamic conflict resolution (focus in on mediation between the various perspectives; being a peacemaker and a unity-builder similar to Nelson Mandela and his Ubuntu philosophy.

The next president should have the ability to facilitate high stakes, open meetings where the best information is shared; political groupthink is stopped in its tracks and moving forward means making a difference in actions and deeds. He or she should make it easy for American citizens to see what actually goes on in government; if coalitions block or resist change, open meetings should be held in front of the American people so we can see who/what is causing the problem. This would clearly reveal the racism and/or foolish unnecessary and unproductive actions of others, which should be to their shame.

The next president should be able to communicate a clear and inspiring vision to his or her administration and our country. Being we're a divided nation when it comes to vision, he or she needs to know that his or her success will fail if he or she just stands and tries to pull others to his or her side. Our next President will need to rise above politics and inspire a vision that includes all, which all will be willing to support. This will require much prayer so as to make good godly judgments in all matters pertaining to the people of this nation. "Where there is no vision the people perish" (Prov. 28:18).

The next president should have the aptitude to handle and manage the effects of constant, complex change and innovation. Collective knowledge is continuously accumulating, bring upon massive change at alarming and unexpected ways and times. He or she must be a change champion of building coalitions of change, the case for change, and a vision for how America is to change in incorporating these changes. As Winston Churchill said, "Courage is the first of human qualities because it is the quality that guarantees all the others." We need a President who demonstrates enormous courage in the face of all that we need to change.

The next president should be capable of communicating the message of motivation that gives confidence to a fatigued nation. We need a President that can motivate with honesty and integrity; not with empty and persuasive words that are meaningless and allusive to deceive. Motivation is an emotional, not logical, force based on competency, autonomy, meaningfulness, and progress. With all that has happened within the last 15 years, including, but not limited to, 9/11, the loss of moral fiber in banking and business, and the economic downturn that goes on and on. Our country needs a president that's first godly, and encouraged to encourage others to stay fast in the faith and our God will provide.

The next president should be capable of establishing and maintaining trust between the people and the government, a trust based on credibility from competency and character. He or she must work diligently and consistently in restoring the trust of the American people in our government. He or she should strive being credible in what he or she is doing, having his or her competency demonstrate excellence and his or her character being above reproach. Efforts must seriously be implemented to restore and to maintain this trust between the people and the government. Only through an honesty and integrity approach is this possible to accomplish.

The next president should have the capability and temperament to cross party lines and negotiate the terms of his or her presidency and the direction of the country. He or she must be a master negotiator who works faithfully and deliberately on both the substantive issues as well as the relationship ones. Fisher and Ury in Getting to Yes, suggest "in fact, the ongoing relationship is far more important than the outcome of any particular negotiation." Imagine a new president who builds from a Zone of Acceptance, rather than accentuating the Zone of Rejection, who acts outside others' expectations so that they will be more open to hearing what he or she has to say.

The next president should be able to implement smart, measurable, attainable, results-oriented and time-bound goals that our country can support and feel enthusiastic about moving upon. John Kennedy moved us out of complacency with his "man on the moon" goal; Lyndon Johnson did the same with his "war on poverty." How about a goal of "restoration of America to great-nation status with God? And how about obedience to Him, being the catalyst or Person that precipitates this restoration in America; how about that?

The next president should be able to manage a multitude of diverse, eccentric, complex personalities both in his or her party and across the aisle. The best leaders know how to manage boundaries, including difficulty personalities. They refuse to let the "toxic" minority cripple the majority. They understand their own personality blind spots and build leadership teams that bring diversity of thought to compensate for those shortcomings.

The next president should be a one-of-kind, an amazing level 5 leader with aspirations to improve upon what's already established for the good of the people; whether it's adding some things, or deleting some things. Such a highly qualified person should be able to bring us together with a clear and commanding picture of all happening within our nation, whether good or bad, and what he or she plans to do about it. He or she needs to be a leader with amazing courage to do what is unlikely; who surprises us with his or her compassion, intellect, humility, unwavering faith and overwhelming commitment to the good of our nation and its people without anyone being excluded.

The next president should work at making our education system work for all children, especially those with disadvantages, and to make college affordable for everyone having a desire and will to go. Continuing along the line of education, the next president should work at getting student debt off the backs of younger people so they can enter the workforce debt-free of student loans. How do college students desire to spell student debt, that is, DEBT-FREE!

The next president should strive to end secret, unaccountable money in politics that's corrupting our political system and drowning out the voices of WE THE PEOPLE. Our next president should be one who appoints Supreme Court Justices who value the "right to vote" over the right of billionaires to buy elections. As such, our next president should be one who pushes for a constitutional amendment to overturn CITIZENS UNITED (a conservative 501 (c) 4 non-profit organization) to restore the government to citizens' control.

The next president should be one who seeks to protect our God-given free-will to choose, that is, the power to act and make our own choices without the constraint of necessity of fate; the ability to act at one's own discretion and according to one's own conscience. Although we may not all agree with another person's choice, we are obligated to acknowledge and respect that person's free-will to make his or her decision according to his or her own conscience.

The next president must be one who is all inclusive, that no matter where you come from, what you look like, who you love, or how much money you make, regardless of your race, color, nationality, your physical ability or disability, your sexual orientation, we as creations of God and members of humanity have a commandment to love one another and not to hate anyone. Although some of us sincerely disagree with behavior practices of some others, we are not to hate but to witness through our love what God requires without forcing anything upon anyone.

The next president must be one who understands our constitutional rights and civil liberties (the freedom of a citizen to exercise customary rights, as of speech or assembly, without unwarranted or arbitrary interference by the government), which do not always agree or concur with godly standards provided by Scripture. Yet, such choices are individual rights of free-will which may be abominations to God according to the Scriptures; yet, even God Himself does not force or coerce anyone to conform to His word; but rather, allows every person to choose the path he or she goes of his or her own free-will. Our choices result in either rewards or consequences. God is the true and righteous Judge, and vengeance belongs to Him, who will repay as He has promised.

The next president must be one who does not divide us, but rather, one who brings us together, because there's strength in unity. Such a person should accomplish this unity by pushing forward on the values that united us as Americans through the process of commitment and tenacity of us all as WE THE PEOPLE.

Our next president needs to be one that sees and understands the inequality that persists in every aspect of our society. Such a person needs to be one able to create more good-paying jobs and raise incomes on existing jobs so that working people can live above the poverty level and take care of their families without working 2 or more jobs. Such a person should strengthen our infrastructure and raise the minimum wage to at least $12 an hour, which would take away the tremendous burden and accompanying anxiety of caring and providing for family.

The next president should stand-up to the gun lobby and get common sense gun safety measures. Enough is enough, and the foolishness associated with this issue has long passed its expiration date. In order to accomplish this and other sensitive issues, our next president has to be one that shows empathy and seeks to guarantee paid family and medical leave by making the wealthiest taxpayers pay their fair share, rather than, pocketing for themselves and paying their executives big unmerited bonuses.

Empathy is a must; staying at home to take care of a sick child or spouse, or an aging parent can now mean losing a paycheck or even a job in some cases; which is a choice that no one should be forced to make; and yet now, many American workers are forced to make such a choice every day that brings upon difficulty and anxiety because of the absence of empathy in upper management. No parent or spouse or care-taker for an elder parent should have to worry about doing that which is morally and ethically right; it's our duty and it's our obligation.

Our next president needs to be one who builds upon what has already been started that's proven good for WE THE PEOPLE. The Affordable Care Act needs to be built upon and expanded, finished to ensure universal health care for every man, woman, and child. Without proper and adequate health care, many people die and suffer unnecessarily before dying. In the best interest of humanity, universal health care for every man, woman, and child is essential.

Our next president needs to understand that climate change is not a hoax, but a reality that should be taken very seriously. Climate change needs to be combated by turning America into a clean energy superpower of the 21st century. Our next president should set national goals for solar panels installation for generating enough renewable energy to power every home in America and to bring greenhouse gas emissions well below what they were a decade ago.

Our next president must not be one who does not bring to WE THE PEOPLE a message of patriotism and hope, but a message stoking our anxieties about the economy, national security, and fears about the country WE THE PEOPLE love. The next president must not have an image of America being an inhabited crippled country because of thousands of immigrants flooding across the borders and stealing hard-earned jobs from Americans. Our next president must not be one who spreads widely discredited rumors, such as, that thousands of Muslims in New Jersey cheered the September 11, 2001 attacks on the Twin Towers and see the Paris attacks followed by the San Bernardino, California shooting as warning signs and President Obama's failure to confront "radical Islamic terrorism;" WE THE PEOPLE cannot and must not have a president with this mindset.

WE THE PEOPLE do not need a president who has misled many be believe that America isn't safe anymore and does not feel like home as it has in the past. The next president does not need to be one who believes he and he alone can restore America's loss of greatness. We do not need a president that's incapable of providing a clear and precise message to WE THE PEOPLE, who have sentences continuously running together, one idea colliding with the next in a rhetorical chain reaction leaving WE THE PEOPLE in a state of confusion about what's said, or rather, unanswered. WE THE People do not need a president who needs a clean-up committee to explain what he really means and to implement damage-control on a continuous basis.

WE THE PEOLE do not need a president who is a demagogue, that is, a political leader who seeks support by appealing to popular desires and prejudices rather than by using rational argument. WE THE PEOPLE do not need a president who exploits the adversities of others, in particularly, senior citizens, in order to fatten his pockets to their pains, sufferings, and ruin. WE THE PEOPLE do not need a president who has committed financial abuse against the elderly (in California over age 65, and in Florida over age 60).

WE THE PEOPLE do not need a president having lawsuit actions where Plaintiffs allege that Trump University and Trump uniformly marketed and misrepresented their Live Events as offering Trump's real estate techniques taught by his "hand-picked" professors and adjunct professors at his elite "university." Plaintiffs allege that these representations were false because Trump had no substantive involvement in the selection of the Live Events instructors or the content of the Live Events and that the New York State Education Department warned Trump not to use the "university" title or to continue operating without a license, but he defied those directives.

WE THE PEOPLE do not need a president having a Cohen (Nationwide) Action alleging that the above fraudulent scheme violates the Racketeer Influenced and Corrupt Organizations Act ("RICO") and each member of the Class is entitled to triple the amount of their purchase price of Trump University Live Events.

WE THE PEOPLE do not need a president having a Low (California/Florida/New York) Action alleging that the above false statements constitute a violation of the unfair trade and competition and false advertising laws of California, Florida, and New York, as well as laws of California and Florida specifically protecting senior citizens from financial abuse.

WE THE PEOPLE do not need a president who vehemently refuses to release his tax returns. For more than four (4) decades or 40 years, presidential candidates have seemed to agree with the release of income tax returns' perspective, and every candidate since former President Carter has released income tax returns voluntarily to the public. A vehemently refusal to follow suite arouses very great suspicion of cheating or wrongdoing which WE THE PEOPLE have the right to know and do not need a president who vehemently refuses not to honor our right.

WE THE PEOPLE know and understand that income tax returns, when considered in conjunction with financial disclosure forms, help paint a fuller picture of the candidate's financial dealings; because it's a snapshot of one's financial positions and interests. From income tax returns WE THE PEOPLE can learn: 1) the yearly income of the candidate, 2) how was paid in taxes and the tax rate, 3) what deductions and tax credits were claimed, 4) real estate taxes and abatements, 5) investments, 6) how much was given to charity (which could shed light on his values and priorities), 7) to whom money is owed, 8) who he's in business with and the financial positions of those companies (whether they have gains or losses), and 8) if there's any indication money is being held offshore).

WE THE PEOPLE know and that the financial disclosure forms provide only: 1) outside income, 2) gifts, 3) assets/property owned, 4) specific investments/trusts, 5) possible conflicts of interest, 6) certain transactions/agreements made with businesses and people, 7) positions held at different companies outside the government, and 8) liabilities. Although presidents, unlike Congress, are exempt from conflict-of-interest laws, is exactly what makes disclosure of income tax returns especially important for shedding light on areas of possible conflicts of interest.

Donald Trump will not ever voluntarily release his tax returns, because this transparency will more than likely disclose wrongful things detrimental to his character and reputation, bring about his demise and ruin. However, I can assure WE THE PEOPLE that the attorneys who are representing the plaintiffs in the Trump University lawsuits will be successful in getting the income tax returns' records from the IRS with a state subpoena. Since the opposing counsels will not be able to get the income tax returns' records with a signed release by Donald Trump, the opposing counsels will file a Motion-to-Compel; and when Trump refuses to conform to the Motion-to-compel, the presiding judge will most likely allow opposing counsels for the plaintiffs to obtain Trump's income tax returns from the IRS; then WE THE PEOPLE and the rest of the world will know exactly what he's been hiding and boasting about.

1

Arrogant Pride a Major Disqualifier

ARROGANT PRIDE MAY be defined as the quality of having or displaying a sense of overbearing self-worth or self-importance. Such people's personality is marked or arisen from feelings or assumptions of their superiority towards others. Arrogant pride people show without hesitation contempt for the weak and/or poor and anyone they consider inferior to them in their own eyes. Because of the unmerited value they place on their self-worth or self-importance, anyone interfering with their selfish ambitions, including God, is a problem and enemy.

In order to be a follower of Christ the Bible says: "Then Jesus said to His disciples, "If anyone desires to come after Me, let him deny himself, and take up his cross, and follow Me" Therefore, because arrogant pride does not give room for self-denial, it's impossible for any arrogant pride person to be a true follower of Jesus Christ. Just going to a church that's Christian doesn't automatically entitle anyone with true Christian status, regardless of what he or she proclaims being. There are many hypocrites in Christian churches for alternative reasons.

The Ku Klux Klan (KKK), White Knights, Aryan nation, Skin heads and other groups who follow the ideology of Adolph Hilter are demon possessed. There's absolutely no where in the Bible that states: "Jews, blacks, and other people of color are inferior to the white race." In fact, Moses married an Ethiopian woman (black woman). These disciples of Satan try to hide behind the Holy Bible and make a mockery of it; in fact, they don't really know what they believe. Most who are members do not even believe in God or in the least, not the God of the Holy Bible.

By their own words they proclaim one must believe in God and the Holy Bible; yet, there are splinter groups that are into Satanism and Witchcraft. There is also a connection to the Masons, as many are members of both groups. These hypocrites claim they are standing for a white America while all the while showing the lost (their followers and potential followers) that it's perfectly alright to hate Jews, blacks, and other people of color. Nowhere does the Holy Bible condone hatred of anyone; but rather, it does condone hatred of sin, but, not the sinner.

Adolph Hitler was a fool, and he is sort of a hero to these fools. Most every page visited by the KKK and these other hate groups has some reference to Hitler and his beliefs. Hitler was fascinated with the occult (magic, witchcraft, sorcery, wizardry, diabolism, and the like); he was a drug addict who used them to achieve a higher consciousness into the spirit world of the dead. Hitler was a follower of Aleister Crowley, the father of today's Satanism. Sarcastically and with disgusting amusement, Hitler claimed being a Christian just as these hate mongers also do.

Christian Identity or Identity Christian (CI or IC) is a white supremacist religion which advocates the view that the Anglo-Saxon, Germanic, Nordic and kindred peoples are the descendants of the ancient Israelites and also the descendants of Abraham, Isaac, and Jacob. It is not an organized religion, instead it is independently practiced by individuals, churches, and some prison gangs. Its white supremacist theology promotes a racial interpretation of Christianity. The White Camelia Knights of the Ku Klux Klan is a Christian Identity Klan.

Christian Identity beliefs were primarily developed and promoted by two (2) authors who considered Europeans to be the "chosen people" and Jews to be the cursed offspring of the "serpent hybrid" (in Dual

Seedline Christian Identity) Cain. Many of these teachings were later adopted by white supremacist sects and gangs. Christian Identity also dictates that all non-whites (people not of wholly European descent) on the planet will either be exterminated or enslaved in order to serve the white race in the new heavenly kingdom on earth under the reign of Jesus Christ. In conclusion, Christian Identity doctrine states that non-whites can never achieve salvation or paradise, instead it states that only "Adamic" (white people) can achieve salvation and paradise.

Christian Identity is a religious ideology popular in extreme right-wing circles. Adherents believe that whites of European descent can be traced back to the "Lost Tribes of Israel." Many consider Jews to be the Satanic offspring of Eve and the Serpent,—while non-whites are "mud peoples" created before Adam and Eve.—Non-whites are referred to as mamzers (in modern Jewish culture is someone who is either born of adultery by a married Jewish woman and a Jewish man who is not her husband, or born of incest (as defined by the Bible), or someone who has a mamzer as a parent); or tares (children of the evil one, the devil).

The KKK and splinter groups are abominations to the Lord. They proclaim believing whole-heartedly in God and His Son Jesus Christ. They claim holding the Bible very dear and its teachings used in KKK thoughts and ideas. In fact, being a Christian is basically necessary for one to become a member of the KKK. As for material realities, the KKK focuses much attention on the physical differences between races and ethnicities; wherein, discriminating against blacks and other people of color because the KKK feel and believe these people being inferior to them.

The _objective of the KKK is to help the White Anglo-Saxon Christian people thrive and be superior to all other races._ They believe that white Christians are morally and spiritually superior. They believe in helping one another in order to keep their people strong as a united race. The KKK uses its elaborate robes and hooded white outfits as a way to hide their identities while also separating members from other ordinary citizens. The power recognized by the KKK does not seem to be strictly reserved for a divine being such as God. Instead, Klansmen feel that God's power is in every white Christian individual and can be realized by every KKK members.

The KKK has a very perverted view of God and Jesus Christ. While holding its perverted view of God the Father and God the Son high; Klansmen also believe in the power of each of its members. Together, these members create what the KKK refers to as "white power." Modern Klan groups are careful to refer to their ritual as "cross lighting" rather than "cross-burning" and insist that their fires symbolize faith in Christ. The days of so-called disciplinary burnings, they add, are long since over. In past times, the KKK burned crosses on hillsides or near homes of those they wished to induce fear and intimidate.

As we all may very well see, calling oneself a Christian and actually being a true born-again Christian, constitutes a tremendous contrast or difference. Without any doubt at all, "all who are members of the KKK and all with KKK mentalities—are of the devil, his children, and his will they desire to do. Do not be deceived: "no KKK member or person with a KKK mentality has the mind of Christ," which, "can only come through a genuine born-again experience of the Holy Spirit." Therefore, do not be deceived!

Scoffers are proud and haughty people who jeer or mock or treat other people with contempt or call out in derision (contemptuous ridicule or mockery). Such people's arrogance is boundless, as they manifest scorning of others in all types of manner. They are flouters, mockers, jeerers, disagreeable and very unpleasant people who should be avoided and/or withdrawn from as quickly as possible. They have no value to the people of God, nor to anyone else that may be seeking to change his or her life for the better. Withdraw from such as quick as possible!

Covertness (eagerness or cravenness to have or possess what some other person has) is a sinful attribute of arrogant pride people. Regardless of what they have, they're never satisfied; always wanting and craving for more. Such people show an intense selfish desire for things of the world, especially, wealth and power. They're never satisfied and are incapable of reaching or coming to a place of contentment, because of their self-ambitiousness and enviousness. They are avaricious, materialistic, progressive and mercenary, grasping at any and everything they can get; as fast as they can, and anything they can get it; regardless of who they might have to hurt to get it. These greedy people feel extremely painful when seeing others having things, money, or power they believe they should have instead, resulting in endless cravings on their behalves.

Arrogant pride people conversations are all about themselves; and when the center of attention moves from themselves to someone else, they get mad and irritated. Their arrogance (conceit, pride, self-importance, and egotism) and smugness (excessive feeling of offensive satisfaction in oneself; self-righteous complacency) are often reflections of limited life experiences and feeling overly concerned that those with greater life experiences have gotten something over on them. Rather than seeking to find out more through questions and learning (actions viewed by them as showing vulnerability); such arrogant pride people tend to generalize from their limited narrow life experiences, and try rather, to impose their small world view on others having considerable more experience in a particular subject matter of serious importance.

Arrogant pride people have an extremely strong need to look good in the presence of others. When anyone makes them look bad, even if it's the slightest offense, they will usually become very angry and mad, and blame the fault upon whoever it was that offended them. For example, when questioned by their appearance, intelligence, athletic ability, leadership ability, or anything else relating to their self-image, they're subject to lose it at any time and respond with outbursts of rage and anger; that's their nature. Their jealousies of other people's achievements or seeming lifestyles cause them to feel smug or arrogant about things they think they can do better than others and/or own or have that others have. They're extremely envious and jealous.

Arrogant pride is a spirit that arrogant pride people cannot control as they wish to control. This ugly spirit raises its racist and destructive head often without warning exposing those who are inhabiting it for who they are. When arrogant pride people's worldviews are challenged, they immediately become enraged from having others question their perfect little worlds. Most people at some point and time come to realize that the world doesn't revolve around them. Not so, for these people; they counteract by creating an atmosphere that does revolve around them; and get angry and mad if they're reminded of the real world (i.e. the world that seek to avoid having to contend with).

Ambiguity (uncertainty or inexactness; a lack of decisiveness or commitment resulting from a failure to make a choice between alternatives) frightens arrogant pride people; because it suggests imperfection, change, and lack of uncertainty (realities we all must contend with as best we can). As such, instead of accepting that the world behaves randomly and at times totally averse to their preferences, arrogant pride people seek to control everything and everybody, which of course, is an impossible mission. Nevertheless, they never stop trying!

Reality seriously hurts arrogant pride people when it intrudes in their lives expectantly. As such, they are less likely than other people to self-reflect and analyze their lives; wherein, never seeking their own imperfections. Such people very often give themselves undue credit for positive achievements, instead of acknowledging the input of others and/or the circumstances contributing to the positive achievements they're taking the credit in causing to happen. This is just the way they are; credit seekers; robbers of other people's achievements; fakes or phonies!

Arrogant pride people don't really have true friends; but rather, only fair-weather friends (i.e. those who stop being friends in times of difficulty). Such people can be happy with someone one day and hateful with the same people on the next day. Whatever mood they're in and whether or not someone is catering to their likes or dislikes determines how they treat their fair-weather friends. Arrogant pride people are struck on themselves, and as such, they're incapable of having truly good friends; egotism does not allow room for such quality friendship.

Such persons have a very strong need to look good and self-sufficiency is an effective way to accomplish this selfish sinful desire. Everybody needs somebody sometime; and the need is more often for some than others.

Since being a good friend to someone usually means helping them, arrogant pride people often cannot stand the thought, much less, the actuality of a good friendship. Ironically, they often cannot understand why they don't have any reliable and supportive friends. How can they with the arrogant and destructive character they bring to the table? Most reasonable people are more than likely anxious to exit their presence. What joy and profit is there being around or in the midst of such obnoxious, intolerable, and despicable people: they're just not worth being around.

Arrogant pride people are inherently negative about those with different beliefs, cultural backgrounds, and ways of seeing the world, due primarily to their own over-zealousness and ignorance of other people. Such people work extremely hard in avoiding those who contradict their fantasy land (i.e. people in their world that caters to them and them only) based upon their general personality and the people they're interacting with. Many time or most often, such people have a very serious "my ways-the only way" attitudes, which is simply, a protective mechanism for their false images or fantasy lands, as demonstrated in their actions, talks, and use of their social statuses. They are usually more than willing to show their cruel side to those whom they dislike; but actually, in reality, hate (which is a primary quality of their character). When being cruel to others, their fair-weather friends will usually ignore it or not do anything to stop it; since they're afraid they'll also be treated bad.

Arrogant pride people see people they don't like as rivalries, annoyances, and enmities. When they hear names of such persons in the mentioned categories, their condemnation is mostly harsh, because they see such persons as threats to their perfect little fantasy worlds.

The more they hate someone, the more dangerous that person or persons are to their fantasy lands; and in turn, the bigger the threat, and the harsher the criticism. They say bad and terrible things about people they don't like. They're very pretentious, wherein, appearing being nice in people's faces, but talking about them behind their backs like it's their favorite hobby. They often, subconsciously know that they don't really have any good friends; so they compensate for this by creating the impression that they have lots of friends. They actually have quantity not quality mentalities; simply insulting their trophy friends when they're not looking or backs are turned.

Arrogant pride people are often trying to hide certain vulnerabilities and fears. Behind their exterior shells of self-confidence, lie weak and frighten people. Most of the time, the need for a strong and unquestionable self-image comes out of deeply rooted pain. Those who push themselves through the brusqueness (abrupt discourteous manners of speech and actions) can possibly free some arrogant pride people to be truer to themselves, rather than, fiercely shielding themselves from what's actually hurting them and causing this type of unacceptable and destructive behavior.

Arrogant pride people tend to have enormous amounts of vulnerability trends hiding behind their arrogant pride, which lends to overcompensating, so that the vulnerability is deeply suppressed. For example, some arrogant pride people grew up poor and later became much better off, and some even rich. As such, they now may be snobbish (i.e. having or exhibiting an exaggerated respect for high social position or wealth who seeks to associate with social superiors and dislikes people or activities regarded as lower-class; believing their tastes in a particular area are superior to those of other people) about everything they can now afford; in doing so, they are now covering-up the fear of poverty from the past.

Arrogant pride involves the doctrine of supremacism (the worldwide view that a particular age, race, species, ethnic group, religion, gender, social class, belief system, or culture is superior to other variations of that same trait, and advocates those identifying with it to being dominate or in control of those who are not). The KKK in America has been the most notorious and infamous of this supremacism. Founded in 1866 after the Civil War, the KKK members adopted masks and robes that hid their identities and added to the drama of their night rides, their chosen time for attacks. Many of them operated in small towns and rural areas where people otherwise knew each other's faces, and sometimes still recognized the attackers by voice and mannerisms. "The kind of thing that men are afraid or ashamed to do openly, and by day, they accomplish secretly, masked, and at night." The KKK night riders "sometimes claimed to be ghosts of Confederate soldiers so, as they claimed, to frighten superstitious blacks. Few freedmen took such nonsense seriously."

The Klan attacked black members of the Loyal Leagues and intimidated southern Republicans and Freedmen's Bureau workers. When they killed black political leaders, they also took heads of families, along with the leaders of churches and community groups, because these people had many roles in society. Agents of the Freedmen's Bureau reported weekly assaults and murders of blacks. "Armed guerrilla warfare killed thousands of Negroes; political riots were staged; their causes or occasions were always obscure, their results always certain: ten to one hundred times as many Negroes were killed as whites." Masked men shot into houses and burned them, sometimes with the occupants still inside. They drove successful black farmers off their land. "Generally, it can be reported that in North and South Carolina, in 18 months ending in June 1867, there were 197 murders and 548 cases of aggravated assault."

Klan violence worked to suppress black voting, and campaign seasons were deadly. More than 2,000 persons were killed, wounded and otherwise injured in Louisiana within a few weeks prior to the Presidential election of November 1868. Although St. Landry Parish had a registered Republican majority of 1,071, after the murders, no Republicans voted in the fall elections. White Democrats cast the full vote of the parish for President Grant's opponent. The KKK killed and wounded more than 200 black Republicans,—hunting and chasing them through the woods. Thirteen (13) captives were taken from jail and shot; a half-buried pile of 25 bodies was found in the woods. The KKK made people vote Democratic and gave them certificates of the fact.

In the April 1868 Georgia gubernatorial election, Columbia cast 1,222 votes for Republican Rufus Bullock. By the November presidential election, Klan intimidation led to suppression of the Republican vote and only one person voted for Ulysses S. Grant. Klansmen killed more than 150 African Americans in a county in Florida, and hundreds more in other counties. Freedmen's Bureau records provided a detailed recounting of Klansmen's beatings and murders of freedmen and their white allies.

Take special note: "the Democratic Party use to be the racial party supported by the KKK, and the Republican Party use to be the non-racial party supporting the Negros and former slaves. Abraham Lincoln was a republican president not a democratic president back in the day. Lincoln set the example for all presidents to follow in treatment of all people. The Republican Party today is not the Republican Party of yesterday! And the Democratic Party of yesterday is not the Democratic Party of today! A tremendous shift has occurred; and the Democratic Party is today's most positive representation for the people. "Vote Democrat!!!"

The next President of the United States of America must first understand that in order to make wise decisions in any area of oval office administration requires understanding of and submission to the principles and rules that governing that particular area of subject matter of the administration. Such a person must have the temperament to listen, submit to God, and apply himself or herself according to the word of God to be successful in performing required duties for the benefit of the people. God's guidance and his or her uniqueness in being called and appointed provide the knowledge, wisdom, and understanding to perform this duty for God and not for oneself.

The office of President is not an office to be grandiose, (impressive or magnificent in appearance or style, especially pretentiously so) especially by anyone unqualified or unfit for the job. This is a very important position of power and authority that should never be trusted into the hands of anyone with arrogant pride having the inability in being humble and listening to God; and definitely not anyone who is racist, not having the best interest of all the people at heart. Our country or nation does not need division; but rather, a working together in uniting us as a people sharing the same purposes and interests so help of God. A narcissistic person is totally unfit and unqualified to accomplish what our nation needs in these critical and perilous times.

ALTERNET, Civil Liberties article entitled "The KKK Has Infiltrated U.S. Police Departments for Decades" The Free Thought Project—December 19, 2015 states: "During the Civil Rights movement, one of the KKK's first orders was to infiltrate police departments around the country. In 1991, a neo-Nazi white supremacist gang was terrorizing the streets of Lynwood in Los Angeles County. The reason these violent thugs could run amok was because they were deputies at the Lynwood Sheriff's station,—having the power of blue privilege.

A federal judge acknowledged that the gang of deputies carried out "systematic acts of shooting, killing, brutality, terrorism, house-trashing and other acts of lawlessness and wanton abuse of power." These maniacs were not the sudden appearance of a unique group of individuals among law enforcement, but the progeny (descendants or off-springs) of a decades-long effort by the KKK to infiltrate police departments wherever possible. That's why it is so difficult to believe the Los Angeles Police Department (LAPD) when it said on Tuesday—that there was no racial profiling in any of the 1,365 allegations leveled against the department from 2012 to 2014.

"I don't think anybody believes that there are actually no incidents of biased policing," said Matt Johnson, president of the Police Commission panel. "The problem is we don't have an effective way of really adjudicating the issue." "While no doubt the vast majority of LAPD officers do not engage in biased policing,—it strains credibility to suggest that ... there were zero instances of biased policing," said Commissioner Robert Saltzman. "It should not be surprising that there is diminished trust in the LAPD given these results." The LAPD seems to think that the influence of neo-Nazi, white supremacist groups—is a thing of the past.

A Florida deputy police chief was exposed as a member of the KKK last year, and no criminal wrongdoing was found as he resigned. In September, a Louisiana police detective was caught in a photo giving a Nazi salute at a KKK rally. An Alabama police officer recently spoke at a League of the South rally. While the South has been fertile ground for racist groups, the KKK has penetrated many police departments around the country, as evidenced by the Lynwood horror.

Larissa Moore and four (4) of her law school colleagues performed an investigation of unsolved civil rights murders from 1946 to 1969, under a Syracuse University program, and confirmed an ugly truth. During the Civil Rights movement, one of the KKK's first orders was to infiltrate police departments, "because the laws don't apply to them if they are the law," according to Moore.

This echoes an FBI statement in 2006 that white supremacist groups "have historically engaged in strategic efforts to infiltrate and recruit from law enforcement communities." The federal agency's concern seems to be selfish, though, as it stated that the hate group's actions cause "investigative breaches and can jeopardize the safety of law enforcement sources and personnel." So far, the FBI has not reviewed any of the 37 cases sent to them from the program in which Moore is involved—The Cold Case Justice Initiative. Since the purview expires in 2017, there seems to be little chance that the FBI will take meaningful action.

"We have discovered hundreds of killings that aren't on the FBI's list that no one's ever done a full accounting of all the people who have been killed either by Klan or by suspicious police shootings," said Janis McDonald, a law professor at Syracuse University who co-founded CCJI with law professor Paula Johnson. The government's disinterest here mirrors a wider problem in law enforcement at all levels. Cops continue to inflict most of their brutality on minority groups, especially blacks. African-Americans make up only 13 percent of the population, yet they are the victims in 26 percent of all police shootings. A young black male is 3 times more likely to be killed by a cop than their white counterparts. Michael Brown, Eric Garner, Walter Scott and Tamir Rice are just a few of the recent examples.

The injustice of the drug war also falls most heavily on minorities. "More than 60% of the people in prison are now racial and ethnic minorities" and "two-thirds (66 2/3%) of all persons in prison for drug offenses are people of color." Clearly, the KKK has had success in establishing a culture within not only police departments but the entire "criminal justice system." With departments like the LAPD continuing to pretend that racism does not motivate any of its officers,—it will be difficult to know just how far the disease of white supremacy has spread into law enforcement.

Mapping police violence, Data from January 1, through December 31, 2015 shows that police killed more than 100 unarmed black people in 2015. Unarmed black people were killed by police at 5 times the rate of unarmed whites in 2015. Police killed at least 102 unarmed blacks in 2015, nearly twice each week. Nearly 1 in 3 black people killed by police in 2015 were identified as unarmed, though the actual number is likely higher due to underreporting. 37% of unarmed people killed by police were black in 2015 despite black people being only 13% of the U.S. population.

Only 10 of the 102 (9.8%) cases in 2015 where an unarmed black person was killed by police resulted in officer(s) being charged with a crime, and only 2 (1.9%) or of these deaths (Matthew Ajibade and Eric Harris) resulted in convictions of officers involved. Only 1 of 2 officers convicted for their involvement in Matthew Ajibade's death received jail time. He was sentenced to 1 year in jail and allowed to serve this time exclusively on weekends. Deputy Bates, who killed Eric Harris, will be sentenced May 31.

CNN News July 7, 2016 entitled "Two police shootings, two videos, two black men dead" states: "Within a day of each other, two men were shot and killed by U.S. police officers. They hailed from different parts of the country—one from Louisiana in the south, the other from Minnesota in the north. But they shared many similarities. Both were black.—Both had their last moments caught on camera. And both of their deaths were watched and shared by millions across the globe. Their deaths have drawn people—brandishing signs emblazoned with the message #BlackLivesMatter—to the streets in their droves,—demanding the world take notice of shootings that feel sadly commonplace in the U.S., yet are no less provocative.

As details continue to emerge, here's what we know so far. Philando Castile was shot by police on Wednesday after being "pulled over for a busted tail light," according to a woman identifying herself as his girlfriend in a live stream on Facebook. Castile's uncle, Clarence Castile, told CNN his nephew worked as a kitchen supervisor for the St. Paul School District. "We all know my nephew was a good kid and we want justice as well as relief," he said. "My nephew has a (concealed carry) permit, and still got killed for carrying a gun ... this needs to stop. This happens so often."

Alton Sterling, 37, known as the "CD man" sold CDs and DVDs outside a convenience store in Baton Rouge, Louisiana—where he was killed by police on Tuesday. "Alton was a respected man. He was beloved in the community. He did not deserve the treatment and this excessive force that was exerted on him by the police department," Edmond Jordan, the Sterling family attorney, told CNN about the father-of-five. Sterling has had encounters with law enforcement before, but there's no evidence that officers at the store were aware of Sterling's criminal history—when they approached him outside the store.

"Stay with me," says Castile's girlfriend Diamond Reynolds, as she turns the phone streaming live to Facebook to her boyfriend slumped in the driver's seat with a blood splattered chest. As with Sterling, it's unclear what happened in the moments before the shooting. Reynolds claims they were "pulled over for a busted tail light." A police officer can be seen pointing a gun through the driver's window, while Reynolds continues narrating the shocking scene streamed live to Facebook. She is then ordered out of the car, pleading for her daughter who appears to be in the arms of a nearby officer. By Thursday morning more than 2.5 million people had watched the stream.

Sterling was shot outside the Triple S Food Mart after an encounter with two police officers. Video footage from a bystander captured officers—wrestling Sterling to the ground and kneeling on him. The camera pans away and gunshots are heard—when it pans back, Sterling is seen sprawled on his back with a large blood stain on his chest. One of the crucial next steps will be to determine what happened before the confrontation ensued. Authorities said that the officers were responding to a 911 report of a man with a gun. A source close to the investigation told CNN the witness who called 911 said Sterling was "brandishing a gun." However Abdullah Muflahi, the owner of the store, told CNN he wasn't aware of any incident Tuesday that would have spurred a 911 call. Muflahi is sure the shooting was caught on his store's surveillance cameras, though he hasn't seen it. Police took the video later Tuesday, he told CNN.

In Minnesota, crowds gathered outside Governor Mark Dayton's home in St. Paul in the early hours of Thursday morning—protesting against the police killing of Castile. They held banners emblazoned with slogans such as "Stop Police Brutality," and chanted "No justice, No sleep."

Earlier in the week, Sterling's death prompted protests Baton Rouge and other parts of the country, including Ferguson, Missouri, Philadelphia. "I, for one, will not rest," Quinyetta McMillon, the mother of one of Sterling's children, said Wednesday, "and will not allow y'll to sweep him in the dirt." As she spoke, McMillon and Sterling's 15-year-old son stood by her side, sobbing.

The killings of Castile and Sterling are just the latest of several incidents that have shocked the United States, igniting yet another debate about the use of deadly force in the line of duty. The U.S. government does not keep national statistics on the number of people killed by police. However, at least two newspapers, the Washington Post and the Guardian, maintain databases based on news reports, public records, social media, and their own reporting. They use slightly different criteria, but both found more than 500 cases of people being killed by police from Jan. 1 to July 5, 2016. The FBI found that 41 law enforcement officers were killed in the line of duty in 2015, down from 51 in 2014. The killers used firearms in 38 of the 41 killings, the FBI reported.

The fatal 2012 shooting of 17-year-old African-American Trayvon Martin by white Hispanic George Zimmerman, a neighborhood watch volunteer, brought arguments about the comparative treatment of African-Americans to the force—with everyone from President Obama on down joining the debate. While Martin was not shot by police, the handling of his killer by authorities and later the judicial system, was key to launching the #BlackLivesMatter movement.

Elsewhere, a perceived racial profiling of African-Americans by police officers continued to bubble just below the surface. The situation reached a tipping point with the death of Michael Brown—an 18-year-old unarmed black man who was shot and killed by a white police officer—in Ferguson, Missouri in 2014. The outrage that followed saw residents take to the streets. Soon these protests had spread coast to coast, and as far as across the Atlantic to London.

A year later, anger erupted again after Freddie Gray, a 25-year-old African-American man, died while in police custody in Baltimore. While at first, peaceful protests were organized—they soon turned violent with reports of stores being looted,—rocks being thrown at police and vehicles being set on fire. These cases have forever changed the conversation on law enforcement procedures as well as police brutality and equality both at home and abroad.

We no longer need to wait and/or perform investigations as to whether racism is a very strong contributing factor in injustices to blacks and people of color in law enforcement systems and judicial systems throughout our country. On the contrary, it's expedient that investigations begin immediately in both systems to detect and punish those who are involved in perverting justice, including, but not limited to, use of excessive force, unnecessary killings or taking of lives, profiling and harassment, unfair sentencing, and any other practice deemed unjustified according to established laws and regulations.

Good cops need to turn-in bad cops (black, white, Hispanic, and any other). Bad cops jeopardize the lives of good cops by causing division between law enforcement and communities being served in good faith by good cops. If there be anyone on the force that's rotten and not fit for the job, such person(s) need to be turned-in and dismissed from the force. Law enforcement is no place the arrogant pride nor anyone else desiring to mistreat or hurt people without cause.

Likewise, bad judges, especially, when it's obvious that their judgments and sentencing are unfair, and sometimes, quite ridiculous, need to be investigated and removed from the bench according to established code of ethics. It's past time for law enforcement officers and judges to be held responsible and accountable to the highest degree. Certain actions should have a zero tolerance requirement, unless otherwise, clearly and cogently justified. Many judges have gotten away being bad and unjust judges for years. They too are responsible for corruption in our country.

2

Trump's Arrogant Pride Behavior

GOD'S WORD IS following Donald Trump to expose him for who he really is; that is, a fake, a deceiver, an imposter, a hypocrite, and a false prophet. Trump is a habitual liar that calls everyone else liars; he's a crooked businessman that calls other people crooked; and he makes promises that are unrealistic that he's unable to bring to past. Trump has floored in on the fears and unrest of the American people and has infused more fear and unrest through his rhetoric and propaganda to gather for himself a huge following that he's sure to disappoint; it's only a matter of time.

The eyes of the Lord are in every place, Keeping watch on the evil and the good. (Prov. 15:3) The Lord's presence chills those who do evil and comforts those who submit to Him. Although Trump has perverted justice against the poor and the needy, in due time, God will bring about justice due to him in the end. Trump has arrogant pride and is adamant in his folly.

Destructive pride has brought down many winners and its sickness is contagious. Just as many other have been brought down in the past, Trump will also follow suit with the rest of them. God is a God of justice who detests those who pervert justice. The Bible says: "Cursed is the one who perverts the justice due the stranger, the fatherless, and widow.' "And all the people shall say, 'Amen!' (Deut. 27:19). A wicked man accepts a bribe behind the back—To pervert the ways of justice. (Prov. 17:23)

To not do justice to students of Trump University who filed lawsuits against him is a perversion of justice, especially, those who are elderly and the educational disadvantaged. In so doing, Trump has declared the innocent guilty and himself with those joining force with him innocent, which constitutes perverted justice. If the will to do righteousness was within him, he could have just given the people their money back and apologized for the promises he had given them that he failed to fulfill. But he, declares he hasn't done anything wrong to them and is basically calling them liars. The Bible says: "He who justifies the wicked, and he who condemns the just, Both of them alike are an abomination to the Lord." (Prov. 17:15) Everyone proud in heart is an abomination to the Lord; Though they join forces, none will go unpunished. (Prov. 16:5)

Trump isolates himself for selfish reasons, thinking himself being above everyone else intellectually. He's actually a recluse that's so intolerant of anyone who disagrees with him that he finds fault with all wise judgment from any of them. He continuously demonstrates himself as being a hasty and compulsive talker; hearing, but never listening, only pausing to plan what he's going to say next. Most every word proceeding out of his mouth confirms how foolish he is and how lacking he is in integrity. There are very high speculations that much of his wealth is marked by cheating and deception. Although, he inherited wealth from his father, even that wealth is suspect as having been produced from possible corruptible activities. When anyone comes close to his vulnerabilities, he quickly displays rashes and violent outbursts to protect himself from being exposed.

Although Trump in his power and wealth feel he's in control of his steps and days,—his life, his very breathe is a gift from God that can be taken anytime as any other person on earth, whether rich or poor. Only a fool assumes he has control of what's happening in his or her life. The Bible says: "The rich and the poor have this in common, The

Lord is the maker of them all." (Prov. 22:2) There are inequities in life, however, that will always be a mystery. The Bible says: "I have seen everything in my days of vanity: There is a just man who perishes in his righteousness, And there is a wicked man who prolongs life in his wickedness." (Prov. 7:15)

God is in control of every person, place, and thing. Even those who refuse to acknowledge Him as God, He has control over them and all possessions in their hands. God has given some over to a debased or reprobate mind to do those things which are not fitting (Rom. 1:28) so that they can go deeper and deeper into sin. God has done this thing so that we have opportunity to see how evil sin really is and how desperately wicked people can become doing what they will to do. In some cases, some of these wicked people have prolonged their lives in their wickedness as God has purposed for examples to our benefit to see just how evil sin really is. They're not getting away with anything; but rather, only building up wrath for themselves.

God's vengeance is certain and perfectly just, which He will execute in His own timing and in His own way. Such persons may believe that they've gotten away with such things for so long that there no repercussions or consequences for the things they've done, because there's no expediency of punishment. However, their calamity will come suddenly without remedy; and in the end, they will be as fools without anyone to redeem them from sins and unrighteousness.

Trump's tongue has a total return of zero (0). He has deceived and convinced himself that he's someone he really isn't at all; and he defends his self-image of himself by exalting himself through his own deceived and fanatical mind. His lies and tricks have no power over God, who only laughs at him as he follows the devil's footsteps with his arrogant pride; the pride that got the devil thrown out of heaven. Trump's influences have proven harmful to a many people; and his foolishness is so bound-up in his heart that he refuses to let it go. Hopefully, before his soul is required of the Lord, he will have a change of heart and humble himself unto the Lord.

But for now, Trump has removed God from the seat of honor and praise and sought that homage unto himself. He praises himself continuously and seeks praises unto himself from his followers. He has presented himself as the savior of America. Only he and he only has what it takes to save America and make it great again, so proclaims; everyone else is not qualified. In his scheme of things, he has incited more fear in America and presented himself as the only person to relieve them of this fear. Nevertheless, in the end, his shame will be revealed before the whole world, just as his hero Saddam Hussein's also was revealed; shame exposed and reputation ruined.

Being proud and haughty is even worse than being a fool. Egotism is the epitome (a person or thing that's a perfect example of a particular quality or type) of folly. Rich people without the Lord are wise in their own eyes and filled with greed. In the end, their money and possessions will mean absolutely nothing; even though they've gain the whole world; but they've lost the most important part of themselves, "their souls." There is no money, no things, no power or anything else worth accumulating and having if it causes one to lose his or her own soul. Such an exchange of the soul for any of these things is foolish, repulsive, and disgusting.

Finally, such people harbor and breathe out hatred, saying one thing, but storing up anger within. These are really mentally troubled and distorted people hurting within because of their own doings. Such persons often find this hatred hurting to hurt them, when in their lives there is so much falsehood that no one believes them—no matter how gracious and truthful they might be at times. But this is a problem they created for themselves and a problem they need to resolve for themselves.

> [18] Whoever hides hatred has lying lips, And whoever spreads slander is a fool. (Prov. 10:18) [24] He who hates, disguises it with his lips, And lays up deceit within himself; [25] When he speaks kindly, do not believe him, For there are seven abominations in his heart; [26] Though his hatred is covered by deceit, His wickedness will be revealed before the assembly. [27] Whoever digs a pit

will fall into it, And he who rolls a stone will have it roll back on him. ²⁸ A lying tongue hates those who are crushed by it, And a flattering mouth works ruin. (Prov. 26:24-28)

¹² A worthless person, a wicked man, Walks with a perverse mouth; ¹³ He winks with his eyes, He shuffles his feet, He points with his fingers; ¹⁴ Perversity is in his heart, He devises evil continually, He sows discord. ¹⁵ Therefore his calamity shall come suddenly; Suddenly he shall be broken without remedy. (Prov. 6:12-15)

¹⁶ These six things the LORD hates, Yes, seven are an abomination to Him: ¹⁷ A proud look, A lying tongue, Hands that shed innocent blood, ¹⁸ A heart that devises wicked plans, Feet that are swift in running to evil, ¹⁹ A false witness who speaks lies, And one who sows discord among brethren. (Prov. 6:16-19)

The above Scriptural references are provided by King Solomon, the wisest man God made and empowered with authority, power, and wealth. Here he gives us characteristic traits of one that is mischievous to man and dangerous to be dealt with. If the slothful are to be condemned that do nothing, much more those that do ill, and contrive to do all the ill they can do. The person Solomon is advising us of here is a naughty person that's referred as "a man of Belial" (simply a worthless lawless person; the personification of all that is evil).

This man Belial is a wicked man that makes a trade of doing evil, especially with his tongue. He walks and works his designs with a forward mouth by lying and perverseness; which are in direct opposition to God and man. He says and does everything he wants to do without any restrictions. He is very artfully and with design; that is, he has the subtlety of the serpent (the devil), and carries on his projects with a great deal of craft and management with his eyes, with his feet, and with his fingers.

He expresses his malice when he dares not speak out (so some), or, rather, as a result or consequence of this, he carries on his plot. Those about him, whom he makes use of as the tools of his wickedness, understand the ill meaning of his wink of the eye, a stamp of his feet, and the least motion of his fingers. He gives orders for evil-doing, and yet would not be thought to do so, but has ways of concealing what he does so that he may not be suspected of doing such.

He is a close man and upon the reserve. Only those let into his secret are those that would do anything he would have them to do. He is a cunning man and upon the trick, he has a language by himself, which an honest man is not acquainted with, nor desires to be. He's very spiteful and with ill design. It's not so much ambition or covetousness that's in his heart, as downright forwardness, malice, and ill nature. He aims not so much to enrich and advance himself as to do an ill turn to those about him.

He is continually devising one mischief or another, purely for mischief's sake. A man of Belial indeed, of the devil, resembling him not only in subtlety, but in malice. Such a person is facing doom; his calamity shall come and he shall be broken. He that devised mischief shall fall into his mischief. His ruin shall come without warning; suddenly, he shall be broken and will be punished for all the wicked arts he had to surprise people into his snares. He shall be irreparably broken and never able to piece again. He shall be broken without remedy. What relief can he expect that has disobliged (offended others by not acting in according to their wishes) all mankind? He shall come to his end, his ruin, exposed for who he is, and none shall help him.

A catalogue of those things which are in a special manner odious to God, all which are generally to be found in those men of Belial whom Solomon described in the foregoing verses; and the last of them (which, being the seventh, seems especially to be intended, because he says they are six, yea, seven) is part of his character, that he sows discord. God hates sin; he hates every sin; he can never be reconciled to it; he hates nothing but sin. But there are some sins which he does in a special manner hate; and all those here mentioned are such as are injurious to our neighbor.

It is an evidence of the good-will God bears to mankind that those sins are in a special manner provoking to Him which is prejudicial to the comfort of human life and society. Therefore, the man of Belial and others like him must expect their ruin to come suddenly, and without remedy, because their practices are such as the Lord hates and are an abomination to Him. Those things which God hates are no thanks to us to hate in others, but we must hate such things within ourselves.

Haughtiness, conceitedness of ourselves, contempt of others—a proud look: There are seven things that God hates, and pride is the first, because it is at the bottom of much sin and gives rise to it. God sees the pride in the heart and hates it there; but, when it prevails to that degree that the show of men's countenance witnesses against them that they overvalue themselves and undervalue all about them, this is in a special manner hateful to God, for then pride is proud of itself and sets shame at defiance.

Falsehood, and fraud, and dissimulation: Next to a proud look nothing is more an abomination to God than a lying tongue; nothing more sacred than truth, nor more necessary to conversation than speaking truth. God and all good men hate and abhor lying. Cruelty and blood-thirstiness: The devil was, from the beginning, a liar and a murderer (Jn. 8:44), and therefore, as a lying tongue, so hands that shed innocent blood are hateful to God, because they have in them the devil's image and do him service. Subtlety in the contrivance of sin, wisdom to do evil, a heart that designs and a head that devises wicked imaginations that is acquainted with the depths of Satan and knows how to carry on a covetous, envious, revengeful plot, most effectually. The more there is of craft and management in sin the more it is an abomination to God.

Vigor and diligence in the prosecution of sin—feet that are swift in running to mischief, as if they were afraid of losing time or were impatient of delay—in a thing they are so greedy of. The policy and vigilance, the eagerness and industry, of sinners in their sinful pursuits, may shame us who go about that which is good so awkwardly and so coldly. False-witness bearing, which is one of the greatest mischiefs that the wicked imagination can devise, and against which there is least fence. There cannot be a greater affront to God (to whom in an oath appeal is made) nor a greater injury to our neighbor (all whose interests in this world, even the dearest, lie open to an attack of this kind) than knowingly to give in a false testimony. There are seven things which God hates, and lying involves two (2) of them;—he hates it, and doubly or twice as much hates it.

Making mischief between relations and neighbors, and using all wicked means possible, not only to alienate their affections one from another, but to irritate their passions one against another. The God of love and peace hates him that sows discord among brethren, for God delights in concord (agreement or harmony). Those that by talebearing and slandering, by carrying ill-natured stories, aggravating everything that is said and done, and suggesting jealousies and evil surmises (conjecture; supposing something is true without having evidence to confirm it) blow the coals of contention (heated conflict, strife, friction, disharmony, and the like) are but preparing for themselves a fire of the same nature.

[5] Even so the tongue is a little member and boasts great things. See how great a forest a little fire kindles! [6] And the tongue is a fire, a world of iniquity. The tongue is so set among our members that it defiles the whole body, and sets on fire the course of nature; and it is set on fire by hell. [7] For every kind of beast and bird, of reptile and creature of the sea is tamed and has been tamed by mankind. (Ja. 3:5-6)

> [8] But no man can tame the tongue. It is an unruly evil, full of deadly poison. [9] With it we bless our God and Father, and with it we curse men, who have been made in the similitude of God. [10] Out of the same mouth proceed blessing and cursing. My brethren, these things ought not to be so. (Ja. 3:8-10) [19] So then, my beloved brethren, let every man be swift to hear, slow to speak, slow to wrath; [20] for the wrath of man does not produce the righteousness of God. (Ja. 1:19-20)

[11]A fool vents all his feelings, But a wise man holds them back. (Prov. 29:11) [20] Do you see a man hasty in his words? There is more hope for a fool than for him. (Prov. 29:20) [22] An angry man stirs up strife, And a furious man abounds in transgression. (Prov. 29:22) [28] The heart of the righteous studies how to answer, But the mouth of the wicked pours forth evil. (Prov. 15:28) [3] It is honorable for a man to stop striving, Since any fool can start a quarrel. (Prov. 20:3)

3

Trump Gives New Life to White Supremacists

THE TRUMP CAMPAIGN has sown discord to such a degree that its devastating results will live on well after the 2016 presidential election and subsequent 2017 presidential inauguration. Trump's rhetoric and propaganda at his campaign sites, social media sites, and news conferences have demonstrated language and behavior practices that have incited White Supremacist groups to pour their support into the Trump Campaign and to increase their activities over the internet, both for fund-raising and to further their primary goal in making America a white America.

Thanks to Trump, White Supremacist groups are excited and enthusiastic about this 2016 presidential campaign/election than they have been in decades. Whites Supremacists groups have typically opposed blacks and other people of color, immigrants, Jews, and Catholics. Their racial ideology is centered upon the belief and promotion of the belief that white people are superior in certain characteristics, traits, and attributes to people of other racial backgrounds; and that therefore, white people should politically, economically, and socially rule non-white people.

Trump has excited and motivated these White Supremacist groups as if his conversations and actions were to them magnetic (having great power to attract and hold their interests). There is no doubt, Trump is playing some sort of music pleasing to their ears; because, they just keep coming back for more and more. It appears almost, as if Trump has arisen and is now being looked upon by them as some sort of Guru (someone that's a teacher, guide, expert, or master of certain knowledge or field) that will help them make America great by cleaning her out from people they've determined and concluded have no right being a part of her.

Obviously, Trump has given White Supremacist groups something (openly and/or in private conversation) that he's with them, but obviously, being strategically careful and very meticulous in handling this matter without damaging himself for this presidential run. No one in his right mind would come out and tell the American people he has ties and/or support White Supremacist ideology and welcome their support to his presidential campaign. Let's just be realistic about this matter and not expect anything from Trump that's reasonable and truthful.

However, there are other ways to analyze known information and to draw some hypothesizes (a set of propositions set forth as an explanation for the occurrence of some specified group of phenomena (facts, occurrences, or circumstances observed or observable), either asserted merely as a provisional conjecture to guide investigation (working hypothesis) or accepted as highly probable in light of established facts). Therefore, this is the manner in which this matter is being approached.

Our first document for analyzing is an article from Mother Jones entitled "Trump Selects a White Nationalist Leader as a Delegate in California" dated May 10, 2016 that states: "Meet William Johnson, head of the American Freedom Party (AFP). On Monday evening, California's secretary of state published a list of delegates chosen by the Trump campaign for the upcoming Republican presidential primary in the state. Trump's slate includes William Johnson, one of the country's most prominent white nationalists. [**Update:** *Responding to this story late Tuesday, the Trump campaign blamed Johnson's selection on* *a "database error," and Johnson told* Mother Jones *he would resign.* Here are documents showing the Trump campaign's personal correspondence with Johnson yesterday.]

Johnson applied to the Trump campaign to be a delegate. He was accepted on Monday. In order to be approved he had to sign this pledge sent to him by the campaign: "I, William Johnson, endorse Donald J. Trump for the office of President of the United States. I pledge to cast ALL of my ballots to elect Donald J. Trump on every round of balloting at the 2016 Republican National Convention so that we can MAKE AMERICA GREAT AGAIN!" After he signed, the Trump campaign added his name to the list of 169 delegates it forwarded to the secretary of state.

Johnson leads the American Freedom Party, a group that "exists to represent the political interests of White Americans" and aims to preserve "the customs and heritage of the European American people." The AFP has never elected a candidate of its own and possesses at most a few thousand members, but it is "arguably the most important white nationalist group in the country," according to Mark Potok, a senior fellow for the Southern Poverty Law Center (SPLC), which tracks hate groups.

Johnson got the news that he had been selected by Trump in a congratulatory email sent to him by the campaign's California delegate coordinator, Katie Lagomarsino. "I just hope to show how I can be mainstream and have these views," Johnson tells *Mother Jones*. "I can be a white nationalist and be a strong supporter of Donald Trump and be a good example to everybody."

Johnson says that in his application to be a delegate for Trump he disclosed multiple details about his background and activism, though he did not specifically use the term "white nationalist." The Trump campaign and Lagomarsino did not immediately respond to requests for comment. Whether or not Johnson was vetted (examined) by the Trump campaign, the GOP front-runner would have a hard time claiming ignorance of Johnson's extreme views: Johnson has gained notice during the presidential primary for funding pro-Trump robocalls that convey a white nationalist message. "The white race is dying out in America and Europe because we are afraid to be called 'racist,'" Johnson says in one robocall pushed out to residential landlines in Vermont and Minnesota. "Donald Trump is not racist, but Donald Trump is not afraid. Don't vote for a Cuban. Vote for Donald Trump."

Armed with cash from affluent donors and staffed by what the movement considers to be its top thinkers, the AFP now dedicates most of its resources to supporting Trump. Johnson claims that the AFP's pro-Trump robocalls, which have delivered Johnson's personal cellphone number to voters in seven states, have helped the party find hundreds of new members. "[Trump] is allowing us to talk about things we've not been able to talk about," Johnson says. "So even if he is not elected, he has achieved great things."

On multiple occasions, Trump has failed to forcefully repudiate this sort of support. After being endorsed by former Ku Klux Klan leader David Duke in August last year, Trump told Bloomberg News, "I don't need his endorsement;—I certainly wouldn't want his endorsement.—I don't need anybody's endorsement." Asked in February about the robocalls, which are funded by Johnson through a super-PAC, a Trump spokeswoman would only tell CNN that the candidate had "disavowed all super-PACs offering their support." In April, the *Huffington Post* reported that Trump returned a $250 donation to his campaign from Johnson.

The SPLC's Potok says Trump has "legitimized and mainstreamed hate" in ways we haven't seen since the days of George Wallace. Though nobody can say for sure how many people belong to America's largest hate groups, the SPLC has found that the number of such groups grew by 14 percent in 2015, reversing years of declines.—Potok worries that Trump could fuel the spread of the AFP's ideas for years to come.

Johnson is a corporate lawyer who grows persimmons and raises chickens at his 67-acre "ranch" in a Los Angeles suburb. When I met him recently outside his law office in downtown LA's World Trade Center, he was in high spirits. He suggested brightly that we walk downstairs to get lunch at a nearby Korean restaurant. As we sat next to a table of immaculately coiffed Korean Air flight attendants, I mentioned that some might find it surprising that a guy who wrote a book advocating the creation of an all-white ethno-state was eating a plate of bulgogi beef with kimchee. "Koreans don't have to make Korean food," he said matter-of-factly. "One of the best Chinese restaurants I went to in the Bay Area is owned by a Mormon and cooked by a Mormon. Really great Chinese food.

Short, graying, and 61 years old, Johnson favors pressed white shirts and bookish black-framed glasses. He grew up in predominantly white neighborhoods in Arizona and Oregon before moving to Japan in 1974 to study the language. It was there that locals engaged him in "open" discussions about differences between the races, and he came to see America's European heritage as its biggest—and most vulnerable—asset.

(This trajectory is not uncommon: Jared Taylor, head of the white nationalist group American Renaissance, also speaks fluent Japanese, and Aryan Nations founder Richard Butler became a white supremacist while immersed in the caste system in India.) In 1985, Johnson published, under a pseudonym, *Amendment to the Constitution: Averting the Decline and Fall of America*, a book calling for the abolition of the 14th and 15th Amendments and the deportation of all nonwhites. He tried to sound a practical tone, allowing, for instance, that African Americans should receive "a rich dowry to enable them to prosper in their homeland."

The book was a hit on the talk show circuit, and Johnson suddenly found himself appearing on television alongside neo-Nazi skinheads and Klansmen. By 1989, his notoriety and clean-cut appeal convinced a group of white nationalists in Wyoming to tap him to run for Dick Cheney's vacant congressional seat. He garnered a flurry of press coverage when he earned enough signatures to qualify for the ballot; around the same time, the building housing his California law office was bombed. Johnson says the FBI accused him of detonating it himself in a bid for more press. (The bureau declined to comment.)

Twenty (20) years later, after unsuccessfully running for various other offices, Johnson became the head of the American Freedom Party (then known as American Third Position), at the request of a group of Southern California skinheads. Johnson's post was supposed to be temporary: "The skinheads thought I was too extreme to run the organization," he explained. But they were the ones who ended up dropping out, replaced by what has become a sort of white nationalist brain trust: Party leaders now include a former Reagan administration appointee and a professor emeritus at California State University-Long Beach.

After our Korean lunch, Johnson rushed back up to his office to host the latest episode of For God and Country, a Christian AM talk show currently broadcast in California, Louisiana, and Texas. His Filipino American co-host, the Rev. Ronald Tan, nodded approvingly as Johnson praised Trump on the air for "busting up the concept of political correctness." The show allows Johnson to push a Trump-centric version of white nationalism to a potentially receptive audience—up to a point. Several radio stations in Iowa recently canceled the program out of objection to its content. During a commercial break, Johnson fidgeted. "Are you going to quote any more Scriptures?" he asked Tan nervously. "Has the station said that we're not Christian enough?" Back on the air, Tan pivoted to 1 Samuel 16, comparing Trump to King David.

In addition to promoting Trump on the radio and over the phone, the AFP streams a podcast called the Daily Trump Phenomenon Hour. It has set up a "political harassment hotline" for Trump supporters who wish to consult with an attorney—about being attacked or verbally abused by anti-Trump protesters. Johnson has personally spent $30,000 on the Trump promotions, including $18,000 for the robocalls. The robocalls, the radio show, and the "harassment hotline" were all things that Johnson mentioned in his application to become a Trump delegate. He specifically cited an anti-Romney robocall commissioned in Utah this past March, which begins, in part, "My name is William Johnson. I am a farmer and a white nationalist."

After wrapping up the radio show, Johnson led me through his office, where a brush-painted screen hangs alongside shelves stacked with Japanese books and dictionaries. Many of his legal clients, it turns out, are foreigners who speak English as a second language. Yet Johnson says he sees no problem with Trump's isolationist foreign policy, even if it hurts his business—ideally, he'd like to give up his practice and serve as Trump's secretary of agriculture.

We ended up in a mirrored conference room to meet with three (3) AFP sympathizers, two (2) middle-aged women and a young man. They talked about how Trump had enabled a new kind of "honest discourse," how he wasn't a racist but a "racialist," and how he had left them feeling "emancipated." Johnson also now finds it easier to be himself: "For many, many years, when I would say these things, other white people would call me names: 'Oh, you're a hatemonger, you're a Nazi, you're like Hitler,'" he confessed. "Now they come in and say, 'Oh, you're like Donald Trump.'"

Our second and final document for analyzing is an article from CNN politics entitled "Donald Trump stumbles on David Duke, KKK" February 29, 2016 which states: "Donald Trump is trying to clean up a racially charged controversy Monday after he refused to disavow former Ku Klux Klan grand wizard David Duke over the weekend. When asked about his comments on CNN's "State of the Union," Trump blamed a "bad earpiece." "I was sitting in a house in Florida, with a bad earpiece," the brash billionaire told NBC's "Today" show. "I could hardly hear what he's saying. I hear various groups. I don't mind disavowing anyone. I disavowed Duke the day before at a major conference."

In the hours that followed Trump's original comments, the real estate mogul used Twitter to explain his remarks amid an outpouring of criticism from his Republican presidential rivals.—Sen. Marco Rubio slammed the remarks, saying they make Trump "unelectable."

The Sunday uproar started when Trump was asked by Tapper whether he would disavow Duke and other white supremacist groups that are supporting his campaign. "Just so you understand, I don't know anything about David Duke, OK?" Trump said. Trump was pressed three (3) times on whether he'd distance himself from the Ku Klux

Klan—but never mentioned the group in his answers. "I don't know anything about what you're even talking about with white supremacy or white supremacists," he said. "So I don't know. I don't know—did he endorse me, or what's going on? Because I know nothing about David Duke; I know nothing about white supremacists."

Duke had detailed his support for Trump in a Facebook post on Thursday. "I think he deserves a close look by those who believe the era of political correctness needs to come to an end," Duke wrote. He touted Trump's strength on immigration, breaking up "Jewish dominated lobbies and super PACS that are corrupting and controlling American politics," preventing war with Russia, exposing media "lies" and ensuring "that White-Americans are allowed to preserve and promote their heritage and interests just as all other groups are allowed to do."

The Anti-Defamation League had called on Trump to repudiate the support of Duke, the former grand wizard of the Ku Klux Klan, and other white supremacist groups. Despite what he said Sunday, Trump apparently did know Duke in 2000—citing him, as well as Pat Buchanan and Lenora Fulani—in a statement that year explaining why he had decided to end his brief flirtation with a Reform Party presidential campaign. "The Reform Party now includes a Klansman, Mr. Duke, a neo-Nazi, Mr. Buchanan, and a communist, Ms. Fulani. "This is not company I wish to keep," Trump said in a statement reported then by The New York Times.

He had also indicated he knew of Duke during a Friday press conference, when he was asked similar questions and said: "David Duke endorsed me? OK, all right. I disavow, OK?" After his appearance on "State of the Union," Trump highlighted that Friday comment in a tweet, saying he does disavow Duke.

During the interview, though, asked if he'd broadly distance himself from Duke and white supremacists, Trump demurred, saying he knew nothing about their support for his bid for the Republican presidential nomination. "I have to look at the group. I mean, I don't know what group you're talking about," Trump said. "You wouldn't want me to condemn a group that I know nothing about. I'd have to look. If you would send me a list of the groups, I will do research on them and certainly I would disavow if I thought there was something wrong. You may have groups in there that are totally fine—it would be very unfair. So give me a list of the groups and I'll let you know." Tapper responded: "OK. I'm just talking about David Duke and the Ku Klux Klan here, but—"

And Trump said: "Honestly, I don't know David Duke. I don't believe I've ever met him. I'm pretty sure I didn't meet him. And I just don't know anything about him." Trump's comments came two days before 12 states—largely Southern—vote on Super Tuesday. If he defeats Texas Sen. Ted Cruz and Rubio in most or all of those states, Trump could become a near lock for the Republican nomination.

Rubio slammed Trump during a rally in Virginia, highlighting Trump's 2000 comment about Duke as he pointed out that Trump did know of the white supremacist leader. "We cannot be the party that nominates someone who refuses to condemn white supremacists and the Ku Klux Klan," Rubio said. "By the way, not only is that wrong, it makes him unelectable. How are we going to grow our party with a nominee that refuses to condemn the Ku Klux Klan?" he said. "Don't tell me he doesn't know what the Ku Klux Klan is. This is serious."

And on Sunday night Sen. Tim Scott, a South Carolina Republican who is backing Rubio—and one of two African-American senators—in a statement blasted Trump's response. "Any candidate who cannot immediately condemn a hate group like the KKK does not represent the Republican Party, and will not unite it. If Donald Trump can't take a stand against the KKK, we cannot trust him to stand up for America against Putin, Iran or ISIS." Cruz hit Trump on Twitter, saying, "Really sad. @realDonaldTrump you're better than this. We should all agree, racism is wrong, KKK is abhorrent." [End of Article]

Let us now compose statements of fact from the two (2) above mentioned sources under scrutiny (careful examination or investigation) to determine whether or not Trump's responses to inquiries or questions concerning David Duke, the KKK, and white supremacists are mostly likely truthful or untruthful, or believable or unbelievable, or can be concluded as moral turpitude (conduct that is considered contrary to community standards of justice, honesty or good morals). Let us now review Trump's responses to draw closure on this particular serious issue of racism.

1. Trump campaign selected White Nationalist Leader William Johnson as a delegate in California for the 2016 Republican National Convention (RNC).
2. Trump campaign, after reviewing data per Johnson's application approved it.
3. Trump campaign added Johnson' name to the list of 169 delegates it forwarded to the Secretary of State of California.
4. Trump campaign sent Johnson a congratulatory email concerning his election as a delegate in California for the 2016 RNC.
5. Johnson had explained a lot of his background in his application prior to his selection.
6. Johnson funded robocalls through a super-Pac in support of Trump.
7. A Trump spokeswoman said Trump had disavowed all super-PACs offering their support.
8. Trump returned a $250 donation to his campaign from Johnson
9. SPLC's Potok says Trump has legitimized and mainstreamed "hate" in ways we haven't seen since the days of George Wallace.
10. Johnson's American Freedom Party (AFP) is arguably the most important white nationalist group in the country according to Mark Potok of the Southern Proverty Law Center (SPLC).
11. Potok worries that Trump could fuel the spread of the AFP's ideas for years to come, as it has grown by 14% in 2015 reversing years of decline.
12. Johnson published a book in 1985 under a pseudonym, Amendment to the Constitution: Averting the Decline and Fall of America, a book calling for the abolition of the 14th and 15th Amendments and the deportation of all nonwhites.
13. Johnson's book was a hit on the talk show circuit, and he suddenly

Trump Gives New Life to White Supremacists

found himself appearing on television alongside neo-Nazi skinheads and Klansmen.
14. In addition to promoting Trump on the radio and over the phone, the APF steams a podcast called the Daily Trump Phenomenon Hour.
15. The Daily Trump Phenomenon Hour has a political harassment hotline for Trump supporters who wish to consult an attorney about being attacked or verbally abused by anti-Trump protester.
16. Johnson has personally spent $30,000 on the Trump promotions, including $18,000 for the robocalls.
17. The robocalls and the radio show and the harassment hotline were things Johnson mentioned in his application that was approved by the Trump campaign that selected him as a delegate.
18. Johnson in his application specifically cited an anti-Romney robocall commissioned in Utah this past March, which begins in part, "My name is William Johnson. I am a farmer and a white nationalist."
19. Three (3) AFP sympathizers (2 middle-aged women and a young man) talked about how Trump had enabled a new kind of honest discourse, and how he wasn't a racist, but a radicalist; and how he left them feeling emancipated.
20. Johnson says he finds it easier now to be himself; for many, many years, when he would say things, other white people would call him names. Oh, you're a hatemonger, you're a Nazi, you're like Hitler; but now they can come in and say, Oh, you're like Donald Trump.
21. Trump initially refused to disavow former KKK grand wizard David Duke.
22. Trump blamed a bad earpiece; saying he was sitting in a house in Florida with a bad earpiece and that he could hardly what was being said.
23. Trump continued by stating he hear various groups and that he didn't mind disavowing anyone; and that he had disavowed Duke the day before at a major conference.

24. Trump was asked whether he would disavow Duke and other white supremacist groups that are supporting his campaign.
25. Trump first response was: just so you understand, I don't know anything about David Duke, OK?
26. Trump was pressed three (3) more times on whether he would distance himself from the KKK.
27. Trump never mentioned the KKK in his answers.
28. Trump's second response was: I don't know anything about what you're even talking about with white supremacy or white supremacists.
29. Trump's third response was: So I don't know. I don't know.
30. Trump's fourth response was: Did he endorse me?
31. Trump's fifth response was: Or what's going on?
32. Trump's sixth response was: Because I know nothing about David Duke.
33. Trump's seventh response was: I know nothing about white supremacists.
34. Duke had detailed his support for Trump in a Facebook post.
35. Duke posted "I think he deserves a close look by those who believe the era of political correctness needs to come to an end."
36. Duke touted Trump's strength on immigration, breaking up Jewish dominated lobbies and super-PACs that are corrupting and controlling American politics, preventing war with Russia, exposing media lies, and ensuring that "White Americans" are allowed to preserve and promote their heritage and interests just as all other groups are allowed to do.
37. The Anti-Defamation League had called on Trump to repudiate the support of Duke and other white supremacist groups.
38. Trump, despite his previous denial of not knowing Duke, apparently did know Duke in 2000.
39. Trump had cited Duke, as well as, Pat Buchanan and Lenora Fulani in a statement that year why he had decided to end his brief flirtation with a Reform Party presidential campaign.
40. The Reform Party now includes a Klansman (Duke), a neo-Nazi (Buchanan), and a communist (Fulani).

41. Trump stated in The New York Times by then that "This is not the company I wish to keep."
42. Trump indicated again that he knew of Duke during a press conference.
43. When asked a similar question about Duke, Trump's response was: "David Duke endorsed me? OK, alright. I disavow, OK?"
44. Trump highlighted his Friday's comment in a tweed "saying he does disavow Duke."
45. Trump was asked during an interview if he had broadly distance himself from Duke and white supremacists.
46. Trump demurred (took exception, showed objection and reluctance) saying firstly: "he knew nothing about their support for his bid for the Republican presidential nomination."
47. Trump's second response was: "I have to look at the group."
48. Trump's third response was: "I mean, I don't know what group you're talking about."
49. Trump's fourth response was: "You wouldn't want me to condemn a group that I know nothing about."
50. Trump's fifth response was: "I'd have to look."
51. Trump's sixth response was: "If you send me a list of the groups, I will do research on them."
52. Trump's seventh response was: "and certainly I would disavow if I thought there was something wrong."
53. Trump's eighth response was: "You may have groups in there that are totally fine."
54. Trump's ninth response was: "it would be very unfair."
55. Trump's tenth response was: "So give me a list of the groups."
56. Trump's eleventh response was: "and I will let you know."
57. CNN's Trapper said: "OK. I'm just talking about David Duke and the KKK."
58. Trump's twelfth response was: "Honestly, I don't know David Duke."
59. Trump's thirteenth response was: "I don't believe I've ever met him."

60. Trump's fourth-teen response was: "And I just don't know anything about him."
61. Rubio pointed out that Trump did know the white supremacist leader (Duke).
62. Rubio also stated: "We cannot be the party that nominates someone who refuses to condemn the KKK."
63. Rubio also stated: "By the way, not only is that wrong, it makes him unelectable."
64. Rubio also stated: "How are we going to grow our party with a nominee that refuses to condemn the KKK?"
65. Rubio also stated: "Don't tell me that he doesn't know what the KKK is; this is serious."
66. Senator Tim Scott one of two African-American senators blasted Trump's response.
67. Sen. Scott stated: "Any candidate who cannot immediately condemn a hate group like the KKK does not represent the Republican Party and will not unite it."
68. Sen. Scott also stated: "If Donald Trump can't take a stand against the KKK, we cannot trust him to stand up for America against Putin, Iran or ISIS."
69. Cruz hit Trump on Twitter saying: "Really sad. @realDonaldTrump you're better than this. We should all agree, racism is wrong, KKK is abhorrent."

The above findings of fact came from: 1) Donald Trump, 2) the Trump Campaign, 3) a Trump Campaign spokeswoman, 4) White Nationalist Leader William Johnson, 5) The American Freedom Party (AFP), 6) APF sympathizers, 7) Southern Poverty Law Center's Mark Potok, 8) The Anti-Defamation League, 9) The Reform Party, 10) Senator Marco Rubio, 11) Senator Ted Cruz, 12) CNN's Jake Trapper, Eric Bradner, and 13) Mother Jones' Journalism. In one way or another, each and every one mentioned has impact on the findings of fact.

I'm strongly inclined to agree with Senator Rubio that "you cannot tell the American people that Donald Trump doesn't know what the

KKK is;" because most everyone in America knows what the KKK is; and to expect American citizens to believe Trump doesn't know is an attempt to play us all as being just stupid. How is it that the presumptive Republican presidential nominee and now Republican nominee doesn't know what the KKK is nor anything about white supremacist groups? Really, does Trump really believe we're that stupid to believe such crazy or ridiculous responses of racism in America, past, present, and future issues.

Trump has played with this issue of racism as if he was playing a sport that has enabled him to avoid giving direct answers and/or fail in honoring questions with respect to their importance and answering such questions only when there's actual proof showing he has previously lied. He plays with questions and answers as if he's the superior intellect and has the power and authority to answer them anyway, anytime, and whenever he so desires doing so. He habitually goes all over the place when responding to willfully and intentionally avoid giving simple, satisfactory, and acceptable answers to interviewers as reflected as following:

1. Trump was asked whether he would disavow Duke and other white supremacist groups that are supporting his campaign.
2. Trump first response was: just so you understand, I don't know anything about David Duke, OK?
3. Trump was pressed three (3) more times on whether he would distance himself from the KKK.
4. Trump never mentioned the KKK in his answers.
5. Trump's second response was: I don't know anything about what you're even talking about with white supremacy or white supremacists.
6. Trump's third response was: So I don't know. I don't know.
7. Trump's fourth response was: Did he endorse me?
8. Trump's fifth response was: Or what's going on?
9. Trump's sixth response was: Because I know nothing about David Duke.

10. Trump's seventh response was: I know nothing about white supremacists.
11. Duke had detailed his support for Trump in a Facebook post.
12. Duke posted "I think he deserves a close look by those who believe the era of political correctness needs to come to an end."

The Trump campaign claims that the approval and selection of White Nationalist Leader William Johnson as a delegate in California for the 2016 Republican National Convention (RNC) was a database error. There also appears to be an error by someone else when it comes to anything involving Trump, as with his income taxes. Trump qualified for the State of New York's Basic STAR School Tax Relief credit, requiring him to have an income between $84,550 and $500,000, and be at least 65 years of age. Trump received this tax credit from 1999 through 2009 and from 2014 on. When asked by Crain's, the Trump Campaign insisted that Trump's receipt of this credit was a mistake and a spokesperson for the city agreed the credit had been mistakenly applied. But later on, the same credit has appeared again for Trump. Obviously, must have been another mistake by the city of New York.

White Nationalist Leader William Johnson is one of the country's most prominent white nationalists, and leads the American Freedom Party (AFP), a racist group that exists to represent the political interests of White America and aims to preserve the customs and heritage of the European American people. The AFP is arguably the most important white nationalist group in the country. For Trump to say he doesn't know William Johnson nor anything about the AFP doesn't only attempt to play upon the American citizens' intelligence; but more than that, would clearly indicate his ignorance of racist groups within our country that's a danger to its citizens.

Therefore, it is highly improbably and almost impossible for Trump nor anyone in the Trump campaign to not have known anything of William Johnson and his AFP before approving his application and selecting him a delegate. As it has been said: "once your hand is caught in the cookie jar, you have to come up with a reason why your hand is there in the first place." The Trump campaign's hand got caught in the cookie jar and its reason was a data base error.

So with David Duke and the KKK; likewise, it is highly improbably and almost impossible for Trump to not to have known of Duke and the KKK. However, he insists on taking interviewers on rollercoaster rides concerning this very serious issue demonstrated as following:

1. Trump was asked whether he would disavow Duke and other white supremacist groups that are supporting his campaign.
2. Trump first response was: just so you understand, I don't know anything about David Duke, OK?
3. Trump was pressed three (3) more times on whether he would distance himself from the KKK.
4. Trump never mentioned the KKK in his answers.
5. Trump's second response was: I don't know anything about what you're even talking about with white supremacy or white supremacists.
6. Trump's third response was: So I don't know. I don't know.
7. Trump's fourth response was: Did he endorse me?
8. Trump's fifth response was: Or what's going on?
9. Trump's sixth response was: Because I know nothing about David Duke.
10. Trump's seventh response was: I know nothing about white supremacists.
11. Duke had detailed his support for Trump in a Facebook post.
12. Duke posted "I think he deserves a close look by those who believe the era of political correctness needs to come to an end."
13. Duke touted Trump's strength on immigration, breaking up Jewish dominated lobbies and super-PACs that are corrupting and controlling American politics, preventing war with Russia, exposing media lies, and ensuring that "White Americans" are allowed to preserve and promote their heritage and interests just as all other groups are allowed to do.

14. The Anti-Defamation League had called on Trump to repudiate the support of Duke and other white supremacist groups.
15. Trump, despite his previous denial of not knowing Duke, apparently did know Duke in 2000.
16. Trump had cited Duke, as well as, Pat Buchanan and Lenora Fulani in a statement that year why he had decided to end his brief flirtation with a Reform Party presidential campaign.
17. The Reform Party now includes a Klansman (Duke), a neo-Nazi (Buchanan), and a communist (Fulani).
18. Trump stated in The New York Times by then that "This is not the company I wish to keep."
19. Trump indicated again that he knew of Duke during a press conference.
20. When asked a similar question about Duke, Trump's response was: "David Duke endorsed me? OK, alright. I disavow, OK?"
21. Trump highlighted his Friday's comment in a tweed "saying he does disavow Duke."
22. Trump was asked during an interview if he had broadly distance himself from Duke and white supremacists.
23. Trump demurred (took exception, showed objection and reluctance) saying firstly: "he knew nothing about their support for his bid for the Republican presidential nomination."
24. Trump's second response was: "I have to look at the group."
25. Trump's third response was: "I mean, I don't know what group you're talking about."
26. Trump's fourth response was: "You wouldn't want me to condemn a group that I know nothing about."
27. Trump's fifth response was: "I'd have to look."
28. Trump's sixth response was: "If you send me a list of the groups, I will do research on them."
29. Trump's seventh response was: "and certainly I would disavow if I thought there was something wrong."
30. Trump's eighth response was: "You may have groups in there that are totally fine."

Trump Gives New Life to White Supremacists

31. Trump's ninth response was: "it would be very unfair."
32. Trump's tenth response was: "So give me a list of the groups."
33. Trump's eleventh response was: "and I will let you know."
34. CNN's Trapper said: "OK. I'm just talking about David Duke and the KKK."
35. Trump's twelfth response was: "Honestly, I don't know David Duke."
36. Trump's thirteenth response was: "I don't believe I've ever met him."
37. Trump's fourth-teen response was: "And I just don't know anything about him."
38. Rubio pointed out that Trump did know the white supremacist leader (Duke).
39. Rubio also stated: "We cannot be the party that nominates someone who refuses to condemn the KKK."
40. Rubio also stated: "By the way, not only is that wrong, it makes him unelectable."
41. Rubio also stated: "How are we going to grow our party with a nominee that refuses to condemn the KKK?"
42. Rubio also stated: "Don't tell me that he doesn't know what the KKK is; this is serious."
43. Senator Tim Scott one of two African-American senators blasted Trump's response.

Trump's hand got caught in the cookie jar of white supremacist groups, in particularly, the KKK and its former grand wizard David Duke and White Nationalist Leader William Johnson and his AFP. Marco Rubio and Ted Cruz have both appealed to Trump concerning this racially charged controversy. The Trump campaign and Trump himself have failed grossly in cleaning up this controversy concerning relationships whether personal or just of common knowledge. As such, answers to serious questions provided by the Trump campaign and Trump himself lack integrity and do not deem worthy of credence (belief in or acceptance of being true).

33 "Either make the tree good and its fruit good, or else make the tree bad and its fruit bad; for a tree is known by its fruit. 34 Brood of vipers! How can you, being evil, speak good things? For out of the abundance of the heart the mouth speaks. 35 A good man out of the good treasure of his heart brings forth good things, and an evil man out of the evil treasure brings forth evil things. 36 But I say to you that for every idle word men may speak, they will give account of it in the day of judgment. 37 For by your words you will be justified, and by your words you will be condemned." (Matt. 12:33-37)

9 Now I rejoice, not that you were made sorry, but that your sorrow led to repentance. For you were made sorry in a godly manner, that you might suffer loss from us in nothing. 10 For godly sorrow produces repentance leading to salvation, not to be regretted; but the sorrow of the world produces death. 11 For observe this very thing, that you sorrowed in a godly manner: What diligence it produced in you, what clearing of yourselves, what indignation, what fear, what vehement desire, what zeal, what vindication! In all things you proved yourselves to be clear in this matter. (2 Cor. 7:9-11)

8 For you were once darkness, but now you are light in the Lord. Walk as children of light 9 (for the fruit of the Spirit is in all goodness, righteousness, and truth), 10 finding out what is acceptable to the Lord. 11 And have no fellowship with the unfruitful works of darkness, but rather expose them. 12 For it is shameful even to speak of those things which are done by them in secret. 13 But all things that are exposed are made manifest by the light, for whatever makes manifest is light. 14 Therefore He says: "Awake, you who sleep, Arise from the dead, And Christ will give you light." (Ephes. 5:8-14)

Trump Gives New Life to White Supremacists

God is always ready and open to hearing a sinner prayer for salvation and/or a Christian's repentance of sin that he or she has committed and acknowledges the Holy Spirit's conviction of whatever the wrong may be. It's never too late to humble oneself unto the LORD and cast your cares upon Him, because He cares. Do not choose staying in darkness concerning any matter; in Christ we come out of darkness into His marvelous light, never to be in darkness again! God gives us free mercies each day and His grace through Jesus Christ is ever sufficient for whatever our need might be, regardless of how difficult or hard the way may seem at the time. Choose the light and refrain yourselves from walking-in and being trapped-in the darkness of this world.

The words that come out of Trump's mouth from his tongue reflect actions he has taken and will most likely take in any given situation or circumstance. He has shown indignity and disrespect to people through his hatred, and has therefore shown no reverence and respect for the God of heaven. His perverse mouth through the aide of his poisonous tongue has poured out deadly venom to crush and paralyze those he hate with a passion. He has captured the attention of other haters of blacks and people of color and has gathered unto himself audiences that he has converted into congregations with itching hears eager to hear his hate rhetoric and believe any propaganda (derogatory information, especially of a biased or misleading nature) he throws out to promote or publicize his political cause or point of views.

Trump has shown repeatedly that he has no problem at all trivializing the word of God and grieving the Holy Spirit for what's in his personal and best interests. Trump has shown and continues to show that his conduct conforms to that of a person with a corrupt spirit whose soul feeds on deceitful lusts. All who are of the faith of God in Christ Jesus know that the corrupt things from his mouth are not from a man which was created according to God by His Holy Spirit in true righteousness and holiness. Trump has shown the world just who he really is by grieving the Holy Spirit without any restrictions nor remorsefulness.

> [25] *Therefore, putting away lying, "Let each one of you speak truth with his neighbor," for we are members of one another.* [26] *"Be angry, and do not sin": do not let the sun go down on your wrath,* [27] *nor give place to the devil.* [28] *Let him who stole steal no longer, but rather let him labor, working with his hands what is good, that he may have something to give him who has need.* [29] *Let no corrupt word proceed out of your mouth, but what is good for necessary edification, that it may impart grace to the hearers. (Ephes. 4:25-29)*

> [30] *And do not grieve the Holy Spirit of God, by whom you were sealed for the day of redemption.* [31] *Let all bitterness, wrath, anger, clamor, and evil speaking be put away from you, with all malice.* [32] *And be kind to one another, tenderhearted, forgiving one another, even as God in Christ forgave you. (Ephes. 4:30-32)*

When we as Christians petition God, we are petitioning to Him who is able to do exceedingly abundantly above all we ask or think, according to the power (the Holy Spirit) that works within us; understanding that all things are possible with Him and that there's nothing too hard for God to bring to past on our behalf. As such, we are to work daily in doing those things that are pleasing in His sight and going boldly to His throne of grace that we may obtain mercy and find grace to help in time of need against Satan whose assaults have "no cease-fire" non-treaty arrangement against the people of God, as Donald Trump's mouth and tongue have labored so painstakingly to execute as to leave us no doubt whatsoever bout his character.

4

God's Truth at Work

IN SCRIPTURE, TRUTH is characterized by both qualitative and quantitative aspects. In the historical narratives of the Old Testament, truth is identified with personal veracity and historical factuality. Before identifying himself to his brothers, Joseph desires to test them by commanding them to send one of their brothers as a prisoner, to see if there is truth in them (Gen. 42:16) Both Joseph's brothers and Achan claim to be speaking the truth when they confess their respective sins (Gen. 42:21; Josh. 7:20)

Truth is also a quality used to describe utterances that are from the Lord. When Elijah intervenes for the son of the widow of Zarephath, bringing the boy back to life, the boy's mother remarks that now she knows that Elijah is a man of God, and that the word of the Lord in his mouth is truth. Ahab becomes angry with Micaiah, his personal incarcerated prophet, because the latter has given a sarcastic favorable forecast for battle. Ahab responds by saying, "How many times must I make you swear to tell me nothing but the truth in the name of the Lord?" (1 Kgs. 22:16; 2 Chron. 18:15)

The Psalter describes truth as a fundamental characteristic of God, a characteristic that the psalmist desires to share. The wicked do not speak truth (Psa. 5:9), whereas the blameless one speaks truth from the heart (Psa. 15:2) The psalmists often depict truth as a quality separate from God, and which God serves by virtue of His nature. In many instances, truth appears to be personified. The psalmist tells God to "guide me in Your truth" (Psa. 25:5); the psalmist asks God to "send forth Your light and Your truth" to lead him (Psa. 43:3); the psalmist asks the Lord to "ride forth victoriously in behalf of truth" (Psa. 45:4). The psalmist desires to walk in God's truth (Prov. 86:11). Indeed, the sum of God's word is truth.

Proverbs seldom speaks of truth, but when it does it defines it as a virtue that the person of God should practice. Truth is to proceed from one's mouth, and wickedness is an abomination to the lips (Prov. 8:7); the one who speaks the truth gives honest evidence (Prov. 12:17); truth is described as a commodity that one should purchase, along with wisdom, instruction, and understanding (Prov. 23:23).

Jeremiah bemoans the fact that in Judah truth is absent. He tells the people that if they can find a man in Jerusalem who does justice and speaks truth, God will pardon the entire city (Jer. 5:1). The Lord looks for truth (Jer. 5:3), but it is notoriously absent from Judah (Jer. 7:28; 9:3; 9:5). In Daniel, truth is an eschatological virtue related to the interpretations of the visions that God shows to Daniel. Daniel inquires of the truth of the vision of the four beasts (Dan. 7:16; 7:19). The casting down of truth allows the little horn to act and prosper (Dan. 8:12); the future dealings of the kings of Persia are referred to as the truth (Dan. 10:21; 11:2). Zechariah commands his readers to speak the truth (Zech. 8:16), and to love truth and peace (Zech. 8:19).

The Synoptic Gospels (Matthew, Mark, Luke, and John) scarcely use the word truth at all, while in John it is an extremely significant term referring to Jesus and His ministry. Jesus, as the Word become flesh, is full of grace and truth (Jn. 1:14), and is the source of grace and truth (Jn. 1:17). In contrast to the woman at the well, who felt geographic location of worship was important, Jesus states that the issue is not whether one should worship God in Moriah or Gerizim, but rather one should worship in spirit and in truth. For John, truth is ultimately identified with, and is personified in the person of, Jesus Christ.

The ministry of John the Baptist is to bear witness to the truth (Jn. 5:33). Jesus speaks the truth, and for this the Jews seek to kill him (Jn. 8:40). This is because the Jews who contended with Jesus were ultimately of their father the devil, who has no truth in him whatsoever (Jn. 8:44-46). Jesus describes Himself as the way, the truth, and the life, and as such He is the only means to the Father (Jn.14:6). Even when Jesus departs, the ministry of truth will continue because the Comforter, who is the Spirit of truth (Jn. 14:17), will be active both in the church as well as in the world.

For Paul, truth is the message of God that all of humanity has repressed (Rom. 1:18) and exchanged (Rom. 1:25) for lie, in that they have directed their worship not to the Creator, but to the creation. All unbelievers ultimately do not obey the truth, which is embodied in the law (Rom. 2:18; Rom. 2:20). In Galatians, truth is synonymous with the gospel, which the Judaizers have perverted by requiring converts to practice law observance (Gal. 2:5; Gal. 2:14; 4:16; 5:7; Ephes. 1:13; Col. 1:5-6). In addition, Paul also uses truth to speak practically of the believer's deportment in following the Lord. Believers are to speak the truth to one another in a loving manner, as we grow up into submission to our head, namely Christ (Ephes. 4:15). The importance of speaking the truth to one another is underscored by the fact that we are members of one another (Ephes. 4:25).

In 2 Thessalonians Paul equates the truth with the believers' salvation. Those who perish do so because they are under a wicked deception, and so refuse to love the truth and be saved (2 Thess. 2:10). Such people are condemned because they did not believe the truth, but instead had pleasure in unrighteousness (2 Thess. 2:12). God's choosing of the Thessalonian believers for salvation came about by means of sanctification by the Spirit as well as belief in the truth.

In the Pastoral Epistles, truth takes on the characteristics of a repository, or official body of beliefs, of which the church is the faithful steward and guardian. Salvation includes, and is likely synonymous with, knowledge of the truth (1 Tim. 2:4). The church of the living God is both the pillar and ground of the truth. Knowledge of and belief in the truth prevents one from becoming entangled in erroneous doctrines, such as the belief that marriage is to be avoided, abstinence from certain foods is to be enjoined, and that godliness is a means of gain (1 Tim. 4:3; 6:5), as well as the belief that the resurrection is past (2 Tim. 2:18).

Paul further encourages Timothy to guard the truth, which the Holy Spirit has entrusted to him (2 Tim. 1:14). The Scriptures are themselves the word of truth (2 Tim. 2:15). Individuals who oppose God and naively listen to others (i.e. Jannes and Jambres, Pharaoh's two magicians) never arrive at the truth, and, in fact, actually oppose it (2 Tim. 3:7-8). Paul informs Titus that the knowledge of the truth goes along with the furtherance of faith and with godliness (Titus 1:1). Paul informs both Timothy and Titus that the only alternative to the truth is to believe in myths (2 Tim. 4:4; Titus 1:14).

While the term "truth" appears only sporadically in most of the General Epistles, it appears repeatedly throughout the Johannine epistles. To claim to have fellowship with God, and to walk in darkness, is not to live according to the truth (1 Jn. 1:6). To claim sinlessness for the believer is to practice self-deceit and thus be void of truth (1 Jn. 1:8). The basic message of Christianity is termed "the truth," and believers know the truth, and can discern that no lie is of the truth (1 Jn. 2:4; 1 Jn. 2:21). Believers are to love in both deed and in truth (1 Jn. 3:18). Believers are of the truth, which no doubt means that they belong to Jesus, who is the truth (1 Jn. 3:19). Likewise, the fact that we are of God allows us to know the Spirit of truth, and to discern Him from the spirit of error (1 Jn. 4:6). The truth abides with us forever (2 Jn. 2), and the Elder rejoices because the elect lady's children follow the truth (2 Jn. 4; 3 Jn. 4). Further references in 3 John indicate that the Elder refers to Jesus Christ as "the truth" (3 Jn. 1:3; 1:4; 1:8; 1:12).

Merriam Webster's Learner's Dictionary defines "truth," the real facts about a person, place, or thing; the things that are true." At some point and time we all have to or should "face the simple truth/hard/honest/plain/naked truth" about a person, place, or thing that profoundly challenges our positions, beliefs, and practices. Nevertheless, "the truth matters more in the eyes of God than" **any of our positions, beliefs, and practices.** God is truth and in practicing truth, He is emulated or personified through our speech and actions; being holy just as He is holy.

Whatever is not of God is a lie; therefore, coming close to the truth and not conveying the whole truth,—"is not of God, and is therefore, a lie." In the communication process, we either "communicate in the truth or in the lie." When communication "is done in truth," God is the source; when communication "is done in lie," the devil, the father of the lie is the source.

> *But outside are dogs and sorcerers and sexually immoral and murderers and idolaters, and whoever loves and practices a lie. (Rev. 22:15) You are of your father the devil, and the desires of your father you want to do. He was a murderer from the beginning, and does not stand in the truth, because there is no truth in him. When he speaks a lie, he speaks from his own resources, for he is a liar and the father of it. (Jn. 4:44)*

> *[31] Then Jesus said to those Jews who believed Him, "If you abide in My word, you are My disciples indeed. [32] And you shall know the truth, and the truth shall make you free." [33] They answered Him, "We are Abraham's descendants, and have never been in bondage to anyone. How can You say, 'You will be made free'?" [34] Jesus answered them, "Most assuredly, I say to you, whoever commits sin is a slave of sin. [35] And a slave does not abide in the house forever, but a son abides forever. [36] Therefore if the Son makes you free, you shall be free indeed. (Jn. 8:31-36)*

> *[37] Pilate therefore said to Him, "Are You a king then?" Jesus answered, "You say rightly that I am a king. For this cause I was born, and for this cause I have come into the world, that I*

should bear witness to the truth.—Everyone who is of the truth hears My voice." ^{38} *Pilate said to Him, "What is truth?" And when he had said this, he went out again to the Jews, and said to them, "I find no fault in Him at all. (Jn. 18:37-38)*

5

The Truth's Transcending Power

PARTY AFFILIATION SHOULD not play a part in distinguishing the truth from a lie; nor should race (physical characteristics), ethnicity (cultural factors, including nationality, regional culture, ancestry, and language), creed (a system of Christian or other religious belief; a faith), national origin (birth nation), religion (belief in and worship of a superhuman controlling power, especially a personal God or gods); sex orientation (enduring pattern of romantic or sexual attraction (or a combination of these) to persons of the opposite sex or gender, the same sex or gender, or to both sexes or more than one gender);

gender identity (one's innermost concept of self as male or female or both, or neither how individuals perceive themselves and what they call themselves; which can be the same or different than the sex assigned at birth); disability (physical or mental condition that limits a person's movements, senses, or activities); marital status (state of being single, married, separated, divorced, or widowed); or socioeconomic status (economic and sociological combined total measure of a person's work experience or family's economic and social position in relation to others, based on income, education, and occupation). The truth is of God; the lie is of Satan!

The kingdom of God is God's way living and during things. The kingdom of darkness (Satan) is Satan's way of living and during things.

The system of this world belongs to the god of this age, Satan, the devil. Those conforming to the system of this world are living and during things the devil's way. Christians are not to be conformed to this world, but transformed by the renewing of the mind, to preform what is that good, and acceptable, and perfect will of God. The ways of the world conform to the lie, which is directly opposed to the truth. Do not be deceived by the lie! Those who live and practice the lie make themselves enemies of God; avoid liars and those who practice lying!!!

Those who do not practice the truth, regardless of their intellectual capacities, degrees, and achievements, are enemies of God and unprofitable to His works in caring and providing for His people. Such people are worthless in God's kingdom works and should never be trusted in doing anything for the benefits of others; they're only interested in themselves and a select few.

We should very heartily abhor lies and carefully avoid those manifesting and promoting lies that will defile our minds and cause us to go in directions unapproved and prohibited of God. The Bible says: "For the wisdom of this world is foolishness with God. For it is written, "He catches the wise in their own craftiness"; and again, "The Lord knows the thoughts of the wise, that they are futile." (1 Cor. 3:9)

Those who practice the lie operate in selfishness, pride and arrogance (promoting self above others, and doing things absolutely contrary to what the word of God teaches). We, and more importantly leaders, who counter this culture, will obtain mercy and find more grace from God in time of need to overcome such persons and wickedness they're promoting. Such persons have no empathy (ability to understand and share the feelings of other), but are, "self-seeking, envious, confused, with every evil thing existing in them for accomplishing their evil desires."

Such wicked persons are very self-centered, wherein, depending on and promoting themselves rather than on God. Humility is definitely not their goal. However, "humility is vitally necessary and should be a goal of everyone seeking God's provision and deliverance."

Everything in God's kingdom operates on this premise of humility;

The Truth's Transcending Power

and without it, you're left out (will not receive grace needed in time of help), passed over because of pride, self-centeredness.

Such prideful persons have forsaken humility and placed a premium and priority on pride, arrogance, and in boasting, follow this pattern by default as a way of life. Those who operate in pride position themselves to fight or battle against God (a battle that only foolish people would be foolish enough to do). The Bible says: "Likewise you younger people, submit yourselves to your elders. Yes, all of you be submissive to one another, and be clothed with humility, for "God resists the proud, But gives grace to the humble." (1 Pet. 5:5) "God pours out His grace on the humble, not the proud!" Therefore, it's absolutely foolish to operate in pride, when the consequences are so costly; however, "fools, scoffers, and those wise in their own eyes do not see nor have any fear of consequences."

Humility is powerful, because it's a divine attribute that has immeasurable value. To the world and those of the world, humility is looked at and presumed as representing weakness, or as having low self-esteem in oneself. Understandable, for the Bible says: "But the natural man does not receive the things of the Spirit of God, for they are foolishness to him; nor can he know them, because they are spiritually discerned. (1 Cor. 2:14) Therefore, it should be very easily seen and understood why natural people (unsaved fleshly minded people) have distorted or perverted views of humility. Only those who know and understand God can appreciate the power of true humility.

The law of gravity (what goes up must come down), just like the law humility,—is a godly law. A person can walk off a tall building, or jump out of an airplane without a parachute, the law of gravity that God created for our benefit can kill them. Likewise, the law of humility that God created for our benefit "can hurt us if we go against it by operating in pride, humility's enemy." The Bible says: "Humble yourselves in the sight of the Lord, and He will lift you up." (Ja. 4:10) Whatever we have need to be lifted up from, or delivered from, or provided for, or protected from; "God will do it for all who humble themselves under His mighty hand!"

Do not expect anything from God if you lie, support liars, and practice a lie. He or she who sows a lie will reap its nasty corruptible fruits. In order to do anything pertaining to a lie, you have to be connected to the father of the lie, the devil. Know this: "to lie is to do the devil's will." We all lied at one time or another, whether intentionally or unintentionally, whether or not we've consider it a big lie or a little lie, we've lied regardless of the size it; falling short of the glory of God. The bottom line is that we shouldn't lie at all, because to lie is to sin.

Nevertheless, lying is definitely not a thing for any of us to continue in and to practice as a way of life. For some, however, lying is like a sport for those who enjoy doing it and have become habitually at it. Such liars maneuver lies around to cover up one lie after another in serious efforts to ensure previous lies are not uncovered and revealed as lies instead of facts. Such persons have no problem at all lying about anything, any person, at anytime and anywhere.

Even when it appears they've been trapped in a lie, their source of escape is attempted by or with another lie. As a leopard stripes never change, neither does he or she who is a habitual liar.

We often, however, wonder and are often at awe, with a mixture of confusion as to how some people right and wrong mindsets are totally off the charts and so ridiculously wrong when compared to what has generally been accepted as morally and ethically right or wrong. But we shouldn't be surprised or shocked at all, considering what the Bible has forewarned us to come and is now here, "perilous times." Therefore, if you're lost, get saved; and if you're saved, live a godly life in Christ Jesus and help someone else to do the same, regardless of what our culture is promoting and what others have chosen to do contrary to the will of the Lord.

> [1]*But know this, that in the last days perilous times will come:* [2]*For men will be lovers of themselves, lovers of money, boasters, proud, blasphemers, disobedient to parents, unthankful, unholy,* [3]*unloving, unforgiving, slanderers, without self-control, brutal, despisers of good,* [4]*traitors, headstrong, haughty,*

> *lovers of pleasure rather than lovers of God, ⁵ having a form of godliness but denying its power. And from such people turn away! (2ⁿᵈ Tim. 3:1-5)*

> *⁶ For of this sort are those who creep into households and make captives of gullible women loaded down with sins, led away by various lusts, ⁷ always learning and never able to come to the knowledge of the truth. ⁸ Now as Jannes and Jambres resisted Moses, so do these also resist the truth: men of corrupt minds, disapproved concerning the faith; ⁹ but they will progress no further, for their folly will be manifest to all, as theirs also was. (2ⁿᵈ Tim. 3:6-9)*

Therefore, don't be surprised or shocked with the number of hypocrites manifesting an outward appearance of reverence to God (a form of godliness), but whose religious activities have no connection to a living relationship with Jesus (denying the power of God). These evil people or imposters will grow worse and worse as their activities will not cease from during evil, because they're of their father the devil, and his will is what they will to do. They have nothing at all to do with a true relationship with God or with individual faith in Jesus Christ as Lord and Savior. Such wicked persons provoke God's anger and we as children of God are to turn away from them and make sure we don't link-up in common cause with them in anything; to do so will also provoke God's anger against us. The Bible says: "It is a fearful thing to fall into the hands of the living God." (Heb. 10:31)

> *¹⁶ They provoked Him to jealousy with foreign gods; With abominations they provoked Him to anger. ¹⁷ They sacrificed to demons, not to God, To gods they did not know, To new gods, new arrivals That your fathers did not fear. ¹⁸ Of the Rock who begot you, you are unmindful, And have forgotten the God who fathered you. ¹⁹ "And when the LORD saw it, He spurned them,*

> *Because of the provocation of His sons and His daughters. ²⁰ And He said: 'I will hide My face from them, I will see what their end will be, For they are a perverse generation, Children in whom is no faith. (Deut. 32:16-20) For the Lord your God is a consuming fire, a jealous God. (Deut. 4:24)*

Being saved by grace through faith, redeemed by the blood of Jesus, we are to step gingerly in this life, watching and being very careful about the paths we choose, so as to avoid contact with all undesirable influences (anything and/or anyone causing unholy or evil influences). We are called in our salvation to live holy and produce fruit worthy of our calling, which is, the fruit of the Spirit (love, joy, peace, longsuffering, kindness, goodness, faithfulness, gentleness, self-control (Gal. 5:22-23)). We are to redeem our time (take advantage of all opportunities for serving God), considering the limited amount of time we are granted on this earth to perform services for God (Ephes. 3:15-16).

We need to make sure we're not wasting our time in folly or foolishness, but rather, spending our time wisely as much as possible, advancing Christ's purposes in the world as He has commanded us (Matt. 28:19-20), understand what the will of the Lord is for us and for those He has called us to witness to. Discerning or understanding the will of the Lord is not a matter of feeling or emotion, but rather, a matter of mental understanding of applying our minds to the Holy Scriptures and doing as we are commanded and instructed.

> *Understanding the goodness of God, we should desire experiencing every facet (dimension, strand) of God's grace or favor, its sufficiency in all things for our profit, which is, abundantly manifested upon us for every good work. The Apostle Paul states: "And He said to me, "My grace is sufficient for you, for My strength is made perfect in weakness." Therefore most gladly I will rather boast in my infirmities, that the power of Christ may rest upon me. (2ⁿᵈ Cor. 12:9) God's grace or favor is poured out upon us to help us live holy in Christ Jesus, and NOT*

The Truth's Transcending Power

for any of us—as a license to sin in ungodliness and uncleanliness to satisfy sinful lusts and prideful aspirations." Sinful people will sin and promote sinful things, the very thing that God hates.

Racism is sin. It is defined as the belief that all members of each race possess characteristics or abilities specific to that race, especially so as to distinguish it as inferior or superior to another race or races. Chauvinism (exaggerated or aggressive patriotism; or excessive or prejudiced loyalty or support for one's own cause, group, or gender) is a form of racism. Bigotry (intolerance toward those who hold different opinions from oneself) is a form of racism. Xenophobia (intense or irrational dislike or fear of people from other countries) is a form of racism.

² The rich and the poor have this in common, The LORD is the maker of them all. (Prov. 22:2) ²³ These things also belong to the wise: It is not good to show partiality in judgment. (Prov 24:23) ¹³ The poor man and the oppressor have this in common: The LORD gives light to the eyes of both. (Prov. 29:13)

²⁸ Then he said to them, "You know how unlawful it is for a Jewish man to keep company with or go to one of another nation. But God has shown me that I should not call any man common or unclean. (Acts 10:28) ³⁴ Then Peter opened his mouth and said: "In truth I perceive that God shows no partiality. ³⁵ But in every nation whoever fears Him and works righteousness is accepted by Him. (Acts 10:34-35) ²⁶ And He has made from one blood every nation of men to dwell on all the face of the earth, and has determined their preappointed times and the boundaries of their dwellings, (Acts 17:26)

¹¹ For the Scripture says, "Whoever believes on Him will not be

> put to shame." ¹² *For there is no distinction between Jew and Greek, for the same Lord over all is rich to all who call upon Him.* ¹³ *For "whoever calls on the name of the* LORD *shall be saved." (Rom. 10:11-13)* ²⁸ *There is neither Jew nor Greek, there is neither slave nor free, there is neither male nor female; for you are all one in Christ Jesus. (Gal. 3:28)*
>
> ¹¹ *where there is neither Greek nor Jew, circumcised nor uncircumcised, barbarian, Scythian, slave nor free, but Christ is all and in all. (Col. 3:11)* ⁸ *If you really fulfill the royal law according to the Scripture, "You shall love your neighbor as yourself," you do well;* ⁹ *but if you show partiality, you commit sin, and are convicted by the law as transgressors. (Ja. 2:8-9)* ¹¹ *But he who hates his brother is in darkness and walks in darkness, and does not know where he is going, because the darkness has blinded his eyes. (1 Jn. 2:11)* ¹⁵ *Whoever hates his brother is a murderer, and you know that no murderer has eternal life abiding in him. (1 Jn. 3:15)*

Because we have people of different religions or no religion, (such as, Islam, Mormons, Jehovah's Witnesses, Catholics, Buddhists, traditional mainstream Christianity, atheists, and others, no one should hate the other because their beliefs, opinions, or practices are different, or because such differences causes one or the other to voice disapproval of the other(s) because of spiritual reasons. To initiate rage and violence against someone because he or she disagrees and speaks negatively against your faith, beliefs, and practices is hatred, and obviously offensive because, "certain matters of truth have touched a nerve that irritates you and makes you feel uncomfortable; if you're certain and comfortable about your faith it shouldn't bother you at all." But, when it bothers you into rage and violence, and even murder, you definitely have a serious problem that discredits your faith and its value to others who will to exercise their own free-will.

Hatred is of the devil, unless it's holy hatred against sin, the thing that God Himself hates. All people, whether they acknowledge God as God or not "are not to be hated, but loved just as God loves them." All people are responsible for their own sins and will have to give an account to God accordingly. We in our love for all God's creation, "are to preach, teach, and witness God's truth without compromise, and without sparing the feelings and emotions of others, because, "it's the truth that benefits and saves; not the giving it and compromising of it."

Therefore, "if we be hated because of the truth, that's a good and profitable thing for us;" just rejoice and be exceedingly glad, "knowing they hate Jesus before they hated us!"

The Apostle Paul encourage Timothy by saying: "But you be watchful in all things, endure afflictions,—do the work of an evangelist, fulfill your ministry." (2 Tim. 4:5) This always remember; Christ called, anointed, and appointed us to be witnesses; for the Bible says:

> [8] *But you shall receive power when the Holy Spirit has come upon you; and you shall be witnesses to Me in Jerusalem, and in all Judea and Samaria, and to the end of the earth." [9] Now when He had spoken these things, while they watched, He was taken up, and a cloud received Him out of their sight. (Acts 1:8-9)*

> [18] *And Jesus came and spoke to them, saying, "All authority has been given to Me in heaven and on earth. [19] Go therefore and make disciples of all the nations, baptizing them in the name of the Father and of the Son and of the Holy Spirit, [20] teaching them to observe all things that I have commanded you; and lo, I am with you always, even to the end of the age." Amen. (Matt. 28:18-20)*

> *"If the world hates you, you know that it hated Me before it hated you. (Jn. 15:18) But even if you should suffer for righteousness' sake, you are blessed. "And do not be afraid of their threats, nor be troubled." (1 Pet. 3:14)*

> *¹⁹ For the wisdom of this world is foolishness with God. For it is written, "He catches the wise in their own craftiness"; ²⁰ and again, "The LORD knows the thoughts of the wise, that they are futile." (1 Cor. 3:19-20) ¹³ Who is wise and understanding among you? Let him show by good conduct that his works are done in the meekness of wisdom. ¹⁴ But if you have bitter envy and self-seeking in your hearts, do not boast and lie against the truth. ¹⁵ This wisdom does not descend from above, but is earthly, sensual, demonic. ¹⁶ For where envy and self-seeking exist, confusion and every evil thing are there. (Ja. 3:13-15)*

> *²⁴ He who hates, disguises it with his lips, And lays up deceit within himself; ²⁵ When he speaks kindly, do not believe him, For there are seven abominations in his heart; ²⁶ Though his hatred is covered by deceit, His wickedness will be revealed before the assembly. ²⁷ Whoever digs a pit will fall into it, And he who rolls a stone will have it roll back on him. ²⁸ A lying tongue hates those who are crushed by it, And a flattering mouth works ruin. (Prov. 26:24-28)*

What Donald Trump and other racists are unable to understand is that God can and does expose racist people at His will whenever He pleases. None of them have any control in the how, when, and where their exposures occur. Even them themselves are sometimes unaware of when they're actually exposing themselves for you they really are. God sometimes give them enough rope to make their own nooses to hang themselves for their own evils. This is exactly what makes their wisdom foolishness to God, and is exactly why God catches them in their own craftiness, knowing their thoughts are futile (incapable of producing any useful results; pointless; fruitless; vain; useless; ineffectual; ineffective). Therefore, to God, such persons are worthless in His sight.

Racists are hypocrites to have as little as possible to do with the true God. They really don't like God, but are willing to tolerate Him for whatever benefits they can get from claiming His name while performing the evil they do against blacks and other people of color, and even their own people who do not agree with their ungodly philosophies and who seek to serve God in spirit and in truth. In reality, they actually despise and hate God because they hate living according to His rules that restrict them from living their ungodly lives and unrestricted lifestyles, especially, when it comes down to accepting blacks and other people of color as their equals. The god they serve and do evil in the name is more racist than they are; because he's the god of this age, Satan himself, the devil.

Jesus told us that "we will know, not possibly, perhaps, or maybe know, but know" a tree by its fruits. Jesus is the One that brought us grace and truth; so then, He knows exactly or absolutely what He's talking about when drawing His conclusion about fruits from a particular tree. Going on Jesus' conclusion, let us look at the Trump family tree and examine the fruits from this tree.

To assist us in "this examination of fruits," an article from American News X entitled, "The Trump Family's Decades-Long History of Racism," April 30, 2016, provides the following vital information in helping all who seriously seek knowing the truth, whether the Trump family tree produces good fruits or bad fruits. Let's look at this article!

Donald Trump's hateful statements towards Mexicans and Muslims are not the earliest examples of his prejudicial worldview. Many Americans are disgusted by Donald Trump's blatant racism, but it comes as no surprise. On January 25, 2016, the New York Times reported that Will Kaufman, a professor of American literature and culture at the University of Central Lancashire in Britain doing research on American folksinger and progressive icon Woody Guthrie, discovered that the latter (Guthrie), who rented an apartment at Beach Haven, a housing complex owned by Donald Trump's father, Frederick Christ Trump in Brooklyn, New York, wrote verse condemning his landlord for spreading racial prejudice:—"I suppose Old Man Trump knows Just how much Racial Hate he stirred up In the blood pot of human hearts When he drawed That color line Here at his Eighteen hundred family project."

TRUMP IS UNFIT

Clearly, Woody Guthrie refers to Fred Trump's refusal to rent to black tenants. Perhaps it's fair to say that the apple doesn't fall far from the tree, considering that throughout Donald Trump's campaign, he has announced intentions to build a wall between the U.S. and Mexico and to mandate Muslims in the U.S. to register in a national database and wear special identification badges. Of course, those two examples of hateful rhetoric are certainly not surprising, considering a bigoted gesture made by Donald Trump in 1989, over 20 years before he first campaigned for President on the Reform Party ticket in 2000.

On April 19, 1989, Trisha Meiji, a white investment banker, 28 years old at the time, went for a jog along the northern section of New York's Central Park and was beaten with a rock, stabbed, gagged, tied, raped and left for dead but survived despite suffering hypothermia and severe brain damage. Five (5) local youths (four (4) black, one (1) Hispanic), 14-year-olds Raymond Santana and Kevin Richardson; 15-year-olds Antron McCray and Yusef Salaam and 16-year-old Korey Wise—later collectively known as the Central Park Five—were arrested for the crime and subjected to violent interrogations.

Four (4) of the accused were forced to sign a confession to the rape and declare on video with no lawyer present that while they had not been the individual to commit the rape they had witnessed one of the others do it, thereby implicating the entire group,—despite the 6th Amendment mandating that people accused of crimes be given the right to an attorney. The youths were convicted and received sentences ranging from five (5) to 10 years and five (5) to 15 years, but in 2002, after their time had been served, DNA evidence linking convicted serial rapist and murderer Matias Reyes—to the attack on Trisha Meiji—proved the Central Park Five innocent.

In the aftermath of the Central Park Five being arrested, Donald Trump paid $85,000 for advertising space in four (4) of the city's newspapers, including the New York Times and the New York Daily News condemning the four (4) teenagers with the headline, "Bring Back The Death Penalty. Bring Back Our Police!" A haranguing paragraph signed by Donald Trump himself was published below the headline in which after Donald Trump laments the disappearance of law and order in New York City over the previous decade, he declares:

"Mayor Koch has stated that hate and rancor should be removed from our hearts. I do not think so. I want to hate these muggers and murderers. They should be forced to suffer, and when they kill, they should be executed for their crimes. They must serve as examples so that others will think long and hard before committing a crime or an act of violence. Yes, Mayor Koch, I want to hate these murderers and I always will. I am not looking to psychoanalyze or understand them, I am looking to punish them. If the punishment is strong, the attacks on innocent people will stop. I recently watched a newscast trying to explain the "anger in these young men". I no longer want to understand their anger. I want them to understand our anger. I want them to be afraid."

The racially motivated demagogy on the part of Donald Trump, certainly was not lost on Yusef Salaam. In a recent interview, he stated: "He was the fire starter. Common citizens were being manipulated and swayed into believing that we were guilty... I knew that this famous person calling for us to die was very serious. We were all afraid. Our families were afraid. Our loved ones were afraid. For us to walk around as if we had a target on our backs, that's how things were... Had this been the 1950s, that sick type of justice that they wanted—somebody from that darker place of society would have most certainly came to our homes, dragged us from our beds and hung us from trees in Central Park. It would have been similar to what they did to Emmett Till."

Michael Warren, who served as defense attorney for the Central Park Five, has no doubt that the advertisements Donald Trump bought to condemn his clients were an important catalyst in them being wrongly convicted.—"He poisoned the minds of many people who lived in New York and who, rightfully, had a natural affinity for the victim. Notwithstanding the jurors' assertions that they could be fair and impartial, some of them or their families, who naturally have influence, had to be affected by the inflammatory rhetoric in the ads."

In 2014, the Central Park Five settled a civil lawsuit with the city for $41 million. In an opinion piece for the New York Daily News published on June 21 of that year, Donald Trump called the settlement a "disgrace" and concurred with an NYPD detective's opinion that the payout was "the heist of the century." Trump also wrote: "Speak to the detectives on the case and try listening to the facts. These young men do not exactly have the pasts of angels." This, despite the fact that the boys were found to be innocent by incontrovertible DNA evidence.

Additionally, according to former Trump Plaza executive John O'Donnell, Donald Trump was not averse to making blatantly racist statements behind closed doors. In his 1991 book Trumped: The Inside Story of the Real Donald Trump—His Cunning Rise and Spectacular Fall, Donald Trump is reported to have said: "I've got black accountants at Trump Castle and at Trump Plaza. Black guys counting my money! I hate it. The only kind of people I want counting my money— are short guys that wear yarmulkes every day." Not one for showing much shame, Donald Trump remarked in an interview with Playboy shortly afterward: "The stuff O'Donnell wrote about me is probably true."

During Trump's first run for President in 2000, he clandestinely bought advertising in local upstate New York newspapers to shut down a rival Native American casino. The ad showed a picture of needles and other narcotics paraphernalia above the following caption: "Are these the new neighbors we want? The St. Regis Mohawk Indian record of criminal activity is well documented." All things considered, electing Donald Trump as the 45th President of the United States would be nothing short of dangerous to say the least. No doubt, Yusef Salaam is concerned by such a prospect. "What would this country look like with Donald Trump as being a president? That's a scary thing. That's a very scary thing."

There are reports that the Trump family has ties or connections with the KKK. Donald Trump has declined to denounce David Duke and the KKK. An article in the New York Times Daily News on Sunday, February 28, 2016, by Adam Edelman states: "Racism reportedly runs in the family, when it comes to the Trump Klan. Trump's late father, Fred Trump, was arrested following a Ku Klux Klan riot in Queens in 1927, according to a bombshell report that further suggests unusual ties between the 2016 front-runner and the notorious white supremacist group.

Fred Trump Sr. was among seven (7) men arrested following a May 30, 1927 brawl between members of the KKK and the New York Police Department, according to the Washington Post, which unearthed news articles from the June 1, 1927 edition of The New York Times.

The elder Trump's role in the brawl was unclear, The Post reported, and there is no proof in the report that he was a member of the KKK. The fights that broke out in Queens occurred after 1,000 KKK members dressed in white hooded robes marched through the Jamaica neighborhood. According to The Post, the address of the elder Trump from the arrest report matched the Jamaica address where he lived, according to a 1930 Census. Trump, who was born in the Bronx to German immigrants, would have been 21 at the time of the arrest. He later became a wealthy real estate developer and died in 1999.

The purpose of the KKK march that day was to rally "Native-born Protestant Americans" who felt targeted by "Roman Catholic police of New York City," according to a flier advertising the protest obtained by The Post. "Liberty and Democracy have been trampled upon," the flier stated, "when native-born Protestant Americans dare to organize to protect one flag, the American flag; one school, the public school; and one language, the English language." Reports of the elder Trump's involvement in the incident initially surfaced last August on tech blog Boing Boing.

When asked to comment Sunday on the latest details surrounding the incident, a spokeswoman for the Trump campaign sent a link to a story from September 2015 story in which the Republican mogul ardently rejected the report. "He was never arrested. He has nothing to do with this. This never happened. This is nonsense and it never happened," Trump said about his father in the September 2015 article. "This never happened. Never took place. He was never arrested, never convicted, never even charged. It's a completely false, ridiculous story. He was never there! It never happened. Never took place." The resurfacing of the report comes at an inopportune time for the bombastic billionaire, who last week received the endorsement of former KKK leader David Duke.

On Sunday Trump repeatedly refused to distance himself from Duke and the KKK and initially declined to disavow the support. Amid mounting pressure to reject the comments, however, he eventually took to twitter to condemn the support. [End of Article] Clearly, in the middle of mounting pressure and the fear of the damage ties with Duke and the KKK could bring against his run for President,—out of this fear and for this purpose only,—"did Trump take to twitter to condemn the support." There's no doubt, whatsoever, that Trump's twit was done out of personal fear to break down amid accusations of him and his father's involvement in the KKK.

Everyone knows that back in the day, Klansmen hid their faces with white hoods and did as much in secret as possible, like the cowards they actually were and still are until this day. As said previously, "you cannot hid that which God chooses to expose!" The facts in a matter will always speak for themselves, when properly and thoroughly weighed for evidence. Hate and bigotry are the "primary or most dominant characteristic traits of KKK members and or racist whites not KKK members having KKK mentalities." Yes, hate and bigotry by far, are out there front and centered to raise their ugly heads, in particularly, to blacks and other people of color, and the whites that support them.

The truth is the Spirit of truth, the Holy Spirit, who brings to us "every word that proceeds from the mouth of God," which "is entirely truthful without one tiny dap of error;" the truth and nothing but the truth. Whatever and however God says what He says is right!!!!!!!

God knows and has declared everything from the beginning to the ending!!!!!!! He knows every person's thoughts, emotions, and wills from the beginning to the ending!!!!!!! His truth breaks down every wall or barrier that divides, discriminates, confuses, and fosters hatred!!!!!!!

White Americans are the racial majority. African Americans are the largest racial minority, amounting to 13.2% of the population. Hispanic and Latino Americans amount to 17% of the population, making up the largest ethnic minority. Native Americans, Alaska Natives, Asian Americans, Native Hawaiians, and Other Pacific Islanders are the other racial minorities in America. The Truth embodies God's love, and as such, "the truth transcends all racial barriers."

> *43 "You have heard that it was said, 'You shall love your neighbor and hate your enemy.' 44 But I say to you, love your enemies, bless those who curse you, do good to those who hate you, and pray for those who spitefully use you and persecute you, 45 that you may be sons of your Father in heaven; for He makes His sun rise on the evil and on the good, and sends rain on the just and on the unjust. 46 For if you love those who love you, what reward have you? Do not even the tax collectors do the same? 47 And if you greet your brethren only, what do you do more than others? Do not even the tax collectors do so? 48 Therefore you shall be perfect, just as your Father in heaven is perfect. (Matt. 5:43-48)*

> *8 Owe no one anything except to love one another, for he who loves another has fulfilled the law. (Rom. 13:8) 10 Love does no harm to a neighbor; therefore love is the fulfillment of the law. (Rom. 13:10) 10In this the children of God and the children of the devil are manifest: Whoever does not practice righteousness is not of God, nor is he who does not love his brother. (1 Jn. 3:10)*

> *14 We know that we have passed from death to life, because we love the brethren. He who does not love his brother abides in death. 15 Whoever hates his brother is a murderer, and you know that no murderer has eternal life abiding in him. (1 Jn.*

3:14-15) [20] *If someone says, "I love God," and hates his brother, he is a liar; for he who does not love his brother whom he has seen, how can he love God whom he has not seen?* [21] *And this commandment we have from Him: that he who loves God must love his brother also. (1 Jn. 4:20-21)*

6

America's Religious Status

AMERICA IS NOT a Christian nation; however, she does have a very strong influence of Christian principles in her midst. She is a melting pot (assimilation of immigrants) of various religious faiths and of all tongues to practice the faiths of their conscious freely without any repercussions. As such, every person in America can of his or her own free-will practice any faith he or she chooses (i.e. Christianity or any other). No one in America is forced or coerced into practicing any faith in opposition or disagreement with his or her conscious or will; which allows every person to exercise his or her own God-given-gift of freewill—to practice, worship, or give homage (show special honor or respect publicly) to whomsoever or whatsoever he or she pleases. This is what America was founded upon (freedom of religion) and not Christianity, as our history clearly reflects and to the contrary to what so many—have been led to believe.

The First Amendment (Amendment I) to the US Constitution prohibits the making of any law respecting: 1) an establishment of religion, 2) impeding the free exercise of religion, 3) abridging the freedom of speech, 4) infringing on the freedom of the press, 5) interfering with the right to peaceably assemble, or 5) prohibiting the petitioning for a governmental redress of grievances. It was adopted on December 15, 1791, as one of the ten (10) amendments that constitute the Bill of Rights.

The freedom of religion (the right to choose a religion or no religion without interference by the government) is guaranteed by this 1st Amendment. Regardless of one's religion or non-religion, he or she has the right to run for any public office on the city, state, and federal levels, including the office of President of the United States of America.

As Christians among many non-Christians and pseudo-Christians (fake or hypocrite Christians), we have unrestricted opportunities in the United States of America to influence others through the Christian principles we believe and practice in our daily lives. Understanding we're in the midst of a mixed culture of various faiths and the impact our faith has on our own decision-making process, we should strongly consider the impact those of other faiths have on their decision-making process.

We should as Christians strive hard to ensure that our elections of politicians are Christians so that their decision-making process includes or factors in Christian principles. When we're successful doing this, our cities, states, and nation as a whole will have legislation (laws set by our governments)—in line or closer in line with Christian principles, than—other non-Christians making and approving legislation according to their own principles, which is to be expected. So then, we shouldn't be wondering or surprised when ungodly laws are enacted (e.g. gay rights, gay marriage, etc.). Nevertheless, passing of ungodly laws should have no impact on Christians who desire to live godly in Christ; they should continue living godly and teach their children and others to do the same.—"God is our guidance not our culture!"—

Is the United States a "Christian nation?" Some Americans think so. Religious Right activists and right-wing television preachers often claim that the United States was founded to be a Christian nation. Even some politicians agree. If the people who make this assertion are merely saying that most Americans are Christians, they might have a point. But those who argue that America is a Christian nation usually mean something more, insisting that the country should be officially Christian. The very character of our country is at stake in the outcome of this debate.

Religious Right groups and their allies insist that the United States was designed to be officially Christian and that our laws should enforce the doctrines of (their version of) Christianity. Is this viewpoint accurate? Is there anything in the Constitution that gives special treatment or preference to Christianity? Did the founders of our government believe this or intend to create a government that gave special recognition to Christianity? The answer to all of these questions is no. The U.S. Constitution is a wholly secular document. It contains no mention of Christianity or Jesus Christ. In fact, the Constitution refers to religion only twice in the First Amendment, which bars laws "respecting an establishment of religion or prohibiting the free exercise thereof," and in Article VI, which prohibits "religious tests" for public office. Both of these provisions are evidence that the country was not founded as officially Christian.

The Founding Fathers did not create a secular government because they disliked religion. Many were believers themselves. Yet they were well aware of the dangers of church-state union. They had studied and even seen first-hand the difficulties that church-state partnerships spawned in Europe. During the American colonial period, alliances between religion and government produced oppression and tyranny on our own shores. Many colonies, for example, had provisions limiting public office to "Trinitarian Protestants" and other types of laws designed to prop up the religious sentiments of the politically powerful. Some colonies had officially established churches and taxed all citizens to support them, whether they were members or not.—Dissenters faced imprisonment, torture and even death.

These arrangements led to bitterness and sectarian division. Many people began agitating for an end to "religious tests" for public office, tax subsidies for churches and other forms of state endorsement of religion. Those who led this charge were not anti-religion. Indeed, many were members of the clergy and people of deep piety. They argued that true faith did not need or want the support of government.

Respect for religious pluralism gradually became the norm. When Thomas Jefferson wrote the Declaration of Independence, for example, he spoke of "unalienable rights endowed by our Creator." He used generic religious language that all religious groups of the day would respond to, not narrowly Christian language traditionally employed by nations with state churches.

While some of the country's founders believed that the government should espouse Christianity, that viewpoint soon became a losing proposition. In Virginia, Patrick Henry argued in favor of tax support for Christian churches. But Henry and his cohorts were in the minority and lost that battle. Jefferson, James Madison and their allies among the state's religious groups ended Virginia's established church and helped pass the Virginia Statute for Religious Liberty,—a 1786 law guaranteeing religious freedom to all. Jefferson and Madison's viewpoint also carried the day when the Constitution, and later, the Bill of Rights, were written. Had an officially Christian nation been the goal of the founders, that concept would appear in the Constitution. It does not. Instead, our nation's governing document ensures religious freedom for everyone.

Maryland representative Luther Martin said that a handful of delegates to the Constitutional Convention argued for formal recognition of Christianity in the Constitution, insisting that such language was necessary in order to "hold out some distinction between the professors of Christianity and downright infidelity or paganism." But that view was not adopted, and the Constitution gave government no authority over religion. Article VI, which allows persons of all religious viewpoints to hold public office, was adopted by a unanimous vote. Through ratification of the First Amendment, observed Jefferson, the American people built a "wall of separation between church and state."

Some pastors who favored church-state union were outraged and delivered sermons asserting that the United States would not be a successful nation because its Constitution did not give special treatment to Christianity. But many others welcomed the new dawn of freedom and praised the Constitution and the First Amendment as true protectors of liberty. Early national leaders understood that separation of church and state would be good for all faiths including Christianity. Jefferson rejoiced that Virginia had passed his religious freedom law, noting that it would ensure religious freedom for "the Jew and the Gentile, the Christian and Mahometan, the Hindoo, the infidel of every denomination."

Other early U.S. leaders echoed that view. President George Washington, in a famous 1790 letter to a Jewish congregation in Newport, R.I., celebrated the fact that Jews had full freedom of worship in America. Noted Washington, "All possess alike liberty of conscience and immunities of citizenship." Washington's administration even negotiated a treaty with the Muslim rulers of North Africa that stated explicitly that the United States was not founded on Christianity. The pact, known as the Treaty with Tripoli, was approved unanimously by the Senate in 1797, under the administration of John Adams. Article 11 of the treaty states, "[T]he government of the United States is not, in any sense, founded on the Christian religion...."

Admittedly, the U.S. government has not always lived up to its constitutional principles. In the late 19th century especially, officials often promoted a *de facto* form of Protestantism. Even the U.S. Supreme Court fell victim to this mentality in 1892, with Justice David Brewer declaring in *Holy Trinity v. United States* that America is "a Christian nation." It should be noted, however, that the *Holy Trinity* decision is a legal anomaly. It has rarely been cited by other courts, and the "Christian nation" declaration appeared in dicta a legal term meaning writing that reflects a judge's personal opinion, not a mandate of the law. Also, it is unclear exactly what Brewer meant. In a book he wrote in 1905, Brewer pointed out that the United States is Christian in a cultural sense, not a legal one.

A more accurate judicial view of the relationship between religion and government is described by Justice John Paul Stevens in his 1985 Wallace v. Jaffree ruling. Commenting on the constitutional right of all Americans to choose their own religious belief, Stevens wrote, "At one time it was thought that this right merely proscribed the preference of one Christian sect over another, but would not require equal respect for the conscience of the infidel, the atheist, or the adherent of a non-Christian faith such as Mohammedism or Judaism. But when the underlying principle has been examined in the crucible of litigation, the Court has unambiguously concluded that the individual freedom of conscience protected by the First Amendment—embraces the right to select any religious faith or none at all."

A determined faction of Christians has fought against this wise and time-tested policy throughout our history. In the mid-19th century, several efforts were made to add specific references to Christianity to the Constitution. One group, the National Reform Association (NRA), pushed a "Christian nation" amendment in Congress in 1864. NRA members believed that the Civil War was divine punishment for failing to mention God in the Constitution and saw the amendment as a way to atone for that omission.

The NRA amendment called for "humbly acknowledging Almighty God as the source of all authority and power in civil government, the Lord Jesus Christ as the Ruler among the nations, [and] His revealed will as the supreme law of the land, in order to constitute a Christian government." Ten years later, the House Judiciary Committee voted against its adoption. The committee noted "the dangers which the union between church and state had imposed upon so many nations of the Old World" and said in light of that it was felt—"inexpedient to put anything into the Constitution which might be construed to be a reference to any religious creed or doctrine."

Similar theocratic proposals resurfaced in Congress sporadically over the years. As late as 1950, a proposal was introduced in the Senate that would have added language to the Constitution that "devoutly recognizes the Authority and Law of Jesus Christ, Saviour and Ruler of nations, through whom are bestowed the blessings of liberty." This amendment was never voted out of committee. Efforts to revive it in the early 1960s were unsuccessful.

Today, America's religious demographics are changing, and diversity has greatly expanded since our nation's founding. The number of Jews has increased, and more Muslims are living in America than ever before. Other religions now represented in America include Hinduism, Buddhism and a myriad others. In addition, many Americans say they have no religious faith or identify themselves as atheists, agnostics or Humanists. According to some scholars, over 2,000 distinct religious groups and denominations exist in the United States.

Also, even though most Americans identify as Christian, this does not mean they would back official government recognition of the Christian faith. Christian denominations disagree on points of doctrine, church structure and stands on social issues. Many Christians take a moderate or liberal perspective on church-state relations and oppose efforts to impose religion by government action.

Americans should be proud that we live in a democracy that welcomes persons of many faiths and none. Around the globe, millions of people still dwell under oppressive regimes where religion and government are harshly commingled. (Iran and the former Taliban regime of Afghanistan are just two examples.) Many residents of those countries look to the United States as beacon of hope and a model for what their own nations—might someday become. Only the principle of church-state separation can protect America's incredible degree of religious freedom. The individual rights and diversity we enjoy cannot be maintained if the government promotes Christianity or if our government takes on the trappings of a "faith-based" state.

The United States, in short, was not founded to be an officially Christian nation or to espouse any official religion. Our government is neutral on religious matters, leaving such decisions to individuals. This democratic and pluralistic system has allowed a broad array of religious groups to grow and flourish and guarantees every individual American the right to determine his or her own spiritual path or to reject religion entirely. As a result of this policy, Americans enjoy more religious freedom than any people in world history. We should be proud of this accomplishment and work to preserve the constitutional principle that made it possible separation of church and state. [Americans United For Separation of Church and State]

God does not force or coerce anyone to choose Him and to worship

Him as Lord and Saviour. Likewise, no city, state, nor federal government should force or coerce anyone to choose a particular person to serve and worship. However, everyone has the right to influence his or her beliefs and practices upon whoever is open and willing to hear them; but—not to aggressively force or coerce anyone by fear, violence, or any other means to become converts of their respective faiths or else. If someone speaks negatively about another's faith, it should not be responded back upon aggressively and violently in any way; because "all have the right to feel, believe, and speak" as their conscious dictates without having to suffer repercussions (unintended consequences occurring sometimes after an event or action, especially an unwelcome one).

One person's faith may be offensive to another's; but, such differences shouldn't create anger and hostility against one another; all negative comments should be taken in strive by both parties and considered through love for future action if such opportunities present themselves again. People do not have to be enemies of destruction because they disagree on faith issues. There are many people of all nations, races, and colors that are good and moral (concerned with the principles of right and wrong behavior and the goodness or badness of human character)—by nature; just as there are many that are bad and immoral (unconcerned with the principles of right and wrong behavior and the goodness or badness of human character)—by nature. This is exactly why: "If it is possible, as much as depends on us, live peaceably with all people" (Rom. 12:18).

However, some are unreasonable and wicked (2 Thess. 3:2) making it impossible to live peaceably with them. Concerning such, we are to pray one another deliverance for the word of the Lord to run swiftly and be glorified in us (2 Thess. 3:1). Here, in our country of the United States of America—Christianity is evangelized through preaching, teaching and sharing the gospel of Jesus Christ without any governmental restraints—wherein, providing unlimited opportunities to fulfill Jesus' great commission as found below in Matthew 28:16-20 and Mark 16:14-18.

[16] Then the eleven disciples went away into Galilee, to the mountain which Jesus had appointed for them. [17] When they saw Him, they worshiped Him; but some doubted. [18] And Jesus came and spoke to them, saying, "All authority has been given to Me in heaven and on earth. [19] Go therefore and make disciples of all the nations, baptizing them in the name of the Father and of the Son and of the Holy Spirit, [20] teaching them to observe all things that I have commanded you; and lo, I am with you always, even to the end of the age." Amen. (Matt. 28:16-20)

[14] Later He appeared to the eleven as they sat at the table; and He rebuked their unbelief and hardness of heart, because they did not believe those who had seen Him after He had risen. [15] And He said to them, "Go into all the world and preach the gospel to every creature. [16] He who believes and is baptized will be saved; but he who does not believe will be condemned. [17] And these signs will follow those who believe:—In My name they will cast out demons; they will speak with new tongues; [18] they will take up serpents; and if they drink anything deadly, it will by no means hurt them; they will lay hands on the sick, and they will recover." (Mk. 16:14-18)

Regardless of people's nationality, race and color,—we are not to discriminate, but as much as possible, live peaceable with them, because, this is the will of the Lord for us,—"to share His gift love to all willing to receive it," and to make all aware and knowledgeable of the fact, that, regardless of how good and morally right they are naturally,—that's not good and morally righteousness enough to be saved from the penalty of sin (spiritual death and eternal separation from God and the Lord Jesus Christ).

"But we are all like an unclean thing, And all our righteousnesses are like filthy rags;—We all fade as a leaf, And our iniquities,—like the wind, Have taken us away. (Isa. 64:6). Everyone, regardless of how good and morally right they might believe themselves being—need their sins redeemed by the precious blood of Christ, God's only begotten Son. This is a must in order to escape the wrath of God to come upon all who rejects His gift of salvation through Jesus Christ;—This is "the message" we are to share with all people of all races, colors, and tongues; when and as often as opportunity presents itself without forcing or coercing anything upon anyone.

As Christians, our behavior practices (speeches and actions) should be done in the meekness of wisdom (Ja. 3:13) and our hearts sanctified in the Lord Jesus Christ (1 Pet. 3:15) conducting ourselves in the world in simplicity and godly sincerity,—not with fleshly wisdom (which is earthly, sensual, demonic). (2 Cor. 1:12; Ja. 3:15) We are to strive continuously in manifesting the fruit of the Spirit (love, joy, peace, longsuffering, kindness, goodness, faithfulness, gentleness, self-control). (Gal. 5:22-23) God's wisdom which He gives to all who asks (Ja. 1:5) is first pure, then peaceable, gentle, willing to yield, full of mercy and good fruits, without partiality and without hypocrisy" (Ja.3:17). Now the fruit of righteousness is sown in peace—by those who make peace (Ja. 3:18).

> *⁷ But as you abound in everything—in faith, in speech, in knowledge, in all diligence, and in your love for us—see that you abound in this grace also. ⁸ I speak not by commandment, but I am testing the sincerity of your love by the diligence of others. ⁹ For you know the grace of our Lord Jesus Christ, that though He was rich, yet for your sakes He became poor, that you through His poverty might become rich. (2 Cor. 8:7-9)*

> *Therefore, if anyone is in Christ, he is a new creation; old things have passed away; behold, all things have become new. (2 Cor. 5:17) For in Christ Jesus neither circumcision nor uncircumcision avails anything, but a new creation. (Gal. 6:15) Let your light so shine before men, that they may see your good works and glorify your Father in heaven. (Matt. 5:16)*

America's Religious Status

We who are Christians in America have a godly responsibility and duty to witness the gospel of Jesus Christ—unto all people of all races, colors, tongues. Whether or not we're in our homes, on our jobs, in our churches, on the streets, in social environments, in politics, and any other place,—"as we have opportunity, we are to witness the gospel of Jesus Christ and let our light shine before all." This is our duty in fulfilling Christ's great commission. In doing so, we will have a continuous or perpetual influence on the good and bad in America. "Our Christian influences makes a difference in all issues and events" occurring in our country.

> [11] *Let us therefore be diligent to enter that rest, lest anyone fall according to the same example of disobedience.* [12] *For the word of God is living and powerful, and sharper than any two-edged sword,—piercing even to the division of soul and spirit, and of joints and marrow, and is a discerner of the thoughts and intents of the heart.* [13] *And there is no creature hidden from His sight, but all things are naked and open—to the eyes of Him to whom we must give account. (Heb. 4:11-13)*

> [6] *Who made heaven and earth, The sea, and all that is in them; Who keeps truth forever,* [7] *Who executes justice for the oppressed, Who gives food to the hungry. The LORD gives freedom to the prisoners.* [8] *The LORD opens the eyes of the blind; The LORD raises those who are bowed down; The LORD loves the righteous.* [9] *The LORD watches over the strangers; He relieves the fatherless and widow; But the way of the wicked He turns upside down. (Psa. 149:6-9)*

> [9] *And let us not grow weary while doing good, for in due season we shall reap if we do not lose heart.* [10] *Therefore, as we have opportunity, let us do good to all, especially to those who are of the household of faith. (Gal. 6:9-10)* [17] *Therefore, to him who knows to do good and does not do it, to him it is sin. (Ja. 4:7)*

> *⁸ If you see the oppression of the poor, and the violent perversion of justice and righteousness in a province, do not marvel at the matter; for high official watches over high official, and higher officials are over them. (Eccles. 5:8)*
>
> *³ The eyes of the Lord are in every place, Keeping watch on the evil and the good. Prov. 15:3) ⁹ For the eyes of the Lord run to and fro throughout the whole earth, to show Himself strong on behalf of those whose heart is loyal to Him. In this you have done foolishly; therefore from now on you shall have wars." (2 Chron. 16:9)*

Every person is required to live peacefully with one another as much as possible. There are some wicked and unreasonable people that make living peacefully with them practically and sometimes altogether impossible. We need to, however, to make sure we've put a serious godly effort into accomplishing this peacefulness; and when such efforts fail, we're pray, separate ourselves, and leave the rest to God. At no time ever are we to hate anyone. We can, however, dislike some for their distasteful and disgusting ways; but to hate, is not an option for godly people. God has everything and everyone under His watch and control; therefore, we are to trust Him,—give way to His vengeance, and He will direct our paths in His will for us.

7
Understanding Mindsets

MINDSET IS DEFINED as a person's way of thinking, his or her opinions, beliefs, and points of view. Mindsets vary from person to person, and some having similar mindsets resulting from their faith or non-faith beliefs and practices. Every individual is influenced by things he or she believes and practices as a way of life, which ultimately determines decisions or choices made. Decisions or choices are just made; but rather, birthed directly from one's faith or non-faith beliefs and practices. Some mindsets can be easily influenced to make bad decisions or choices; while other mindsets are not so easily influenced because they're more careful, painstaking, and meticulous about things they hear and act upon.

Imposter or deceivers bring their trickery with persuasive words to entice through their cunning craftiness and deceitful plotting. Some mindsets are easily broken down, infiltrated, and caught-up in webs of deception; while other mindsets are not so easily entrapped; because they're more sober and vigilant of the devil's temptations; so they submit to God, resist the devil and he flees from them. All of us, in order to prevent being deceived must guard our hearts and minds from worldly things (the lust of the flesh, the lust of the eyes, and the pride of life). The devil and his representatives will use every available means to bring about deception, division, hatred, contention, strife, and the like wherever and whenever possible.

⁹ "The heart is deceitful above all things, And desperately wicked; Who can know it?

¹⁰ I, the LORD, search the heart, I test the mind, Even to give every man according to his ways, According to the fruit of his doings. (Jer. 17:9-10)

⁶ Be anxious for nothing, but in everything by prayer and supplication, with thanksgiving, let your requests be made known to God; ⁷ and the peace of God, which surpasses all understanding,—will guard your hearts and minds through Christ Jesus. (Phil. 4:6-7)

[The Humbled and Exalted Christ] Let this mind be in you which was also in Christ Jesus, (Phil. 2:5) Therefore let us, as many as are mature, have this mind; and if in anything you think otherwise,—God will reveal even this to you. (Phil 3:15)

⁵ Trust in the LORD with all your heart, And lean not on your own understanding; ⁶ In all your ways acknowledge Him, And He shall direct your paths. ⁷ Do not be wise in your own eyes;— Fear the LORD and depart from evil. (Prov. 3:5-7)

Most politicians would not have us to trust in the Lord and not lean on our own understanding; because all who was to do so, would detect their fruitless rhetoric (art of effective speaking in lying and deceiving with persuasive words carrying empty promises). If we were to have the mind which was also in Christ Jesus, it would be very easy for us to identify imposters, pretenders, and those who are arrogant and prideful, and those having no empathy for other. But, if we were to trust the Holy Spirit, no doubt, many politicians would be disqualified and dismissed from our consideration in the voting process.

[13] However, when He, the Spirit of truth, has come, He will guide you into all truth; for He will not speak on His own authority, but whatever He hears He will speak; and He will tell you things to come. [14] He will glorify Me, for He will take of what is Mine and declare it to you. [15] All things that the Father has are Mine. Therefore I said that He will take of Mine and declare it to you. (Jn. 16:13-15)

The truthful lip shall be established forever, But a lying tongue is but for a moment. (Prov. 12:19) He who speaks truth declares righteousness, But a false witness, deceit. (Prov. 12:17) A false witness will not go unpunished, And he who speaks lies will not escape. (Prov. 19:5) A false witness will not go unpunished, And he who speaks lies shall perish. (Prov. 19:9)

In the political process, "Voting" provides the opportunity and means to "Vote" to "Elect" the most qualified candidate to perform the duty at hand in the best interest of the people. As, "the people," we all have a duty and a responsibility to cast individually our "Vote" in an "unbiased, indiscriminative, moral and ethical manner," in the best interest of all the people. Since most people know very little about politicians, it's our duty/responsibility to learn and inform others of what they might not know and what they might need to know so that "their Votes" have been made rightfully to the best of their knowledge and understanding, with the Holy Spirit's help for the most qualified candidate to perform the duty at hand in the best interest of the people.

[1]Therefore if there is any consolation in Christ, if any comfort of love, if any fellowship of the Spirit, if any affection and mercy, [2] fulfill my joy by being like-minded, having the same love, being of one accord, of one mind. [3] Let nothing be done through selfish ambition or conceit, but in lowliness of mind let each esteem others better than himself. [4] Let each of you look out

> not only for his own interests, but also for the interests of others. (Phil. 2:1-4)

When it's time to "Vote," whether on the city, state, or federal levels, we all need the best guidance possible so that our "Votes" aren't cast for unqualified candidates full of envy and selfish ambition, who are interested in themselves only and a select few. Therefore, we all have need to be quick to hear and slow to speak before "Voting" on our candidate of choice!

> [20] But you have an anointing from the Holy One, and you know all things. [21] I have not written to you because you do not know the truth, but because you know it, and that no lie is of the truth. (1 Jn. 2:20-21)

> [26] These things I have written to you concerning those who try to deceive you. [27] But the anointing which you have received from Him abides in you, and you do not need that anyone teach you; but as the same anointing teaches you concerning all things, and is true, and is not a lie, and just as it has taught you, you will abide in Him. (1 Jn. 2:26-27)

> [6]This is He who came by water and blood—Jesus Christ; not only by water, but by water and blood. And it is the Spirit who bears witness, because the Spirit is truth. [7] For there are three that bear witness in heaven: the Father, the Word, and the Holy Spirit; and these three are one. [8] And there are three that bear witness on earth: the Spirit, the water, and the blood; and these three agree as one. (1 Jn. 5:6-8)

Therefore, to avoid being trapped in the web of liars and deceivers,—trust the Holy Spirit, the Spirit of truth, and He will guide us in all truth to cast the best "Vote!"

8

A Fool's Profile and Actions

A FOOL IS defined by many dictionaries as someone who acts unwisely or imprudently; a silly person; an idiot or ignoramus. Biblically, the word "fool" occurs in several forms (fools, foolish, etc.). The Hebrew word for fool is "nabal," meaning stupid, wicked (especially impious (not showing respect or reverence to God)). The Greek word "aphone" is similar, but adds the idea of someone who is "mindless, egotistic, practically rash or moral unbelieving, and unwise. Nevertheless, it's never a good thing to be a fool or to act foolishly; avoid being and/or doing so always!

Based on the above descriptions, we provide the following characteristics of a fool as referenced in the Holy Bible: 1) Fools are unwise (Deut. 32:6; Psa. 94:8; Prov. 14:33; Prov. 23:9); 2) Fools are immoral (2 Sam. 13:11-18; Job 30:8; Psa. 53:1; Psa. 74:18; Prov. 10:18; Prov. 14:9; Mk. 7:18-23); 3) Fools are prideful (Psa. 49:6-11; Psa. 73:3-13; Prov. 14:3; Prov. 30:32; Rom. 1:19-23; 2 Cor. 11:17); Fools despise parental teaching (Prov. 15:15; Prov. 15:20; Prov. 17: 21-25); Fools run their mouths with nonsense (Eccles. 5:3; Eccles. 7:6; Eccles. 10:12-14); Matt. 5:22); Fools reject God and what His word teaches (1 Sam. 13:13; Job 2:7-10; Psa. 14:1; Prov. 1:7; Prov. 10:8; Prov. 12:15; Matt. 7:26; Lu. 24:25; 1 Cor. 1:18-27); Fools cannot understand God's Word (Psa. 92:6; Prov. 1:22; Jer. 5:21; 1 Cor. 2:14); Foolish thinking deceives and leads the way of sin and destruction (2 Sam. 24:10; 1 Chron. 21:8; Psa. 5:5; Psa. 38:4-8; Psa. 107:17; Prov. 17:28; Prov. 26:11; Eccles. 7:9; Ezek. 13:3; Matt. 25:1-13); Foolish people are sometimes used by God to rebuke His people (Deut. 32:21; Hos. 9:7; Rom. 10:19-21); Fools and foolish thinking should be avoided (Prov. 9:6; Prov. 13:20; Prov. 26:5; Prov. 28:9; Eccles. 5:1; Eccles. 7:5; 2 Tim. 2:23; Titus 3:9).

Sin is exceedingly sinful, manifesting its wickedness of folly, even of foolishness and madness. Sin is the disease of mankind and is malignant and epidemic. In its malignance, it puts contempt upon the honour of God, in that, there is something of practical atheism at the bottom or root of all sin. The fool has said in his or her heart, "there is no God," which constitute atheistism (disbelief or lack of believe in God). Fools believe: 1) there's no Judge or Governor of the world, and 2) there's no providence (presiding care of God) presiding over the affairs of mankind. Yes, even during biblical times, there were those who had arrived at such a height of impiety (lack of piety or reverence, especially for God) as to deny the very being of God, which constitutes the first and self-evident principles of religion (a pursuit or interest to which a person ascribes supreme importance, whether of the God of the Bible or something or someone other than God, including, but not limited to, oneself).

Fools cannot doubt of the being of God, but will question His dominion. What they said in their hearts (there's no God) is not their judgment, but rather, their imagination. They cannot satisfy themselves that there is no God, but wish there was none; so as, to please themselves with the fancy that it's possible that there may be no God. Being a fool, he or she cannot be sure there is a God; therefore, he or she is willing to think there is no God. He or she dares not speak it out (there's no God), lest he or she be confuted (proved to be wrong), and so undeceived (clearly shown his or her idea or belief is mistaken or wrong in his or her opinion); therefore, he or she whispers it (there's no God) in his or her heart, for the silencing of the clamors (loud and confused noises, especially that of people yelling vehemently or with very strong feelings) of their consciences and the emboldening of themselves in their evil ways.

They are actually convicted by their own consciences that there is a God, but refuse to allow this fact to process in their minds. Being simple and unwise, this is an evidence of it; they are wicked and profane, and their state of being simple and unwise is the cause of their inability to accept and process the truth in their minds and hearts. Their athestical thoughts are very foolish and are at the bottom or root of a great deal of wickedness occurring in the world today. No person comes to the point of saying there's no God until he or she is so harden in sin that sin has become his or her interest that there should be none to call him or her out to an account of this sinful position.

Nature itself teaches and confirms there's a God. Nature speaks very eloquently of its Creator. God's divine attributes are not only clearly seen or revealed in humanity, but also in the material universe. From the intricate design of the human cell to the majestic strength of the Rocky Mountains, all of God's works testify of His infinite knowledge, understanding, wisdom, and power. God's invisible attributes, such as His eternal power and Godhead (Divine Nature) can be clearly seen by contemplating (looking thoughtfully or examining) His awesome works in all of creation. Only a fool and nothing but a fool could say "there's no God." Someone much greater and wiser than us altogether, would have had to create the earth and all that's in it.

The word of God is a discerner of these foolish thoughts (Heb. 4:12), and puts a just brand on the person that harbors them in his or her heart. Folly is with such people who think against the clearest light (truth), against their own knowledge and convictions, and the common sentiments (feelings or emotions; views or attitudes) of the wise and sober part of mankind's conscience, which places disgrace and debasement upon the nature of man. No doubt, sinners are corrupt, quite degenerated (having lost the physical, mental, and moral qualities considered normal and desirable) from what God created them (male and female) in His image in their innocent estate. Nevertheless, their consciences still have the ability to convict them of those things that are naturally wrong or right; whether of an action or a belief that is out of order (there's no God).

Fools have become filthy, putrid (rotten, repulsive, or extremely unpleasant). All their facilities are so disordered that they have become odious (despicable, contemptible, or sickening) to God their Maker and are utterly incapable of answering the ends of their creation (they are wretched, condemned, and unrepresented by Christ before the great white throne judgment). They are corrupt indeed, do no good, and represent the unprofitable burdens of the earth; they do God no service, bring Him no honor, nor do they do themselves any real kindness. They do a great deal of hurt in the earth; doing abominable works, for such are all sinful works. Sin is an abomination to God, and is that abominable thing which He hates (Jer. 44:4), and sooner or later, it will be found to be hateful (Psa. 36:2), and abomination of desolation, that is, making desolate (Matt. 24:15).

The Scriptures follow up on the fool's saying (there's no God); "for those that profess they know God, but in works deny Him, are abominable, and to every work reprobate" (Titus 1:16). This clearly shows how epidemic this sin disease really is, in that, it has infected the whole race of mankind (from one generation to another). To prove this prevailing sickness, God Himself brought Himself in as an eye-witness, and His question was, as He viewed all the children of men, was whether there were any among them that did understand themselves alright, their duty and interests, and did seek Him and set Him before them. God was not only One that could find out a good man if there was one to be found, though ever so obscure, but One that would be glad to find a good man, and would definitely be sure to take notice of him, just as He did of Noah in the old world.

When looking down from heaven, a place of prospect, which commands the lower world (earth and below), His search revealed they had all gone astray, the apostasy of the universe, there is none that does good, not one, no, not one, till the free and mighty grace of God has wrought a change. Whatever good is any of the children of men, or is done by them, it is not of themselves; but rather, it is of God's work through them. When God had made the world, He looked upon His work and all was very good (Gen. 1:31); and sometime after, He looked upon man's work, and behold, it was very bad (Gen. 6:5), every operation of the thoughts of man's heart was evil, only evil, and that continually.

Mankind have gone aside from the right way of their duty, the way that leads to happiness, and have turned into the paths of the destroyer (Satan). In singing this, let us lament the corruption of our own nature, and see what need all have of the grace of God; and, since that which is born of flesh is flesh, let us not marvel that we are told we must be born again. For, without the born again experience (regeneration), the sinner state of being a fool does not and will not change, which is a very dangerous and deadly state to remain, knowing there is a coming judgment for all before the judgment seat of Christ.

We often wonder and are caught-up with surprise, amazement, and confusion as to how some of the people are in the positions of power and authority in our work places, schools, politics, judicial and law enforcement systems, and even our churches, where we expect no evil to being occurring. In resolving this wonder and confusion, we have to understand that there are more people of the world (unsaved and under the influence of the devil) than there are people in Christ (born again of the Holy Spirit). Therefore, Satan has his workers of iniquity in every place to accomplish his mission to kill, and to steal, and to destroy; even in the churches that we run to for help and safety.

The great work of Satan is to disrupt justice; and the way he disrupts justice is by accusing, lying, false witnessing, and the like. His primary objective is to cause people to judge others based on accusation, not reality. We all judge in some way or another, whether as a parent, employee or employer, neighbor, friend, associate, church member, lawyer, judge, or in some other capacity of life, all of us participate in the judging process. However, Satan's primary objective is to get all of us in our judging process to pervert justice by thinking and believing evil about people that based upon accusations and not facts, which, actually paralyzes

God's system of justice in all arenas of life from the home to the White House, and even the U.S. Supreme Court. Satan has personnel everywhere to ensue justice is perverted wherever, however, and whenever it may; he is ruthless and has regard for God nor the people of God.

Our real battle in this life is not against flesh and blood, but against the four (4) powers of Satan that he has spread out throughout the world: 1) principalities, 2) powers, 3) rulers of the darkness of this age, and 4) spiritual hosts of wickedness in heavenly places (Ephes. 6:12). In bringing across this understanding, we believe that: 1) principalities are Satan himself; 2) powers are generals and/or captains of Satan's armies; 3) rulers of the darkness of this world are Satan's princes which are appointed over each country, and 4) spiritual wickedness in high places are all the demons that work individually against us.

Yes, indeed; our real battle in this life is not against flesh and blood, but against: 1) human cultists (leaders of religious groups that are exclusive, secretive, and authoritarian, that is, expecting total loyalty and unquestioned obedience); false religions (all religions rejecting Christ as Lord and Savior); atheists (those proclaiming there's no God); agnostics (those who believe that nothing is known or can be known of the existence or nature of God or anything beyond material phenomena; those who claim neither faith nor disbelief in God); and pseudo-Christians (those who gather around an individual (a false prophet or leader of an organization), who, while claiming to be the true Christian Church and teach the true Christian doctrine, actually or in reality, distorts and denies the foundational and distinctive doctrines of the mainstream traditional Christian Church founded by Jesus Christ and built upon by His apostles; these are they, and there be many, who sincerely believe they are Christians and even have a level of righteousness in their actions, but are really and truly motivated by their own self-righteousness through deceiving spirits and doctrines of demons, speaking lies in hypocrisy).

Our battle is against demonic beings working through these various people, of which, even them being our flesh and blood opponents are sometimes unaware of what they're doing because they've been so deceived into believing Satan's lies, that they themselves believe the things they're doing is right. Well their wrongs are rights, because, that's what they actually believe being right. Regardless of how stupid and ridiculous their thoughts, ideas, speeches, and actions appear being to us, they see absolutely nothing at all wrong with anything they've said and/or action they've take. They personify the devil and exemplify his pride and arrogance; simply because, they're his representatives missioned throughout the world to accomplish his will. Satan utilizes all willing vessels and does reward them for practicing and promoting his will.

Maybe now, a clearer understanding has been brought about as to why we see and hear about people saying and doing things that don't make sense to us. Such things as these wicked people do shouldn't make sense to us; but we should understand that they are doing what they do because they're fools and belong to the devil; and his will is exactly what they desire doing. As mentioned before, some aren't even aware they're under the sway or influence of the devil; they are just self-righteous people who believe themselves being wiser than most people. They compare themselves among themselves and measure themselves among themselves, while looking down on all other people, and commending themselves (2 Cor. 10:12).

Even a fool is considered wise when he holds his or her peace and shuts his or her mouth (Prov. 17:28). But a person who is wise in his or her own eyes, cannot be told or reprimanded about anything; for such a person, there's more help for a fool than for him or her (Prov. 26:12). According to the Bible, if there's more help for a fool than a person that's wise in his or her own eyes, then, a person that's wise in his or her own eyes has a problem more serious than a fool. It is possible for a person who's a fool to also be wise in his or her own eye (being one in the same). It's also apparent that a fool does not have to be wise in his or her own eyes; just a simple fool without understanding that's able from time to time hold his or her peace and shut his or her mouth. Obviously, those having the attribute of being wise in their own eyes are unable to hold their peace nor able to shut their mouths from time to time when necessary.

A fool or a person who is wise in his or her own eyes doesn't need the wisdom of God, he or she has his or her own wisdom (the wisdom of the world, which is earthly, sensual, and demonic). The wisdom of God is too high for such persons, because it addresses the simple ones, or open ones, the naïve; those who have not made up their minds yet about life or the direction they will take in life. God's wisdom ridicules those who reject it when they come to face the inevitable judgment of their foolishness. When fools and/or persons wise in their own eyes despise wisdom, they must face the results of their choices. Their hatred of wisdom arise out of a willful, intentional, and deliberate refusal to fear God (Prov. 1:29). Fools and those wise in their own eyes bring about their own destruction; their rejection of wisdom will slay them.

Those who seek wisdom will find it in the fear of the Lord (the knowledge of God), that brings about knowing God and fearing or reverencing Him as God. To do so brings about abiding success or victory in the name of Jesus Christ, His only begotten Son, our Savior. His eyes are in every place watching everything at the same time, which chills those who do evil, and comforts those who submit to Him and trust Him (Prov. 15:3) Wisdom is not for a scoffer (one who mocks or scorns), delight in scorning the things of God (Prov. 1:22); and he is incapable of responding to discipline, reproof, or rebuke (Prov. 9:7-8; Prov. 13:1). A scoffer's basic problem is displayed in his or her response to correction (Prov. 12:1), which he or she does not learn from it nor does he or she seek it. Scoffers are adamant in their folly. Wicked and foolish people like scoffers stir up strife, contentions, and troubles where there is none; they will bring them on!

The nature instinct for self-preservation is dangerous when it's time to listen to necessary rebuke that will prevent and save us from troubles and afflictions. Knowledge alone to itself does not make a person wise, except maybe in his or her own eyes; the fear of the Lord must be accompanied with such knowledge to make a person wise in the Lord; and the same is true with honor. It is vitally important to understand that pride has everything backwards, in that, it takes due credit away from God who gives us all our need graciously, and awards

A Fool's Profile and Actions

it to oneself, who takes without being thankful; caught-up with conceit or pompousness. This is exactly the reason God sees pride as an abomination (a thing detestable disgusting, repulsive) to Him. (Prov. 15:26). God resists the proud, but gives grace to the humble; therefore humble yourselves under the mighty hand of God, that He may exalt you in due time,—casting all your care upon Him, for He cares for you (1 Pet. 5:5-7).

Prideful people are their own worst enemy; given enough rope, they will prepare a noose for their own hanging (Prov. 14:3). To do evil is like a sport to a fool (Prov. 10:23); Everyone proud in heart is an abomination to the Lord; Though they join forces, none will go unpunished (Prov. 16:5). Those who pursue evil pursue it to their own death (Prov. 11:19). Destruction will come upon the workers of iniquity (Prov. 10:29). An evildoer gives heed to false lips; A liar listens eagerly to a spiteful tongue (Prov. 17:4). Even a child is known by his deeds,

Whether what he does is pure and right (Prov. 20:11). A haughty look, a proud heart, And the plowing of the wicked are sin (Prov. 21:4). The violence of the wicked will destroy them,

Because they refuse to do justice (Prov. 21:7). Evil men do not understand justice, But those who seek the LORD understand all (Prov. 28:5).

> *¹Do not be envious of evil men, Nor desire to be with them; ² For their heart devises violence, And their lips talk of troublemaking (Prov. 24:1-2). ⁷ Wisdom is too lofty for a fool; He does not open his mouth in the gate. ⁸ He who plots to do evil Will be called a schemer. ⁹ The devising of foolishness is sin, And the scoffer is an abomination to men. (Prov. 24:7-9) ¹⁹ Do not fret because of evildoers, Nor be envious of the wicked; ²⁰ For there will be no prospect for the evil man; The lamp of the wicked will be put out. (Prov. 24:19-20)*

When we take the time to thoroughly examine this profile of a fool, we should understand much better why many people are doing the foolish and senseless things they're doing. Failure in understanding the evil attitudes and actions of most inhabitants of this earth will cause us to remain blind, naïve, shocked, and confused as to why so many people are doing so much wickedness and evilness everywhere, even in the houses of God. Remember, when God is not feared, He's disrespected and dishonored in people's hearts, meaning everywhere people exist across the world.

Wickedness and evilness do not depart from a person, place, or thing that welcomes them; but rather, they take up residence and make their home right there in that person, place, or thing; and manifest their works through these willing vessels. These willing vessels profit and enjoy the fruits of wickedness and evilness, becoming one with whom they have joined themselves. "Or do you not know that he who is joined to a harlot is one body with her? For "the two," He says, "shall become one flesh (1 Cor. 6:16)." The devil knows that a three (3) fold cord is not quickly broken (Eccles. 4:12); therefore, where he has 1) a willing vessel, 2) himself, and 3) his wickedness and evilness joined together as one, he accomplishes his will until, 1) the saint, 2) his wife or her husband, and 3) through Lord Jesus Christ resist him and his demons—and, prevail over any assaults brought upon them. Glory be to God and His Son Jesus Christ, now and forevermore!

To glorify God is to worship Him in spirit and in truth (Jn. 4:24), which is the only way God, who is Spirit, can be worshipped. This is the only way we can come forth a glorify Him in our bodies and in our spirits, which are His. However, those who have made spiritual images of Him, or have imagined Him being a God they have fantasied in their corrupt demoralized minds, that fits their vain fancies and meets with their selfish desires, do not glorify God; nor can they glorify God, because they are not of God. To respect Him as a creature, and not the Creator, is not to glorify Him, but, to disrespect and dishonor Him.

Satan has come to us with great wrath (Rev. 12:12); but we, the people of God have overcome him by the blood of the Lamb (Jesus), and the word of our testimony (Rev. 12:11). Satan only has but a short time before he and his demons met with their doom in the lake of fire burning with brimstone, where the Antichrist and false prophet would have already been cast (Rev. Rev. 12:12; Rev. 20:10). This is a done deal and Satan knows that very well; so does his demons, who believe there's one God and tremble! (Ja. 2:19) God has given us power and authority over all demons and to cure diseases (Lu. 9:1). When we submit to God, resist the devil, he and all his representatives will flee from us according to God's promised word (Ja. 4:7).

We only need to remain faithful, steadfast in His word, and in all these things we are more than conquerors through Christ Jesus, our Lord and Savior who first loved us and gave His life for us (Rom. 8:37; 1 Jn. 4:19). He loved us and washed us from our sins in His own blood (Rev. 1:5). The Lord our God is faithful; He will never leave us alone to fight against the devil on our own; He will establish us and guard us from the evil one (2 Thess. 3:3; Jn. 14:18). We can be ever so secure, because we are encamped about with holy angels (Psa. 34:7). Our enemies are like chaff before the wind, and the angel of the Lord chases them away (Psa. 35:5). The peace of God which surpasses all understanding guards our hearts and minds through Christ Jesus (Phil. 4:7). What consolation in Christ, what comfort of love; what fellowship of the Spirit; what affection and mercy; what amazing grace to us from God through Christ Jesus (Phil 2:1-2).

9
Republican Delegate Refuses to Vote for Trump

CNN POLITICS ARTICLE entitled "RNC delegate files lawsuit in order to avoid voting for Trump," June 24, 2016 states: A delegate to the Republican National Convention has filed a lawsuit against Virginia officials as part of a long-shot attempt to avoid voting for Donald Trump this summer in Cleveland. Carroll Correll is suing Virginia election officials in federal court, arguing that his right to free speech is infringed upon by legal requirements that he cast his ballot for Trump. His suit comes as efforts to unbind delegates and subvert Trump at the convention intensify, though remain very unlikely to succeed.

Correll is bound to vote for Trump on the first ballot at the convention. Trump won Virginia's primary on Super Tuesday. "Correll believes that Donald Trump is unfit to serve as President of the United States and that voting for Donald Trump would therefore violate Correll's conscience," the complaint reads. "Accordingly, Correll will not vote for Donald Trump on the first ballot, or any other ballot, at the national convention. He will cast his vote on the first ballot, and on any additional ballots,—for a candidate whom he believes is fit to serve as President."

Anti-Trump Republicans are exhausting every possible step to nominate someone who is not Trump, with the most recent effort being television ads that encourage delegates to vote their "conscience."

But the Rules Committee at the Republican convention is stocked with party stalwarts, and ousting Trump would require a series of extraordinary changes to the RNC nomination rules. Several delegates have led an effort to create enough pressure to permit a majority of Republican delegates to vote however they choose. But their path is uphill, in part due to the make-up of the committee announced this week.

THE HILL article entitled "Va. GOP delegate files lawsuit over bound convention votes," June 24, 2016 by Jessie Hellmann states: "A Virginia Republican delegate has filed a class-action lawsuit in federal court Friday challenging a state law that requires delegates to the national convention to vote for the winner of the primary, in this case Donald Trump. A Virginia law dictates that delegates vote for the candidate who wins the state primary, NBC News reported, although the Virginia Republican Party rules call for voting proportional to the primary results.

"The First Amendment to the United States Constitution guarantees delegates to the Republican Party's and Democratic Party's national conventions the right to vote their conscience, free from government compulsion, when participating in the selection of their party's presidential nominee," the complaint reads. "Nonetheless, Virginia law acts to strip them of that right, imposing criminal penalties on delegates who vote for anyone other than the primary winner on the first ballot at a national convention. That law cannot be sustained under the First Amendment or as a legitimate exercise of Virginia's authority under the United States Constitution."

Beau Correll, a Republican delegate who served as one of Ted Cruz's campaign co-chairs in Virginia, is the only named plaintiff in the lawsuit but filed on behalf of all of Virginia's Republican and Democratic delegates. His attorneys wrote in the complaint that Correll is concerned Trump may sue him when he votes against him at the convention this summer, based on Trump's reputation of being litigious. The attorneys have asked for the case to be expedited because the Republican's nomination convention is only a month away.

"Correll, like many other Republicans, refuses to cast his first-ballot vote—or any other vote—for Virginia primary winner Donald Trump because Correll believes that Trump is unfit to serve as President of the United States," the suit reads. "Correll is concerned that voting against Trump at the convention may subject him to retaliatory litigation by Trump, Trump's campaign, or other persons or entities associated with Trump."—Trump won Virginia's primary with about 34 percent of the vote,—besting Marco Rubio by 3 points. [End of Article]

CNN politics article entitled "Donald Trump lavishes praise on 'leader' Putin," December 18, 2015 states: "Donald Trump on Friday praised Vladimir Putin and appeared to defend the autocratic Russian president when pressed about his alleged killing of journalists and political opponents critical of his rule." One day after Putin called Trump a "bright and talented" and the "absolute leader of the presidential race," the Republican presidential front-runner returned the compliments, hailing Putin as a "leader" and pointing to his high favorability numbers in Russia.

"He's running his country and at least he's a leader, unlike what we have in this country," Trump said when asked by "Morning Jo'"" Republican host Joe Scarborough about Putin's alleged killing of journalists and political opponents.—"I think our country does plenty of killing also, Joe, so you know. There's a lot of stupidity going on in the world right now, a lot of killing, a lot of stupidity," he said. Finally, when asked whether he would condemn Putin's alleged brutal tactics, Trump responded: "Sure, absolutely." Trump noted that Putin had called him smart, which Trump said is "always good, especially when the person heads up Russia."

While Republicans have hammered President Barack Obama for failing to do enough to halt Russian aggression in eastern Ukraine, Trump called for decreased U.S. involvement in the Ukrainian conflict. "I think maybe we should do a little following and let the neighbors take a little bit more of an active role in the Ukraine," Trump said, calling for European countries like Germany to take the lead, despite Germany's deep involvement in brokering a political settlement to the conflict in Ukraine.

Trump also suggested that as president he would herald a new era of relations between the U.S. and Russia, which have plummeted to levels not seen since the Cold War, experts say. Trump pointed to his experience as a dealmaker and said that while some see Russia as a problem for the United States—most in the Republican Party have described Russia as the U.S.'s top global adversary—Trump said "one could also see Russia being a really big asset to our country."—"A lot of good things could happen with Russia if we get along with Russia and if they respect us," Trump said. "Putin doesn't respect our president."

CNN politics article entitled "Trump praises Saddam Hussein's efficient killing of 'terrorists,' calls today's Iraq 'Harvard for terrorism,'" July 6, 2016 states: "Donald Trump on Tuesday once again expressed his preference for keeping dictators in power in the Middle East.

While acknowledging that Saddam Hussein "was a bad guy," Trump praised the former Iraqi dictator's efficient killing of "terrorists"—despite the fact that Iraq was listed as a state sponsor of terrorism during Hussein's time in power. Trump, who supported the Iraq War before the invasion and in the early months of the war, said the U.S. "shouldn't have destabilized" Iraq—before pivoting to praising Hussein.—"He was a bad guy—really bad guy. But you know what? He did well? He killed terrorists. He did that so good. They didn't read them the rights. They didn't talk. They were terrorists. Over. Today, Iraq is Harvard for terrorism," Trump said.

Asked Tuesday night on Fox News about the comments, House Speaker Paul Ryan appeared taken aback by Trump's words. "He was one of the 20th century's most evil people," Ryan said of the former Iraqi strongman. The Clinton campaign jumped on the remarks, with senior campaign adviser Jake Sullivan saying "Trump's praise for brutal strongmen seemingly knows no bounds."

Trump yet again lauded Saddam Hussein as a great killer of terrorists, noting with approval that he never bothered to read anyone their rights," Sullivan said in a statement, after noting Trump has also praised North Korea's Kim Jong Un and Russia's Vladimir Putin. "In reality, Hussein's regime was a sponsor of terrorism—one that paid families of suicide bombers who attacked Israelis, among other crimes," he said. "Trump's cavalier compliments for brutal dictators, and the twisted lessons he seems to have learned from their history,—again demonstrate, how dangerous he would be as commander-in-chief and how unworthy he is of the office he seeks."

The presumptive Republican nominee has previously said that Iraq and Libya—two countries that have become ISIS strongholds—would be better off if Hussein and Libyan dictator Moammar Gadhafi were still alive and in power in their respective countries. Trump has also previously praised Hussein's prowess at killing terrorists.—Hussein was notoriously effective at suppressing dissent in his country, but he frequently targeted civilians and minority groups while in power, which earned him widespread condemnation from the international community—as one of the world's worst human rights abusers. Hussein also financed and supported terrorism around the world. Yet, Hussein is still being praised by Trump today!!!

An ABC News article of January 10, 2016 entitled "Trump on North Korean Leader Kim Jong-un: 'You Gotta Give Him Credit'" states: "Republican presidential front-runner Donald Trump appeared to praise North Korean leader Kim Jong-un, saying at a rally Saturday that "it's incredible" how he was able to dispatch his political opponents. Trump called Jong-Un a "maniac" during remarks about North Korea's nuclear program during a rally at Ottumwa, Iowa, but conceded, "You gotta give him credit." "How many young guys—he was like 26 or 25 when his father died—take over these tough generals, and all of a sudden ... he goes in, he takes over, and he's the boss," Trump said. "It's incredible. He wiped out the uncle, he wiped out this one, that one. I mean this guy doesn't play games. And we can't play games with him."

Last week North Korea announced it had successfully detonated a hydrogen bomb after an earthquake was detected near previous test sites, though the White House quickly disputed the claim. North Korea released an image of Jong-un personally authorizing the test. The next morning Trump said that North Korea was under the "total control" of China. Yesterday's remarks were not the first time Trump has been complimentary of an antagonist of the U.S. The real estate mogul has previously drawn criticism for accepting praise from Russian President Vladimir Putin, calling it a "great honor to be so nicely complimented by a man so highly respected within his own country and beyond."

Trump is a Presbyterian. In an April 2011 interview, on the 700 Club, Trump said, "I'm a Protestant, I'm a Presbyterian. And you know I've had a good relationship with the church over the years. I think religion is a wonderful thing." "When I look at the present state of things in the world I realize that Vladimir Putin is the sole defender of Christian civilization one can rely on," declared Assad during an interview with the French magazine Valeurs Actuelles earlier this week. [The Christian Post, Ray Nothstine, November 20, 2015]

Orthodox Christians believe in a single God who is both three and one (triune); the Father, Son, and Holy Spirit,—"one in essence and undivided." The Holy Trinity is three "unconfused" and distinct divine persons (hypostases), who share one divine essence (ousia); uncreated, immaterial and eternal. This is "the faith" Vladimir Putin proclaims."

State atheism was an official policy of anti-clericalism in the Soviet Union and other Marxist-Leninist states. The Soviet Union used the term "gosateizm," a syllabic abbreviation of "state" (gosudarstvo) and "atheism" (ateizm), to refer to a policy of expropriation of religious property, publication of information against religion and the official promotion of anti-religious materials in the education system. Governments that have implemented official policies of ant-clericalism oppose religious institutional power and influence in all aspects of public and political life, including the involvement of religion in the everyday life of the citizen. [From Wikipedia, the free encyclopedia]

There are no known official statistics of religions in North Korea. North Korea is an atheist state where public religion is discouraged. North Korea is mostly atheist and agnostic, with the religious life dominated by the traditions of Korean shamanism and Chondoism. At the dawn of the 20th century, almost the totality of the population of Korea believed in the indigenous shamanic religion and practiced

Confucian rites and ancestral worship.—Christianity became very popular in northern Korea from the late 18th century to the 19th century. The first Catholic missionaries arrived in 1794, a decade after the return of Yi Sung-hun, a diplomat who was the first baptized Korean in Beijing. [From Wikipedia, the free encyclopedia]

10

Donald Trump's Hero— Saddam Hussein

I FOUND IT vitally important for us to look into and explore the mindset of Donald Trump and some of the leaders of the world—he has spoken in admiration. The term "birds of a feather flock together" is an idiomatic phrase (expression nature to our country) meaning "people having similar characters, backgrounds, interests, and/or beliefs are admired by and/or congregate with one another physically and/or in mind. Likewise, the idiomatic phrase "If it looks like a duck, swims like a duck, and quacks like a duck, then it probably is a duck" implies that "a person can identify another person by listening and observing his or her habitual characteristics, in this case, Donald Trump's and those he so admire!

Saddam Hussein Abd al-Majid al-Tikriti (28 April 1937 – 30 December 2006) was the fifth (5th) President of Iraq, serving in this capacity from 16 July 1979 until 9 April 2003. A leading member of the revolutionary Arab Socialist Ba'ath Party, and later, the Baghdad-based Ba'ath Party and its regional organization the Iraqi Ba'ath Party—which espoused Ba'athism, a mix of Arab nationalism and socialism—Saddam played a key role in the 1968 coup (later referred to as the 17 July Revolution) that brought the party to power in Iraq. The total number of Iraqis killed by the security services of Saddam's government in various purges and genocides is unknown, but the lowest estimate is 250,000. [From Wikipedia, the free encyclopedia]

Trump's praise of Saddam Hussein is abomination to the Lord, and should be abomination to every American, in particularly, all of the truly traditional mainstream Christian faith. Inspired by his uncle's tales of heroism in the service of the Arab nation, Saddam was consumed by dreams of glory since his earliest days. He identified himself with the King of Babylonia Nebuchadnezzar who conquered Jerusalem (586 B.C.) and Joseph Saladin who regained Jerusalem in 1187 by defeating the Crusaders. Often affixed to Saddam was the labels "madman of the Middle East" and "megalomaniac."

Hitler shot himself before capture; Stalin received a grand state funeral, and Pol Pot died while under house arrest. The brutal leader of Turkmenistan, Saparmurat Niyazov, died of natural causes. In fact, when the noose tightened around Saddam's neck on December 30, 2006, Saddam Hussein became one of a surprisingly small number of modern dictators actually executed by their own people: 1) Benito Mussolini, 2) Nicolae Ceausescu—and now the man who once called himself Iraq's president for life. Of those three (3), Saddam was the only one who had anything resembling a trial. America brought justice against him.

Saddam saw himself as part of the pantheon of modern dictators. Allegedly, he boasted to KGB agents in Baghdad of his personal admiration for Stalin. Certainly, he took their advice: Historians who have worked on Iraqi documents captured during the first Gulf War have clearly shown how Saddam's secret police force was clearly organized along Soviet lines.

Saddam kept his people in a state of constant terror, as did Hitler and Stalin at the height of their powers. Iraqi writer Kanan Makiya, whose book Republic of Fear remains the definitive account of Saddam's Iraq, estimates that in 1980, one-fifth (1/5) of the economically active Iraqi labor force was a member of the army, the political militias, the secret police, or the police. One in five people, in other words, was employed to carry out institutional violence.

The result was a country in which the families of political victims received their body parts in the mail; in which tens of thousands of Kurds could be murdered with chemical weapons; and in which, as Saddam's truncated trial demonstrated, the dictator could sign a document randomly condemning 148 people to death—among them an 11-year-old boy—and feel no remorse or regret whatsoever. As his defense team argued, "he believed this was his prerogative as head of state." NO REMORSE!!!

Throughout his rule, Saddam unsettled the ranks of the Baath Party with bloody purges and packed his jails with political prisoners to defuse real or imagined plots. In one of his most brutal acts, he rained poison gas on the northern Kurdish village of Halabja in 1988, killing an estimated 5,000 of his own citizens suspected of being disloyal and wounding 10,000 more. No praise does this morbid and ungodly act deserve.

Even at the end, Saddam showed no remorse!!! When four (4) Iraqi politicians visited him after his capture in December 2003, they asked about his more brutal acts. He called the Halabja attack Iran's handiwork; he said that Kuwait was rightfully part of Iraq and that the mass graves were filled with thieves who fled the battlefields, according to Adnan Pachachi, a former Iraqi foreign minister. Saddam declared that he had been "just but firm" because Iraqis needed a tough ruler, Pachachi said. It was a favorite theme, one even espoused in a novel attributed to Saddam called "Zabibah and the King." At one point, the king asks the comely Zabibah whether the people needed strict measures from their leader. "Yes, Your Majesty," Zabibah replies. "The people need strict measures so that they can feel protected by this strictness."

Iraq under Saddam had a stifled quality. Imprisonment, torture, mutilation and execution were frequent occurrences, at least for those who chose to dabble in anything vaguely political. Simple information like the weather report was classified. There was no freedom of expression—even foreign newspapers were banned—and no freedom to travel. Contact with foreigners was proscribed. There were widespread reports that Saddam himself periodically carried out the torture or even execution of those he felt had crossed him. This doesn't deserve any praise.

Saddam and Stalin were similar in many ways: 1) both were 20th century rulers of large, relatively economically developed states, 2) both headed one-party regimes and propagated cults of personality, 3) both perpetrated mass political violence against their citizens; 4) both fought bloody external wars, 5) both relished violence, but only Saddam personally engaged in violence as leader. Clearly, we can see that Saddam admired and emulated Stalin.

Saddam studied Stalin (his hero) and modeled himself after Stalin more than any other man in history. Saddam had a full library of books about Stalin and studied him in full. Even before Saddam obtained any measurement of power, he use to wonder around the offices of the Ba'ath Party telling people: "Wait until I take over this country; I will make it a Stalinist state out of it yet." People use to just laugh him off; they shouldn't have; his proposition was a very serious one indeed. Saddam, although illiterate until age 10,—made his dream as leader become true.

Saddam became a gunman, a thug for the Ba'ath Party and participated in the assassination attempt on Iraq's strong man, Gen. Kassem in 1959. Saddam went into exile in Cairo and returned back to Iraq after the Ba'ath Party took power and proceeded to organize the Party and give it supremacy over the army, which was a most important development in Iraq's history and future. Saddam believed that family and tribal connections were supreme, and came ahead of ideology, commitment to nation-state, and all other commitments. Therefore, Saddam transferred power from the Ba'ath Party that had put him in power,—to his family, because he decided family could be trusted, but, the Ba'ath Party could not be trusted. As such, that's the way it was in Iraq until his death of December 30, 2006.

Saddam Played the Faith Card! Many see the Iraqi leader's decade religious campaign as just another political ploy. March 2003—He's peppered his speeches with references to Muslim scripture, built some of Baghdad's most opulent—and militant—mosques, and reportedly had a Qur'an written in his blood. Yet most commentators say Saddam Hussein is not religious. Rather, the once avowedly secular Iraqi leader has used Islam to increase support for his regime. When he came to power 30 years ago, Hussein's Baath Party was identified with a strongly secular Arab nationalism. Despite some concessions to the Muslim faithful made during the Khomeini era—including Hussein's inventing a lineage that connected him to a descendant of the Prophet Muhammad—the regime downplayed religion in the public square. In Baghdad, for example, women were less likely to wear headscarves than in neighboring Middle Eastern countries.

After the first Gulf War, pressure from several sides apparently forced him to rethink his policy. An embargo-weary populace was vulnerable to ultraconservative Muslim preachers from Iran and Saudi Arabia. To counter this influence, Hussein began manipulating religion for political ends. As anti-Western sentiment grew throughout the Middle East, he also saw in Islam a propaganda tool in his ongoing fight with the United States and the United Nations over his weapons programs.

Under his "faith campaign," begun in 1994, government money goes to promote mandatory Qur'an studies in schools. The campaign built training centers for imams (Muslim teachers), including Saddam College (for Iraqis) and Saddam University of Islamic Studies (for foreigners). Radio stations were dedicated to airing Qur'anic lessons, and alcohol was banned in restaurants. Even Baath party officials began taking courses in the Qur'an, and in the ubiquitous murals of the Iraqi leader, Saddam himself was often shown in prayer.

Mosque attendance had begun to increase when the sanctions were first imposed; it continued to rise, and more women began wearing veils. Contests in Qur'an recitation were held, with cash prizes given to the best reciters. The "faith campaign" also encouraged mosque-building; Saddam himself planned to construct three (3) gigantic mosques, which do as much to commemorate his regime as they do to honor the Prophet. The first one built, the "Mother of All

Battles," opened in 2001. Its Scud-shaped minarets, 37 meters high (Hussein was born in 1937), surround a central structure where a 605-page Qur'an is encased in glass. According to Iraqi officials, Hussein donated 50 pints of blood over three years to mix with ink for the book.

Saddam Hussein was a phony, a cult leader, a false prophet, a defiant dictator who ruled Iraq with fear and violence. He oppressed Iraq for more than 30 years, wherein, unleashing devastating regional wars and reducing his once promising oil-rich nation to a claustrophobic (extremely or irrationally fearful) police state; what a failure and most terrible disappointment to the people of Iraq. Yet, this is a man praised by Donald Trump, which should make all Americans suspicious of Trump's praises to such a villain and failure to his people.

Saddam was not a true follower of the Islamic faith; he was a pseudo-Islamic and claimed and portrayed his loyalty—"only when "this faith" proved beneficial for him doing so.

Saddam's mindset was Baathism, for he was a member of the Ba'ath Party. The ideology of Baathism is exactly what the coup leader says it is; or what Michael Aflag chose to say, which, after Aflag is done with pure blood lineages, and the "external mission and Arab spirit," began to sound in the mid-50s and afterwards, evermore left-wing, as if his philo-communist origins were stirring into renewed life.

Saddam was Aflag's protégée. According to Aflag, Baathism is scientific socialism plus spirit, which suggests that Baathism, already claimed to as addendum to Islam, was also an addendum to Karl Marx's Marxism. In Baathism, the party leaders think of themselves as the ultimate authority, instead of invoking Qur'an sacred texts and religious interpretations. To Aflag and Saddam, the Qur'an and its interpretations meant little to nothing; the irksome little details of theology (sharia) and ritual (prayer, etc.) interested Aflag and Saddam not at all. Aflag's Baathism was about Islam, but never claimed to be Islam itself. Aflag created for himself an unpredictable position to maneuver as to benefit his purpose for himself.

Aflag with his talks of socialism, reserved for himself the option of veering flexibly in different directions entirely,—all of which, has meant that, on doctrinal grounds—Baathists and Islamics could look upon one another as either friends or enemies—depending upon whether Baathists chose to emphasize the overlap, or lack of overlap. The Arab East has offered examples of Baathists/Islamics alliances and enmities in roughly equal measures down through history. The alliance/enmity status is predicated on the Baath Party leader's mindset.

Aflag was born in Damascus to a middle class Greek Orthodox Christian family, his father, Joseph, working as a grain merchant. Aflaq was first educated in the westernized schools of the French Mandate of Syria. In 1929, he left Syria to study philosophy abroad at the Sorbonne in Paris. During his stay Aflaq was influenced by the works of Henri Bergson, and met his longtime collaborator Salah al-Din al-Bitar, a fellow Syrian nationalist. Aflaq founded an Arab Student Union at the Sorbonne, and discovered the writings of Karl Marx. He returned to Syria in 1932, and became active in communist politics, but left the movement when the government of Leon Blum, supported by the French Communist Party (FCP), continued France's old politics towards its colonies.

Aflaq, and others, had believed that the FCP followed pro-independence policies towards the French colonies. It had not helped that the Syrian-Lebanese Communist Party (SLCP) supported the FCP's decision. From then on Aflaq saw the communist movement as a tool of the Soviet Union. He was impressed by the organization and ideology of Antun Saadeh's Syrian Social Nationalist Party (ASSSNP).

Although Aflag was born in a Christian environment,—his words and actions—didn't evidence those of a born-again Christian. Therefore, we can rightfully conclude, being born in a certain environment (Christian, Islamic, etc.) does not automatically mean one is a true believer of a specific faith. As in the cases of Aflag and Saddam, one of Christian and the other of Islamic environments, "neither were true believers of their environmental faiths." Both were imposters or counterfeits of confessions and utilized faith only when it was advantageous in doing so.

Aflag was pseudo-Christian/Islamic and Saddam was pseudo-Islamic; both phonies. Baram fails to understand how hypocrites will do whatever is necessary to deceive and to convince others of being people whom they're not truly; as in the cases of Aflag and Saddam.

Amatzia Baram's 2014 book, "Saddam Husayn and Islam, 1968-2003: Ba'thi Iraq from Secularism to Faith," which argues that Saddam *did* become a born-again Muslim, and Joseph Sassoon's 2012 book, "Saddam Hussein's Ba'th Party: Inside an Authoritarian Regime," which argues that Saddam remained hostile to Islamism to the very end.

Saddam's public rhetoric took on a more Islamist tone as his long war with the Iranian revolution wore on, Baram notes, and the patronizing and proliferation of the clergy began in the same period. Among other things, Saddam began to present Khomeini as *masih ad-dajjal* (the false messiah), a figure akin to the antichrist. Atheism was loudly condemned in the State media and as early as 1982 Saddam spoke of the war with Iran as a *jihad*.

After Saddam annexed Kuwait in August 1990, intending to solve Iraq's financial woes and catapult himself into regional and even global leadership status—with increased oil reserves at his command,—it became clear that the initial conquest would be difficult to sustain. In response, the Islamization of rhetoric was super-charged, and Saddam himself began a psychological alteration that shifted responsibility to god. What is interesting is that Saddam's reliance on god becomes evident first in private, telling his generals that god had willed the abolition of Kuwait, and only in late October/early November 1990 does Saddam begin to speak in Islamic terms in public to justify—what he has done.

Still, it is correct to be cynical about Saddam's initial turn to Islamist rhetoric, which seems to have been an exercise in blame-shifting, from Saddam to the Almighty. One notable feature of the Islamist rhetoric was Saddam claiming to have a direct line to god, and the cynicism around this claim was increased by the fact that the line "became progressively busier as the war against the Allies forces in Kuwait approached," as Baram puts it.

Baram lays out the steps Saddam was taking toward Islam. The public statements of Saddam Hussein toward the end of 1990 laid claim to the conquest of Kuwait as a means of renewing Islam through *jihad* and purifying Islam by removing a corrupt government that operated in the religion's name. Kuwait "has been returned to the Faith," Saddam said. Foreshadowing the rhetoric of Osama bin Laden, Saddam condemned the Saudis for putting the holy places under the protection of unbelievers, and even had Iraqi State media disseminate stories that the Saudi and Kuwaiti monarchies were of Jewish origin. Saddam was now the redeemer of the entire Islamic religion.

Saddam reiterated miracle stories from the Qur'an—in the run-up to his expulsion from Kuwait, and introduced a concept that would become more and more marked as the 1990s went on: *at-tawakkul ala Allah* (reliance on god). When Saddam promised that a retinue of angels was on-hand—seemingly to make up for the lack of close-air cover after Saddam sent his air force to Iran—some of his cynical lieutenants took this as a reference to weapons of mass destruction that could equalize the Americans' technological edge, but the WMD never materialized. Instead, in private settings as well as in public, dreams and *ruya* (visions) came to preoccupy Saddam, who impressed upon his deputies how much meaning he attached to them.

Himself a Sunni Muslim, Saddam has oppressed Shiite Muslims throughout his tenure as president. (Politically, the two sects are not unlike Catholics and Protestants in the West.) But he has made clear that his cause is not a sectarian one. In a 1978 speech following a Shiite uprising, Saddam argued that the party must "oppose the institutionalization of religion in the state and society......Let us return to the roots of our religion, glorifying them—but not introduce it into politics." [Go to Saddam plays faith card]

Sassoon argues that the Faith Campaign was a cynical smokescreen by which the Saddam regime sought to win support from Muslim conservatives, while continuing to engage in "anti-religious activities." Sassoon's argument against Saddam being a believer is that "Saddam Hussein was always wary of any religious movement; even though, when necessary, Saddam "publicly supported all religious activities, and called for more conservatism and religiosity within society. That Saddam's personal tastes, rather than a strict religious interpretation,—shaped the Faith Campaign is hardly novel. Ruhollah Khomeini, after he seized power, ruled that the survival of his revolution took precedent over the strict interpretation of shari'a jurisprudence.

Saddam did dislike Wahhabism, Khomeini'ism, the Muslim Brotherhood and the Taliban. Saddam's reasons for disliking these movements break down into broadly two (2): he saw them as a threat to his power or a personal distaste. Khomeini'ism was undoubtedly seen as a both a threat and was personally disliked—it was associated in Saddam's mind with Iran and he was an anti-Persian bigot, among other things. But in the case of the Taliban,—Saddam despised them for being so primitive, specifically blowing up the Bamiyan Buddhas.

Sassoon takes Saddam's distrust of independent Islamist groups and trends to mean Saddam opposed all Islamism, which as noted he did not: Saddam's own Islamists were keenly supported. Moreover, alongside the Ba'athist-Salafists, the "pure" Salafi Trend, which had long opposed the regime, was strengthened,—partly by commission and partly by commission. When Sassoon writes that Saddam "wanted to infiltrate" the religious movements "to ensure [the regime's] control," what he is describing is Saddam's approach to power, not Saddam's ideology. *Of course* Saddam's regime infiltrated the Salafi Trend and tried to bring it under control, and even assassinated some of its leaders.

Saddam still believed that only *his* movement was the true one,— even if others were complementary. In a regime where the intelligence agencies spied on one-another, Saddam's approach to the Salafi Trend is hardly a surprise. The Salafi Trend largely made its peace with the Islamized Saddam regime but it remained independent of the regime, and therefore a possible threat. That said, there is no evidence Saddam ever made any effort to seriously restrain, let alone destroy, the Salafi Trend, and in fact Saddam seems to have seen the "pure" Salafis as a complement to his Ba'athist-Salafists. Sassoon writes that "anyone showing an inclination toward Wahhabism was considered an enemy of the state."

"When [Saddam's] public record is read together with his confidential conversations and documents it appears that eventually he began to believe all those inventions," Baram writes. The Shi'a rebellion that erupted after the Iraqi army had been expelled from Kuwait was a total shock to Saddam, and he reacted by isolating himself—physically and politically—relying on an inner-core of kinsmen and Sunni clans that he trusted. When it finally came time for the end of the Gulf War, the internal advice Saddam gave to his military suggested that Saddam had again ceded responsibility to god.

Five (5) days into the invasion in March 2003, Saddam gave this speech to his troops: "Those who are believers will be victorious. ... We have been promised by God in our struggle with the enemies of humanity that God will support his soldiers and [the enemy] will be defeated. ... We are the soldiers of God. ... The victory of God is very close. ... God is great! God is great! Long live our country! Long live Palestine, free and Arab. Long live Iraq! Long live Iraq! Long live Iraq, the country of jihad and virtue! ... God is great! God is great!" As strategic or even tactical advise—it left the Iraqi leadership—somewhat in the dark.

The final message Saddam sent to his troops, on March 29, eleven (11) days before the collapse of the regime, was mostly Islamic incantation, but gave some instructions on preparing ambushes, which were duly carried out by the Fedayeen Saddam, before returning to religious themes, telling soldiers that they would be victorious if they relied on god because the enemy believed in "infidelity and atheism and crime."

Also in 1995, there is a recorded conversation with Culture Minister Latif Nusayyif Jasim in which Jasim said Saddam was becoming very religious. Saddam had said that no matter how much god punished him—and Saddam felt that the heavenly treatment since 1990 had been on the harsh side—Saddam would never waver in his love for god. One of the most convincing pieces of evidence that Saddam became a believer comes from the memoir of Yevgeny Primakov, the Russian foreign minister between 1996 and 1998, who spoke Arabic and met with Saddam more than any other foreign diplomat. Primakov concluded: *"Russia did everything in its power to get Saddam to pull back from the brink ... But ... Saddam continued to believe in his lucky star ... and ultimately Allah, who would save him from harm."*

Saddam had nothing to gain by pretending to be pious around Primakov. To the contrary, as Saddam would well have known, a profession of religiosity and a belief that matters of State could be left in god's hands—would have convinced Primakov, a life-long atheist and apparatchik of the Soviet State, that Saddam was losing his mind. Baram notes that not only Saddam's "public speeches" but his "words in closed-door meetings and his top-secret military communiqués since 1999-2000 imply a similar change [towards religion]."

Another very powerful indicator that a change had come over Saddam is from the private diary of Barzan al-Ibrahim, a younger brother of the dictator's and the head of the Iraqi Intelligence Service, the infamous *Mukhabarat*. Al-Ibrahim, in the entry dated Oct. 21, 2000, states plainly that Saddam had undergone a mental metamorphosis and now thought "similar to the way of ... a monk who is sitting in a sanctuary and worshiping [god.] ... I told the president ... of the danger of an alliance with the religious trend domestically and externally." The Salafi Trend would not hold to its side of the alliance, al-Ibrahim said; when they are powerful enough the Salafis will topple the regime. But Saddam pressed on with the alliance with the Salafi Trend regardless—as he had over the objections of Tariq Aziz, a member of the "Quartet," and his eldest son, Uday.

Perhaps the clinching evidence, uncovered by Baram, comes from a letter Saddam wrote to god, dated May 22, 2002. The letter, written in a clearly anxious hand and as far as can be told never supposed to be made public, was then to be cast in pure gold and affixed to a granite tablet, which would be placed in a steel box with an unbreakable glass front and a lead lining so it could withstand anything, including radiation. This letter was then to be placed in the *Umm al-Ma'arik* (Mother of All Battles) Mosque, the splendidly ornate monument Saddam had built himself in honour of his "victory" in 1991. Saddam then planned to place a smaller box, also with one glass wall, inside this larger box—containing several moustache hairs.

In times gone by, moustache hairs had served in Iraq as a handshake would in the West, and the deal Saddam was trying to seal with god was laid out in his letter. Saddam beseeched god to protect Iraq, by which he also meant himself—like most dictators, Saddam imagined his own fate and interests were identical with the country he tyrannized—and asked that, in considering Saddam's request, god "remember my history together with all the meanings that I placed with you." This was a reference to the Islamization measures: the imposition of the Holy Law, the mosque-building, the empowerment of the clergy, and the personal sacrifices of many pints of blood to write a Qur'an. With these measures, Saddam hoped he had earned god's grace. [End of Article]

Saddam's pursuit of power for himself and Iraq was boundless. In fact, in his mind,—his destiny and Iraq's were one and indistinguishable.—His exalted concept of himself was fused with his Ba'thist political ideology. As such, Ba'thist dreams were to be realized when the Arab nation was unified under one (1) strong leader (himself).—In his mind, he was destined for the role of leader of the Arab nation,—him and him only.

In pursuit of his messianic dreams, he was not constrained by conscience;—his only loyalty was to Saddam. In pursuing his goals, he used aggression instrumentally and whatever force was necessary, and—did, when he deemed it expedient, go to extremes of violence, including the use of weapons of mass destruction. His unconstrained aggression was instrumental in pursuing his goals, but it was also at the same time defensive aggression, for his grandiose façade masks underlying insecurity. While he was psychotic, he had strong paranoid orientation. He was ready for retaliation and, not without reason, saw himself as surrounded by enemies. He completely ignored his personal role in creating enemies, and self-righteously threatened his targets.

The conspiracy theories he envisioned were not merely for popular consumption in the Arab world, but genuinely reflected his paranoid mindset. He was convinced that the United States, Israel and Iran had been in league for the purpose of eliminating him, and found a persuasive chain of evidence for this conclusion. His minister of information, Latif Hassif Jasin, who was responsible for propaganda and public statements, helped him to reinforce his paranoid disposition and in a sense was the implementer of his paranoia.

It is this political personality constellation—messianic ambition for unlimited power, absence of conscience, unconstrained aggression, and a paranoid outlook—which made Saddam so dangerous.—Conceptualized as malignant narcissism, this is the personality configuration of the destructive charismatic who unified and rallied his downtrodden supporters by blaming outside enemies. While he was not charismatic, this psychological stance was the basis of his particular appeal to the Palestinians who saw him as a strongman who shared their intense anti-Zionism and would champion their cause.

Saddam genuinely saw himself as one of the great leaders of history, ranking himself with Nasser, Castro, Tito, Ho Chi Minh, and Mao Zedong, each of whom he admired for adapting socialism to his environment, free of foreign domination. Saddam saw himself as transforming his society. He believed youth must be "fashioned" to "safeguard the future" and that Iraqi children must be transformed into a "radiating light that will expel" traditional family backwardness. Like Mao, Saddam encouraged youth to inform on their parents' anti-revolutionary activity.

As God-like status was ascribed to Mao, and giant pictures and statues of him were placed throughout China, so too giant pictures and statues of Saddam abound in Iraq. Asked about this cult of personality, Saddam shrug and said: "he cannot help it if that is what they want to do." While he was in power, 1) his statue guarded the entrance to every village, 2) his portrait watched over each government office and 3) he peered down from at least one wall in every home. His picture was so widespread that a joke quietly circulating among his detractors in 1988 put the country's population at 34 million—17 million people and 17 million portraits of Saddam.

Mosques, airports, neighborhoods and entire cities were named after him. A military arch erected in Baghdad in 1989 was modeled on his forearms and then enlarged 40 times to hold two giant crossed swords. In school, pupils learned songs with lyrics like "Saddam, oh Saddam, you carry the nation's dawn in your eyes." The entertainment at public events often consisted of outpourings of praise for Saddam Hussein. At the January 2003 inauguration of a recreational lake in Baghdad, poets spouted spontaneous verse and the official translators struggled to keep up with lines like, "We will stimulate ourselves by saying your name, Saddam Hussein, when we say Saddam Hussein, we stimulate ourselves."

Saddam often tried to draw parallels between himself and the famous leaders of Mesopotamia, the earliest civilization in the region, as well as Saladin, the 12th century Kurdish Muslim military commander who expelled the crusaders from Jerusalem. He stated at one point that he was preoccupied about what people would be thinking about him in 500 years. To the horror of historic preservationists, he had the ancient walls of the former capital, Babylon, completely reconstructed using tens of thousands of newly fired bricks. An archaeologist had shown him bricks stamped with the name of Nebuchadnezzar II in 605 B.C.

After the reconstruction, the small Arabic script on thousands of bricks read in part, "In the reign of the victorious Saddam Hussein, the president of the Republic, may God keep him, the guardian of the great Iraq and the renovator of its renaissance and the builder of its great civilization,—the rebuilding of the great city of Babylon was done."

Aside from his secret police, he held power by filling the government's upper ranks with members of his extended clan. Their Corleone-like feuds became the stuff of gory public soap operas. Saddam Hussein once sentenced his elder son, Uday, to be executed after he beat Saddam's food taster to death—in front of scores of horrified party guests, but later rescinded the order. The husbands of his two (2) eldest daughters, whom he had promoted to important military positions, were gunned down after they defected and then inexplicably returned to Iraq.

Saddam was so consumed with his messianic mission that he over-read the degree of his support in the rest of the Arab world. He psychologically assumed that many in the Arab world, especially the downtrodden, shared his views and saw him as their hero. He was genuinely surprised at the nearly unanimous condemnation of his invasion of Kuwait. He probably to a degree persuaded himself of his oft repeated assertion that the United Nations was controlled by the United States, and denied the degree of international disapproval of his invasion of Kuwait.

Continual wars sapped Iraq's wealth and decimated its people. In 1980, Saddam dragged his country into a disastrous attempt to overthrow the new Islamic government in neighboring Iran. By the time the war ended in stalemate in 1988, more than 200,000 Iraqis were dead and hundreds of thousands more wounded. Iran suffered a similar toll. Iraq's staggering war debt, pegged around $70 billion, soon had wealthy Arab neighbors demanding repayment. Enraged, Saddam invaded Kuwait in August 1990, only to be expelled by an American-led coalition in the Persian Gulf War seven (7) months later.

Yet in the language of his Orwellian government, Saddam Hussein never suffered a setback. After the gulf war ended with the deaths of an estimated 150,000 Iraqis, he called "the Mother of All Battles" his biggest victory and maintained that Iraq had actually repulsed an American attack. Saddam stated: "Iraq has punched a hole in the myth of American superiority and rubbed the nose of the United States in the dust."

In Iraq, the Baath ruled for 35 years, chiefly under the leadership of Saddam Hussein, and this meant repeated military campaigns and acts of extermination against Iraq's Kurdish population (Baathism is anti-Kurd), against Iran (Baathism, in its Iraqi version, is anti-Persian), against Kuwait, and against Iraq's Shiite population,—not to mention the protracted two-act war with the United States and its allies—from all of which the poor and suffering Iraqis—will need a 100 years or more to recover; what a shame.

In Saddam speeches from the 70s—they appear as if a communist was hectoring from the podium. Here was a left-wing oscillation (swinging to and fro) that appeared to have been more enthusiastic even than Aflaq. And then, a few years later, Comrade Saddam oscillated back into the renewed emphasis on Islam that can be seen in his final literary composition—his novel Demons, Be Gone! (or, in the Google translation from the Arabic, Get Out of My Damned), from early in 2003, pre-invasion—a Koranic action-hero melodrama, climaxing in a barely disguised burst of Baathist applause for Al Qaeda's destruction of the World Trade Center.

Something in the Baathist doctrine is insane, and this is worth emphasizing. The Arab Baath Socialist Party has slaughtered more Arabs than any institution in modern history. No one has definitively tallied up the deaths committed by the Baath in Syria, not in 1981, when Hafez Al Assad presided over executions by the hundreds,—nor when he leveled entire neighborhoods in Hama back in 1982,—nor in 2011 and 2012, when his son has gone about doing the same on what appears to be an even bigger scale. It is a matter of tens of thousands, though (and worse may be to come).

The Iraqi Baath achieved a toll of many hundreds of thousands. The Baath in Iraq was the only government in the world, after the Nazis,—to use poison gas on its own people. And here was the Bashar's Syrian Baath threatening to make use of its own stocks of poison gas, if only against foreign invaders—meaning, from a Baathist standpoint, against anyone at all who has taken up arms against them.

Someone may argue that, in Syria and Iraq, the Baath never succeeded in establishing total control, therefore should not be considered a totalitarian movement. But totalitarians never achieve total control. They merely give it an honest try. What marks a totalitarian movement is the vigor and lunacy that animates the honest try. Ultimately a totalitarian movement is a political tendency that, in a spirit of nihilism, is committed to achieving the opposite of whatever it says it is going to achieve, and will stop at nothing to bring this about. Soviet communism in the age of Stalin was ruthlessly devoted to constructing a gigantic slave-labor system in the prison camps. Nazism left no stone unturned to bring about the ruination of Germany. Baathism is an anti-Arab movement; but this did not prevent the Baath from thriving, in its day. It's been obvious that totalitarian movements have proven unsuccessful.

Saddam has led Iraq into two (2) disastrous wars. Regimes rarely survive losing one war, let alone two in rapid succession. The Federation of American Scientists estimates that the Iran-Iraq War (1980-1988) produced approximately one million Iranian casualties and 375,000 Iraqi casualties. And Iraq failed to gain new oil-rich territory in southeastern Iran that was the goal of the Iraqi invasion. The Gulf War (1990-1991) resulted in approximately 150,000 Iraqi military dead and the subsequent UN economic sanctions may have resulted in as many or more civilian dead. Once again, Iraq failed to gain the new oil-rich territory of Kuwait.

Iraq sits on the second (2nd) largest lake of oil in the Persian Gulf, after Saudi Arabia, and yet its people now are the poorest in the region. Per capita GDP in Iraq is less than one-half (1/2) that of Iran and less than one-sixth (1/6) that of Kuwait. The infant mortality rate in Iraq is three (3) times that of Iran and six (6) times that of Kuwait. This is a record of failure which would have brought down several dictators, and yet, Saddam Hussein remained firmly in power until December 3, 2003.

And then Saddam blew it all by invading Kuwait, the small, rich neighboring emirate, on August 2, 1990. Asked in later years, following his capture in a "spider hole" by American invaders, why he had done this, Saddam first blustered that it was because Kuwait was rightfully Iraq's 19th province. Then, in his slightly nasal whine, he growled, "When I get something into my head I act. That's just the way I am."

UN economic sanctions notwithstanding, Iraq continues to be one of the world's largest oil exporters. Neighboring Syria, Jordan, and Turkey have become so dependent on Iraqi oil that they fear that a change of regime in Baghdad would interrupt supplies. Even the U.S. imports large amounts of Iraqi oil. Gulf Coast refiners prefer Iraqi crude because of its low sulphur content. In 2000, the U.S. imported roughly $6 billion in oil from Iraq. Granted, that was less than half (1/2) the $13 billion in oil imported from Saudi Arabia, but it was double the $3 billion in oil imported from Kuwait. (The bulk of Iraqi oil purchased by the U.S.—is sold through Russian middlemen, which gives the Russian government added incentive to do Saddam's bidding.)

Saddam knew how to exploit world public opinion. Iraqi's propaganda didn't have to be terribly sophisticated to take advantage of the widespread perception that economic sanctions unfairly punish the people of Iraq. And across the Islamic world, Saddam's regime is applauded for having successfully defied the UN and the US. For many, Saddam personifies their sense of historic victimization—at the hands of the imperialist West.

Like Enver Hoxha of Albania or North Korea's Kim Il Sung and son,—Saddam succeeded in turning the entire apparatus of the state into an expression of his own paranoia.—Saddam's rule cost the lives of perhaps half (1/2) a million Iraqis; wherein, two-thirds (2/3) fell in unnecessary wars; and the rest were civilian "enemies,"—rounded up and shot,—usually by firing squad.

Saddam's showy return to the faith was perhaps not entirely cynical; but in some ways an expression of his feeling of having been used, then betrayed, by the West. Back in the late 1950s, when Saddam consecrated his party membership by wielding a pistol in a botched assassination attempt against Iraq's then president, Abdul Karim Qasim, the Baath was favored by Western powers as a foil to both the powerful Iraqi Communist Party and to the pro-Russian Nasserists. The West welcomed the 1968 coup that brought Saddam into power. When he invaded revolutionary Iran in 1980, America and its allies helped quietly but generously with credits, arms and satellite intelligence. Later, America and its allies turned a blind eye to his use of chemical weapons,—first against Iranian soldiers and—then against his own unruly Kurds.

In Saddam's final communication to the world, a letter released following his conviction for crimes against humanity, he adopted the role of a martyr to the nation,—calling nobly for Iraqis to unite and to forgive invaders for their leaders' folly. It is difficult to judge what Saddam's legacy will be. Many Iraqis, especially among the Kurds and Shias, rejoiced at his death. Others simply shrugged at the inevitable passing of a delusional has-been. But quite a few regret his departure,—less out of admiration for the man than out of sadness for the deeply flawed but at least secure and predictable Iraq they have lost. And in Iraq and beyond the rage against the world felt by many other Arabs and Muslims, which Saddam the dictator once harnessed,—has yet to be assuaged (made less intense; eased, alleviated; soothed; abated).

The Iraqi state that Saddam had created was dismantled, but with such crudeness that the wider polity he had built also began to fall apart. As it did so, cracking with ever greater force into Sunni, Shia and Kurdish components, a slogan appeared on Baghdad's walls: "Better the tyranny of Saddam than the chaos of the Amerkan." In captivity and then during a messy, ill-conducted trial, the Saddam, the reviled dictator began to regain stature among his core Sunni constituents. The sordidness of his hanging, and its ugly timing on the day of the Muslim Feast of Sacrifice—contrasting with his composure before death—reinforced the Sunni sense of injury—at the hands of what many see—as a puppet sectarian regime.

Saddam sporting a bushy salt-and-pepper beard was first shown on television December 13, 2003 undergoing a medical exam for head lice. The pictures electrified and shocked Iraqis and the larger Arab world, with some cheering and some appalled to see the captive Arab leader, Saddam Hussein put on undignified display. He was imprisoned at Camp Cropper, near the international airport some 10 miles from Baghdad, on the grounds of a former palace complex that the United States military turned into a prison for senior members of the government.

The prison consisted of three (3) rows of single-story buildings surrounded by a double ring of razor wire. Saddam was kept in solitary confinement—letters and care packages including cigars sent via the Red Cross from his wife and daughters living in Qatar or Jordan were his main contact with the outside world. He lived in a relatively spartan cell consisting of: 1) a bed, 2) a toilet, 3) a chair, 4) a towel, 5) some books and 6) a prayer rug. He claimed that President Bush had always known he had no unconventional weapons. His favorite snack was Doritos corn chips, his guards said.

He was executed Saturday, December 30, 2006. The Iraqi government released an official videotape of his execution,—showing him being led to the gallows and ending after his head was in a hangman's noose. His fall from his glory and fame for him was a sudden unexpected calamity that—fell upon him without any opportunity of recovery.

The White House, September 2003, President George Bush, article entitled "Tales of Saddam's Brutality," the Iraqi people talk about mass graves and Saddam's crimes against humanity. The cruelty of Saddam's regime is evident in its brutality towards Iraqi citizens. Mass grave sites across Iraq provide further evidence of Saddam's atrocities. Within this article, the Iraqi people share their stories of brutality, torture, fear, and death. Be warned: these are some extremely horrible and most inhumane testimonies. [Go to George Bush Whitehouse]

The Syrian Intifada article entitled "Donald Trump is Wrong (Again): Saddam Hussein Supported Terrorism" by Kyle Orton, dated July 6, 2016 states: "Last night Donald Trump unburdened himself of the view that Saddam Hussein was an efficient anti-terrorist operator. It is a statement Trump has made before, and it is one of such staggering ignorance—yet one which has such wide sympathy—that it seemed worth examining the multiple ways in which it was wrong!!! Trump's praise for Saddam having "made a living off killing terrorists" in February followed a statement in December 2015, *"Saddam Hussein throws a little gas, everyone goes crazy, 'oh he's using gas!'" Trump said. Describing the way stability was maintained in the region during that time, Trump said "they go back, forth, it's the same. And they were stabilized."*

One might wonder if the use of chemical weapons of mass destruction against the Iranians during the eight-year war Saddam started can really be called "stability," and the genocidal use of such weapons as part of the Anfal campaign that murdered at least 100,000 Kurds hardly seems to have helped regional stability either. Trump's exact statement from last night was: "*Saddam Hussein was a bad guy ... really bad guy. But you know what he did well? He killed terrorists. He did that so good. They didn't read them the rights. They didn't talk. They were terrorists. It was over. —Today, Iraq is Harvard for terrorism. —You want to be a terrorist, you go to Iraq.*"

Christopher Hitchens used to say that anyone who would content themselves with saying only that Saddam Hussein was "a bad guy" did not know anything about that man, his regime, or Iraq, and that rule can be safely said to hold in this case. It does accidentally contain a truth, however: If you "want to be a terrorist, you go to Iraq," was in fact a well-known maxim for international terrorists for many decades. It might be felt that this record, bad as it is, doesn't exactly contradict Trump because this terrorism was not Islamist or jihadist in nature. Not to fear: Saddam supported Islamist and jihadist terrorism, too—a lot.

Saddam's regime supported the Syrian Muslim Brotherhood (SMB) from when they initially rebelled against the Assad regime in 1976. Al-Banna was even tasked with training Syrian Ikhwans in camps at Hit, in Anbar Province. One man trained in these camps—which evidently operated even after al-Banna departed the country—was Ahmed Barodi, who later resided in the U.S. before being deported partly for these ties. In the wake of the crushing of the SMB rebellion in 1982 at Hama, Saddam took in the survivors—the "most radical" ones anyway (many others went to Europe), including Eddin Barakat Yarkas and Mustafa Nasar (Abu Musab al-Suri). Yarkas became a roommate of Mohamed Atta—the lead death pilot on 9/11—and was swept up in Spain after the 9/11 massacre, later convicted of helping to plan and finance that atrocity. Nasar went on to become probably the greatest strategist in the Jihadi-Salafist world, a guide for both the Islamic State (IS)* and al-Qaeda. Furthermore, there's lots and lots of more proof.

Trump has shown on the one hand a near-perfect illiteracy in foreign policy, and on the other a very disturbing sympathy for authoritarians, not just in Iraq but Syria, Libya, China, North Korea, and Russia.—This admiration has been returned, notably by North Korea, and Russia, and even more disturbingly Trump's entourage includes powerful Kremlin-linked figures. Trump has said he will "bomb the s*it" out of IS and take the oilfields currently under their control, and that he will leave Syria as a "free zone" for IS. Who knows which, if any, of those statements represents his true view? One probably should be able to say, four months from an election, what the position of a candidate is on the major national security questions of the day—and when one cannot,—that is its own judgment.

It was notable, in terms of Trump's simple political competence, that Trump chose to praise Saddam on the day the FBI released a damning report about Hillary Clinton's "extremely careless ... handling of very sensitive, highly classified information" that almost certainly led to "hostile actors" having access to it. As flabbergasting as this must have been for Republicans, they have only themselves to blame for Trump: their message has ceased to resonate and they allowed Trump to pick up issues that matter to the public, notably the welfare safety net and economic nationalism.

Trump's campaign has attracted the "Alt-Right"—the white supremacists with a thing for internet snark—and he has engaged in demagogy of the crudest kind on any number of subjects. But his is not a fascist candidacy, either in inception or support; its driving energy comes from millions of people who feel, essentially correctly, they have been left behind by the recent economic growth and have been disenfranchised politically.

These issues are so important, indeed, that Trump's disastrous foreign policy might well be overlooked "by voters" who not-unreasonably do not make the connection between international security and personal security. In the last few years, after all, security abroad and security at home—has been set up as an antagonistic, rather than reinforcing, relationship. The reality still is that the world needs

American leadership, and a man who concludes that Saddam Hussein was a bulwark against terrorism—is unlikely to be fit to provide it. [End of Article]

For informational purposes, I thought it necessary from an educational perspective to provide some background information about Islam to help us in understanding things when hearing and reading about Islam. Therefore, the following information is being provided for this purpose.

Jihadism or Jihadist-Salafism is a transnational religious-political ideology based on a belief in "physical" jjhadism and the Salafi movement of returning to (what adherents believe to be) "true" Sunni Islam. Sunni Islam is a denomination of Islam which holds that the Islamic prophet Muhammad's first Caliph was his father-in-law Abu Bakr. Sunni Islam primarily contrasts with Shi'a Islam, which holds that Muhammad's son-in-law and cousin, Ali ibn Abi Talib, not Abu Bakr, was his first caliph. Sunni Islam is by far the largest denomination of Islam. As of 2009, Sunni Muslims constituted 87–90% of the world's Muslim population. Its adherents are referred to in Arabic as ahl as-sunnah wa l-jamā☐ah (Arabic: أهل السنة والجماعة), "people of the tradition of Muhammad and the consensus of the Ummah" or ahl as-sunnah (Arabic أهل السنة) for short.

In English, Jihadism or Jihadist-Salafism theological study or doctrine is called Sunnism, while adherents are known as Sunni Muslims, Sunnis, Sunnites and Ahlus Sunnah.

Sunni Islam is the world's largest religious denomination, followed by Roman Catholicism.

Sunni Islam is sometimes referred to as "orthodox Islam." The word "Sunni" comes from the term Sunnah, which referes to the sayings and actions of the prophet Muhammad as recorded in the Arabic hadith (News or Story), also spelled Hadit (record of the traditions or sayings of the Prophet Muhammad,—revered and received as a major source of religious law and moral guidance,—second only to the authority of the Qur☐ān, the holy book of Islam).

11

U.S. Supreme Court Justice Calls Trump a Fake

DONALD TRUMP HAS proven himself as being unpredictable; manifesting a temperament through his behavior practices that's given the world a very clear reading of his disposition and general outlook people and things;—manifesting behavior practices that have been unusually moody and disgustingly unpredictable. Such unpredictable is not a good or positive quality for anyone, especially, and in particularly, persons seeking leadership positions, especially, for the office of President of the United States of America.

There are some things that come in our heads that we need to keep in our heads; simply, because, such things are not good and profitable for ourselves nor the people with whom we're to communicate and/or serve. As such, it's wise and profitable to give due thought and filter the things coming from our heads. However, Trump's temperament is unrestrained with anger and excessive aggressiveness that brings whatever's in his head out of his head, clearly and cogently setting and confirming a destructive quality making him unquestionably unfit for president.

The following Scriptural references are provided for us to examine and test ourselves and to examine and test Donald Trump as to whether things manifested in his behavior practices are good or bad and acceptable or unacceptable unto the Lord. The only way we can truly see who we are, Donald Trump or any other person—is by faith through God's spiritual lens of the Holy Scriptures.

> *[16] A wise man fears and departs from evil, But a fool rages and is self-confident. [17] A quick-tempered man acts foolishly, And a man of wicked intentions is hated. (Prov. 14:16-17) [29] He who is slow to wrath has great understanding, But he who is impulsive exalts folly. [30] A sound heart is life to the body, But envy is rottenness to the bones. (Prov. 14:29-30)*

> *[1] A soft answer turns away wrath, But a harsh word stirs up anger. [2] The tongue of the wise uses knowledge rightly, But the mouth of fools pours forth foolishness. (Prov. 15:1-2) [18] A wrathful man stirs up strife, But he who is slow to anger allays contention. (Prov. 15:18) [21] Folly is joy to him who is destitute of discernment, But a man of understanding walks uprightly. (Prov. 15:21) [23] A man has joy by the answer of his mouth, And a word spoken in due season, how good it is! (Prov. 15:23)*

> *[18] Pride goes before destruction, And a haughty spirit before a fall. (Prov. 16:18) [27] An ungodly man digs up evil, And it is on his lips like a burning fire. [28] A perverse man sows strife, And a whisperer separates the best of friends. [29] A violent man entices his neighbor, And leads him in a way that is not good. (Prov. 16:27-29) [32] He who is slow to anger is better than the mighty, And he who rules his spirit than he who takes a city. (Prov. 16:32)*

> *[1] A man who isolates himself seeks his own desire; He rages against all wise judgment. [2] A fool has no delight in understanding, But in expressing his own heart. (Prov. 18:1-2) [7] A fool's mouth is his destruction, And his lips are the snare of*

his soul. (Prov. 18:7) **¹²** *Before destruction the heart of a man is haughty, And before honor is humility.* **¹³** *He who answers a matter before he hears it, It is folly and shame to him. (Prov. 18:12-13)*

⁴ *A haughty look, a proud heart, And the plowing of the wicked are sin. (Prov. 21:4)* **⁷** *The violence of the wicked will destroy them, Because they refuse to do justice.* **⁸** *The way of a guilty man is perverse; But as for the pure, his work is right. (Prov. 21:7-8)* **²³** *Whoever guards his mouth and tongue Keeps his soul from troubles.* **²⁴** *A proud and haughty man—"Scoffer" is his name; He acts with arrogant pride. (Prov. 21:23-24)*

¹ *A good name is to be chosen rather than great riches, Loving favor rather than silver and gold. (Prov. 22:1)* **⁴** *By humility and the fear of the* LORD *Are riches and honor and life. Thorns and snares are in the way of the perverse; He who guards his soul will be far from them. (Prov. 22:4-5)* **⁸** *He who sows iniquity will reap sorrow, And the rod of his anger will fail. (Prov. 22:8)* **¹⁶** *He who oppresses the poor to increase his riches, And he who gives to the rich, will surely come to poverty. (Prov. 22:16)*

⁴ *Do not overwork to be rich; Because of your own understanding, cease!* **⁵** *Will you set your eyes on that which is not? For riches certainly make themselves wings; They fly away like an eagle toward heaven. (Prov. 23:4-5)* **⁷** *For as he thinks in his heart, so is he. "Eat and drink!" he says to you, But his heart is not with you. (Prov. 23:7)* **²³** *Buy the truth, and do not sell it, Also wisdom and instruction and understanding. (Prov. 23:23)*

¹⁹ *Confidence in an unfaithful man in time of trouble Is like a bad tooth and a foot out of joint. (Prov. 25:19)* **²⁸** *Whoever has no rule over his own spirit Is like a city broken down, without walls.*

(Prov. 25:28) *⁵ Evil men do not understand justice, But those who seek the LORD understand all. Better is the poor who walks in his integrity Than one perverse in his ways, though he be rich. (Prov. 28:5-6) ⁸ One who increases his possessions by usury and extortion Gathers it for him who will pity the poor. ⁹ One who turns away his ear from hearing the law, Even his prayer is an abomination. (Prov. 28:8-9) ¹¹ The rich man is wise in his own eyes, But the poor who has understanding searches him out. (Prov. 28:11)*

¹⁶ A ruler who lacks understanding is a great oppressor, But he who hates covetousness will prolong his days. (Prov. 28:16) ²² A man with an evil eye hastens after riches, And does not consider that poverty will come upon him. (Prov. 28:22) ²⁵ He who is of a proud heart stirs up strife, But he who trusts in the LORD will be prospered. ²⁶ He who trusts in his own heart is a fool, But whoever walks wisely will be delivered. (Prov. 28:25-26)

¹⁵The way of a fool is right in his own eyes, But he who heeds counsel is wise. (Prov. 12:15) ²⁰ Do you see a man hasty in his words? There is more hope for a fool than for him. (Prov. 29:20) ¹¹ As a dog returns to his own vomit, So a fool repeats his folly. ¹² Do you see a man wise in his own eyes? There is more hope for a fool than for him. (Prov. 26:11-12) ²⁷ Whoever digs a pit will fall into it, And he who rolls a stone will have it roll back on him. ²⁸ A lying tongue hates those who are crushed by it, And a flattering mouth works ruin. (Prov. 26:27-28)

³³ "Either make the tree good and its fruit good, or else make the tree bad and its fruit bad; for a tree is known by its fruit. ³⁴ Brood of vipers! How can you, being evil, speak good things? For out of the abundance of the heart the mouth speaks. (Matt. 12:33-34) ³⁷ For by your words you will be justified, and by your words you will be condemned." (Matt. 12:37)

> *⁵ If any of you lacks wisdom, let him ask of God, who gives to all liberally and without reproach, and it will be given to him. (Ja. 1:5) ¹⁹ So then, my beloved brethren, let every man be swift to hear, slow to speak, slow to wrath; ²⁰ for the wrath of man does not produce the righteousness of God. (Ja. 1:19-20) ⁶ But without faith it is impossible to please Him, for he who comes to God must believe that He is, and that He is a rewarder of those who diligently seek Him. (Heb. 11:6)*

When Donald Trump is interviewed and asked questions, he has habitually gone all over the country and world to avoid giving direct responses to questions asked. In this avoidance of asking questions directly and clearly, he's willfully and intentionally implemented a process with designed technique to avoid disclosure, in particularly, but not limited to, his income tax returns and Trump University cases that could and most likely bring serious harm to his status and reputation.

However, Trump should not have been given and continue to be given special treatment concerning these vitally important issues. It's obvious that his accounting team and lawyers have used every means possible to create degrees of difficulty for the IRS in ongoing audits at the tax payers' expense; and that lawsuits against Trump University, which appear very strongly to be open and closed cases by the preponderance of evidence available to the general public, that Trump is in "very hot water," and that any honesty and/or integrity from him has taken a very long vacation and can now be classified as Missing-in-Action (MIA).

We the People of the United States, in Order to form a more perfect Union, establish Justice, insure domestic Tranquility, provide for the common defence, promote the general Welfare, and secure the Blessings of Liberty to ourselves and our Posterity,—should not have to wait any longer in being provided Trump's tax returns and closure on Trump University lawsuits.

We the People have the right to know whether or not Trump is a tax cheat and/or a con man (one who has willfully and intentionally cheated and tricked seniors and uneducated disadvantaged out of their funds by a confident game he himself designed and promoted). We the People have the right to know these answers to these issues before the President of the United States is elected in November 2016 and subsequently inaugurated in January 2017.

It should be noted, if Donald Trump is innocent, he has nothing to lose; however, if he is guilty, Trump has a very, very, lot to lose. His clearly visible and obvious fight to not reveal his income tax returns is a very indication that he has something extremely damaging that he's really hoping he has to never ever disclose. Yes, Trump has no intentions at all of releasing his income tax returns because, in them, exist a bombshell (an unexpected and shattering discovery) that will bring destruction to his status and reputation. Trump is very, very, fearful of this and will do all within his power to avoid any release of his tax returns and/or settlement agreements with the IRS.

> *[10] Fear not, for I am with you; Be not dismayed, for I am your God. I will strengthen you, Yes, I will help you, I will uphold you with My righteous right hand.' (Isa. 41:10) [13] For I, the LORD your God, will hold your right hand, Saying to you, 'Fear not, I will help you.' (Isa. 41:13) [8] I am the LORD, that is My name; And My glory I will not give to another, Nor My praise to carved images. [9] Behold, the former things have come to pass, And new things I declare; Before they spring forth I tell you of them." (Isa. 42:8-9)*

> *[8] "Remember this, and show yourselves men; Recall to mind, O you transgressors. [9] Remember the former things of old, For I am God, and there is no other; I am God, and there is none like Me, [10] Declaring the end from the beginning, And from ancient times things that are not yet done, Saying, 'My counsel shall stand, And I will do all My pleasure,' (Isa. 46:8-11)*

¹¹ I, even I, am the Lord, And besides Me there is no savior. ¹² I have declared and saved, I have proclaimed, And there was no foreign god among you; Therefore you are My witnesses," Says the Lord, "that I am God. ¹³ Indeed before the day was, I am He; And there is no one who can deliver out of My hand; I work, and who will reverse it?" (Isa. 43:11-13) ²⁶ Put Me in remembrance; Let us contend together; State your case, that you may be acquitted. (Isa. 43:26) ²⁴ But let justice run down like water, And righteousness like a mighty stream. (Amos 5:24)

We the People want justice and righteous in our land. However, Trump does not seek justice, but rather, to pervert it by whatever means possible to accomplish his own selfish ambitions. Trumps knows if justice was rendered upon him it would disclose his true deeds as inappropriately and most likely criminal, which will have severe consequences most likely causing disgrace and disrespect to himself from We the People.

As we all know, Trump has very aggressively called for justice and jail time for Hillary Clinton, whose two (2) issues have been investigated and resolved. NOW, what about Trump's two (2) issues that hasn't been resolved? Will it turn out that Trump who aggressively demanded jail-time for Hillary Clinton will himself be going to jail? Let's get it over with, that the truth be known and justice be served.

¹Dishonest scales are an abomination to the Lord, But a just weight is His delight. ² When pride comes, then comes shame; But with the humble is wisdom. (Prov. 11:1-2) ⁷ There is one who makes himself rich, yet has nothing; And one who makes himself poor, yet has great riches. (Prov. 13:7) ¹¹ Wealth gained by dishonesty will be diminished, But he who gathers by labor will increase. (Prov. 13:11) ²⁷ He who is greedy for gain troubles his own house, But he who hates bribes will live. (Prov. 15:27)

⁵ Everyone proud in heart is an abomination to the LORD; Though they join forces, none will go unpunished. ⁶ In mercy and truth Atonement is provided for iniquity; And by the fear of the LORD one departs from evil. (Prov. 16:5-6) ¹¹ An evil man seeks only rebellion; Therefore a cruel messenger will be sent against him. (Prov. 17:11) ¹³ Whoever rewards evil for good, Evil will not depart from his house. (Prov. 17:13) ²⁰ He who has a deceitful heart finds no good, And he who has a perverse tongue falls into evil. (Prov. 17:20)

¹⁷ Bread gained by deceit is sweet to a man, But afterward his mouth will be filled with gravel. (Prov. 20:17) ⁶ Getting treasures by a lying tongue Is the fleeting fantasy of those who seek death. (Prov. 21:6) ¹⁴ A gift in secret pacifies anger, And a bribe behind the back, strong wrath. ¹⁵ It is a joy for the just to do justice, But destruction will come to the workers of iniquity. (Prov. 21:14-15) ¹¹ "As a partridge that broods but does not hatch, So is he who gets riches, but not by right; It will leave him in the midst of his days, And at his end he will be a fool." (Jer. 17:11)

⁶ Now godliness with contentment is great gain. ⁷ For we brought nothing into this world, and it is certain we can carry nothing out. ⁸ And having food and clothing, with these we shall be content. ⁹ But those who desire to be rich fall into temptation and a snare, and into many foolish and harmful lusts which drown men in destruction and perdition. ¹⁰ For the love of money is a root of all kinds of evil, for which some have strayed from the faith in their greediness, and pierced themselves through with many sorrows. (1 Tim. 6:6-10)

The above Scriptural references are provided for further examination and evaluation of ourselves, Donald Trump, and others. We are living in perilous times when evil men who are "imposters or fakers"

U.S. Supreme Court Justice Calls Trump a Fake

grow worst and worst, deceiving and being deceived. (2 Tim. 3:13) As such, it calls for we who are protectors of the flock of God to help the sheep and lambs so that they are not taken advantaged and devoured by workers of iniquity. As such, we Christians have the inherited responsibility of detecting and exposing them to aid in their safety and welfare. Times such as these call for exceptional and unusual efforts that may be unprecedented, but yet, vitally necessary for the benefit of all the people.

This Book is a prime example of an exceptional or extraordinary effort towards this mission. However, Supreme Court Justice Ruth Bader Ginsburg, in her personal call of duty to We the People has implemented an extraordinary and unusual effort to expose Donald Trump for who he really is; and I believe we should commend her for her conviction and courage. Some of us are called upon to take extraordinary and unusual efforts for the benefit of We the People.

CNN politics on Wednesday, July 13, 2016 in an article entitled "Justice Ruth Bader Ginsburg calls Trump a 'faker,' he says she should resign" states: "Supreme Court Justice Ruth Bader Ginsburg's well-known candor was on display in her chambers late Monday, when she declined to retreat from her earlier criticism of Donald Trump and even elaborated on it. "He is a faker," she said of the presumptive Republican presidential nominee, going point by point, as if presenting a legal brief. "He has no consistency about him. He says whatever comes into his head at the moment. He really has an ego. ... How has he gotten away with not turning over his tax returns? ... The press seems to be very gentle with him on that." ...

Ginsburg's comments came in a previously scheduled interview related to my research for a book on Chief Justice John Roberts. I took a detour to raise the reverberations from her criticism of Trump to The Associated Press and The New York Times in recent interviews. "I can't imagine what this place would be—I can't imagine what the country would be—with Donald Trump as our president," she had said in the Times interview published Monday. Trump responded Wednesday morning by calling on Ginsburg to resign. "Justice Ginsburg of the U.S.

Supreme Court has embarrassed all by making very dumb political statements about me. Her mind is shot—resign!" Trump tweeted.

It is highly unusual for a justice to make such politically charged remarks, and some critics said she crossed the line. House Speaker Paul Ryan told CNN's Jake Tapper on Tuesday night the comments were "out of place."—"For someone on the Supreme Court who is going to be calling balls and strikes in the future based upon whatever the next president and Congress does,—that strikes me as inherently biased and out of the realm."

Having met with Ginsburg on a regular basis for more than a decade and sometimes been struck by her frankness, I found her response classic. The 83-year-old justice expressed no regret on Monday for the comments or surprise that she would be criticized. Any disbelief she expressed stemmed from the fact that Trump has gotten so far in the election cycle.

"At first I thought it was funny," she said of Trump's early candidacy. "To think that there'' a possibility that he could be president ..." Her voice trailed off gloomily. "I think he has gotten so much free publicity," she added, drawing a contrast between what she believes is tougher media treatment of Democratic candidate Hillary Clinton and returning to an overriding complaint: "Every other presidential candidate has turned over tax returns." I

Ginsburg was appointed to the high court by President Bill Clinton in 1993, and is now the senior member of the liberal wing and leading voice countering conservative Chief Justice Roberts. She has drawn a cult-like following among young people who have nicknamed her The Notorious R.B.G., a play on American rapper The Notorious B.I.G.

I have witnessed her off-bench bluntness many times through the years. During 2009 oral arguments in a case involving a 13-year-old Arizona girl who had been strip-searched by school administrators looking for drugs, she was troubled that some male justices played down any harm to the student.—"They have never been a 13-year-old girl," Ginsburg told me. "It's a very sensitive age for a girl.—I didn't think that my colleagues, some of them,—quite understood."

Earlier in 2009, she was being treated for pancreatic cancer—yet made sure to attend President Barack Obama's televised speech to a joint session of Congress, explaining that she wanted people to know the Supreme Court was not all men.—"I also wanted them to see I was alive and well," contrary to that senator who said I'd be dead within nine (9) months." She was referring to Sen. Jim Bunning, a Kentucky Republican, who had said she would likely die within nine (9) months from the pancreatic cancer. Bunning later apologized.

It was evident in our interview on Monday that when Ginsburg imagines who would succeed Obama, she does not expect Trump to prevail over Clinton. Acknowledging her own age and that Justices Anthony Kennedy and Stephen Breyer will turn 80 and 78, respectively, Ginsburg said of the possible next president: "She is bound to have a few appointments (to the Supreme Court) in her term."

Hypocrites dress, walk, and talk somewhat Christian, some more so than other; but they do not have the love of God abiding in them. Hypocrites sit in the congregation of the saints singing, praying, shouting, and doing Christian-like things (i.e. pretending to hear or listen to the word), but in reality; don't really like God, much less love Him; but tolerate Him by granting their presence or appearance in the Christian environment and in some Christian-like works in seeking the benefits of being called and accepted as Christians.

Hypocrites really hate and despise God, because they hate and despise His rules of morality that prohibit and restrain them from living according to their own wills and ways. But in their cunning craftiness of deceitful plotting, they very reluctantly go along with things publically that they actually hate in private. But that's the way they play the game; trickery and deceit is like a sport to them; and when they're successful, they celebrate!!!

> [7] *Hypocrites! Well did Isaiah prophesy about you, saying:* [8] *'These people draw near to Me with their mouth, And honor Me with their lips, But their heart is far from Me.* [9] *And in vain they worship Me,—Teaching as doctrines the commandments*

of men.' " (Matt. 15:7-9) ²¹ "Not everyone who says to Me, 'Lord, Lord,'—shall enter the kingdom of heaven, but he who does the will of My Father in heaven. ²² Many will say to Me in that day, 'Lord, Lord, have we not prophesied in Your name, cast out demons in Your name, and done many wonders in Your name?'²³ And then I will declare to them, 'I never knew you; depart from Me, you who practice lawlessness!' (Matt. 7:21-23)

Saul of Tarus was a Roman who persecuted and killed people of the way, later called Christians. However, when he had a one-on-one encounter with Christ on the road to Damascus, his life was changed, renewed by the Holy Spirit and he became the Apostle Paul, an ex-persecutor/killer of Christians—to now supporter and protector of Christians. The Apostle Paul's fruits were no longer evil, but good and profitable for life and not bad and unprofitable for death. When a person is truly born-again of the Holy Spirit, there will be a change in his or her production of fruits, as the Apostle Paul has clearly demonstrated in his works for the gospel of Jesus Christ. Some may fake it for a while; but sooner or later, the true person comes out, and many times unexpectedly.

> ¹But know this, that in the last days perilous times will come: ² For men will be lovers of themselves,—lovers of money,—boasters, proud, blasphemers,—disobedient to parents,—unthankful, unholy, ³ unloving, unforgiving, slanderers,—without self-control,—brutal,—despisers of good,—⁴ traitors, headstrong,—haughty, lovers of pleasure rather than lovers of God,—⁵ having a form of godliness but denying its power.—And from such people turn away! (2 Tim. 3:1-5)

> ¹Beloved, do not believe every spirit, but test the spirits, whether they are of God; because many false prophets have gone

out into the world.² By this you know the Spirit of God: Every spirit that confesses that Jesus Christ has come in the flesh is of God, ³ and every spirit that does not confess that Jesus Christ has come in the flesh is not of God. And this is the spirit of the Antichrist, which you have heard was coming, and is now already in the world. (1 Jn. 4:1-3)

12

Trump University a Fake/ a True Con

THE NEW YORKER article June 2, 2016 entitled TRUMP UNIVERSITY: IT'S WORSE THAN YOU THINK, states: "Following the release, earlier this week, of testimony filed in a federal lawsuit against Trump University, the United States is facing a high-stakes social-science experiment. Will one of the world's leading democracies elect as its President a businessman—who founded and operated a for-profit learning annex that some of its own employees regarded as a giant rip-off, and that the highest legal officer in New York State has described as a classic bait-and-switch scheme?"

If anyone still has any doubt about the troubling nature of Donald Trump's record, he or she should be obliged to read the affidavit of Ronald Schnackenberg, a former salesman for Trump University. Schnackenberg's testimony was one of the documents unsealed by a judge in the class-action suit, which was brought in California by some of Trump University's disgruntled former attendees.

Schnackenberg, who worked in Trump's office at 40 Wall Street, testified that "while Trump University claimed it wanted to help consumers make money in real estate, in fact Trump University was only interested in selling every person the most expensive seminars they possibly could." The affidavit concludes, "Based upon my personal experience and employment, I believe that Trump University was a fraudulent scheme, and that it preyed upon the elderly and uneducated to separate them from their money."

In one sense, the latest revelations don't break much new ground. Back in 2013, when the office of Eric Schneiderman, New York's Attorney General, filed a civil lawsuit against Trump and some of his associates, the complaint, which is also worth reading in full, made perfectly clear what sort of organization it was targeting. Despite Trump University's claim that it offered "graduate programs, post graduate programs, doctorate programs," it wasn't a university at all. It was a company that purported to be selling Trump's secret insights into how to make money in real estate. From the time Trump University began operating, in 2005, the A.G.'s office repeatedly warned the company that it was breaking the law by calling itself a university. (In New York State, universities have to obtain a state charter.)

That was the bait—or, rather, the initial bait. According to the Attorney General's complaint, the free classes were merely a marketing device. There, Trump University's instructors "engaged in a methodical, Systematic Series of misrepresentations" designed to convince students to sign up for a three-day seminar, where they would learn Trump's personal techniques and strategies for investing, at a cost of about fifteen hundred dollars ($1,500).

When it began, Trump University offered online classes, but it quickly switched its focus to live classes and seminars, the first of which was free to attend. One of the company's ads said of Trump, "He's the most celebrated entrepreneur on earth. . . . And now he's ready to share—with Americans like you—the Trump process for investing in today's once-in-a-lifetime real estate market." The ad said that Trump had "hand-picked" Trump University's instructors, and it ended with a quote from him: "I can turn anyone into a successful real estate investor, including you."

In fact, Trump hadn't handpicked the instructors, and he didn't attend the three-day seminars. Moreover, the complaint said, "no specific Donald Trump techniques or strategies were taught during the seminars, Donald Trump 'never' reviewed any of Trump University's curricula or programming materials, nor did he review any of the content for the free seminars or the three day seminars." So what were the attendees taught? According to the complaint, "the contents and material presented by Trump University were developed in large part by a third-party company that creates and develops materials for an array of motivational speakers and Seminar and timeshare rental companies." The closest that the attendees at the seminars got to Trump was when they were encouraged to have their picture taken with a life-size photo of him.

The alleged scam didn't stop there. Trump University instructors told people who attended the three-day seminars that this wasn't enough time to learn how to succeed, and encouraged them to purchase additional "mentorship" programs, which cost up to thirty-five thousand ($35,000) dollars. The complaint explained,

This bait and switch was laid out in the Trump University Playbook ("Playbook"), which provided step-to-step directions to Trump University instructors on what to tell students during the seminars. . . . Trump University instructors and staff were given detailed guidance as to how to build rapport and approach consumers one-on-one to encourage further purchases. Trump University representatives were explicitly instructed to push the highest priced Elite programs. Even when students hesitated to purchase the expensive programs, Trump representatives were provided stock responses to encourage purchases, including encouraging students to go into debt to pay for the Elite programs.

The newly released documents, which included actual Trump University playbooks (one was also uncovered by Politico earlier this year), provide more detail about the sales tactics that its employees used. Some of these methods, such as encouraging customers to max out their credit cards and playing psychological tricks on them, are familiar from the world of time-shares and other dodgy industries. "If they can afford the gold elite don't allow them to think about doing anything besides the gold elite," one of the playbooks advised the sales staff. At another point, the manual said, "Don't ask people what they think about something you've said. Instead, always ask them how they feel about it. People buy emotionally and justify it logically."

One of Schnackenberg's contributions, in his testimony, was to illustrate how these tactics worked with individuals. Recounting his experience with one couple, which included a man who was on disability, he said, "After the hard-sell sales presentation, they were considering purchasing the $35,000 Elite program. I did not feel it was an appropriate program for them because of their precarious financial condition." Far from being commended by his bosses for his honesty, Schnackenberg said that he was reprimanded. Another salesperson then "talked them into buying the $35,000 program after I refused to sell this program to them," he testified. "I was disgusted by this conduct and decided to resign."

Trump denies any wrongdoing. Citing surveys that he claims show that Trump University got high approval ratings from its customers, he has set up a Web site at 98percentapproval.com, which features testimonials from Trump University attendees and attacks on the Attorney General. Trump's lawyers also told the Times that other testimony in the California case had discredited the charges made by former employees. Hope Hicks, Trump's campaign spokesperson, said that he was looking forward to his day in court.

> [8] *Do not go hastily to court; For what will you do in the end, When your neighbor has put you to shame?* [9] *Debate your case with your neighbor, And do not disclose the secret to another;* [10] *Lest he who hears it expose your shame, And your reputation be ruined. (Prov. 25:8-10)*

So far, though, Trump has failed in his efforts to have the lawsuits in California and New York thrown out. And, whatever happens to the legal cases, the allegations will dog him all the way to November. On Wednesday, Hillary Clinton offered a preview of what is to come, calling Trump a "fraud" who is "trying to scam America the way he scammed all those people at Trump University."

The Clinton campaign is clearly hoping that Trump University will be to Trump as Bain Capital was to Mitt Romney—a way to portray him as just another selfish rich guy who is out to profit at the expense of ordinary folk. Commenting on Twitter, Clinton's press secretary, Brian Fallon, wrote, "Trump U is devastating because it's metaphor for his whole campaign: promising hardworking Americans way to get ahead, but all based on lies."

So will Trump University be the thing that brings Trump down? In a post for *The New Republic*, Brian Beutler argued that it will be "devastating" to him. On my Twitter feed, some people reacted more skeptically, pointing out that many of Trump's supporters appear oblivious to any criticisms of him, and that Clinton isn't necessarily the ideal prosecutor. It is also worth recalling that, in Italy, Silvio Berlusconi, another populist businessman, served as Prime Minister four times despite a list of allegations against him that included bribery, tax evasion, sexual misconduct, and having ties to the mafia.

One thing is clear, though. If the revelations about Trump University *don't* do any damage to Trump, it's time to worry—or worry even more—about American democracy. John Cassidy has been a staff writer at *The New Yorker* since 1995. He also writes a column about politics, economics, and more, for newyorker.com.

The affidavit (Declaration of Ronald Schnackenberg in Support of Plaintiff's Motion for Class Certification), United States District Court, Southern District of California, Case Number: 3:10-CV-00940-CAB (WVG) reads as follows: I Ronald Schnackenberg, hereby declare and state the follows:

1. I am a residen of San Francisco, Califorina. If called a witness, I could and would competently testify as to all facts within my personal knowledge.
2. I worked for Trump University from October 2006 through May 2007. My title was Sales Manager. I worked at Trump University headquarters located at 40 Wall Street, New York, New York. My job duties included selling Trump University programs to

Trump University a Fake/a True Con

all consumers who called to inquire about Trump University, and to sell courses to consumers who attended live events.

3. I resigned from my position in May 2007 because I believed that Trump University was engaging in misleading fraudulent, and dishonest conduct. I found it particularly offensive that, while Trump University claimed it wanted to help consumers make money in real estate, in fact Trump University was only interested in selling every person the most expensive seminars they possible could.

4. For example, at a live event in New York City in April 2007, I spoke to a couple whose names I believe are Chris and Carla (or Clara) Moore. After the hard-sell sales presentation, they were considering purchasing the $35,000 Elite program. I did not feel it was an appropriate program for them because of their precarious financial condition—they had no money to pay for the program, but would have had to pay for the program using his disability income and taking out a loan based on the equity in his apartment. Trump University reprimanded me for not trying harder to sell the program to this couple. Another sales person, I believe his name is Tad Lignell, talked them into buying the $35,000 seminar after I refused to sell this program to them.—I was disgusted by this conduct and decided to resign.

5. I never saw Donald Trump at the University. In the seven months that I worked at Trump University, I did not see him once.

6. In my experience, the primary goal of Trump University was not to educate students regarding real estate investing. The primary focus seemed to make money, as quickly and easily as possible. An example of this was the drastic discourse they took from their prior line of business.

7. Gary Eldred wrote the "Real Estate Investor Training Program," which was an online program with some interactive aspects (conference calls and video conferences). When I accepted a

job with Trump University, they were focused on selling the Real Estate Investor Training Program.

8. However, around February 2007, the direction of Trump University's business drastically changed to a "live events" and seminar driven by high-pressure front-end salesmen, inexperienced in real estate, making high-pressure sales. If consumers attended the event and did not purchase a seminar, the Trump University sales team followed up with them.

9. Trump University's live seminars and events were not based on the content of Eldred's Real Estate Investor Training Program. Instead, Mark Dove, who essentially owns that "front-end high-pressure speaker scam" world, provides speakers, instructors, mentors and salespeople to Trump University, and these people brought their own programs, which turned into Trump University programs.

10. I was very uncomfortable with this new direction of business, as I believed it to be very unethical.

11. While Trump University claimed that its teachers and mentors were all experts in real estate, I believe that most of the instructors, mentors, and coaches had very little or no personal experience in real estate techniques they were teaching, and that Trump University misrepresented their experiences and successes to the public. I know this because I received complaints from Trump University students about this. For example, David Stamper was a mentor and front end speaker, but his background was in jewelry making and he did not have any personal real estate experience when he was hired by Trump University.

12. From the very beginning, Trump University speakers told students to raise their credit card limits so that they could be ready to purchase real estate. In fact, the speakers then told students to use their increased credit limits to purchase the next level of Trump University seminar.

13. In my position as sales manager, I received calls from many

Trump University a Fake/a True Con

students after they had taken the Trump University seminars. In my experience, virtually all students who purchased a Trump University seminar were dissatisfied with the program they purchased. To my knowledge, not a single consumer who paid for a Trump University seminar programs went on to successfully invest in real estate based upon the techniques that were taught.
14. Trump University seminars were a scheme involving a constant upsell. Based upon my experience at Trump University, the whole goal of the free seminar was to persuade consumers to sign up for the $1,500 seminar. Also based upon my experience at Trump University, the whole purpose of the $1,500 seminar was to get people to sign up for the $35,000 Elite seminars. And the whole purpose for the $35,000 Elite seminars was to get people to buy additional books, seminars and products.
15. Based upon my personal experience and employment, I believe that Trump University was a fraudulent scheme, and that it preyed upon the elderly and uneducated to separate them from their money.

I declare under the penalty of perjury under the laws of the United States of America that the foregoing is true and correct. Executed this 16 day of September, 2012, at San Francisco, California. Signed, Ronald Schnackenburg.

From what I have read and examined, the preponderance of evidence against Trump University is clear and cogent, not frivolous, injudicious, irresponsible, or unreasonable, and without any merit for summary judgment. I truly believe that—"Donald Trump and Trump University I profoundly believe will be found guilty of implementing a fraudulent scheme."

The Washington Post article on June 7, 2016 entitled, "Sorry, Donald Trump, The Trump University Judge was Just following the law;" states: "Republican presidential candidate Donald Trump told CBS's "Face the Nation" that the judge overseeing the Trump University case has treated him "very unfairly," and that "there is something going on" adding that he is biased. (Reuters) "He [Judge Gonzalo Curiel] is giving us very unfair rulings, rulings that people can't even believe. This case should have ended years ago on summary judgment. The best lawyers—I have spoken to so many lawyers—they said, this is not a case. This is a case that should have ended."

Trump has been blasting U.S. District Court Judge Gonzalo Curiel for having an "inherent conflict of interest," because of his Mexican heritage and Trump's plan to build a wall along the U.S.-Mexico border. Curiel, who is presiding over two of three lawsuits against Trump and Trump University, was born in Indiana to parents who emigrated from Mexico. But the presumptive Republican presidential nominee continues to rail against the judge for biased, negative and unfair rulings.

In particular, Trump points to Curiel's use of a procedural move—a summary judgment—as evidence: "I should have easily won the Trump University case on summary judgement but have a judge, Gonzalo Curiel, who is totally biased against me."

Trump University marketed its seminars and mentorship packages that cost up to $35,000 as opportunities for "students" to learn tricks of the real estate trade from mentors and instructors said to be "hand-picked" by Trump. Both cases before Curiel are class-action lawsuits from former students, claiming fraud and demanding their money back. One lawsuit was filed in 2010 by students in California, Florida and New York, and the other in 2013 by a plaintiff who alleged he was misled and upsold to pay for a $35,000 upgrade.

Trump is named as a defendant in both lawsuits and has filed for a motion for summary judgment in both. Last year, Curiel ruled on the motion in the 2010 lawsuit. The motion in the 2013 lawsuit is pending a court hearing next month, as noted in this explainer by the Popehat blog. A "summary judgment" is a procedural move that allows a judge to dismiss a case before going to trial. If summary judgment is granted, that means the judge found there's "no genuine dispute of material fact" that requires a full trial. So all the judge is deciding is whether the two sides agree or disagree on facts—a pretty low bar. When a judge grants a summary judgment, it's usually for a narrow and straightforward issue, said Kevin Johnson, dean of the University of California at Davis School of Law.

For example, a judge may grant it if someone is suing a defendant who has immunity from that specific lawsuit. Or a judge may grant it if someone was bringing an asbestos lawsuit against a manufacturer—but the manufacturer wasn't making any products during the time that person claims they were injured. "In any kind of complex factual case, it's very hard to get summary judgment," Johnson said. "The [Supreme] Court has made it clear that only in certain, limited cases will summary judgment be granted.... We have a Constitution that requires civil cases to be submitted to a jury if there's enough fact and dispute—and that's a pretty important right to most people."

Trump says this case "should have ended years ago on summary judgment." But historically, fewer than 10 percent of total cases in six key federal district courts between 1975 and 2000 were resolved as a result of such a motion, according to a December 2007 on summary judgment practices by researchers at the Federal Judicial Center. Further, out of the total number of federal cases during that time, summary judgments were granted in part or in full for less than 15 percent of all cases. In cases where there was such a motion, summary judgments were fully granted less than 40 percent of the time.

"These findings offer solid evidence that summary judgment is a weak filter designed to resolve only the most lopsided of cases where no reasonable jury could find for the other side," said David Freeman Engstrom, Stanford University law professor and expert in civil procedure. Unless the case is a slam dunk for one side or the other, summary judgment is not appropriate.

In fact, Trump's own defense team said that Curiel "is doing his job" and that it had no plans to file a motion for the judge to be recused. Lead defense attorney Daniel Petrocelli told reporters after a May 6 pre-trial hearing in San Diego that Curiel was doing a "good job of trying to balance out competing interests" by pushing the trial date to the end of November so that the case does not interfere with

Trump's campaign, Yahoo News reported. . (Side note: We debunked Trump supporters' false, repeated claim that Curiel is affiliated with a pro-immigrant group.)

Curiel actually granted partial summary judgment for Trump, in the 44-page ruling published November 2015. The former students made an array of claims in the 2010 lawsuit, including one requesting an injunction against Trump and Trump University from selling the same services so that the same thing can't happen again in the future. But Trump asked for a summary judgment, since Trump University stopped enrolling students after July 2010 and isn't selling the same seminars or mentorships anymore.—Curiel granted Trump the summary judgment and dismissed that claim.

For other claims, Curiel dismissed Trump's request for a summary judgment because he found a genuine factual dispute. For example, the former students claimed that Trump and Trump University used deceptive practices and misrepresentation in advertisements, thereby violating consumer protection and business laws in California, Florida and New York. One of the "core" misrepresentations Trump made, they claimed, was that they would be taught by real estate experts who were "hand-selected" by Trump.

Trump asked the judge to throw out that claim by granting him summary judgment, saying he never personally misrepresented the program to those individual students. But the students disagreed, showing advertisements featuring Trump's statements such as, "You'll learn inside secrets from me" and from hand-picked instructors. Plus, ads were reviewed and approved by Trump himself. So Curiel denied Trump's motion—since the two sides disagreed on the basic facts—and allowed it to go to a jury trial. The two sides now have to argue their case before a jury.

Once again, Trump greatly stretches the facts to the point of Four-Pinocchio inaccuracy. We can't fact-check whether Curiel has a bias against Trump; that's Trump's opinion. But what is clear is that Curiel made a straightforward legal judgment as to whether two sides agreed or disagreed on facts, and whether those should be presented to a jury. Further, Trump says the case should have been ended with a summary judgment, but fewer than 10 percent of federal court cases in key districts between 1975 and 2000 were resolved that way. Judges make this decision for narrow circumstances, to filter out cases that should not be taken to a jury. Trump also overlooks that Curiel, in his November 2015 ruling, did grant him partial summary judgment.

Trump can disagree with the judge's decision all he wants, but Curiel didn't really have a choice: The students provided evidence that could dispute Trump's reason for requesting a summary judgment. So Curiel had to do his job—and let the case go forward to a jury. [End of Article]

I believe Donald Trump to be exceedingly frightful about the consequences of these lawsuits, because "justice will demand his guilt and cause great devastation to his reputation."

In other words, Donald trump will be proven the schemer and liar as alleged by his accusers.

An inner lack of godliness and contentment leaves a vacuum in the heart filled with greed for those who desire to be rich, which drive such persons into temptation, snares, and foolish and harmful lusts (2 Tim. 6:9) which drown or drag such ones eventually to the bottom. The bottom line is that "greed is a tremendous weight or material desires that drown or drag greedy people into destruction and perdition (irretrievable loss)," which may be experienced in this life; but definitely, the life in the hereafter.

Money in and of itself is not a problem; but, the love of money is a very serious problem. The love of money is a root, though not the root, of all evil; the devil is the root of all evil. The love of money can drive a person into all types of evil. Greediness may cause a believer even to stray from the faith; that is, being blinded by greed and materialism to such a point that he or she breaks away from the faith and focuses on material things rather than God; producing for such a person pain and sorrows. No one can serve two (2) masters (Matt. 6:24) Christians who yield to this temptation are disciplined by God that repentance might be implemented and a turn away from evil and a return to what is good and right is accomplished. God's discipline sometimes involves turning disobedient Christians over to the devil for a time; and sometimes His discipline may even involve death, if He sees it necessary for the good of disobedient Christians.

Those who pursue the things of the world rather than the things of God make themselves enemies of God. Pursuing the things of the world can cause all who do such to mistreat and disrespect other in order to obtain their own selfish desires. The only interests such worldly people have are their own, and whatever it takes, regardless of who they might have to mistreat and disrespect is no problem; no one, no one!!! Is going to stand in their way of preventing them from getting the selfish things desired by their evil hearts. No one, absolutely, **no one!!!**

Christians are to pursue producing the fruit of the Spirit (love, joy, peace, longsuffering, kindness, goodness, faithfulness, gentleness, self-control); we who walk in the Spirit will have a Spirit-controlled life, and not produce the works of the flesh (adultery, fornication, uncleanness, lewdness, idolatry, sorcery, hatred, contentions, jealousies, outbursts of wrath, selfish ambitions, dissensions, heresies, envy, murders, drunkenness, revelries, and the like); by walking in the flesh and fulfilling its lusts. Christians are to pursue walking in the Spirit with all our heart, mind, soul, and strength; "not just in an every now and then or a moderate or not very good manner."

To be blessed here on earth is to be faithful to Him here on earth; so that our faithfulness in our works in Him will be rewarded when we stand before His judgment seat. Do not be deceived: Christians cannot live any type of life in sin and stilled expect to be blessed God in their sinfulness. If it's God's will for Christians to live holy, then, we will be blessed through our holiness in doing those things that're pleasing in His sight; do not be deceived: unholy lifestyles have consequences; not rewards from God. Therefore, do not sin; avoid sin as much as possible; do good and not evil.

The fear of the Lord is our mark of reverence and awe on the part of all Christians who recognize and honor Him as God. No one but He and He alone is God; no power, no matter how evil, has not ever nor can ever, be a threat to His control (Job. 26:10-14; Prov. 8:28-29). The fear of the Lord is the beginning of knowledge (Prov. 1:7). The fear of the Lord is the beginning of wisdom, And the knowledge of the Holy One is understanding (Prov. 9:10). For the LORD gives wisdom; From His mouth come knowledge and understanding (Prov. 2:6). "Only from the fear of the Lord is provision and protection provided for our causes!"

To fear the Lord we must acknowledge and honor Him as God; and believe His word is all powerful and the sole source of all creation (Psa. 24:1). His word is the controlling element in creation (Psa. 33:4-5). It was Gods breath (Psa. 33:6) that He made all things. All the imaginations, thoughts, intentions, and counsels of all people from all nations all together, He brings to nothing and makes their plans of no effect (Psa. 33:10), displaying just how powerful and awesome He is. There's no wisdom or understanding or counsel against the Lord (Prov. 21:30). Blessed is the nation whose God is the Lord, The people He has chosen as His own inheritance. (Pas. 33:12) What then shall we say to these things? If God is for us, who can be against us? (Rom. 8:31)

We are currently experiencing unrest, riots, and completely shattered societies around the world. Such occurrences are happening because many have and many continue to turn further and further away from God and chosen to follow their own imaginations and ways that seem right to them, but they are the ways of destruction and death. Fear can be attributed to the unrest, riots, and completely shattered societies. The Holy Bible has made is very clear about fear, stating: For God has not given us a spirit of fear, but of power and of love and of a sound mind (2 Tim. 1:7). There is no fear in love; but perfect love casts out fear, because fear involves torment. But he who fears has not been made perfect in love (1 Jn. 4:18).

Fear is of the devil, Satan, the evil one, who infuses fear in others and takes advantage through fear to motivate and drive others into more and more fear to produce more and more unrighteousness, which satisfies his egotistical diabolical nature. He's and murder and liar from the beginning, and these evil things are promoted and implemented through those whom he deceives into doing them. Satan promises peace and security through those who cannot deliver, simply because, they have no interest in peace and security, and that's no in their nature. "No one can deliver what he or she is incapable of delivering, that a fact!"

There are other practitioners and promoters of unrighteousness, in particularly, LGBTs who yell and scream in getting their own way in promoting vile behavior practices with benefits and end up getting those things, in particularly, but not limited to, Gay Marriage, that are without doubt abominations very displeasing and distasteful to God. Nevertheless, they get their way because the world hears their cries, and LGBT's being of the world, are received and rewarded of the world. "No Christian should ever take part in approving and/or promoting any sin, in particularly, those being demanded by the LGBT community." Remember, "Whoever therefore wants to be a friend of the world makes himself an enemy of God" (Ja. 4:4).

> And Elijah came to all the people, and said, "_How long will you falter between two opinions? If the Lord is God, follow Him; but if Baal, follow him._" But the people answered him not a word. (1 Kgs. 18:21). _For do I now persuade men, or God? Or do I seek to please men?_ For if I still pleased men, I would not be a bondservant of Christ. (Gal. 1:10)

CNN article entitled "Will Congress compel Trump to release his tax returns? May 25, 2016 states: "Donald Trump has refused to release his tax returns until, he says, the IRS completes its audit. There is, of course, no indication of when that will be. And the IRS is required by law to say nothing publicly about anyone's tax return ... ever. But on Wednesday one of the Senate's top tax writers—Democrat Ron Wyden of Oregon—introduced a bill that would compel all presidential nominees to publicly disclose their three most recent tax returns. And if they don't, Wyden's bill would authorize the Treasury to do so for them—audit or no.

"Since the days of Watergate, the American people have had an expectation that nominees to be the leader of the free world not hide their finances and personal tax returns," Wyden said. Currently, presidential candidates are only legally required to disclose broad information on their income, assets, liabilities and outside employment, among other things, to get a beat on whether the person would have any potential conflicts of interest in office.

Tax returns offer a different take on a candidate's financial behaviors. "Tax returns deliver honest answers to key questions from the American public," Wyden said. "Do you even pay taxes? Do you give to charity? Are you abusing tax loopholes at the expense of middle class families? Are you keeping your money offshore? People have a right to know." The prospects for Wyden's bill aren't clear yet. He is collecting cosponsors for the bill this week, his spokeswoman told CNN Money. And while it is proposed as a standalone measure, she said, it may also be offered as an amendment to the National Defense Authorization Act. Regardless of the bill's fate, it's another example of political efforts to pressure Trump to release his tax returns.

Meanwhile, Trump's most likely Democratic opponent in the general election—Hillary Clinton—has already released eight (8) years of tax returns for this election cycle, and more than 30 years' worth over the course of her public life.

RAWSTORY article entitled "Is that called ripping off an old couple," July 13, 2016 states: "James Harris told CNN's Drew Griffin that his job was to upsell even if older people were "putting up their last dollar." During an interview that he will likely later regret, Harris beamed when Griffin pointed out that he was the "top guy" for bringing in revenue.—"Do you remember when you said this?" Griffin asked, quoting the former instructor: "I'm a former licensed agent/broker. At 29, I became the top 1 percent broker in the country.—I've built homes in Atlanta, Georgia and I used to live in Beverly Hills." "Yes," Harris replied. "If I said those things, they are true. I did live in Beverly Hills." "We have no record of you ever living in Beverly Hills," Griffin pointed out. "Okay," Harris shrugged."

"We can't find your broker's license anywhere," the CNN correspondent continued. "And I have no idea what homes you built in Atlanta, Georgia. Did you build homes in Georgia?"—"I'm not prepared to answer those questions today," Harris stuttered. "This is part of you pitch," Griffin observed. "Is any of that true?"—"Again, I'm not going to answer those questions," Harris repeated. "Well, you certainly know what you've done in your life," Griffin quipped. "What do you know about real estate?"—"Again, I'm not prepared to answer those questions today," Harris said.

Pressing Harris, Griffin asked him to confirm that the Trump University business model was "upsell by upsell by upsell."—"Kinda, sorta, yep," Harris admitted. "It's an upsell from if you pay this amount, we're going to teach you this much; if you pay this amount, we're going to go further with you."—"Is that called ripping off an old couple?" Griffin wondered. "That is sales," the former Trump employee said. "I don't know if those people had the money or not, they could have been putting up their last dollar. I don't know." "Do you care?" Griffin shot back.

"Of course, we care," Harris insisted. "But I was doing my job."—"Regardless of if they could afford it or not?" the CNN reporter asked. "Regardless if they could afford it or not," Harris confirmed. "I don't know if they could afford it or not. That was not my position, that was not my job.—Other people did that. I don't know if they could afford it or not.—We were told to show them all the ways that they could afford it—and could come up with the finances to get into the business. Period. End of story."

Following the interview, Griffin speculated to CNN's Poppy Harlow and Chris Cuomo about why Harris agreed to speak.—"He's all over the Internet. He calls himself Uncle Jim and he likes to sell this idea that you could make so much money from home," Griffin explained. "I think the guy just has a huge ego.—He didn't understand what was about to be happening in that CNN interview." "And many of us thought he would just get up and walk out," the reporter added. "He stayed there, he answered the questions... sort of."

13

Trump's Income Tax Returns—Bombshells

THE POLITICO MAGAZINE article entitled "What to Look for in Donald Trump's Taxes" May 18, 2016 states: "The methods of tax abuse among egotistical real estate magnates are as predictable as they are inviting. There is an adage among longtime prosecutors and criminal defense attorneys that says, "A prosecutor can indict a ham sandwich." What the adage doesn't mention is that often the easiest-to-indict, juiciest ham sandwiches are wealthy real estate developers—the ones with overinflated egos and enduring senses of entitlement—people exactly like Donald J. Trump. As a former 27-year defense attorney, I can tell you the opportunities for tax abuse in this crowd are as predictable as they are inviting.

Trump has been waffling recently on whether he'll release his tax returns, which has prompted much speculation about what he might be hiding in them. People have mentioned potential crooked real estate deals, an embarrassingly low tax rate and foreign investments. But their searches will lead nowhere. If you want to discover fraud, don't bother plumbing the depths of his real estate deals. The thousands of pages of mumbo jumbo associated with one hotel deal or another probably don't reveal anything. These finances are handled by attorneys and accountants on both sides and are pretty routine.

And you cannot embarrass Trump by pointing to his likely next-to-zero tax rate. As a real estate developer, Trump undoubtedly uses every lawful financial tool available to bring his taxes as close as possible to zero. More power to him; that is the American way. Foreign investments? Plainly, he will just blame those on the Democrats. No, none of these areas is likely to bear any fruit. That's because, to expose a wrong-hearted real estate developer as a tax cheat, it is often more important to focus not on what the developer reports on his returns, but on what he leaves off.

You see, the goal of tax cheats is usually not to save money for some corporation, but to avoid using their own shekels to pay for personal expenses. Why pay for their own homes, food, golf rounds, cars or flights—or the taxes thereon—when their companies can pick up the tab? But personal expenses charged to a company counts as compensation, and failing to report such perks as taxable income is illegal.

This kind of personal and professional line-blurring is a hallmark of the real estate tax cheat—those people who control whole construction firms, golf courses and hotel crews and who don't get 1099s and W-2s for all the work they order and the perks they get. Perhaps the most famous example of this kind of fraud comes from New York real estate billionaire Leona Helmsley, who, in 1989 was convicted of having her real estate company pay for personal improvements, including a new dance floor, at her 21-room weekend home in Connecticut, without paying taxes on such benefits. (Helmsley, by the way, is famous for saying, "We don't pay taxes. Only little guys pay taxes.")

Focusing therefore simply on Trump's response to three or four topics—the finances and taxes relating to his primary and any vacation residence, including repairs, insurance and the like; the source of payment for and taxes on any benefits for food, golf fees, staff and the like at such homes; and the payment for and taxes on private car usage and plane trips—should provide a ready shorthand by which to assess Trump's financial ethics. Regardless of whether Trump discloses his tax rate or produces all of his tax returns, Americans most certainly have the right to receive answers to and the proof regarding such basic questions concerning Trump's financial integrity. And Trump has no excuse to fob off this request: Production of this information would be relatively simple and inexpensive.

Any scrutiny should focus first on Mar-A-Largo, Trump's weekend and vacation oasis in Palm Beach, Florida, and former estate of Marjorie Merriweather Post. As the East Coast financial elite will attest, having a second home for leisure in Palm Beach is a pretty expensive luxury. Trump explains the financial status of Mar-A-Largo on the home page of the Mar-A-Largo website: "Since purchasing this landmark in 1985, I spend many weekends and holidays at this home away from home. When I made it a club in 1995, (126 rooms made it a very big house), I kept private quarters and designed the club to provide the best amenities possible for our members."

The relevant questions are few and should be quite easy for Trump to answer and to prove: Did Trump pay personally when he bought Mar-A-Largo in 1985? During the time that it was his personal vacation residence from 1985-1995, did his company deduct any of the acquisition costs, real estate taxes, insurance or utilities as a corporate expense? In other words, did he and his family alone live in this vacation home for 10 years while having the government and the rest of us pay for all or some as a business expense? Or, if a corporation bought Mar-A-Largo and provided it as a corporate perk, did Trump pay taxes on the benefit?

For the past 20 years since Mar-A-Largo has functioned as a club, how much has Trump personally paid for his "private quarters," his "home away from home," any improvements thereto, and for his staff, food and golf in Palm Beach? Once again, were these amenities provided as a corporate perk? If so, did Trump pay the millions of dollars that would be owed in taxes on this income?

Second, his primary residence at Trump Tower: Did Trump personally pay for his condo, and does he pay for the condo fees, utilities, improvements and expenses? If not—if the company pays—does he report that on his tax return?

Third, everyone pays for his or her own car or must pay taxes on the personal use of a company car. Tom Daschle, a good and honest man, withdrew himself from consideration as secretary of the Department of Health and Human Services when a friend and client claimed that he allowed Daschle part-time use of an extra car, and Daschle hadn't paid taxes on such "benefit." Has Trump, like the rest of us, paid for his personal travel?

And then, of course, there's personal air travel, which we know Trump does often. Is Trump's plane a personal or corporate jet? If personal, did he pay for the plane and for all of the expenses out of his own pocket? If corporate, has he reimbursed the owner for personal travel or paid the taxes on the perk? The plane records could be gathered in an hour.

In pursuing the answers to and proof concerning such basic questions, the media, the Democratic National Committee and even the Republican National Committee—which in the long run would be equally hurt, were any negative information subsequently to emerge—should be focused and unrelenting. Of course, Trump will decry such focused questioning as an invasion of privacy. But the louder the outrage, the greater the confirmation that something is likely amiss within these limited records. (And we already know that Trump has a tendency to blur the business and the personal when it comes to finance: Trump once brashly announced that he had donated large sums to charity. But it turned out that he had made virtually no charitable contributions from his own pocket; he simply was taking credit for corporate contributions.)

Trump doesn't deserve any special treatment here. Prior to being confirmed for any senior government position, every presidential appointee has to produce and authorize access to every W-2, 1099, tax filing, mortgage payment, loan or investment document, and brokerage statement ever signed or received. During my personal background investigation to become a U.S. ambassador, two IRS agents arrived at my office unannounced one day to grill me about $210 of income—a check for appearing for two days in a movie—that they thought I had failed to report. Only by proving that the $210 was earned that

Trump's Income Tax Returns—Bombshells

January—and thus would be reported on the following year's return—was my confirmation assured.

If appointees are forced to go through that, finalists for the most important job in the world should at least have to disclose and prove who pays their rent and bills. Donald Trump may well be a very honest man. But he has to prove it. Based on my experience, proving so is a relatively easy undertaking. Howard Gutman is the former U.S. ambassador to Belgium, the managing director of the Gutman Group and a frequent guest on Fox News.

> *¹ "You shall not circulate a false report. Do not put your hand with the wicked to be an unrighteous witness. ² You shall not follow a crowd to do evil; nor shall you testify in a dispute so as to turn aside after many to pervert justice. ³ You shall not show partiality to a poor man in his dispute. (Exod. 23:1)*

> *¹Do not keep silent, O God of my praise! ² For the mouth of the wicked and the mouth of the deceitful Have opened against me; They have spoken against me with a lying tongue. ³ They have also surrounded me with words of hatred, And fought against me without a cause. ⁴ In return for my love they are my accusers, But I give myself to prayer. ⁵ Thus they have rewarded me evil for good, And hatred for my love. (Psa. 109:1-5)*

> *¹In my distress I cried to the LORD, And He heard me. ² Deliver my soul, O LORD, from lying lips And from a deceitful tongue. (Psa. 120:1-2) ⁶ My soul has dwelt too long With one who hates peace. ⁷ I am for peace; But when I speak, they are for war. (Psa. 120:6-7)*

> *¹⁶ These six things the LORD hates, Yes, seven are an abomination to Him: ¹⁷ A proud look, A lying tongue,—Hands that shed innocent blood, ¹⁸ A heart that devises wicked plans, Feet that*

are swift in running to evil, ¹⁹ A false witness who speaks lies, And one who sows discord among brethren. (Prov. 6:16-19)

The truthful lip shall be established forever, But a lying tongue is but for a moment. (Prov. 12:19) Deceit is in the heart of those who devise evil, But counselors of peace have joy. (Prov. 12:20) Getting treasures by a lying tongue Is the fleeting fantasy of those who seek death. (Prov. 21:6) Whoever digs a pit will fall into it, And he who rolls a stone will have it roll back on him. (Prov. 26:27) A lying tongue hates those who are crushed by it, And a flattering mouth works ruin. (Prov. 26:28)

A faithful witness does not lie, But a false witness will utter lies. (Prov. 14:5) A false witness will not go unpunished, And he who speaks lies will not escape. (Prov. 19:5) A gift in secret pacifies anger, And a bribe behind the back, strong wrath. (Prov. 21:14) A man who wanders from the way of understanding Will rest in the assembly of the dead. (Prov. 21:16) "As a partridge that broods but does not hatch, So is he who gets riches, but not by right; It will leave him in the midst of his days, And at his end he will be a fool." (Jer. 17:11)

Today, as the presumptive Republican presidential nominee, Trump regularly denounces corporate executives for using loopholes and "false deductions" to "get away with murder" when it comes to avoiding taxes. "They make a fortune. They pay no tax," Trump said last year on CBS. "It's ridiculous, okay?"

The contrast highlights a potentially awkward challenge for Trump. He has built a political identity around his reputation as a financial whiz, even bragging about his ability to game the tax code to pay as little as possible to the government—a practice he has called the "American way." Moreover, he has aggressively pursued tax breaks and other government supports to bolster his real estate empire. But that

Trump's Income Tax Returns—Bombshells

history threatens to collide with his efforts to woo working-class voters who resent that they often pay higher tax rates than the wealthy who benefit from special loopholes.

Trump's personal taxes are a mystery. He has refused to release any recent returns, meaning the public cannot see how much money he makes,—how much he gives to charity—and how aggressively he uses deductions, shelters and other tactics to shrink his tax bill. Trump, who said last week on ABC that his tax rate is "none of your business," would be the first major-party nominee in 40 years to not release his returns. In an interview this week, Trump said that he has paid "substantial" taxes but declined to provide specifics. He reiterated that he fights "very hard to pay as little tax as possible." "One of the reasons is because the government takes your money and wastes it in the Middle East and all over the place," he said.

Trump's contradictory approaches have been apparent for years. He criticized 2012 Republican nominee Mitt Romney for delaying the release of his returns. Romney, a former private-equity executive, had come under fire for paying a low tax rate because most of his income came from investments. Trump said at the time. "It's a great thing when you can show that you've been successful and that you've made a lot of money,"

Romney eventually released returns showing that, for his 2011 taxes, he chose not to take certain deductions, bringing his tax rate more in line with that of average Americans. Trump, early in his campaign, seemed ready to give voters a look at his tax filings. In January, he said on NBC's "Meet the Press" that he was ready to disclose his "very big ... very beautiful" returns. But as his campaign gained momentum, Trump backed away from his declaration. He first claimed that ongoing audits by the Internal Revenue Service prevent disclosure.

Then last week, he told the Associated Press that voters are not interested in seeing his tax filings and that "there's nothing to learn from them." Trump's new position has unnerved some tax experts, who see value in the tradition of transparency by presidential contenders. "At some point, he could be the tax collector in chief. He'd supervise the

IRS, making sure all of us live up to our own tax responsibilities," said Joe Thorndike, a director at Tax Analysts, a nonpartisan, nonprofit group that specializes in tax policy. "People deserve to know. ... how a person like that plays the game." Trump's stance has become an issue in the campaign.

Romney said on Facebook last week that refusing to release tax returns should be "disqualifying" for any nominee and speculated that Trump's returns could be hiding a "bombshell of unusual size." Senate Majority Leader Mitch McConnell (R-Ky.) weighed in this week, telling reporters that Trump will "have to make that decision himself" but that presidential candidates' releasing their returns has "certainly been the pattern for quite some time."

Trump's likely Democratic opponent, Hillary Clinton, who has disclosed decades of tax returns, released a 60-second ad last week asking, "What's Donald Trump hiding?" "You've got to ask yourself: 'Why doesn't he want to release it?' " Clinton said at a New Jersey rally last week. "Yeah, well, we're gonna find out."

Bob McIntyre of the liberal group Citizens for Tax Justice suspects Trump's tax returns, if made public, would undermine the political image the candidate has crafted of a brilliant businessman with what his campaign has called "tremendous cash flow." Trump may be worried that "he'd show very little income on his tax returns compared to his wealth claims," McIntyre said, adding that Trump's returns could also show that he "writes off everything he has in his life—the hairdo, the plane—as business expenses."

Trump has repeatedly said that he would be open to sharing his returns. In 2011, he said he would release them after President Obama released his long-form birth certificate but never did after the certificate's release. In 2014, he said he would "absolutely" release them "if I decide to run for office." Last year, he said he would release them when "we find out the true story on Hillary's emails." To back his refusal, Trump has released a letter from his tax attorneys that said his tax returns had been audited by the IRS since 2002, and that audits on the returns since 2009 were still underway.

The attorneys' letter also said returns from 2002 to 2008 had been closed administratively by the IRS, meaning their audits had been completed. Trump said in an interview that he would still not release those returns because "they're all linked." But experts say that Trump is free to release his tax records. President Richard Nixon released his returns while under audit. Nothing, including an audit, "prevents individuals from sharing their own tax information," an IRS spokesman said.

The only window into Trump's handling of his income taxes came during the 1981 New Jersey gambling commission report. Trump had submitted his 1978 and 1979 returns to the regulators as part of an application for a casino license. State records summarizing the returns show that Trump claimed that his combined income during those two years was negative $3.8 million, allowing him to pay no taxes. A few years earlier, he had told the New York Times he was worth more than $200 million.

Tax analysts say it is possible that Trump pays very low income taxes, or no taxes at all, using tactics available to wealthy investors and developers, such as depreciating the value of real estate. When asked this week whether he pays income taxes, Trump said, "I will give that to you as soon as I get my audit finished." He added later, "But with that being said, when you're in the real estate business, you do have certain tax advantages."

Trump has benefited from public money by aggressively seeking large tax reductions at developments including Trump Tower. His first major development, the Grand Hyatt Hotel in midtown Manhattan, built in partnership with Chicago's wealthy Pritzker family, was made possible with the help of a New York City tax subsidy worth $400 million over 40 years, according to city records. It was New York's first-ever tax abatement for a commercial property, secured by Trump with help from his developer father's political allies, according to "Trump: The Deals and the Downfalls," a biography on Trump's developments by investigative reporter Wayne Barrett.

Trump has defended his use of public tax assistance to boost private projects. He said opponents of such government supports, including some conservatives, are out of touch with reality. "The true conservative philosophy is that a thing like that shouldn't happen. But they're in the world of the make-believe," Trump said in an interview. "The real world is that without certain tax abatements, you have a choice. The job could get built ... or you don't have to have anything. It could just go stagnant, and a town can die."

Trump's strategy to ease his company's tax burden has resulted in sore feelings in some communities, where local governments rely heavily on tax receipts from large businesses. In Ossining, N.Y., home to a Trump National Golf Club, town officials say that a tax break being sought by the company would cost their coffers more than $200,000 a year. In seeking the reduction, Trump's attorneys have claimed that the club is worth far less than the roughly $15 million value assessed by the city.

Trump's attorneys have filed papers with the state claiming that the "full market value" of the property is $1.4 million. The same golf course appears on Trump's new financial disclosure form released this week as part of his presidential campaign—valued by him at more than $50 million. Ossining Town Supervisor Dana Levenberg, a Democrat, expressed frustration that Trump seemed to be gaining "at other people's loss." "It's hard to look at someone who talks about their wealth frequently and think they got that successful on other people's backs," she said.

Crain's New York dug up Trump's quarterly property tax bill from the city of New York, from which that snippet is taken. He owes about $97,000 by July 1, if he hasn't already paid it, or about $192,000 in total. That large figure is nonetheless about $304 less than it wouldn't have been without the "Basic STAR—School Tax Relief" credit for which Trump was eligible.

What's interesting about the STAR credit, though, is that there's an income requirement that applies. In order to be eligible for the basic version, you must meet three qualificiations: You must own your own home, it must be your primary residence, and you and your spouse can't have an annual combined income of more than

$500,000. There's an "enhanced" STAR credit, too, with an income limit of $84,550 and a required age of at least 65 (which Trump meets). This suggests that Trump's income in 2014 (the applicable year) was between $84,550 and $500,000—somewhat more modest than you might have expected.

Earlier this year, Crain's looked at Trump's 2015 filing and found the same credit. In fact, he received it from 1999 through 2009 and from 2014 on. (In 2011, the state introduced the $500,000 limit, using income from the 2009 tax year.) When asked by Crain's, the Trump campaign insisted that his receipt of the credit was a mistake—and a spokesperson for the city agreed that the credit had been mistakenly applied. But earlier this month, the credit re-appeared.

What we do know about Trump's stated income is sketchy. Last month, The Post reported that Trump tax filings from the late 1970s showed that the businessman's income was zero. Those returns were made public during a legal proceeding and appear to be the only such returns that have come to light. Trump has refused to release more recent filings, arguing that the returns are under audit and therefore his lawyers think he should keep them private. (We spoke with tax attorney Steven Goldburd, who agreed.) Asked to prove that his filings were under audit, Trump released a letter from his attorneys suggesting that the audit applied to his returns from 2009 on—meaning that those from earlier could potentially be released. Trump has refused to do so.

So what's going on here? Is this a continued failure of bureaucracy? Or is it the case that Trump actually earned less than $500,001 in 2014? It could be the former. "There is supposed to be a clerical check for income over $500,000," tax attorney Goldburd wrote when we reached him again by email on Monday. "However, things like this are often overlooked. When dealing with the government, anything is feasible." Trump has released personal financial disclosure documents for his candidacy which detail a great deal of wealth, much of which is in the form of real estate holdings. (That's different than income, of course, which is the amount of money Trump is earning each year.) And that real estate could be the key to the question.

Goldburd pointed out that it's hard to know how Trump might have come in under the $500,000 limit. It's possible, he said, that Trump "could have sold interest in a partnership or a building that he was not actively involved in (passive income), which would have released 'suspended losses' from prior years which would only be allowable after sale. "In other words," that he could have taken a step that resulted in his taking a big loss that, when combined with his annual income, reduced that income below the $500,000 mark.

Or he may have seen less income thanks to depreciation. We explored this a bit in March, looking at how tax law mandates that the value of a property decrease each year. That's its depreciation—and the amount of the depreciation is a loss to the property owner. Here's how we described it at the time. Let's say you buy a building for $10 million. Every year, the value of that property depreciates. Say it depreciates $1 million a year. (The IRS mandates such a depreciation schedule.) After year one, it's worth $9 million. After year two, $8 million, and so on. After nine years, it has depreciated $9 million. If it were sold at that point for more than you paid—say, $11 million—you'd pay taxes on the $10 million difference between the $11 million you got and the $1 million value to which it had depreciated.

But there's benefit! That $1 million a year counts as a loss. So if you make $10 million a year in income, but also own 10 properties that are each depreciating at $1 million a year, your income and your losses are equivalent. Boom. No net income, no income tax. And on top of that, you put yourself in the running for the STAR tax credit. No matter how much Trump may have made from "The Apprentice" in 2014, for example, his real estate holdings could have dropped his net income to less than $500,000.

The whole point here is we don't know what's happening. Without Trump releasing his tax documents, we're left to speculate about how much he earns and how he earns it. We don't know if the STAR credit is a function of Trump's savvy tax maneuvers or if it's a function of New York's tax department repeating the mistake of giving away money for three years in a row. Trump can answer that question easily by

Trump's Income Tax Returns—Bombshells

releasing his tax returns. That he chooses not to leaves us to speculate on particular line items in quarterly tax documents from the city where he lives.

In my personal opinion and experience working as an accountant/auditor for the US government, Donald Trump has utilized every tax loophole available and charged every personal expense possible against his corporations, wherein, implementing illegal income tax processing for his personal gain. He has made his income tax filings as difficult as possible to decipher (grasp, interpret, understand, comprehend), creating the greatest degree of difficulty possible for those assigned to auditing his tax returns. However, the US government should have qualified persons capable of during the job in an excellent manner.

I profoundly believe that Donald Trump's schemes in acquiring his wealth (proclaimed wealth) is at the point of being revealed for the person he really is, that is, a liar, con artist, and self-righteous pompous, hypocritical bragger hiding behind a very great lie. Trump is running scared and is extremely fearful of his true falsehood identity being revealed before the world, which will destroy his established reputation as being a smart successful businessman; which,

"he has deceived and convinced the world that he's the best in the world at what he does"

He is, however, a master in the art of deception. He firstly he himself has been deceived into believing his own lies, which in turn, has made him successful in making it easy for him to deceive others into believing his lies. Lying is a sport for Trump; when he is successful in deceiving and reaping the wicked prosperity of his deception, he celebrates his victories over those whom he has caused hurt and harm to accomplish his wealth. He has absolutely no regrets or remorsefulness for those whom he has caused hurt and harm, regardless of race, color, sex, religion, age, or disability; all are targets and potential victims for a master of deception as he, who perverts justice against the poor, aged, and uneducated he has deceived for financial gain.

Following his corrupt nature, particularly, that of lying, he's seeking to deceive the world into electing him into the highest office of our nation, the President of the United States of America. He's promising things he cannot make good upon, but sound good to those he has used the fear factor to infuse more fear and declared himself as savior from their fears. He has deceived many, in particularly, those who are racist, into believing he's their deliverer and will make America great again as it was in the grand old days when blacks and people of color were more looked upon as second class citizens and/or in some cases less than humans. This is the nature of this beast that's running for President and looking to rule from the oval office.

Jeffrey Batchelder, SEO Manager at That Company, September 7, 2014 wrote an article at Linkedin entitled Self Deceivers and How to Recognize Their Lies well worth sharing, stating: "In a recent Study Lamba S, Nityananda V (2014) titled Self-Deceived Individuals Are Better at Deceiving Others. Published in PLoS ONE 9(8):e104562. doi.10 .1371 /journal.pone. 0104562 the researchers found that there are several key factors to successfully lying to others when we believe the lie ourselves. These key factors are very useful when trying to identify self-deceivers and protect ourselves from their deception.

There is no correlation to actual natural abilities in the area of the deception and the liars lie. So, in other words, self-liars may not be good at or well informed about the lie they are perpetrating and a simple "calling their bluff" test of the lie may easily reveal them as liars. Remember, if they are skilled, they will wrap the failure in another lie. The longer you spend with the self-deceiver, the more likely you are to come to the conclusion that they are a liar. Liars "web" of deceit is not usually well formed and the longer you spend with the deceiver, the more likely you are to see kinks in the armor. What is important here is to remember, when you realize they are lying, don't beat yourself up, just move on.

Self-Deceivers often lie close to the truth. This is where the deception gets difficult to recognize. If the person is an assistant manager, they can easily lie about being the general manager and that is where they shine. In close to truth lies. However, over time, they tend to move on from a close lie to a further lie and that is where the web begins to falter. Self-liars can't detect other liars well. If you know someone who is a self-deceiver, their perception of another self-deceiver will often be that they believe that persons lies. This is an important constraint on being a self-deceived, the impaired ability to detect deception by others. Because of the need to keep one's own "house of cards" in order, self-deceivers are often deceived themselves and this may be how they attained the ability in the first place, starting out as gullible and eventually learning to self-lie.

An interesting outcrop of this is the "fake it till you make it" attitude. When taught to people who are naturally confident, this attitude allows them to push their boundaries. However, when people with weak internal structures learn this technique, a failure causes an internal strife that is difficult to compensate for and they often begin the process of self-lying. This leads to a false reality, which eventually leads to a self-deceptive lifestyle.

An interesting correlation can be found between the narcissistic personality and the self-deception paradigm. While not addressed in the above study, it has been recognized by a large part of the psychological community for some time that narcissistic people are actually damaged self-loathing personalities shielded in a barrier of false self-love. Because they are in constant need of psychological reinforcement, they seek out people whom they deem significant to hear and value them. When the self-deception it tested in a narcissistic personality, they RAGE and ATTACK IN A WAY that often show WHAT WEAKNESS THEY FEAR will be attacked.

The DSM—IV defines Narcissistic Personality Disorder (NPD) as follows: "A pervasive pattern of grandiosity (in fantasy or behavior), need for admiration, and lack of empathy, beginning by early adulthood and present in a variety of contexts." This fits well with the self-deceiver and build on a framework of self and external deception which can be recognized as follow:

These personalities have a grandiose sense of self-importance and will build a false persona to enhance this, by exaggeration of achievements or talents and demands or expects to be recognized as superior regardless of the lack of commensurate achievements. Will often lie about levels or degrees and certifications, etc. These people are preoccupied with self-deceptions of success, power, brilliance, beauty, or perfect love and will often speak and act as if they possess these attributes already. They express themselves as people of the "special/unique" people, who "can only be understood by other special or high-status people or institutions." Again, falsely identifying with some level of degree or specialty that they do not really possess.

Such NPD persons have a constant requirement of excessive admiration, seeking positions and professions where they are consistently recognized and often demanding attention when it is not forthcoming. People with this disorder display a pathological sense of entitlement and favorable treatment. They often expect automatic compliance with their expectations and will RAGE at any denial of this entitlement.

NPD persons are by their nature interpersonally EXPLOITATIVE and CONSISTENTLY TAKES ADVANTAGE OF OTHER to achieve their goals.—Narcissist lacks empathy (the ability to understand and share the feelings of another) and are unwilling to recognize or identify with the feelings and needs of others. Some will feign empathy (give a false appearance for caring) to garner more attention and admiration, but—will shift beliefs when outside of the circumstance that would have brought them attention. This group is envy driven, assuming and seeking others to be envious of them and being envious of others.—People displaying NPD are ARROGANT, acting haughty in their behaviors and attitudes.

Grandiosity refers to an unrealistic sense of superiority—a sustained view of oneself as better than others that causes the narcissist to view others with disdain or as inferior—as well as to a sense of uniqueness: the belief that few others have anything in common with oneself and that one can only be understood by a few or very special people.

Donald Trump has an unrealistic sense of superiority and a sustained view that he is better than others, which causes him to view others with disdain or as inferior. He has an inner sense of uniqueness, that is, that he is better than and wiser than anyone else in the world, and that there are very few (a very, very, few) in the world having anything in common with him and that he can only be understood by this very, very, few population.

Trump is a stone narcissist lacking empathy for anyone, but fakes empathy when necessary to garner attention and admiration from others whom he cares absolutely nothing at all about. He is exploitative and consistently takes advantage of others without discrimination to achieve his self-centered and conceited sinful goals. He is self-ambitioned and enviously consumed with greed and will through whatever deceptive means possible, he will implement to achieve.

Trump is self-consumed with arrogant-pride. He exaggerates his achievements and talents, and demands or expects to be recognized as superior in what he does, regardless of his lack of commensurate (comparable, proportionate, corresponding) achievements. He has preoccupied himself with an array or collection of lies which he himself has been self-deceived into believing, such as, his success, power, brilliance, beauty or perfect love, very often speaking as if he already possesses these attributes. To himself he believes he's a god that everyone else should be looking up to and giving homage to him for who he is. "Trump is a bonafide fool!"

Trump places himself at a level well above everyone else, in particularly, those whom he seek preying on to achieve dishonest gains. Trump does not respect authority because he believes he is the authority. He complicates and argues matters which he opposes, especially, matters dealing with his illegal business practices and taxes, to willfully and intentionally create long drawn out processes through his attorneys. He actually believes he can win, because he's smarter than all who seek justice against him; and he enjoys the long drawn out processes he creates and the suffering of those awaiting justice against him. He will do anything to pervert justice, anything!

Trump doesn't feel that anyone has the right to bring any charge against him, because whatever he does in his own eyes is right; he has only himself and himself only to answer. Trump's false reality has led to his self-deceptive lifestyle. When Trump's self-deception is tested, he rages and attacks consistently in ways that often, without his awareness, show what weaknesses he fears about himself will be attacked. Therefore, to protect himself from being exposed, he rages and initiates attacks against others to avoid issues about himself and to prevent himself from being a victim of demise, which will be far too great of fall from glory of the world for Trump to handle. Nevertheless, that's not Trump's call, that's God's call!

Remember, most deceivers are fragile at the core, they never received recognition or love as a child and so they are missing true self-worth. This weakness has created a pathological disorder that left them with a false self-worth shell built around the broken child core. That shell is what is doing the self-deceiving and external deception. The "shell has a job,"—"to protect the deceiver's complete lack of self-esteem,"—and, "Anytime! You threaten that, the beast will RAGE, look for this RAGE,"—"it is a PRIMARY IDENTIFIER of Narcissistic Personality Disorder (NPD).

> *You shall not follow a crowd to do evil; nor shall you testify in a dispute so as to turn aside after many to pervert justice. (Exod. 23:2) "You shall not pervert the judgment of your poor in his dispute. (Exod. 23:6) And you shall take no bribe, for a bribe blinds the discerning and perverts the words of the righteous. (Exod. 23:8) You shall not pervert justice; you shall not show partiality, nor take a bribe, for a bribe blinds the eyes of the wise and twists the words of the righteous. (Deut. 16:19)*

> *"You shall not pervert justice due the stranger or the fatherless, nor take a widow's garment as a pledge. (Deut. 24:7) 'Cursed is the one who perverts the justice due the stranger, the fatherless, and widow.' "And all the people shall say, 'Amen!' (Deut. 27:19) Does God subvert judgment? Or does the Almighty pervert justice? (Job 8:3) [4] It is not for kings, O Lemuel, It is not for*

kings to drink wine, Nor for princes intoxicating drink; *⁵ Lest they drink and forget the law, And pervert the justice of all the afflicted. (Prov. 31:4-5)*

²⁶ I also will laugh at your calamity; I will mock when your terror comes, ²⁷ When your terror comes like a storm, And your destruction comes like a whirlwind, When distress and anguish come upon you. ²⁸ "Then they will call on me, but I will not answer; They will seek me diligently, but they will not find me. ²⁹ Because they hated knowledge And did not choose the fear of the LORD, ³⁰ They would have none of my counsel And despised my every rebuke. ³¹ Therefore they shall eat the fruit of their own way, And be filled to the full with their own fancies. (Prov. 1:26-31)

¹² A worthless person, a wicked man, Walks with a perverse mouth; ¹³ He winks with his eyes, He shuffles his feet, He points with his fingers; ¹⁴ Perversity is in his heart, He devises evil continually, He sows discord. ¹⁵ Therefore his calamity shall come suddenly; Suddenly he shall be broken without remedy. (Prov. 6:12-15)

⁴ An evildoer gives heed to false lips; A liar listens eagerly to a spiteful tongue. ⁵ He who mocks the poor reproaches his Maker; He who is glad at calamity will not go unpunished. (Prov. 17:4-5) ¹⁵ Do not lie in wait, O wicked man, against the dwelling of the righteous; Do not plunder his resting place; ¹⁶ For a righteous man may fall seven times And rise again, But the wicked shall fall by calamity. (Prov. 24:15-16)

And whoever exalts himself will be humbled, and he who humbles himself will be exalted. (Matt. 23:12; Lu. 14:11) ¹⁹ For you put up with fools gladly, since you yourselves are wise! ²⁰ For you put up with it if one brings you into bondage, if one devours you, if one takes from you, if one exalts himself, if one strikes you on the face. ²¹ To our shame I say that we were too weak for that! But in whatever anyone is bold—I speak foolishly—I am bold also. (2 Cor. 11:19-21)

⁵ Or do you think that the Scripture says in vain, "The Spirit who dwells in us yearns jealously"? ⁶ But He gives more grace. Therefore He says: "God resists the proud, But gives grace to the humble." (Ja. 4:5-6) ¹⁰ Humble yourselves in the sight of the Lord, and He will lift you up. (Ja. 4:10) Do not be deceived, God is not mocked; for whatever a man sows, that he will also reap. (Gal. 6:7) But he who does wrong will be repaid for what he has done, and there is no partiality. (Col. 3:25)

Vengeance is Mine, and recompense; Their foot shall slip in due time; For the day of their calamity is at hand, And the things to come hasten upon them.' (Deut. 32:35) Beloved, do not avenge yourselves, but rather give place to wrath; for it is written, "Vengeance is Mine, I will repay," says the Lord. (Rom. 12:19) For we know Him who said, "Vengeance is Mine, I will repay," says the Lord. And again, "The LORD will judge His people." (Heb. 10:30)

Donald Trump is very proud of himself for forcing President Obama to release his birth certificate, ending the debate over whether Obama was legally fit to lead the country. But not everything the Donald has put his name behind has succeeded. TIME for Family takes a look at some Trump gambles that went bust, as reflected below.

The Trump Airlines, April 29, 2011, states: In October 1988, Donald Trump threw his wallet into the airline business by purchasing Eastern Air Shuttle, a service that for 27 years had run hourly flights between Boston, New York City and Washington, D.C. For roughly $365 million,

Trump got a fleet of 17 Boeing 727s, landing facilities in each of the three cities and the right to paint his name on an airplane.

Trump pushed to give the airline the Trump touch, making the previously no-muss, no-fuss shuttle service into a luxury experience. To this end, he added maple-wood veneer to the floors, chrome seat-belt latches and gold-colored bathroom fixtures. But his gamble was a bust. A lack of increased interest from customers (who favored the airline for its convenience not its fancy new look) combined with high pre–Gulf War fuel prices meant the shuttle never turned a profit. The high debt forced Trump to default on his loans, and ownership of the company was turned over to creditors. The Trump Shuttle ceased to exist in 1992 when it was merged into a new corporation, Shuttle Inc. No word on whether the gold-plated faucets survived the merger."

Trump Vodka April 29, 2011, states: "The Donald had a vodka. Trump vodka (labeled super premium, naturally) was introduced in 2006 to much fanfare. Under the slogan "Success Distilled," the liquor was touted as the "epitome of vodka" that would "demand the same respect and inspire the same awe as the international legacy and brand of Donald Trump himself." At the time, Trump predicted the T&T (Trump and Tonic) would become the most requested drink in America, surpassed only by the Trump Martini. On Larry King Live, he said he got into the vodka business to outdo his friends at Grey Goose. Six years later, Grey Goose is still on top shelves throughout the country.

As for Trump vodka? Yeah, we'd never heard of it either. The New York City blog Gothamist reports the vodka has stopped production "because the company failed to meet the threshold requirements." Two weeks ago, Trump's company filed an injunction to prevent an Israeli company from selling Trump vodka without his consent or authorization. Meaning the Donald stopped the only people in world who wanted to drink his vodka from doing so."

The Bankruptcies April, 29, 2011, states: "I don't like the B word," Donald Trump said in 2010 while testifying in a New Jersey bankruptcy courtroom about his gambling company, Trump Entertainment Resorts

Inc., which had filed for bankruptcy for the third (3rd) time. Given the number of times Trump has flirted with bankruptcy, you'd think he'd be used to that word by now.

In 1990, the banking institutions that backed his real estate investments had to bail him out with a $65 million "rescue package" that contained new loans and credit. But it wasn't enough, and nine (9) months later the famous developer was nearly $4 billion in debt. He didn't declare personal bankruptcy, although his famous Taj Mahal casino in Atlantic City, N.J., did have to file for it (bondholders ended up taking a 50% stake in the investment). Trump's economic troubles continued through the early 90s, while he was personally leveraged to nearly $1 billion. In 2004, Trump Hotels & Casino Resorts also filed for bankruptcy. The company was only a small portion of Trump's real estate empire, but he did still have to personally cough up $72 million to keep it afloat. In 2009, the same company (by then renamed Trump Entertainment Resorts Inc.) filed for bankruptcy again. Yet during all of this, no one ever told Trump, "You're fired!" Probably because no one could.

The Hair April 29, 2011, states: "Trump isn't fooling anyone with that hairdo. That's not his real hairline, he just blow-dried it forward and then combed it backward. Surprisingly, his hair started out kind of normal in the 1980s. It appeared to be hair sprayed into a pouf, but that was to be expected in the decade in which everything went big. But as the real estate mogul aged, he tried to will himself younger with his hair. It got blonder and blonder until it went yellow. Then it turned into—well, whatever it is that it is now."

The Marriages April 29, 2011, states: "For all his success in the boardroom, Donald Trump's life in the bedroom has been messy at best. The real estate magnate married his first wife, Ivana, in 1977, but things got rocky after Trump's affair with actress Marla Maples surfaced in New York City tabloids. "You bitch, leave my husband alone!" Ivana (pictured) told Maples on a ski trip in Aspen, Colo. Ivana's warning fell on deaf ears, and in 1992, Trump left her with a reported $25 million settlement and married his mistress one year later. His marriage to Maples was even shorter-lived, and the couple divorced in 1999. These days, Trump's married to Slovenian supermodel Melania Knauss. Together in marital bliss since 2005, this relationship's proving the third (3rd) time really is a charm—so far anyway."

Trump Mortgage April 29, 2011, states: "In April 2006, Trump announced that, after years in the real estate business, he was launching a mortgage company. He held a glitzy press conference at which his son Donald Jr. predicted that Trump Mortgage would soon be the nation's No. 1 home-loan lender. Trump told CNBC, "Who knows more about financing than me?" Apparently, plenty. Within a year and a half, Trump Mortgage had closed shop. The would-be lending powerhouse was done in by timing (the housing market cratered in 2007) and ironically enough, given Trump's Apprentice TV show, poor hiring. The executive Trump selected to run his loan company, E.J. Ridings, claimed to have been a top executive at a prestigious investment bank. In reality, Ridings' highest role on Wall Street was as a registered broker, a position he held for a mere six days."

Trump: The Game April 29, 2011, states: "In 1989, the Donald teamed up with Milton Bradley to release Trump: The Game, a Monopolyesque board game in which three to four players must buy and sell real estate and try to trump one another in business deals. A year later Trump admitted the game was vastly underselling the predicted 2 million units he and the toy company had hoped for. Not one to abandon ridiculous ideas, Trump revived the game 15 years later after his success on The Apprentice, making sure to incorporate the series catchphrase "You're fired!" into the game. Other updated features included a sterner-looking Trump on the box cover, somewhat simpler rules and cards with business tips. Enduring feature? The considerable tack factor of a Donald Trump board game.

The China Connection April 29, 2011, states: "The problem with our country is we don't manufacture anything anymore," Donald Trump told Fox News a year ago. "The stuff that's been sent over from China," he complained, "falls apart after a year and a half. It's crap." That very same Donald Trump has his own line of clothing, and it's made in ... China. (O.K., O.K.—not all of it. Salon, which reported this intriguing, head-scratching fact, notes that some of his apparel is from Mexico and Bangladesh.)"

Trump Casinos April 29, 2011, states: "Donald Trump's gambles don't always go as planned. Especially when that gamble is gambling itself. In February 2009, Trump Entertainment Resorts Inc. filed for Chapter 11 bankruptcy protection for the third (3rd) time in a row—an extremely rare feat in American business. The casino company, founded in the 1980s, runs the Taj Mahal, the Trump Plaza and the Trump Marina. All three casinos are located in Atlantic City, N.J., where the gambling industry has faced a decline in tourists who prefer gambling in Pennsylvania and Connecticut instead. Trump defended himself by distancing himself from the company, though he owned 28% of its stock. "Other than the fact that it has my name on it—which I'm not thrilled about—I have nothing to do with the company," he said. He resigned from Trump Entertainment soon after that third (3rd) filing, and in August of that year he, along with an affiliate of Beal Bank Nevada, agreed to buy the company for $100 million. The company reported it emerged from bankruptcy in July 2010.

The Middle East 'Policy' April 29, 2011, states: When recently discussing oil prices on air with ABC's George Stephanopoulos, Donald Trump blustered on about the scheming malfeasance of OPEC and the kingdom of Saudi Arabia. Trump insisted the U.S. could leverage its military supremacy to persuade OPEC to lower prices. In his words: "I'm going to look'em in the eye and say, 'Fellas, you'd have your fun.' Your fun is over.'" But this rather naive suggestion of bullying one of the U.S.'s most longstanding and essential allies in the Middle East—not to mention the recent customer in a megabillion-dollar U.S. weapons sale that would create tens of thousands of American jobs—was comparatively harmless when set against his next suggestion.

Trump bemoaned U.S. costs sustained during its wars in the Middle East and floated the idea of "taking" Iraqi oil. Stephanopoulos countered incredulously, "So, we steal an oil field?" Trump responded, "Excuse me. You're not stealing anything. You're taking—we're

Trump's Income Tax Returns—Bombshells

reimbursing ourselves." Given how many U.S. leaders have had to stress to their Middle East interlocutors that they're not in it simply for the oil, Trump would be starting off regional relations on pretty slippery ground.

Trump once said in a court deposition that "his wealth goes up and down with markets and with attitudes and with feelings, even my own feeling. But you can't fudge a tax return—unless, of course, you're willing to risk getting caught for fraud." The gambling and lying Trump most likely has taken the risk to fudge his tax returns and when a properly through, appropriate, and sufficient audit of his tax returns has been completed, I believe the results will prove beyond a reasonable doubt that Trump is a willful, intentional, and deliberate tax fraud criminal.

The New York City property-tax records show that for several years Trump has received a $300 tax credit aimed at qualified New Yorkers whose household income is under $500,000 a year. Trump's staff has said it's a mistake by the New York City property-tax office. However, the New York City and state tax officials have stated they regularly check to ensure only qualified filers receive the credit. There isn't anyone in New York who does not recognize the name Donald Trump, including, but not limited to, New York City and state tax officials. Surely, if Donald Trump disqualified for this $300 tax credit, a red flag should have gone off and the credit discontinued with a follow-up notice of disqualification to Donald Trump.

Furthermore, both Trump and his accountants should have known this $300 tax credit was an invalid credit, and in the interest of honesty and integrity, initiated the action to have it discontinued. This tax-credit issue is a very important and should be investigated thoroughly as to whether or not Trump actually qualified for this credit according to figures his reported income reflected, or if it was actually an administrative error(s) by New York City and state tax officials. How did a man of Trump's wealth (or alleged wealth) qualified for this middle-class $300 tax credit?

Real estate professionals as Trump have extraordinary leeway when it comes to tallying up their incomes and reporting their gross adjusted income for tax purposes. For instance, they can accelerate depreciation rates on properties and in the process create losses to offset gains, which, Trump more than likely has done to minimize his adjusted gross income as low as possible, even to zero (0) or some negative number. We all have heard him state that he does as much as possible to pay as little as possible. It's also possible that Trump may have sheltered some income in offshore entities, like Shell companies, which he may own some controlling interest.

Personal expenses, this is a major issue of great concern. Many of Trump's personal expenses may have been paid by his company, the Trump Organization, which, by tax law, must be taxed as personal income. Celebrities like Trump often deduct expenses associated with promoting and maintaining their personal image. Trump's brand and his company's brand are closely connected, which makes it very likely for a person who does as much as possible to pay no taxes, to have his personal brand expenses charged to his company brand expenses. This is a serious issue that government auditors are most likely scrutinizing (examining or inspecting closely and thoroughly).

Trump has said that his tax returns are being audited every year by the IRS. Has the IRS found valid reason to audit Trump's tax returns every year, and if not, then why is the IRS doing these ongoing audits on Trump? Has the IRS raised any objections in this or prior years to the way Trump's returns have been prepared and filed? If so, has Trump and his accountants at Weiser Mazars responded?

It is vitally important to know that Weiser Mazars is an accounting firm that virtually no one has heard of, is privy (sharing in the knowledge of something secret or private) that almost everyone wants to know (Donald Trump's net worth). Weiser Mazars' clients include a taxi-medallion lender and a small perfume maker. It's also Trump's accounting firm, Crain has ascertained, although the Republican front-runner won't name it, referring to it only as a "big accounting firm-one of the most respected." It is in fact, the nation's 24th largest such firm. Respected? Certainly Big? No.

7 Reasons the IRS Will Audit You by Romona Paden, Contributing Writer Nnerdwallet, December 18, 20115, wrote: "Nothing is inherently sinister about a tax audit. An audit is simply the Internal Revenue Service double-checking your numbers to make sure you don't have any discrepancies in your return. If you're telling the truth (and the whole truth) you need not worry. However, people who are consciously cheating the system do have reason to be concerned.

The IRS conducts audits to minimize the "tax gap," or the difference between what the IRS is owed and what the IRS actually receives. Sometimes audits are random, but the IRS often selects taxpayers based on suspicious activity. We're against subterfuge. But we're also against paying more than you owe. As you walk the line this tax season, here are seven (7)of the biggest red flags likely to land you in the audit hot seat.

Making math errors: When the IRS starts investigating, "oops" isn't going to cut it. Don't make mistakes. This applies to everyone who must file taxes. Don't accidentally write a 3 instead of an 8. Don't get distracted and forget to include that final zero. Mistakes happen, but make sure you double- and triple-check your numbers if you're doing your own taxes. You'll be hit with fines regardless of whether your mistake was intentional. If your math is a little shaky, using an online tax preparer or a tax professional can help you avoid unfortunate errors.

Failing to include a Form 1099 or additional income: Easy way to score an audit? Don't report part of your income. Let's say you're employed herding sheep for Farmer Joe and pick up a little extra cash writing articles for a sheep-shearing publication on a freelance basis. You may be tempted to submit only the W-2 from your herding job and keep the freelance writing income on your Form 1099 under wraps. (Form 1099 reports the nonwage income you get from things like freelancing, stock dividends and interest.) Well, guess what? The IRS already knows about income listed on your 1099, so it's only a matter of time before it discovers your omission.

Claiming too many charitable donations: If you made significant contributions to charity in 2015, you're eligible for some well-deserved deductions. Most taxpayers who itemize deductions claim charitable deductions at an average of 3% of their income. This bit of advice is common sense: Don't report false donations. If you don't have the proper documentation to prove the validity of your contribution, don't claim it. Pretty simple. Claiming $10,000 in charitable deductions on your $40,000 salary is likely to raise some eyebrows.

Reporting too many losses on a Schedule C: This one is for the self-employed. If you are your own boss, you might be tempted to hide income by filing personal expenses as business losses. But before you write off your new ski boots, consider the suspicion too many reported losses can arouse. The IRS may begin wonder how your business is staying afloat.

Claiming too many business expenses: Along the same lines as reporting too many losses is reporting too many expenses. To be eligible for a deduction, purchases must be 1) ordinary and 2) necessary to your line of work. A professional artist could claim paint and paintbrushes because such items meet both requirements. A lawyer who paints for fun and doesn't turn a profit on the works couldn't claim art supplies as a deduction. The question to ask is: Was the purchase absolutely necessary to performing my work duties?

Claiming a home office deduction: Home office deductions are rife with fraud. It may be tempting to give yourself undeserved deductions for expenses that don't technically qualify. The IRS narrowly defines the home office deduction as reserved for people who use part of their home "exclusively and regularly for your trade or business." That means a home office can qualify if you use it for work and work only. Occasionally answering e-mails on your laptop in front of your 72-inch flat screen TV doesn't qualify your living room as a deductible office space. Only claim a home office deduction if you have set off a section of your home strictly for business purposes. Be honest when you report expenses and measurements.

Using nice, neat, round numbers: In all likelihood, the numbers on your 1040 and supporting documents will not be in simple, clean intervals of $100. When making your calculations, be precise and avoid making estimations. Round to the nearest dollar, not the nearest hundred. Say you're a photographer claiming a $495.25 lens as a business expense; round that to $495, not to $500. An even $500 is somewhat unlikely, and the IRS may ask for proof.

If Donald Trump is being audited by the IRS on and ongoing or continuous basis, year after year, the "IRS is auditing Trump based on suspicious activity and to detect subterfuge" (deceit, dishonesty, cheating, craftiness, or fraud) in order to achieve one's selfish goal. No doubt, something is going on extremely bad for there to be consistent conflict between the IRS and Trump. Trump's financial statement filed last year with the Federal Election Commission, Trump claimed he made $362 million in income in 2014. However, Fortune demonstrated that figure overlooks a flood of expenses, and, is actually, REVENUE. Therefore, "what is Trump's actual income; is there any valid reason he and his accountants cannot report an income tax return without problems or errors? How much was his actual income in 2014 and other years?"

> *⁸But truly I am full of power by the Spirit of the LORD, And of justice and might, To declare to Jacob his transgression And to Israel his sin. ⁹ Now hear this, You heads of the house of Jacob And rulers of the house of Israel, Who abhor justice And pervert all equity, ¹⁰ Who build up Zion with bloodshed And Jerusalem with iniquity: ¹¹ Her heads judge for a bribe, Her priests teach for pay, And her prophets divine for money. Yet they lean on the LORD, and say, "Is not the LORD among us? No harm can come upon us." ¹² Therefore because of you Zion shall be plowed like a field, Jerusalem shall become heaps of ruins, And the mountain of the temple Like the bare hills of the forest. (Micah 3:8-12)*

How is it that much of the evangelical population supports Donald Trump with all inappropriate conducts he has manifested, in addition to his total unfitness for the office of President of the United States of America? Evangelicals' faith is in the Bible and Jesus, evangelical Christians may seem similar to other Christian denominations, even bearing some of the same names. But, Evangelicals unique beliefs and interpretations of Christianity make them a distinct worldwide movement, "emphasizing the "born again" experience, the infallibility of the Bible, salvation by faith in Jesus alone, the need to evangelize or spread the gospel of Jesus Christ, and the RAPTURE of the church in the end times, immediately followed by the 7-years tribulation, the Second Coming of Christ, Christ's 1,000 years reign on earth (Millennial Kingdom), and the Battle of Armageddon. Does his practiced ungodly Christian conduct have any bearing on their judgment and support of him; or does just being a Republican the most concerned issue?

14

Trump verses Truth

IN SCRIPTURE, TRUTH is characterized by both qualitative and quantitative aspects. In the historical narratives of the Old Testament, truth is identified with personal veracity and historical factuality. Before identifying himself to his brothers, Joseph desires to test them by commanding them to send one of their brothers as a prisoner, to see if there is truth in them (Gen. 42:16) Both Joseph's brothers and Achan claim to be speaking the truth when they confess their respective sins (Gen. 42:21; Josh. 7:20)

Truth is also a quality used to describe utterances that are from the Lord. When Elijah intervenes for the son of the widow of Zarephath, bringing the boy back to life, the boy's mother remarks that now she knows that Elijah is a man of God, and that the word of the Lord in his mouth is truth. Ahab becomes angry with Micaiah, his personal incarcerated prophet, because the latter has given a sarcastic favorable forecast for battle. Ahab responds by saying, "How many times must I make you swear to tell me nothing but the truth in the name of the Lord?" (1 Kgs. 22:16; 2 Chron. 18:15)

The Psalter describes truth as a fundamental characteristic of God, a characteristic that the psalmist desires to share. The wicked do not speak truth (Psa. 5:9), whereas the blameless one speaks truth from the heart (Psa. 15:2) The psalmists often depict truth as a quality separate from God, and which God serves by virtue of His nature. In many instances, truth appears to be personified. The psalmist tells God to "guide me in Your truth" (Psa. 25:5); the psalmist asks God to "send forth Your light and Your truth" to lead him (Psa. 43:3); the psalmist asks the Lord to "ride forth victoriously in behalf of truth" (Psa. 45:4). The psalmist desires to walk in God's truth (Prov. 86:11). Indeed, the sum of God's word is truth.

Proverbs seldom speaks of truth, but when it does it defines it as a virtue that the person of God should practice. Truth is to proceed from one's mouth, and wickedness is an abomination to the lips (Prov. 8:7); the one who speaks the truth gives honest evidence (Prov. 12:17); truth is described as a commodity that one should purchase, along with wisdom, instruction, and understanding (Prov. 23:23).

Jeremiah bemoans the fact that in Judah truth is absent. He tells the people that if they can find a man in Jerusalem who does justice and speaks truth, God will pardon the entire city (Jer. 5:1). The Lord looks for truth (Jer. 5:3), but it is notoriously absent from Judah (Jer. 7:28; 9:3; 9:5). In Daniel, truth is an eschatological virtue related to the interpretations of the visions that God shows to Daniel. Daniel inquires of the truth of the vision of the four beasts (Dan. 7:16; 7:19). The casting down of truth allows the little horn to act and prosper (Dan. 8:12); the future dealings of the kings of Persia are referred to as the truth (Dan. 10:21; 11:2). Zechariah commands his readers to speak the truth (Zech. 8:16), and to love truth and peace (Zech. 8:19).

The Synoptic Gospels (Matthew, Mark, Luke, and John) scarcely use the word truth at all, while in John it is an extremely significant term referring to Jesus and His ministry. Jesus, as the Word become flesh, is full of grace and truth (Jn. 1:14), and is the source of grace and truth (Jn. 1:17). In contrast to the woman at the well, who felt geographic location of worship was important, Jesus states that the issue is not whether one should worship God in Moriah or Gerizim, but rather one should worship in spirit and in truth. For John, truth is ultimately identified with, and is personified in the person of, Jesus Christ.

The ministry of John the Baptist is to bear witness to the truth (Jn.

5:33). Jesus speaks the truth, and for this the Jews seek to kill him (Jn. 8:40). This is because the Jews who contended with Jesus were ultimately of their father the devil, who has no truth in him whatsoever (Jn. 8:44-46). Jesus describes Himself as the way, the truth, and the life, and as such He is the only means to the Father (Jn.14:6). Even when Jesus departs, the ministry of truth will continue because the Comforter, who is the Spirit of truth (Jn. 14:17), will be active both in the church as well as in the world.

For Paul, truth is the message of God that all of humanity has repressed (Rom. 1:18) and exchanged (Rom. 1:25) for lie, in that they have directed their worship not to the Creator, but to the creation. All unbelievers ultimately do not obey the truth, which is embodied in the law (Rom. 2:18; Rom. 2:20). In Galatians, truth is synonymous with the gospel, which the Judaizers have perverted by requiring converts to practice law observance (Gal. 2:5; Gal. 2:14; 4:16; 5:7; Ephes. 1:13; Col. 1:5-6). In addition, Paul also uses truth to speak practically of the believer's deportment in following the Lord. Believers are to speak the truth to one another in a loving manner, as we grow up into submission to our head, namely Christ (Ephes. 4:15). The importance of speaking the truth to one another is underscored by the fact that we are members of one another (Ephes. 4:25).

In 2 Thessalonians Paul equates the truth with the believers' salvation. Those who perish do so because they are under a wicked deception, and so refuse to love the truth and be saved (2 Thess. 2:10). Such people are condemned because they did not believe the truth, but instead had pleasure in unrighteousness (2 Thess. 2:12). God's choosing of the Thessalonian believers for salvation came about by means of sanctification by the Spirit as well as belief in the truth.

In the Pastoral Epistles, truth takes on the characteristics of a repository, or official body of beliefs, of which the church is the faithful steward and guardian. Salvation includes, and is likely synonymous with, knowledge of the truth (1 Tim. 2:4). The church of the living God is both the pillar and ground of the truth. Knowledge of and belief in the truth prevents one from becoming entangled in erroneous doctrines, such as the belief that marriage is to be avoided, abstinence from certain foods is to be enjoined, and that godliness is a means of gain (1 Tim. 4:3; 6:5), as well as the belief that the resurrection is past (2 Tim. 2:18).

Paul further encourages Timothy to guard the truth, which the Holy Spirit has entrusted to him (2 Tim. 1:14). The Scriptures are themselves the word of truth (2 Tim. 2:15). Individuals who oppose God and naively listen to others (i.e. Jannes and Jambres, Pharaoh's two magicians) never arrive at the truth, and, in fact, actually oppose it (2 Tim. 3:7-8). Paul informs Titus that the knowledge of the truth goes along with the furtherance of faith and with godliness (Titus 1:1). Paul informs both Timothy and Titus that the only alternative to the truth is to believe in myths (2 Tim. 4:4; Titus 1:14).

While the term "truth" appears only sporadically in most of the General Epistles, it appears repeatedly throughout the Johannine epistles. To claim to have fellowship with God, and to walk in darkness, is not to live according to the truth (1 Jn. 1:6). To claim sinlessness for the believer is to practice self-deceit and thus be void of truth (1 Jn. 1:8). The basic message of Christianity is termed "the truth," and believers know the truth, and can discern that no lie is of the truth (1 Jn. 2:4; 1 Jn. 2:21). Believers are to love in both deed and in truth (1 Jn. 3:18). Believers are of the truth, which no doubt means that they belong to Jesus, who is the truth (1 Jn. 3:19). Likewise, the fact that we are of God allows us to know the Spirit of truth, and to discern Him from the spirit of error (1 Jn. 4:6). The truth abides with us forever (2 Jn. 2), and the Elder rejoices because the elect lady's children follow the truth (2 Jn. 4; 3 Jn. 4). Further references in 3 John indicate that the Elder refers to Jesus Christ as "the truth" (3 Jn. 1:3; 1:4; 1:8; 1:12).

Merriam Webster's Learner's Dictionary defines "truth," the real facts about a person, place, or thing; the things that are true." At some point and time we all have to or should "face the simple truth/hard/honest/plain/naked truth" about a person, place, or thing that profoundly challenges our positions, beliefs, and practices. Nevertheless, "the truth matters more in the eyes of God than" any of our positions, beliefs, and practices. God is truth and in practicing truth, He is emulated or personified through our speech and actions; being holy just as He is holy.

Whatever is not of God is a lie; therefore, coming close to the truth and not conveying the whole truth,—"is not of God, and is therefore, a lie." In the communication process, we either "communicate in the truth or in the lie." We communication "is done in truth," God is the source; when communication "is done in lie," the devil, the father of the lie is the source.

But outside are dogs and sorcerers and sexually immoral and murderers and idolaters, and whoever loves and practices a lie. (Rev. 22:15) You are of your father the devil, and the desires of your father you want to do. He was a murderer from the beginning, and does not stand in the truth, because there is no truth in him. When he speaks a lie, he speaks from his own resources, for he is a liar and the father of it. (Jn. 4:44)

Satan has given liars a professional technique to use to avoid speaking truth and at the same time deceive others into believing the lie. Satan has given his followers "a class or seminar in cunning craftiness to make lies appear as truths." Some politicians and top managers "have mastered the art of avoiding answers to difficult media interview questions or questions when in debate with one another." This art of avoiding questions and responding with partial and/or inaccurate answers constitutes a lie.

Trained politicians in cunning craftiness cringe (feel disgusted or embarrassed and often show their feelings by a movement of their face or body) every time one of their own increases the impact of an awkward or difficult question by repeating it with denial that only reinforces the accusation in the minds of the audience. These politicians skilled in cunning craftiness shrink in fear or servility (of or befitting a slave or a menial position) when one of their own fail to answer questions in a way to deceive people into believing the lie rather than the truth. Their sudden movements from fear of their party being negatively hit or hurt are clearly and cogently manifested. Lying to deceive is a lifestyle for politicians and their supporters trained in cunning craftiness.

To acquire this deceptive lifestyle with its craft just doesn't happen; it takes preparation and practice. The traditional news media still dominate the news sector ahead of social media; therefore, "such persons keep themselves prepared with a cunning craftiness skill set to ensue" they're not ambushed in news interviews or political debate platforms to their own and/or party's detriment (damage or injury). To save face for themselves and/or their party, for them, lying and deception are the only options!!!

In implementing their cunning craftiness, they: 1) acknowledge questions without answering them (saying, that's a good question, and I think we should consider the implications by looking at ... something other than what the question was actually about); 2) ignore questions completely (saying, however, this is a high-ranking approach because the interviewer may repeat the question or reword it slightly to return to the subject; which tends to make the interviewee look evasive;) 3) question the questions (a) request clarification or further information about the question; b) reflect the question back to the interviewer (why do you ask me that?) Some years ago an interviewer was floored by UK Prime Minister Margaret Thatcher, when in a famous response to "Some people are saying you are too autocratic," she said "Name some of them." The interviewer was caught by surprise and wasn't able to think of a suitable response, which made him look a bit silly.)

4) attack the questions, on the basis of a) the questions fail to tackle the important issues; b) the questions are based on false assumptions; c) the questions are factually inaccurate; d) the questions are too personal or objectionable; 5) decline to answer; refuse to answer on the basis that it's not your area of responsibility (saying, "you will have to ask [give a name or just say someone else] about that because I'm not involved at all in that part of the situation.") 6) Give an incomplete answer; a) give a partial answer; b) start to answer but change the subject, c) Give a negative answer; state what won't happen instead of what will happen. 7) State or imply the question has

already been answered (I'm not going to go over old ground); and 8) Defer to the will of others; (Refer to the will of constituents or shareholders, etc. and imply you're doing your duty by complying with their will.)

One of the most successful tricks is that of answering a question with a question.—"Why do you ask that?" or "Is that issue something that concerns you?" Anything which—can make your questioner drop the difficult question and come up with a new one which might be easier to answer. If you get really good at this, you can eventually turn an interview into a conversation. The natural back-and-forth of a conversation can help blur the lines between question and response,—making it harder for the other party to realize that you're not actually saying anything of substance. Even if that doesn't work, you'll have bought yourself a little bit of time.

That's right! Time to regroup and come forth with more of the same (lies and deceptions) to captivate and to motivate those who are already deceived and those susceptible to being deceived. Those having a lifestyle of this craft enjoy their evil works; although to them, there nothing at all evil about what they're doing; because they're self-righteous and "their righteousness is of themselves and not of God." So, do not be at all surprised about what's happening in our world, and in particularly, during this Presidential election; no, no more surprised, than what happened during Obama's elections. "The devil is still the devil and his followers will continue during his will."

A sign to us all that "a politician is seeking to avoid a question" that will potentially damage or hurt him or her, or his or her party's reputation, is when the politician or his or her supporter asks for the question to be repeated or clarified in detail. An example would be for specific terms to be defined, such as "gross negligence;" What constitutes "gross" negligence? Is it "gross" as in "large," or as in "disgusting?"

Two (2) things will tell you which meaning is the right one with a word like gross, the part of speech and the context. If you're talking about awful, sickening, vile things such as dissecting an animal or filthy behavior, you're looking at the adjective gross. That guy is gross. If you're talking about, say, how much money a movie made, that's the noun gross. That was the biggest gross in history! Likewise, the verb to gross is to pull in money. The bake sale grossed 29 bucks! But remember, the gross is how much you made in total, not how much you cleared—the "net" or "profit." Politicians "seeking to avoid the question or give themselves time to answer deceitfully" already know the part of speech and context the question was asked; just as most of us hearing the question ourselves understood clearly and expected a sensible answer. s

The major political parties in the United States are: 1) Democratic (founded in 1828), 2) Republican (founded in 1854), 3) Libertarian (founded in 1971) and 4) Green Party (founding in 1991). The largest of these four (4) parties are the Democratic and Republican. As Christians, we all have the responsibility to be more loyal to God than whatever party we are affiliated; but, that's not the case, because, regardless of how some politicians speak and act, because they're of a certain party, "Christians with party loyalty still back and support them regardless!" What's even more disturbing and somewhat frustrating "is hearing and seeing prominent or well-known TV evangelists voicing their support and promoting them for office."

Many of us know these evangelists to both teach and preach the truth; how then is it that these same preachers and teachers of the truth can turn deaf ears and blind eyes to the truth being manifested right before them? There's a very interesting article in THE HILL entitled "Blind loyalty to political party" February 26, 2013 states: "People who are unaffiliated with a political party, while sometimes thought of as being indecisive, are actually people who demonstrate the ability to think for themselves. Anyone who is blindly loyal to the platform of a political party has given up their God-given right to exercise their independent thought processes. They degrade their own worth.

If we are to solve the massive economic problems facing our nation, we will need innovative independent thinkers from all walks of life. They can contribute to solutions that will eventually benefit all of us, rather than blindly following the dictates of a political power structure that is only interested in its own self-aggrandizement.

"We the People" need to awaken to the sad fact that our nation is being exploited by both political power structures. They pass laws that apply to the masses and not themselves. They become adolescents and point fingers when this nation face devastating challenges and cries out for principle leadership. They manipulate the American people with lies, rhetoric and deceit, and continuously exploit the ignorance and lack of understanding of the people who elected them.

How is it possible that the best and brightest in the executive and legislative branches of our government can't find common-sense solutions on the critical issues that confront us today? We need to focus less on electing the intellectual and Ivy League elite of our nation and return farmers, factory workers, carpenters, teachers, law enforcement and military leaders to the highest offices of the land. When electing the individuals that our Congress envisioned during our founding, we will return a modicum (a small quantity) of common sense and true leadership to our nation. When this happens, then and only then will America return to a pinnacle of spiritual and economic success."

I believe Donald Trump to be a liar, deceiver, untrustworthy, pompous, and totally unqualified for the office of President of the United States of America. U.S. News and World Report article on May 17, 2016 states: "When did we resign ourselves to the idea that Donald Trump could be president of the United States? Not that he should be, but that he possesses the intellectual capacity or experience to theoretically be up to the task? Earlier on Tuesday, I wrote about how the billionaire personifies all the sexism and stereotypes aimed to keep women in their place—and that's all definitely true. But it is also beside the point, as are his compulsive lies and proclivity for racist and nationalistic rhetoric.

Strip all that away; none of it matters. Because fundamentally, what matters is this: Donald Trump is manifestly unqualified to be president. Trump is a businessman fortunate enough to be born into one of the richest families in America. He's done well for himself, as far as we know without accessing his tax returns, though not always as well for his business ventures. He transferred into the University of

Pennsylvania after two years at Fordham, and went straight to work for the family business upon college graduation. He's never held elected office, never worked in the public sector, never served in the military.

Safeguards built into our nuclear command contain a fatal flaw, one that's particularly susceptible to a Donald Trump presidency. And he appears wholly uninterested in mitigating this lack of experience with learning. Trump has demonstrated staggering unfamiliarity with our system of separation of powers, the nuclear triad, the First Amendment, the role of the federal government, our educational system, our responsibilities under the Geneva Convention, or how the national debt works—basic Government 101 concepts. Beyond disregarding the fundamentals of the job he seeks, Trump even failed to acquaint himself with the mechanics of the primary process, leaving him blindsided by the Republican delegate apportionment.

This lack of understanding is showcased nowhere more clearly than in Trump's vague, waffling policy platforms. Lacking a comprehensive grasp of the national abortion debate, Trump wrapped himself in knots trying to settle on a stance on consequences for women who choose abortion. Trump's economic plan is so erratic and full of wild promises, my colleague Pat Garofalo explained, that it's impossible to decipher which is the real position, "the plans he's put out or the last sentence to come out of his mouth?" Put another way, "his policy proposals are ridiculous and inconsistent to the extent that it's almost a category error to critique them," wrote Vox's Matt Yglesias.

But again, this doesn't bother the front-runner. He doesn't want to "waste time on policy," a source close to him told Politico. We're inundated with so much Trump news meant to shock our consciences these days, it's tempting to dismiss concerns over his qualifications as routine election year chattering. Then-Sen. Obama was young in 2008, and people deemed him inexperienced—now it's just Trump's turn. Obama was a sitting U.S. senator, of course, and previously a state senator. But Trump is also sometimes compared to Andrew Jackson, who was similarly deemed unfit for the presidency before he was elected. "In a conversation with Daniel Webster in 1824, Thomas Jefferson described Jackson as 'one of the most unfit men I know of' to become president of the United States,' psychologist Dan McAdams wrote in The Atlantic this month. This initially made me feel slightly better, until I remembered that Jackson, for all his faults, was a major general in the Army, a hero in the War of 1812, before taking the Oval Office.

In sharp contrast, Trump is an amateur by historic proportions. Every president in U.S. history, in fact, has had either government or military experience. And as a dilettante who's shown remarkably little curiosity about the ways of governing, it's unlikely Trump would seek to improve once in office. There's no shortage of literature on how partisan our politics have become and the dangers such siloing can hold. But surely even the cynics were surprised at how quickly the Republican establishment laid down its pitchforks and began to justify Trump as the GOP's likely presidential nominee.

There are still some conservative holdouts who recognize Trump's unfitness for office, but the party elites are increasingly calling for conservatives to rally around him, "to unite and focus on defeating [likely Democratic nominee] Hillary Clinton," as RNC chair Reince Priebus tweeted. It's winning the election over Democrats that matters at any cost, in other words, not the governing that comes after. Fitness for office be damned, I guess. And that's perhaps what should most frighten those of us who value intellect. That Trump is acutely unqualified would be true even if he were Mr. Congeniality, a champion of the people with the aspirations of Jimmy Stewart in "Mr. Smith Goes to Washington." His temperament, morality and judgment are irrelevant if he's not even competent at a fundamental level.

15

Trump's Call for Violence at Rallies

AFTER HE CANCELLED a rally at a Chicago university Friday night due to safety concerns, on CNN Tonight, 9:30 PM, March 11, 2016, Trump told Don Lemon: "I certainly don't incite violence and …. I don't condone violence." Trump, however, has a history of calling for violent acts against those who protest at his events that goes back until at least August of last year. So then, is the history of Trump's call for violence a lie, or is Trump a habitual liar? The record or preponderance of evidence "consistently shows and confirms Trump being a habitual liar!"

And after canceling the rally at the University of Illinois at Chicago Pavilion, which devolved into mayhem when protesters and supporters faced off, Trump pointed the finger at detractors for the violence that erupted. Below are the recorded instances in which the Republican presidential candidate has called for, rejoiced in, or otherwise encouraged combat between supporters and detractors, in reverse chronological order.

At a campaign rally in Kansas City on Saturday, the day after the unrest in Chicago, Trump addressed an earlier event in Dayton, Ohio, when a protester tried to storm the stage. The candidate said he would have fought the person had he reached the lectern and mimed punching him a few times. "I'll beat the crap out of you," he then mouthed. "Part of the problem ... is nobody wants to hurt each other anymore."

Demonstrators interrupted a Trump rally in St. Louis, Missouri, Friday. As they were being escorted out of the venue, the candidate bemoaned the fact that there were no longer "consequences" to protesting and insisted the "country has to toughen up."—"You know, part of the problem and part of the reason it takes so long is nobody wants to hurt each other anymore, right?" he explained. His remarks are heard just after the seven-minute mark in the video above in this article. Outside the event, people screamed profanity and anti-Muslim rhetoric at each other while a bloodied protestor was given medical treatment.—Thirty two (32) people were arrested.

At a press conference in Florida earlier on Friday, Trump was asked about his rhetoric in the wake of an incident in which a supporter at a rally in Fayetteville, North Carolina sucker-punched a black man in the face. While he wasn't asked about that specific altercation, Trump said of violent behavior in general at his events: "The audience hit back and that's what we need a little bit more of." He also praised people using physical force at his rallies as "appropriate." On NBC's Meet the Press on Sunday, Trump said he would have his team look into paying the legal fees of 78-year-old John McGraw, who was charged with assault and disorderly conduct after attacking the protester.

As protesters were being escorted out of the rally in Fayetteville on Wednesday, Trump told the crowd that the protesters were not being treated poorly enough.—"They used to treat them very, very rough, and when they protested once, they would not do it again so easily," he said, before lamenting "we've become weak."

At a rally in Michigan in early March, Trump again seemed to give the green light to violent behavior. As a protester was being escorted out of the building, Trump marveled at what a "fun time" everyone was having. "Get him out," he then said. "Try not to hurt him. If you do, I'll defend you in court, don't worry about it." He then told an anecdote about a brawl at a prior rally that was "amazing to watch."

At a Las Vegas rally in late February, as a protester was again being removed from the premises, Trump lamented that "we're not allowed to punch back anymore" and reminisced about the halcyon "old days," when a protester would "be carried out on a stretcher." The crowd is delighted, cheering, clapping and laughing. He then said "he'd like to punch the man in the face, again to cheers."

After a protester threw a tomato at Trump at a previous event, he encouraged fighting at a later campaign stop in Cedar Rapids, Iowa, in early February. "If you see somebody getting ready to throw a tomato, knock the crap out of them, would you? Seriously." He again promised to pay for any legal fees associated with an assault.

After a Black Lives Matter activist was kicked, punched and, he said, called the N-word at a campaign event in Birmingham, Alabama, in November, Trump expressed his approval. "Maybe he should have been roughed up because it was absolutely disgusting what he was doing," the now frontrunner for the GOP presidential nomination told Fox & Friends the next day. Trump said the man deserved the treatment because he had been "very obnoxious" and "so loud." The remarks can be heard just after the 11-minute mark in the video above in this article.

Black Lives Matter activists took over a Bernie Sanders campaign event in Seattle in August, asking for a moment of silence for Michael Brown, the teenager who was killed by a policeman in Ferguson, Missouri, in 2014. Trump was asked how he would respond to a similar situation. The candidate was defiant, and curious about who would get into a physical altercation when faced with protesters—him or his supporters, Trump stated: "I don't know if I'll do the fighting myself or if other people will."

I performed an analysis (detailed examination) of Trump's rhetoric speeches and comments at his rallies as to whether or not he has with cunning craftiness persuaded disgruntled racist Americans to engage in violence by willfully having them reminisce (indulge in enjoyable recollection of past events), the "halcyon old day" (endless sunny days of slavery and Jim Crow) when people of color, in particularly, blacks could be treated any way whites so desired without any serious repercussions from the law. This analysis was implemented to prove whether or not the findings of fact show without doubt, that Donald Trump incites violence and certainly condone violence; and whether or not he's a habitual liar. The facts for examination are as follows:

1. Trump points his finger at detractors for the violence that erupts.
2. Trump said he would have fought the person had he reached the lectern.
3. Trump mimed (used body movements and facial expressions) punching him a few times; then mouthed: "I'll beat the crap out of you."
4. Trump stated: "Part of the problem is nobody wants to hurt each other anymore."
5. Trump bemoaned (expressed discontent or sorrow over) the fact that there were no longer consequences to protesting.
6. Trump insisted the country has need to toughen up.
7. Trump stated: "You know, part of the problem and part of the reason it takes so long is nobody wants to hurt each other anymore, right?"
8. A black man was sucker-punched in the face by a white man in Fayetteville, N.C.
9. Trump told the crowd in Fayetteville that "protestors were not being treated poorly enough."
10. Trump stated: "They used to treat them very, very, rough, and when they protested once, they would not do it again so easily; we've become weak.
11. Trump marveled at what a fun time everyone is having, then stated: "Get him out!"
12. Trump then stated: "Try not to hurt him. If you do, I'll defend you in court, don't worry about it."
13. Trump then told an anecdote (a short and amusing or interesting story) about a brawl at a prior rally that was "amazing to watch."

14. Trump said of violent behavior in general at his events: "The audience hit back and that's what we need a little bit more of."
15. Trump praised people using physical force at his rallies as "appropriate."
16. Trump on NBC's Meet the Press, said he would have his team look into paying the legal fees of 78-year-old John McGraw (the white man), who was charged with assault and disorderly conduct after attacking the black protestor.
17. Trump lamented that "we're not allowed to punch back anymore."
18. Trump reminisced about the halcyon "old days," when a protester would be "carried out on a stretcher;" the crowd is delighted, cheering, clapping, and laughing.
19. Trump then states: "he'd like to punch the man in the face;" again the crowd cheers.
20. Trump stated: If you see somebody getting ready to throw a tomato, knock the crap out of them, would you? Seriously."
21. Trump again promised to pay for any legal fees associated with an assault.
22. A Black Lives Matter activist was kicked, punched and called the N-word, and Trump expressed his approval.
23. Trump stated: "Maybe he should have been roughed up because it was absolutely disgusting what he was doing."
24. Trump stated the man deserved the treatment because he had been "very obnoxious and so loud."
25. Black Lives Matter activists took over a Bernie Sanders campaign event in Seattle, asking for a moment of silence for Michael Brown, the black teenager killed by a white policeman in Ferguson, Missouri, in 2014.
26. Trump was asked how he would respond to a similar situation.
27. Trump's was defiant (in bold opposition and rebellious).
28. Trump was curious about who would get into a physical altercation when faced with Black Lives Matter activists, him or his supporters.

29. Trump then stated: "I don't know if I'll do the fighting or if other people will."

According to the Black's Law Dictionary Second Edition, "incite" means to arouse; stir up; instigate; sec in motion; as to "incite" a riot. Also, generally, in criminal law, to instigate, persuade, or move another to commit a crime; iu this sense nearly synonymous with "abet." (See Long v. State, 23 Neb. 33, 30 N. W. 310) Aid and Abet in criminal law is that kind of connection with the commission of a crime which, at common law, render the person guilty as a principle in the second (2nd) degree. It consisted in being present at the time and place, and doing some act to render aid to the actual perpetrator of the crime,------- though without taking a direct share in its commission. See 4 Bl. Comm. 34; People v. Dole, 122 Cal. 486, 55 Pac. 5S1, 68 Am. St. Rep. 50; State v. Tally, 102 Ala. 25, 15 South. 722; State v. Jones, 115 Iowa, 113, 88 N. W. 196; State v. Cox, 65 Mo. 29, 33.

Did Donald Trump in and through his speeches and actions have anything at all to do with "a white man named John McGraw," who was charged with assault and disorderly conduct after attacking "a black male protester" in Fayetteville, N.C. Did Donald Trump's promises after this attack, to have his team look into paying the legal fees of 78-year-old John McGraw, and, in reference to another protester, saying: "Try not to hurt him. If you do, I'll defend you in court, don't worry about it;" and yet, in reference to another protester, saying: "If you see somebody getting ready to throw a tomato, knock the crap out of them, would you? Seriously." Trump again promised to pay for any legal fees associated with an assault; do any of these things amount to "inciting violence, as to a riot," and "condoning such violence," by clearly "promising to pay legal fees for his supporters that assault protestors?" "If not, why not?"

Donald Trump's racially motivated demagogy (practice of gaining power, wealth, and popularity by arousing the emotions, passions, and prejudices of the people) certainly was not lost on Yusef Salaam (a black man that served 5 ½ years for a crime against a white woman he did not commit). On the night of April 19, 1989, a 28-year-old female jogger was brutally attacked and raped in New York's Central Park. She was found unconscious with her skull fractured, her body temperature at 84 degrees, and 75 percent of her blood drained from her body. When she recovered, she had no memory of the assault. Initial police investigations quickly focused on a group of African American and Latino youths who were in police custody for a series of other attacks perpetrated in the park that night.

The following year, all five (5) teenagers were convicted, in two separate trials, of charges stemming from the attack. Yusef Salaam was tried as a juvenile and convicted of rape and assault. He was sentenced to five (5) to ten (10) years. In early 2002, Matias Reyes, a convicted murderer and rapist, admitted that he alone was responsible for the attack on the Central Park jogger. Reyes had already committed another rape near Central Park days earlier in 1989, using the same modus operandi. The victim of that rape had described the rapist as having fresh stitches in his chin and an investigator quickly linked Reyes to this description. Although the police had Reyes's name on file, they failed to connect Reyes to the rape and assault of the Central Park jogger.

Donald Trump need to be reminded, that eventually, the evidence from the crime was subjected to DNA testing. The DNA profile obtained from the spermatozoa found in the rape kit matched the profile of Reyes. Mitochondrial DNA testing on the hairs found on one of the defendants revealed that the hairs were not related to the victim or the crime. Further testing on hairs found on the victim also matched Reyes. Neither blood nor the hair found on the rock matched the victim. The evidence corroborates Reyes's confession to the crime and is consistent with the other crimes committed by Reyes. He is currently serving a life sentence for those crimes.

Donald trump need to be reminded that on December 19, 2002, on the recommendation of the Manhattan District Attorney, the convictions of the five (5) men were overturned. Yusef Salaam had served 5 ½ years for a crime he did not commit. The investigation of the convictions of these five teenagers has raised questions regarding police coercion and false confessions, as well as, the vulnerability of juveniles during police interrogations. Donald Trump need to be reminded because of reasons as following:

In the aftermath of the Central Park Five being arrested, Donald Trump paid $85,000 for advertising space in four (4) of the city's newspapers, including the New York Times and the New York Daily News condemning the four (4) teenagers with the headline, "Bring Back The Death Penalty. Bring Back Our Police!" A haranguing paragraph signed by Donald Trump himself was published below the headline in which after Donald Trump laments the disappearance of law and order in New York City over the previous decade, he declares:

"Mayor Koch has stated that hate and rancor should be removed from our hearts. I do not think so. I want to hate these muggers and murderers. They should be forced to suffer, and when they kill, they should be executed for their crimes. They must serve as examples so that others will think long and hard before committing a crime or an act of violence. Yes, Mayor Koch, I want to hate these murderers and I always will. I am not looking to psychoanalyze or understand them, I am looking to punish them. If the punishment is strong, the attacks on innocent people will stop. I recently watched a newscast trying to explain the "anger in these young men". I no longer want to understand their anger. I want them to understand our anger. I want them to be afraid."

The racially motivated demagogy on the part of Donald Trump, certainly was not lost on Yusef Salaam. In a recent interview, he stated: "He was the fire starter. Common citizens were being manipulated and swayed into believing that we were guilty... I knew that this famous person calling for us to die was very serious. We were all afraid. Our families were afraid. Our loved ones were afraid. For us to walk around as if we had a target on our backs, that's how things were... Had this been the 1950s, that sick type of justice that they wanted—somebody from that darker place of society would have most certainly came to our homes, dragged us from our beds and hung us from trees in Central Park. It would have been similar to what they did to Emmett Till."

Michael Warren, who served as defense attorney for the Central Park Five, has no doubt that the advertisements Donald Trump bought to condemn his clients were an important catalyst in them being wrongly convicted.—"He poisoned the minds of many people who lived in New York and who, rightfully, had a natural affinity for the victim. Notwithstanding the jurors' assertions that they could be fair and impartial, some of them or their families, who naturally have influence, had to be affected by the inflammatory rhetoric in the ads."

The inflammatory rhetoric in the ads" that Donald Trump paid $85,000 to be published, had a very profound influence on the wrongful convictions of Yusef Salaam and the other four (4) people of color. Yet, Donald Trump manifested his hatred and bigotry that only a true racist, as himself, whose "primary or most dominant characteristic traits are hate and bigotry, did without empathy. Without any remorsefulness whatsoever for the wrongfully convicted victims and their families,—Donald Trump called the $41 million settle a "disgrace," and concurred with an NYPD detective's opinion that the payout was "the heist of the century." Trump also wrote: "Speak to the detectives on the case and try listening to the facts. These young men do not exactly have the pasts of angels." This, despite the fact that the boys were found to be innocent by incontrovertible DNA evidence

Donald Trump seeks continuously through fear and intimidation with his position of power and authority as one of the world's most successful businessmen, and by some, one of the world's most notorious businessmen, "to get things done how he wants them done, his way." He believes in his position of power and authority that "through fear and intimidation make anyone who challenges him afraid enough to back up off him." This is exactly the reason that he rages quickly and threats with lawsuits if his challengers or those in opposition to him don't back up off him. Because of his status and his wealth, many, including the IRS, fear him and intimidated by him.

I believe the IRS has had and continue to have some very nasty and most distasteful encounters with Donald Trump, in particularly, because I believe him to be a cheat of the highest degree, and an abuser of the elderly and uneducated to remove them of their funds in illegal manners. However, my beliefs are hypotheses (suppositions or proposed explanations on the basis of limited evidence as a starting point for further investigation), until his tax returns are made public and the Trump University case litigation is completed. In both matters, in what evidence the general public has been privileged, I believe Donald Trump guilty as accused and, as believed to be by many Americans.

Vocatic article entitled "Everyone Donald Trump, Truth Warrior, Has Called a Liar," No one is safe from the Human Lie Detector, December 22, 2015, states: "Donald Trump watched teeming crowds of Muslims cheer the falling Twin Towers, sees the hordes of rapists steaming across our border, and has the robust health of a teenage athlete. He also loves the truth—and hates those lying liars who violate it.

On Monday, the possible future Republican Pinocchio-in-chief called Hillary Clinton a liar and demanded she apologize for saying that ISIS is using Trump's statements to recruit jihadists. But it was far from the first time Trump has called Hillary a Liar Liar Pantsuits On Fire—he has challenged her truthfulness on Twitter eight (8) times.

Donald J. Trump@davenorthYV: Does anybody ever realize that Hillary Clinton doesn't make eye contact with anyone, even the camera. That's a sign of lying." 7:25 PM-15 Nov 2015 But Clinton isn't the Human Lie Detector's main focus. Trump's Twitter spends most of its time going after the honesty of President Obama, whose lies Trump has vilified (spoken or written about in an abusively disparaging manner) 43 times on Twitter since 2012. Donald J. Trump @realDonaldTrump 10:08 AM—8 Jun 2014: No president in history has lied to the American people more than President Obama; in fact, it is not even close!

Trump has policed the truths of Republican presidential candidates Jeb Bush, Ben Carson, and John Kaisich, and Marco Rubio, as well as other Republicans like Sen. John McCain and former President George W. Bush. Outside of Washington, Trump's favorite targets are in the media. He has outed liars like "dopey" Megyn Kelly, Dana Perino, CNN, and The Daily "Snooze," but usually he just denounces all mainstream media and so-called "journalists." (Full disclosure: this article was written by a so-called "journalist.")

While most of Trump's attention goes towards politicians and pundits, it seems no one is safe. The Knight of Integrity has also attacked "the doctors," Star Jones, disgraced New York Yankee Alex Rodriguez, Edward Snowden, the fraud and Ebola patient Thomas Eric Duncan. In total, Trump has called out people for lying 93 times since the beginning of 2012. Here's a breakdown of every lie he has caught.

Everyone Donald Trump has called a liar of twitter: MEDIA: "I truly love all the millions of people who are sticking with me, despite so many media lies. There is a great silent majority looming!" Mainstream Media: 7 times; New York Post: 3 times; New York Daily News: 2 times; CBS: 1 time; Megyn Kelly: 1 time; CNN: 1 time; George Will: 1 time; Dan Hanninger: 1 time; Dana Perion: 1 time; Ed Schutlz: 1 time; Glen Thrush: 1 time; John Hardwood: 1 time; total 21 lies.

Everyone Donald Trump has called a liar of twitter: POLITICIANS: "No president in history has lied to the American people more than President Obama; in fact, it is not even close!" Barrack Obama: 43 times; Hillary Clinton: 8 times; Jeff Bush: 3 times; Marco Rubio: 2 times; Ben Carson: 2 times; Jonathan Gruber: 1 time; George W. Bush: 1 time; John Kasich: 1 time; John McCain: 1 time; The Senate: 1 time; total 63 lies.

Everyone Donald Trump has called a liar of twitter: OTHERS: "Ebola patient Duncan lied on his exit papers by saying he never came in contact with a person with Ebola. He knew he did and person died." Alex Rodriguez: 2 times; Chinese government: 2 times; Edward Sowden: 2 times; The doctors: 1 time; Thomas Eric Duncan: 1 time; Star Jones: 1 time; total 9 lies. So think before you lie, tweet or come down with Ebola. The Donald is watching. And he's out to make America honest again.

ABC News, May 11, 2016 an article entitled "From 'Crooked Hillary' to 'Little Marco,' Donald Trump's Many Nicknames" states: "Donald Trump loves nicknames. Throughout the presidential primary season, he has become known for bestowing catchy nicknames upon his friends and foes. Actually, mostly foes. From "Little Marco" to "Crooked Hillary" and everyone in between, here's a look at Trump's top pet names:

Crazy Bernie' **Origin:** Campaign rally in Pensacola, Florida, on Jan. 13, 2016. **Famous use case:** "What do you do? Concede the election to Hillary Clinton or to Crazy Bernie? Right? I mean Bernie. I don't know who I want to run against more, I don't know," Trump said back then. Trump rehashed the nickname for the Vermont senator this morning, tweeting, "I don't want to hit Crazy Bernie Sanders too hard yet because I love watching what he is doing to Crooked Hillary." "Crazy Bernie" then began trending on Twitter.

@realDonaldTrump 3:31 PM 10 May 2016: "The Clintons spend millions on negative ads on me & I can't tell the truth about her husband? Don't feel sorry for crooked Hillary!" 'Crooked Hillary' Origin: Campaign rally in Watertown, New York, on April 16, 2016. Famous use case: "So, I'm self-funding. All of this is mine. When I fly in, it's on my dime, right, it's on mine. And what does that mean? That means I'm not controlled by the special interests, by the lobbyists. They control crooked Hillary and they control lyin' Ted Cruz, right?" Trump said in New York in April. Trump also likes to use this attack on Twitter and has been using the nickname for Clinton even more on the campaign trail now that he is the presumptive Republican nominee.

'Little Marco' **Origin:** Campaign rally in Columbus, Ohio, on March 1, 2016. **Famous use case:** "I call him little Marco. Little Marco. Hello, Marco," Trump said in response to the Florida senator's joke about Trump's "small hands." After the 11th GOP debate, social media had a field day when they were introduced to Trump's belittling taunt for Rubio. "Don't worry about it, little Marco," Trump said when challenged by the Florida senator to answer a policy question on March 3. Rubio hit Trump back, calling him "Big Donald."

'Lyin' Ted' **Origin:** Campaign rally in Columbus, Ohio, on March 1, 2016. **Famous use case:** "I call him lying Ted," Trump said about the Texas senator on Super Tuesday. Trump debuted Cruz's new nickname on a national stage, shortly after revealing Rubio's, at the Republican debate on March 3, 2016. "Excuse me, I have given my answer, lyin' Ted," Trump called Cruz after the Texas senator taunted him about releasing tapes of an off-the-record conversation with the New York Times about immigration.

'Low Energy' Jeb **Origin:** August 2015. **Famous use case:** "Let's say, this is impossible to imagine, low-energy Jeb Bush becomes president," Trump said of his fellow GOP candidate back in January at a rally in Burlington, Vermont. "Hello, I'm Jeb," Trump said imitating Bush. "He's afraid to use his last name. Can you believe it? I'm Jeb with an exclamation point. I said to him, 'Use your last name. I think you'll do better.'" It was more of a label than a nickname, but regardless, it was effective in branding Bush.

'1 for 38 Kasich' **Origin:** Twitter, on April 25, 2016. Famous use case: "Lyin' Ted Cruz and 1 for 38 Kasich are unable to beat me on their own so they have to team up (collusion) in a two on one. Shows weakness!" "1 for 38 Kasich" never quite took off as well as Trump's other nicknames for his opponents. The "1 for 38" referred to Kasich's only win in the Ohio Republican primary out of all the contests up to that point. Trump later called the Ohio governor "1 for 41 Kasich" and "1 for 44 Kasich" as more states held their primaries.

Goofy Elizabeth Warren' **Origin:** May 6, 2016. **Famous use case:** "I hope corrupt Hillary Clinton chooses Goofy Elizabeth Warren as her running mate. I will defeat them both," Trump wrote on Twitter on May 6. The real estate mogul's tweet came just days after the Massachusetts senator went on a Twitter spree, calling Trump a narcissist and a racist. Later that day, Warren responded to Trump's "lame" nickname with a series of tweets and noted she "called out" the presumptive Republican nominee on May 3. I called out @realDonaldTrump on Tuesday. 45 million saw it.—He's so confident about his "counter punch"—"he waited until Friday night. Lame." May 6, 2016 8:36 PM

Trump in my personal opinion is a narcissist racist bully who attempts to bully whoever he can with fear and intimidation, but, when

Trump's Call for Violence at Rallies

stood up to as he should be, he becomes "his own victim of fear and intimidation he sought to impose," because, like any other bully, when stood up to firmly, he's actually "too weak and incompetent" (deficient; inferior; unprofessional; inept; amateurish; not having or showing the necessary skills) to do what's necessary in in appropriate, proper, and acceptable manner.

Without his primary tools (hatred and bigotry) and his fiery bullets of rage to infuse fear and intimidation,—"he's weakened without any real resolve for who or what he faces." That's just the way most bullies are, especially those frighten and afraid of blacks and people of color when they believe they longer have an advantage. Such racists and bigots are "constantly in fear of a black and people of color takeover," which is exactly why they "work exceedingly hard at hindering blacks and people of color progress and/or stopping it altogether." Having to "answer to and/or under the administrative control of blacks and people of color"—is unquestionably, the "most disgusting, distasteful, repulsive, terrible, dreadful thing" that could happen to them.

As a matter of fact, "to them it's abomination for blacks and people of color to have any control over whites in any capacity," especially, the office of President of the USA, which explains exactly why "Trump went after and continues to go after Obama so aggressively and abusively; he hates Obama with a passion because of his race and the color his skin! And seeks to persuade and influence all other "whites" to do the same. This course of action will not change for Donald Trump,—"that's who he really, really, really, is!"

16

Trump the Cult Leader

THE TERM "CULT" is confusing because it is ambiguous—infused with a variety of meanings depending on who uses it—and for which purpose it is used. For example, the term "cult" can be used in a theological and/or a sociological sense. The word takes on different meanings depending on the context in which it is used. The theological sense is used when discussing major religious differences: a group or movement is theologically a cult if it identifies itself as belonging to a mainstream, recognized religion—and yet rejects or otherwise violates one or more of the central, essential teachings of that religion.—Essential teachings are those doctrines that define a given religion's basic essence.

A silly example, but one that illustrates this concept: You cannot call something a tomato sauce if it does not include tomatoes—because tomatoes are a central, essential ingredient (teaching or doctrine) of tomato sauce.—A sauce that is made with apples instead of tomatoes but—is sold as 'tomato sauce' is a 'cult of tomato sauce', because—it rejects one of the essential ingredients of tomato sauce, and thus—"misrepresents itself as something it is not."

The sociological sense is used when discussing behavior or other sociological aspects: a group or movement may be a cult if it acts in ways that are illegal or otherwise unacceptable in a civilized society.—A silly example, but one that illustrates this concept:

A restaurant that serves a perfectly acceptable, genuine tomato soup by pouring it into your lap—is sociologically a cult restaurant.

When most people hear the term "cult," they tend to think about destructive cults they have read or heard about. For instance, Scientology, Branch Davidians, Aum Shinrikyo, Peoples Temple, Solar Temple, the Manson Family, and so on. Psychiatrist Robert Jay Lifton, M.D., said that cults can be identified by three (3) characteristics: 1) a charismatic leader who increasingly becomes an object of worship as the general principles that may have originally sustained the group lose their power; 2) a process call coercive persuasion or thought reform; and 3) economic, sexual, and other exploitation of group members by the leader and the ruling coterie (clique; inner circle; crowd; gang).

The International Cultic Studies Association (ICSA) utilizes Benjamin Zablocki's definition of the term cult:—"an ideological organization held together by charismatic relations and demanding total commitment." Russel H. Bradshaw—who together with his wife works for ICSA's New York Educational Outreach Committee—notes:

Even in cultic groups that score at the high end of the control/demand continuum, however, not all members are abused or equally affected. [...] In general, some people in the same cultic group will be hurt more than others, some may not be affected at all, and some may actually benefit. Groups change over time and from one branch or subgroup to another; leaders' personalities change, as do the personalities of various members.—Even persons with secure and intelligent personalities—may encounter problems at times,—especially during times of transition and crisis—and they may become vulnerable to unethical psychosocial influence and control.

As a result of all these interwoven variables, it is very difficult to say that a particular group, in all branches, at all times, affects all members in a particular way. Nevertheless, trained social workers and therapists know a dangerous cultic group environment when they encounter it—and so treat former members in various degrees of suffering. These helping professionals know it is the intense psychosocial dynamic of these high-demand/high-control cultic groups and their charismatic (and often narcissistic) leaders that are—at the core of their clients' sense of abuse and trauma.—Source: Russell H. Bradshaw: What is a cult? Definitional Preface, ICSA Today, Vol. 6, No. 3, 2015, 8-9

Donald Trump, cult leader, absolutely! Even persons with secure and intelligent personalities, during our country's time of transition and crisis, unquestionably, have become vulnerable and victimized by Trump's unethical psychosocial influence and control; wherein, Trump has and continue utilizing their fears to abuse and infuse trauma,—bring them under his sole sway or control. The "charismatic narcissistic bigot Trump"—has transformed minds of millions into following his concept of rejection and hatred, especially, towards blacks and other people of color, and the whites who reject his concept and refuse going backwards with him—which, grievously disturbs him with intense passion.

Trump is a false prophet—promising easy ways out of difficult situation—he cannot deliver upon, which, are nothing more than lies and deceptions,—his profile in full color! He will lie at anytime, anyplace, and in any way—he sees beneficial to himself. That's Trump and that's not going to change; he believes he's the smartest in the world and can deceive anyone in the world; that's not going to change. He desires desperately to be President and to oval office's position to rule the USA and to have influence over the entire world of his way of doing things.

Donald Trump gravitate attention to himself!!!! And to himself, again and again!! Praising and exalting himself on his accomplishments, his brilliancy or profound brightness, and his ability to make America great again;—exalting himself and demeaning everyone else!!! He presents himself greater and more perfect than all before him and "all existing now, who dare compare themselves to him."

Trump proclaims "all before him were failures and "all existing now seeking to accomplish what needs to be done are failures."—There's "no one qualified" to do what needs to be done except himself; he's the only one capable and qualified to make America great again. Trump promises that the "many things that need to be done are just so simple," but, we have idiots trying to get them done and "idiots claiming they know how to get what needs to be done that are just not qualified."

The Washington Post, January 22, 2016, article entitled, "Here are 76 of Donald Trump's many campaign promises," states: Here are some of the most memorable campaign promises Republican presidential candidate Donald Trump has made since he declared his candidacy in June 2015. (Sarah Parnass/The Washington Post) Most presidential candidates are careful to not promise too much on the campaign trail. That's not at all the case for Republican front-runner Donald Trump. Listed below are 76 things that Trump has said he would do if elected, or, has predicted would occur as a result of his election. If he were to win the White House, Trump has promised to:

1. Build a wall along the southern border that's taller than the arenas where Trump holds his rallies, taller than any ladder and one foot taller than the Great Wall of China. This "artistically beautiful" wall will be constructed out of hardened concrete, rebar and steel, and it will be "the greatest wall that you've ever seen"—so great that the nation will likely one day name it "The Trump Wall."
2. Make Mexico pay for the wall. If Mexico refuses, then the United States will impound all remittance payments taken from the wages of illegal immigrants, cut foreign aid, institute tariffs, cancel visas for Mexican business leaders and diplomats, and increase fees for visas, border-crossing cards and port use.
3. "If I become president, we're all going to be saying 'Merry Christmas' again."
4. Get rid of Common Core because it's "a disaster" and a "very bad thing." Trump says he wants to give local school districts more control and might even eliminate the Department of Education.
5. The Environmental Protection Agency might also disappear.

6. Get rid of Obamacare and replace it with something "terrific" that is "so much better, so much better, so much better."
7. Knock down the regulatory walls between states for health insurance, making plans available nationally instead of regionally.
8. Rebuild the country's aging infrastructure—especially bridges and airports that look like they belong in a third-world country—for one-third of what the United States is currently paying for such projects.
9. Save Medicare, Medicaid and Social Security without cutting benefits.
10. Defund Planned Parenthood.
11. "I will take care of women, and I have great respect for women. I do cherish women, and I will take care of women."
12. Frequently use the term "radical Islamic terrorism."
13. Temporarily ban most foreign Muslims from entering the United States "until our country's representatives can figure out what is going on." Trump would allow exceptions for dignitaries, business people, athletes and others who have "proven" themselves.
14. Bar Syrian refugees from entering the country and kick out any who are already living here. Trump says wealthy Persian Gulf nations like Saudi Arabia should pay to set up a heavily guarded "safe zone" in Syria.
15. Heavily surveil mosques in the United States. Trump has said he's open to the idea of closing some mosques.
16. Create a database of Syrian refugees. Trump hasn't ruled out creating a database of Muslims in the country.
17. Never take a vacation while serving as president.
18. Prosecute Hillary Clinton for her use of a private e-mail server while serving as secretary of state.
19. Make medical marijuana widely available to patients, and allow states to decide if they want to fully legalize pot or not.
20. Stop spending money on space exploration until the United States can fix its potholes. Encourage private space-exploration companies to expand.

21. Pick Supreme Court justices who are "really great legal scholars."
22. Ensure that Iowa continues to host the nation's first presidential nominating contest.
23. Strengthen the military so that it's "so big and so strong and so great" that "nobody's going to mess with us."
24. Be unpredictable. "No one is going to touch us, because I'm so unpredictable."
25. Allow Russia to deal with the Islamic State in Syria and/or work with Russian President Vladimir Putin to wipe out shared enemies.
26. "Bomb the s—out of ISIS." Also bomb oil fields controlled by the Islamic State, then seize the oil and give the profits to military veterans who were wounded while fighting.
27. Target and kill the relatives of terrorists.
28. Shut down parts of the Internet so that Islamic State terrorists cannot use it to recruit American children.
29. Bring back waterboarding, which the Obama administration considers torture. Trump has said he's willing to use interrogation techniques that go even further than waterboarding. Even if such tactics don't work, "they deserve it anyway, for what they're doing."
30. Leave troops in Afghanistan because it's such "a mess." Protect Israel. And increase U.S. military presence in the East and South China Seas.
31. Find an "out" clause in the Iran deal and then "totally" renegotiate the whole thing.
32. "I promise I will never be in a bicycle race. That I can tell you." (This promise is connected to criticism of Secretary of State John F. Kerry, who was injured while riding a bicycle amid the Iran negotiations.)
33. Refuse to call Iran's leader by his preferred title. "I guarantee you I will be never calling him the Supreme Leader... I'll say, 'Hey baby, how ya doing?' I will never call him the Supreme Leader."

34. Negotiate the release of all U.S. prisoners held in Iran before taking office. (Five hostages were recently released, including Washington Post reporter Jason Rezaian; Trump has taken some credit for this.)
35. Oppose the killing of journalists: "I hate some of these people, but I would never kill them."
36. Find great generals—like the next Gen. Patton or Gen. MacArthur—and do not allow them to go onto television news shows to explain their military strategy: "I don't want my generals being interviewed, I want my generals kicking a—." Trump likes generals who are rough, foul-mouthed and beloved by their troops.
37. Drop that "dirty, rotten traitor" Bowe Bergdahl out of an airplane into desolate Afghanistan without a parachute.
38. **Fire "the corrupt and incompetent" leaders of the U.S. Department of Veterans Affairs** and dramatically reform the agency. Allow veterans to take their military identification card to any medical facility that accepts Medicaid patients to receive care. Embed satellite VA clinics in rural hospitals and underserved areas, and ensure than every VA hospital is permanently staffed with OBGYN doctors.
39. Invest more heavily in programs that help military veterans transition back to civilian life, including job training and placement services. Also increase funding for the treatment of post-traumatic stress disorder, traumatic brain injuries and mental health issues. Veterans who apply for a job at a VA facility will have five points added to their qualifying scores.
40. Bring back jobs from China—and Mexico, Japan and elsewhere.
41. "I will be the greatest jobs president that God ever created." Trump says cities like Reno, Nev., will "be a big fat beautiful beneficiary" of these new jobs.
42. Students at Wofford College in South Carolina, where Trump attended a town hall, will all have jobs at graduation.
43. Aggressively challenge China's power in the world by declaring

the country a currency manipulator, adopting a "zero tolerance policy on intellectual property theft and forced technology transfer" and cracking down on China's "lax labor and environmental standards."
44. Rather than throw the Chinese president a state dinner, buy him "a McDonald's hamburger and say we've got to get down to work."
45. Replace "free trade" with "fair trade." Gather together the "smartest negotiators in the world," assign them each a country and renegotiate all foreign trade deals.
46. Put billionaire hedge fund manager Carl Icahn in charge of trade negotiations with China and Japan, and pick an ambassador to Japan who is "a killer," unlike the current ambassador, Caroline Kennedy.
47. Tell Ford Motor Co.'s president that unless he cancels plans to build a massive plant in Mexico, the company will face a 35 percent tax on cars imported back into the United States. Trump is confident he can get this done before taking office. (Last year he incorrectly said this had already happened.)
48. Force Nabisco to once again make Oreos in the United States. And bully Apple into making its "damn computers" and other products here.
49. Impose new taxes on many imports into the country. Numbers thrown around have included 32 percent, 34 percent and 35 percent.
50. Grow the nation's economy by at least 6 percent.
51. Reduce the $18 trillion national debt by "vigorously eliminating waste, fraud and abuse in the federal government, ending redundant government programs and growing the economy to increase tax revenues."
52. Cut the budget by 20 percent by simply renegotiating.
53. Get rid of the Dodd-Frank Wall Street Reform and Consumer Protection Act.
54. Simplify the U.S. tax code and reduce the number of tax

brackets from seven to four. The highest earners would pay a 25-percent tax. The corporate tax rate would fall to 15 percent. Eliminate the "marriage penalty" for taxpayers and get rid of the alternate minimum tax.
55. No longer charge income tax to single individuals earning less than $25,000 per year or couples earning less than $50,000. These people will, however, be required to file a one-page form with the Internal Revenue Service that states: "I win."
56. Ensure that Americans can still afford to golf.
57. Allow corporations a one-time window to transfer money being held overseas, charging a much-reduced 10 percent tax.
58. Get rid of most corporate tax loopholes or incentives, but continue to allow taxpayers to deduct mortgage interest and charitable donations from their taxes.
59. On his first day in office, Trump would get rid of gun-free zones at military bases and in schools.
60. Use "common sense" to fix the mental health system and prevent mass shootings. Find ways to arm more of the "good guys" like him who can take out the "sickos." Get rid of bans on certain types of guns and magazines so that "good, honest people" can own the guns of their choice.
61. Impose a minimum sentence of five years in federal prison for any violent felon who commits a crime using a gun, with no chance for parole or early release.
62. Fix the background check system used when purchasing guns to ensure states are properly uploading criminal and health records.
63. Allow concealed-carry permits to be recognized in all 50 states.
64. Sign an executive order calling for the death penalty for anyone found guilty of killing a police officer.
65. Provide more funding for police training.
66. And provide more funding for drug treatment, especially for heroin addicts.
67. On the first day in office, terminate President Obama's

executive orders related to immigration. This includes getting rid of "sanctuary cities" that Trump says have become refuges for criminals.
68. Deport the almost 11 million immigrants illegally living in the United States.
69. Triple the number of U.S. Immigration and Customs Enforcement officers.
70. Continue to allow lowly paid foreign workers to come to the United States on temporary works visas because Trump says they are the only ones who want to pick grapes.
71. End birthright citizenship.
72. Say things that are politically incorrect, because the country does not have time to waste with political correctness.
73. **Make America great again**—and strong again, as it has become too weak.
74. Be a cheerleader for America and bring the country's spirit back. "Take the brand of the United States and make it great again."
75. Bring back the American Dream.
76. Start winning again. "We're going to win so much—win after win after win—that you're going to be begging me: 'Please, Mr. President, let us lose once or twice. We can't stand it anymore.'—And I'm going to say: 'No way. We're going to keep winning. We're never going to lose. We're never, ever going to lose."

Donald J. Trump @ realDonaldTrump received from "@ LegacyRealtorsJ: "You will come out tops Mr Trump. You are sincere, genuine, hardworking, honest, and will DO WHAT YOU PROMISE THE PEOPLE." 10:52 AM—27 Dec 2015

Dr. Robert Hare, one of the world's foremost experts in the field of criminal psychology, developer a "the Hare Psychopathy Checklist" used to assess cases of psychopathy, estimates that there are at least

2 million psychopaths in North America. He writes: "Psychopaths are social predators who charm, manipulate, and ruthlessly plow their way through life,—leaving a broad trail of broken hearts, shattered expectations, and empty wallets. Completely lacking in conscience and in feelings for others,—they selfishly take what they want and do as they please,—violating social norms and expectations—without the slightest sense of guilt or regret." The psychopath is characterized by a mixture of criminal and socially deviant behavior (departure from usual or acceptable standards).

At the very core of the psychopath is a deep-seated rage which is a split off (i.e. psychological separation from the rest of oneself) and repression (the act of subduing oneself by force). Some researchers theorize that this is caused by feeling abandoned in infancy or early childhood. Whatever the emotional or psychological source, psychopaths see those around them as objects, targets, or opportunities,—"not as people!" Such persons do not have friends; but rather, "victims and accomplices," and "their accomplices frequently end-up as victims." For the psychopath, the end always justifies the means; therefore, there's no place for feelings of remorse, shame, or guilt.—Psychopaths are cold, with shallow emotions,—living in a very dark world of their own.

> [22] "The lamp of the body is the eye. If therefore your eye is good, your whole body will be full of light. [23] But if your eye is bad, your whole body will be full of darkness. If therefore the light that is in you is darkness, how great is that darkness! (Matt. 6:22-23) [12] Then Jesus spoke to them again, saying, "I am the light of the world. He who follows Me shall not walk in darkness, but have the light of life." (Jn. 8:12)

As living embodiments of God's love, psychopaths are tragically flawed in being unable to either give or receive love; instead, appearances of love or substitutes for love are given. They cannot, regardless of how hard they try, duplicate the love of God, which is agape love from God Himself, and, which, they are unqualified to receive. Their nature is of the devil, their father.

Psychopaths readily take advantage of others; expressing utter contempt for anyone else's feelings. They are unable to empathize with the pain and suffering of their victims; they use their people skills of evil to exploit, abuse, and wield (flourish, exert, maintain, and control) power. Meanwhile, part of the victims' denial system is the inability to believe that someone they love so much could consciously and callously hurt them; wherein, making themselves the victims.

Most, if not all, cult leaders are psychopaths. A cult leader is a master manipulator who has the outstanding ability to charm and win over followers. Such a person beguiles (charms or enchants in deceptive ways) and seduces (attracts and lures people to a belief or into a course of action that's inadvisable or foolhardy). Such persons enter a room and garner (gathers or collects) all the attention; wherein, commanding the upmost respect and obedience. These are individuals whose "narcissism is so extreme and grandiose" that they exist in a kind of splendid isolation in which the creation of the "grandiose self takes precedence over legal, moral, and/or interpersonal commitments."

Paranoia (a mental condition characterized by delusions of persecution, unwarranted jealousy, or exaggerated self-importance, typically elaborated into an organized system. It may be an aspect of chronic personality disorder, of drug abuse, or of a serious condition such as schizophrenia in which the person loses touch with reality) may be evident in simple or elaborate delusions of persecution.— Highly suspicious, such persons may feel: 1) conspired against, 2) or spied upon, 3) or cheated, and 4) or maligned by a person, group, or governmental agency.

Any real or suspected unfavorable reaction may be interpreted as a deliberate attack upon them or the group. (Considering the criminal nature of some groups and the antisocial behavior of others, some of these fears may have more of a basis in reality than delusion!) Harder to evaluate, of course, is whether these leaders' belief in their magical powers, omnipotence, and connection to God (or whatever higher power or belief system they are espousing) is delusional or simply part of the con.—Megalomania (the belief that one is able or entitled to rule the world) is equally hard to evaluate without psychological testing of the individual; although numerous cult leaders state quite readily that their goal is to rule the world. In any case, beneath the surface gloss of intelligence, charm, and professed humility—seethes an inner world of rage, depression, and fear.

In reading the following Profile of a Psychopath by Robert Lifton, bear in mind, that these three (3) characteristic traits are seen common to a cultic situation. These 3 characteristic traits are: 1) a charismatic leader who...increasingly becomes the object of worship, 2) a series of processes that can be associated with "coercive persuasion" or "thought reform," and 3) the tendency toward manipulation with exploitation, economic, sexual, or other, often of genuine seekers who bring idealism.

The purpose of a cult (whether group or one-on-one) is to serve the emotional, financial, sexual, and power needs of the leader. The single most important word here is power. The dynamic around which cults are formed is similar to that of other power relationships and is essentially ultra-authoritarian, based on a power imbalance. The cult leader by definition must have an authoritarian personality—in order to fulfill his half of the power dynamic. Traditional elements of authoritarian personalities include the following: 1) the tendency to hierarchy, 2) the drive for power (and wealth), 3) hostility, hatred, prejudice, 4) superficial judgments of people and events, 5) a one-sided scale of values favoring the one in power, 6) interpreting kindness as weakness, 7) the tendency to use people and see others as inferior, 8) a sadistic-masochistic tendency, 9) incapability of being ultimately satisfied, and 10) paranoia.

Donald Trump is a cult leader that has utilize the media as his platform to spread his propaganda (information, especially of a biased or misleading nature, used to promote or publicize a particular political cause or point of view). Trump's narcissism has been extreme and grandiose, so much so, that his "grandiose self" takes precedence over legal, moral, and/or interpersonal commitments. He has through persuasive messages and false promises—beguiled and seduced millions of followers into coming aboard and dividing America as it once was before the Civil War and during the Black Codes and Jim Crow days, so that, "America can be great again!"

Donald Trump has a very serious paranoia condition, directly resulting from his delusions of persecution, unwarranted jealously or exaggerated self-importance. He is highly suspicious of people—conspiring against him, spying on him, cheating him, and maligning or bringing evil or harm against him, individually or collectively, including, but not limited to the media (radio, TV, newspapers, magazines, books, internet, government, etc.) and other persons of celebrity status and politicians in or seeking office, Trump has persuaded and convinced his followers that "anything said negatively publically and/or in writing are lies" and "not worthy of any credence whatsoever, all lies; just don't believe anything anyone has to say negatively."

It's clearly obvious and understandably that Donald Trump has factored God entirely out of the process; in that, God has promised to let his people know the difference between the "truth" and the "lie." Therefore, "liars are exposed for who they really are" by the promise of God. Therefore, those of the world may be deceived and drawn into Trump's web; however, "no so for those "not of the world" that listen and follow the promptings (sayings, persuasions, encouragements, reminders, etc.) of the Holy Spirit. It is God's will that that his people do His will, and not follow the lie and do the devil's will.

The Spirit of truth (Holy Spirit) guides us into all truth, and tells us things to come (Jn. 16:13). All truth means any truth necessary to mature us so that we're not tossed to and fro and carried away by every wind of doctrine by the trickery of men, in cunning of craftiness of deceitful plotting (Ephes. 4:14), such as, Donald John Trump, American businessman, author, TV personality, politician, and 2016 Presumptive Republican Presidential Nominee, who is a narcissist and pathological liar, that all should withdraw from, especially, Christians of the household of faith.

Christians have an anointing from God and know all things (whether of the truth or of the lie) (1 Jn. 1:20). This anointing (the Holy Spirit) is our protection against liars, deceivers, imposters, false prophets/teachers/preachers, because God cares and His love is infinite. As such, we who have His Holy Spirit are without excuse, because, "we know the truth and know that no lie is of the truth." (1 Jn. 1:21) The Holy Spirit reveals whether Trump's accusations, promises, actions (i.e. Trump University, Income Tax filings, etc.) are lies or not. There's no greater witness than the Holy Spirit here on earth; He is the highest power and authority, as every Christian knows.

Christians have one great Shepherd of the sheep, the Lord Jesus Christ (Heb. 13:20). His sheep hears His voice (Jn. 10:16) and voices of strangers (liars, imposters, false prophets/ teacher/ preachers, hypocrites) they will not follow, but flee from them (Jn. 10:5). As Christians, we are not to follow the lie, but the truth; yet, knowing the truth, many have suppressed the truth in unrighteousness (Rom. 1:18), because, what may be known of God concerning Trump,—is manifested in them, for God has shown it to them (Rom. 1:18); therefore, they are without excuse! (Rom. 1:20; Rom. 2:1)

Trump, like all other psychopaths, lie coolly and easily, even when it is obvious he being untruthful. It's almost impossible for him to be consistently truthful about either a major or minor issue. He lies for no apparent reason, even when it would seem easier and safer to tell the truth. This type of lying has sometimes been called "crazy lying," just lying to lie, because that's his true nature. Confronting him or any other pathological liar, with his lies often provokes an unpredictable behavior response of rage or simply a Buddha like smile;—with egg, fear, and arrogance over his face.

Trump has created a complex belief system about his powers and abilities, which he has gotten caught-up in many times. It's often difficult to determine whether his lies are actually delusional distortions of reality or are expressed with the conscious or unconscious intent to deceive. For him, as with all other pathological liars, objective truth (a proposition when its truth conditions are met without biases caused by feelings, ideas, opinions, etc.) does not exist. The only truth to Trump is whatever will best achieve the outcome that meets his needs. Anything, whatever it may be, he disapproves or rejects, he seeks persuading and deceiving his followers into doing the same;—regardless of existence of objective truths on the matter. His truth is the only truth!!!

Trump is about mastering the environment and controlling it in an unpredictable, capriciously, inconsistently, and irrationally manner. This approach serves to render all others dependent solely upon his next twist and turn, his next inexplicable whim, his next outburst, his denial, his next smile, or his next whatever. He wants to make very sure and certain that he is the only reliable person for advice and action; and in doing so, he shatters all other people's knowledge, skills, and abilities—through his seemingly insane behavior practices.

Trump perpetuates his own stable presence in the lives of others by destabilizing their own through fear and whatever means possible. He reacts with supreme rage to the slightest and seeks to punish severely for what he perceives to be an offense against him; wherein, seeking to persuade and deceive his followers that "any offense against him is an offense against them" and "his plans for their betterment." He, as we have often seen, throws temper tantrums over any discord or disagreement, however gently and considerately expressed; or, he acts inordinately attentive, charming, and tempting.

His "ever-shifting code of conduct" is done willfully and intentionally to keep everybody off-guard and in suspense as to his next action, and his unusually harsh and arbitrary applied penalties are premeditated. His victims are kept in the dark just as he is in darkness; therefore, neediness and dependence on him and him only of justice meted (administered or allotted) and judgment passed by him (ability to make considerate decisions or come to sensible conclusions based on his mindset) on violators of his rules are guaranteed. The combination of charisma and psychopathy—"is a lethal mixture for destruction and death" of our country and all of its inhabitants.

Trump is very strong-will and very persuasive in his pursuit for the oval office, and truly believes this is his time to take charge. He has been very successful in gathering new converts to promote his racially motivated concepts. His skills of persuasion are far more important than his charisma; his ability to habitually lie and have people support and follow his lies just show how much in the dark many of the American citizens remain. His dehumanization and objectification of people by attacking the very foundation of human interaction is cruel and most distasteful. "We as a people have a need to believe in the empathic skills and basic good-heartedness of others." Trump, however, is incapable of this empathy,—being an excellent imitator of a fully formed adult; but yet, in actuality, emotionally absent and immature as to the needs of others.

Trump's abuse is horrid (rough; bristling; causing horror), so repulsive (intensely distasteful or disgusting), so phantasmagoric (having a fantastic or deceptive appearance, as something in a dream or created by the imagination), which causes many of us as people to recoil (suddenly spring or flinch back in fear, horror, or disgust). It's here at this point and time, when such people with their defenses absolutely down, that they are most susceptible and vulnerable to his control. His rhetoric references slavery and associated cruelty of those times; and America's greatness when blacks and people of color were kept in their inferior places.

17

Trump's Acceptance Speech Confirms His Hatred

GOD PROMISED US that hatred covered by deceit would be revealed before the whole assembly (Prov. 26). Prior to Trump making his acceptance speech for the 2016 Republican presidential nominee, many came before him attempting to give America a more impressive view of his humbleness and kindness as a family man, an employer, a friend, and as a benevolent giver preferring his giving to others being left anonymous. Through the tremendous efforts of others trying desperately to give America a more positive image of him; he himself took stage before America and the world and showed clearly and cogently just how hateful and unfit he is—to be President of our country.

With pure hatred he crushed those he hated with his tongue as if with venom from a poisonous snake's bite. All that others said to possible bring about a more positive image of him was destroyed by his own selfish, envious, and hateful manifestations; which, after all, constitute true nature. The Bible says: **"Can the Ethiopian** <u>change his skin or the leopard its spots?</u> **Then may you also** <u>do good who are accustomed to do evil</u> (Jer. 13:23)."** A person cannot change who he or she really is (i.e. his or her character or behavior practices), no matter how hard he or she tries to cover it up; it will manifest itself because it does exactly what it wants to do;—self is its own governing authority.

Trump in his narcissism revealed to the world his character and the direction he intends to lead our country, which is, frightening and most destructive; as previously proven in other countries with leaders practicing narcissism. He most definitely cleared up any questions as to whether or not he was a narcissist. Now, is should be very clear to all that "Trump is out of control; an impulsive, unpredictable want-a-be-dictator, that's totally unfit for the oval office.

POLITICO Staff at politico.com/story/2016/07 provides a full transcript of Donald Trump's presidential nomination acceptance speech at the Republican National Convention, Cleveland, Ohio. For each person's own review and evaluation, a very small portion of his speech is provided as following:

Friends, delegates and fellow Americans: I humbly and gratefully accept your nomination for the presidency of the United States. Together, we will lead our party back to the White House, and we will lead our country back to safety, prosperity, and peace. We will be a country of generosity and warmth. But we will also be a country of law and order.

Our Convention occurs at a moment of crisis for our nation. The attacks on our police, and the terrorism in our cities, threaten our very way of life. Any politician who does not grasp this danger is not fit to lead our country. Americans watching this address tonight have seen the recent images of violence in our streets and the chaos in our communities. Many have witnessed this violence personally; some have even been its victims.

I have a message for you all: the crime and violence today that afflicts our nation will soon come to an end. Beginning on January 20, 2017, safety will be restored. The most basic duty of government is to defend the lives of its own citizens. Any government that fails to do so is a government unworthy to lead. It is finally time for a straightforward assessment of the state of our union. I will present the facts plainly and honestly. We cannot afford to be so politically correct anymore.

So if you want to hear the corporate spin, the carefully-crafted lies, and the media myths the Democrats are holding their convention next week. But here at our convention there will be no lies. We will honor the American people—with the truth, and nothing else.

When the FBI Director says that the Secretary of State was "extremely careless" and "negligent," in handling our classified secrets, I also know that these terms are minor compared to what she actually did. They were just used to save her from facing justice for her terrible crimes. In fact, her single greatest accomplishment may be committing such an egregious crime and getting away with it—especially when others have paid so dearly. When that same Secretary of State rakes in millions of dollars trading access and favors to special interests and foreign powers I know the time for action has come.

This is the legacy of Hillary Clinton: death, destruction and weakness. But Hillary Clinton's legacy does not have to be America's legacy. The problems we face now—poverty and violence at home, war and destruction abroad—will last only as long as we continue relying on the same politicians who created them. A change in leadership is required to change these outcomes. Tonight, I will share with you my plan of action for America.

I have joined the political arena so that the powerful can no longer beat up on people that cannot defend themselves. Nobody knows the system better than me, which is why I alone can fix it. I have seen firsthand how the system is rigged against our citizens, just like it was rigged against Bernie Sanders—he never had a chance.

But his supporters will join our movement, because we will fix his biggest issue: trade. Millions of Democrats will join our movement because we are going to fix the system so it works for all Americans. In this cause, I am proud to have at my side the next Vice President of the United States: Governor Mike Pence of Indiana.

It's time to show the whole world that America Is Back-bigger, and better and stronger than ever before. But now, my soul and exclusive mission is to go to work for our country—to go to work for all of you. It's time to deliver a victory to the American people. But to do that, we must break free from the petty politics of the past. America is a nation of believers, dreamers, and strivers that is being led by a group of censors, critics, and cynics.

My opponent asks her supporters to recite a three-word loyalty pledge. It reads: "I'm With Her." I choose to recite a different pledge. My pledge reads: "I'M WITH YOU—THE AMERICAN PEOPLE." I am your voice. So to every parent who dreams for their child, and every child who dreams for their future, I say these words to you tonight: I'm With You, and I will fight for you, and I will win for you.

To all Americans tonight, in all our cities and towns, I make this promise. We Will Make America Strong Again. We Will Make America Proud Again. We Will Make America Safe Again. And We Will Make America Great Again. Thank You.

The New York Times' article entitled "His Tone Dark, Donald Trump Takes G.O.P. Mantle" July 21, 2016 states: "Donald John Trump accepted the Republican presidential nomination on Thursday night with an unusually vehement appeal to Americans who feel that their country is spiraling out of control and yearn for a leader who will take aggressive, even extreme, actions to protect them. Mr. Trump, 70, a New York real estate developer and reality television star who leveraged his fame and forceful persona to become the rare political outsider to lead the ticket of a major party, drew exuberant cheers from Republican convention delegates as he strode onto the stage of the Quicken Loans Arena and delivered a speech as fiery as his candidacy.

With dark imagery and an almost angry tone, Mr. Trump portrayed the United States as a diminished and even humiliated nation, and offered himself as an all-powerful savior who could resurrect the country's standing in the eyes of both enemies and law-abiding Americans. "Our convention occurs at a moment of crisis for our nation," an ominous-sounding Mr. Trump said, standing against a backdrop of American flags. "The attacks on our police, and the terrorism in our cities, threaten our very way of life. Any politician who does not grasp this danger is not fit to lead our country."

Mr. Trump nearly shouted the names of states where police officers had been killed recently, as the crowd erupted in applause, and

Trump's Acceptance Speech Confirms His Hatred

returned repeatedly to the major theme of the speech: "Law and order," he said four (4) times, each time drawing out the syllables. Evoking the tumult of the 1960s and the uncertainty that followed the Sept. 11 terrorist attacks, Mr. Trump made a sharp departure from the optimistic talk about American possibility that has characterized Republican presidential candidates since Ronald Reagan redefined the party over 30 years ago. In promoting his hardline views on crime, immigration and hostile nations, Mr. Trump was wagering that voters would embrace his style of populism and his promises of safety if they feel even less secure by Election Day.

But his speech—the longest, at an hour and 15 minutes, since at least 1972—had relatively little new to offer women, Hispanics, blacks and others who have been turned off by Mr. Trump's incendiary brand of politics. He did sound like a different sort of Republican at times, though, making no mention of abortion—a core issue for many Republicans—and saying of his support among evangelical voters,— "I'm not sure I totally deserve it."

Mr. Trump also challenged Republican orthodoxy as he promised to end multilateral trade deals and limit American intervention in global crises. He denounced "15 years of wars in the Middle East"—a rebuke of his party's last president, George W. Bush—and pledged to help union members, coal miners and other low-wage Americans— who have historically supported Democrats. "These are the forgotten men and women of our country," said Mr. Trump, a billionaire with a mixed record of job creation and layoffs. "People who work hard but no longer have a voice—I am your voice."

He even vowed "to do everything in my power to protect our L.G.B.T.Q. citizens from the violence and oppression of a hateful foreign ideology." As the audience applauded, Mr. Trump made a deviation from his prepared text, observing: "I have to say, that as a Republican, it is so nice to hear you cheering for what I just said."' Facing a restive party on the final night of a convention that has been unusually turbulent and divided, Mr. Trump seemed to make headway in galvanizing and unifying at least those Republicans gathered in the hall. The nearly full arena was rapt as Mr. Trump spoke, and when he began discussing illegal immigration, a familiar chant quickly broke out in the arena: "Build the wall, build the wall!"

And when he vowed to tell the truth "plainly and honestly," a delegate cried from the floor: "Bring it, Donald!" Mr. Trump dwelled at length on illegal immigrants and lawless Americans, saying they are as dangerous for the nation's security as the Islamic State and Syrian refugees. In doing so, Trump advisers said, he sought to win over undecided voters who are sickened by the recent violence against police officers and worried about safety yet are unsure if Mr. Trump has the temperament and abilities to be commander in chief. "I have a message to every last person threatening the peace on our streets and the safety of our police: When I take the oath of office next year, I will restore law and order to our country."

While nomination speeches are traditionally optimistic and personal, full of hope and revelations that cast candidates in the best possible light for voters, Mr. Trump sounded like a wartime president, using the word "threat" seven times and promising to "defeat the barbarians of ISIS." He also recited homicide rates in American cities and the thousands of illegal immigrants with criminal records, promising to control violence at home and abroad. "It is time to show the whole world that America is back—bigger, and better and stronger than ever before," Mr. Trump said.

He was blistering about Hillary Clinton, his Democratic opponent, and her tenure as secretary of state, arguing that her diplomatic strategy in Syria, Iraq, Egypt, Libya and other countries had led to civil unrest and political chaos and rendered her unfit to be president. "America is far less safe—and the world is far less stable—than when Obama made the decision to put Hillary Clinton in charge of America's foreign policy," Mr. Trump said.

I once thought the email scandal was overblown, but I've been troubled by Clinton's handling of it:"... Hillary Clinton made a blunder by... Strangely missing from his acceptance speech (and Amtrak is certainly relieved!): Trump did not promise to make the trains run on

Trump's Acceptance Speech Confirms His Hatred

time. Well; The more I ponder the statement, "I am your voice," the more-creepy it sounds. As if Trump could be inside one's mind, could read it or...

Mr. Trump said Americans had "lived through one international humiliation after another" under President Obama: the Navy sailors "being forced to their knees" by Iranian captors in January; the destruction of the American consulate in Benghazi, Libya; and Mr. Obama's decision not to defend his "red line" on Syria. Mrs. Clinton shared the blame, too, he added. "This is the legacy of Hillary Clinton: death, destruction, terrorism, and weakness," Mr. Trump said.

In a bid to appeal to Democrats unhappy with their party's embrace of Mrs. Clinton, he invoked the political message of her chief rival, Senator Bernie Sanders, and suggested that Mr. Sanders shared Republicans' critique of her record. Mr. Trump's elder daughter, Ivanka, also sought to reach out to Democrats and moderates, extolling him as a champion of women in the workplace, and a leader who would "take on the bold and worthy fights, who will be unafraid to set lofty goals and relentless in his determination to achieve them." This week's convention, which typically would have been choreographed carefully, was itself a departure from the norm. But if Mr. Trump injected drama and even spontaneity back into the formulaic gathering, he also tested the limits of improvisation over the last week.

The operatic quality of the first three days of the convention worried some Republicans. Presidential candidates have two major issues to deal with over the summer, their vice-presidential selection and their convention, and they felt he had bungled both. Mr. Trump chose his running mate haphazardly and then overshadowed the announcement of Gov. Mike Pence of Indiana by indulging in a rambling speech that revived questions about his seriousness.

The party staged a convention that reflected just how fractured it is. There were, to be sure, effective attacks on the character and record of Mrs. Clinton, whose unpopularity among modern presidential nominees is exceeded only by Mr. Trump's. But some of the anti-Clinton language spilled into ugliness and catcalls. The party at times seemed unified only around a shared determination to imprison the former secretary of state.

But the speeches dedicated to promoting Mr. Trump and the party's governing vision were hazy and at times collided with the candidate's own beliefs. Many of the elected officials who spoke extolled a traditional conservative platform that bears little relation to the nationalist agenda on which Mr. Trump is basing his campaign. For example, just hours before Mr. Pence, a committed internationalist, assured delegates and millions of voters that America would defend its allies, Mr. Trump gave an interview in which he balked at defending NATO countries, a policy that has been the cornerstone of the alliance for 70 years.

Even as Republicans prepared to leave Cleveland, they were still straining to come to terms with the views and personality of their newly minted nominee. "I'm going to vote for Mike Pence," said Gov. Gary Herbert of Utah, pausing for effect: "And Donald Trump comes along with the package." Candidates who are trailing—as Mr. Trump is, according to national polling averages—must maximize the bump they typically enjoy in the polls after their conventions. Mr. Trump may see his standing improve after he leaves Cleveland on Friday, even though he did not fully seize the opportunity he was afforded after Mrs. Clinton was upbraided by the F.B.I. director over her private email server.

In many ways, the convention's formality was an awkward fit for Mr. Trump, who soared in the primaries by energizing voters at freewheeling rallies with his off-the-cuff and frequently entertaining remarks. Instead, for Thursday night, he relied on a teleprompter and a speech heavy with familiar Republican themes like cutting taxes, creating jobs, and pushing for education reforms to give parents more choice in schools for their children.

Yet he also made more personal promises as well, like being the ultimate safeguard for the younger generations of Americans. "To every parent who dreams for their child, and every child who dreams for their future, I say these words to you tonight: I'm with you, I will fight for you, and I will win for you," Mr. Trump said.

Trump's Acceptance Speech Confirms His Hatred

BREITBART's article entitled "Black Lives Matter Responds to Trump Speech: 'Terrorists; 'Fascist'" July 21, 2016 by states: "CLEVELAND, Ohio—The Black Lives Matter movement issued an official response to Donald Trump's acceptance speech at the Republican National Convention on Thursday evening, calling him among the "worst fascists in history" and the "terrorist on our televisions." Trump emphasized law-and-order themes in his speech, pledging to stand with law enforcement. At one point, he interrupted his speech to thank police as they removed a heckler. The full Black Lives Matter statement is as follows (original emphasis):

Cleveland, OH—Tonight's acceptance speech from Republican Presidential nominee, Donald J. Trump was possibly the most negative acceptance speech in recorded history. In his 75 minutes on stage, the nominee—whether couched in dog-whistling or outright yelling—managed to vilify and criminalize good people of all walks ranging from Latino immigrants, to Muslims, to Black people to which the co-founders of Black Lives Matter have issued the following response:

"The terrifying vision that Donald J. Trump is putting forward casts him alongside some of the worst fascists in history. "Black people and our allies have unequivocally demanded a new path forward for safety in our communities, one that involves real accountability for police. "While our movement envisions a bright future where everyone is treated with dignity and respect, Trump is proposing a new, dark age where police have carte blanche authority to terrorize our communities.—"Whether it was Richard Nixon unleashing a war on drugs or George Wallace's more overt war on Black people, we've heard it all before and won't be fooled again," said Alicia Garza, Co-Founder of Black Lives Matter.

"The terrorist on our televisions tonight was Donald Trump. He pledged to fight for Americans, while threatening the vast majority of this country with imprisonment, deportation and a culture of abject fear. "His doublespeak belies his true nature: a charlatan who will embolden racists and destroy communities of color. He is a disgrace. White people of conscience must forcefully reject this hatred immediately," said Patrisse Cullors, Co-Founder of Black Lives Matter." [End of Article]

CBS News article entitled "Celebrities react to Donald Trump's RNC Speech" July 22, 2016 states: "Stars tuned in to watch the final night of the Republican National Convention in Cleveland on Thursday, and most of them did not take kindly to the words of Republican presidential nominee Donald Trump in his dark acceptance speech that spanned more than an hour.

Celebrities like Rosie O'Donnell and Julia Louis-Dreyfus used caps in their tweets to emphasize their frustration toward the billionaire, while others, like "The Fault in Our Stars" author John Green used statistics to take down the GOP nominee. A couple of stars, like Eric Benet and Josh Gad, even went as far as to compare Trump to Hitler. Read on to see the NSFW things angry celebrities had to say about the presidential nominee.

Rosie@Rosie: SAME "S" HE SAID ABOUT SCOTLAND AND HIS ABSURD GOLF COURSE—HE IS A "F" ING LIAR—EVERY WORD HE SPEAKS PURE B.S.—RICH SPOILED PRICK 10:40 PM 21 Jul 2016

Julia Louis Dreyfus@officialJLD: And THAT is the reason to NOT VOTE for @realDonaldTrump. #SCOTUS 11:25 PM 21 Jul 2016

John Green @JohnGreen: Trump's speech tonight says "safety will be restored." In fact, U.S. crime rates are at their lowest in 40+ years. 6:49 PM 21 Jul 2016

Troian @SleepintheGardn: As I watch Trump's speech to the #RNC I just keep shouting "BUT HOW" at my screen. Please say something, sir, what do you plan to DO? 10:26 PM 21 Jul 2016

Josh Gag @joshgad: Eh. Trump's speech sounded much better in German. 10:38 PM 21 Jul 2016

Michael Ian Black @michaellanblack: On a scale of 1-10, I would rate Trump's acceptance speech a solid "Go FYS." 11:30 PM 21 Jul 2016

Eric Benet @ericbenet: I give it 4 out of 5 swastikas. #RNCinCLE 11:48 PM 21 Jul 2016 Calabasas, CA, United States

Rashinda Jones @rashindajones: You're right. Trump promotes love. And the ventilation of refugees. 11:27 PM 21 Jul 2016

Marlon Wayans @marlonwayans: Trump's daughter just gave a great speech ... Who the "f" was she talking about 10:19 PM 21 Jul 2016

Meghan McCain @MeganMcCain: The party I was part of is dead. 11:39 PM 21 Jul 2016

George Lopez @georgelopez: Cough "B.S." cough @realDonaldTrump 10:19 PM 21 Jul 2016

Clay Aiken @clayaiken: So @realDonaldTrump who's gonna protect the LGBT citizens from the hatred of DOMESTIC violence???? 10:57 PM 21 Jul 2016

Michael Moore @michaelmoore: First Republican ever to use the word "peace" in any speech. So I guess that means, war. 10:22 PM 21 Jul 2016

Ronan Farrow @RonanFarrow: Donald Trump emphasizing deadly toll of gun violence. This is where he announces support for common sense gun control. Right? ...Right? 10:28 PM 21 Jul 2016

Jon Law @RonRAS2: speech is a speech ... his actual actions have been crap and he hasn't been a good man at all! 22 Jul 2016 6:6 PM

Keote_Poet@Jon Law: ditto here... Cruz has somehow risen to the top of the crap pile. trump is the smelliest of them all.. cruz told and stood up to these fools. 22 Jul 2016 5:5 PM

When a major party selects a reality TV personality as a "legitimate" candidate, one should also expect celebrity commentary on such selection. Hello! I agree with these comments—I think it probably did sound better 70 years ago in German. I too was sitting on the couch screaming—HOW are you going to do that? Simply saying words like "believe me" and "so fast" don't MEAN anything! I did, however get a considerable hangover from tequila shots for every empty phrase like that...

I'm an on-the-fence-about-Hillary voter. I could have been enlightened by a substantive, informative, FACTUALLY BASED speech. Instead, we were subjected to more or the same-old, same-old and had it screamed at us for over an hour. That was so fun. Instead of winning hearts and minds—he continued to rant and rave like the lunatic that he is. Major loser turn-off. Now Ivanka's hawking her RNC dresses over twitter—that's what this whole insane alternate universe is all about—how to increase the value of the Chump brand. Get a grip disciples. (Flowerlady 1025 22 Jul 2016)

> [14] *Now we exhort you, brethren, warn those who are unruly, comfort the fainthearted, uphold the weak, be patient with all.* [15] *See that no one renders evil for evil to anyone, but always pursue what is good both for yourselves and for all.* [16] *Rejoice always,* [17] *pray without ceasing,* [18] *in everything give thanks; for this is the will of God in Christ Jesus for you.* [19] *Do not quench the Spirit.* [20] *Do not despise prophecies.* [21] *Test all things; hold*

fast what is good. ²² Abstain from every form of evil. (1 Thess. 5:14-21)

¹¹ "Now therefore, speak to the men of Judah and to the inhabitants of Jerusalem, saying, 'Thus says the LORD: "Behold, I am fashioning a disaster and devising a plan against you. Return now everyone from his evil way, and make your ways and your doings good."'" (Jer. 18:11) ³⁴ Brood of vipers! How can you, being evil, speak good things? For out of the abundance of the heart—the mouth speaks. (Matt. 12:34)

The New York Times' article entitled "The Biggest Challenges of 2016" January 6, 2016 states: "At the end of 2015, we asked what you felt was the greatest challenge facing the United States in the coming year. Over a thousand readers responded, and while their answers varied widely, a few common themes emerged. Below are some of the issues readers brought up the most frequently:

Climate change, Stephen Woolpert, Berkeley: "The climate crisis dwarfs all other issues. Climate change has put weather on steroids. The oceans are becoming acidified. The adverse consequences are already having a disparate impact on the poor. And it will only get worse. We need to use less energy, replace fossil fuels with renewable energy (like wind and solar) for our remaining energy needs, and adopt land use practices that stop deforestation and unsustainable agriculture. Even if we stopped all carbon pollution today, impacts would continue to increase for some time due to the time lag in our climate system. It is important that we both move to eliminate fossil fuels, and begin to prepare for the impacts we can't avoid through smarter planning and actions to improve the resilience of communities to stronger and more frequent storms, droughts, heat waves and sea level rise."

Wharton, Chicago: "The biggest challenge faced by America in 2016 is that of moving our energy use away from fossil fuels in order to address climate change. There is overwhelming scientific consensus that the increase in atmospheric greenhouse gases due to use of fossil fuels is warming earth's climate, and will result in sea level rise, loss of agricultural areas and increasingly severe weather events. The challenge is to create the political will to take aggressive action consistent with this knowledge by reducing our reliance on fossil fuels.

The EPA's Clean Power Plan, and recent Paris agreement are steps in the right direction, but aren't sufficient to put us on a safe path. We can achieve a greater reduction of carbon emissions by creating incentives which work throughout the economy to encourage conservation and a shift to low-carbon energy. Incentives such as a tax on fossil carbon can accomplish this without damaging the economy, if carbon-tax revenues are returned to households, for example as a dividend similar to a tax refund. Douglas McLane, Plymouth, N.H.: As Bernie Sanders so simply said in the debate, "Terrorism can't bring down our civilization, but climate change can."

Money in politics Jefflz, San Francisco: "The biggest problem the United States faces in 2016 is the restoration of a constitutional democracy run by the people and for the people. We are on a slippery slope where gerrymandering, voter suppression and above all, limitless dark money in elections, has placed our country in the hands of a powerful ruling oligarchy. If any of the G.O.P. candidates is elected in 2016, through subsequent appointments, the Supreme Court will become an even more powerful tool of corporations and the super-rich. America will definitely continue on an irreversible slide into corporate fascism."

Blue State: There are many important issues (guns, terrorism, climate change, labor, immigration, globalization, infrastructure, defense, investment, taxation, healthcare, education, research) but they are all at the mercy of campaign finance reform. Fix the fixing of elections by the wealthy and corporations, and we can fix anything.

Education: DC Smith, Pennsylvania: "The greatest challenge is to change our educational system so that it encourages and teaches critical thinking, the evaluation of claims and evidence, and the understanding of logical argument. American citizens could then understand the evidence for and consequences of global climate change, understand other cultures and their values, and understand how to evaluate candidates' and legislators' claims and lies. We could then move beyond ignorance and hatred to empathy, compassion, and more active participation in ridding ourselves of injustice and inequality."

Adrian, Cincinnati: "Education reform—not just in 2016, but in every year. If we're really serious about giving every child an opportunity in this country, then we will work to have quality education—good teachers, adequate resources, diverse classes—available to all communities. This should require creative solutions, maybe more charter schools, or integration policies between districts, and above all, a greater commitment to change. It is a tragedy that with every passing year, more and more kids go through the American school system with a semblance of an education and little opportunity to attain more."

Meredith, Massachusetts: "America's biggest challenge is our shortfall in civic education. Its absence and the resulting dysfunction make us more vulnerable to every foreign and domestic threat. The whole country, from Senators to voters to candidates, needs remedial classes in basic governance. This lack of understanding leads to disappointment, a sense of betrayal, powerlessness and cynicism. Congress is certainly not modeling good government, but I suspect the uninformed electorate, lacking the information to direct its outrage, helps perpetuate the problem.

Some years ago the teaching of Civics (how-a-bill-becomes-a-law, the balance of powers, and the basics of the electoral process) as a required course was ended. It was supposed to be integrated into other classes, but in many cases was simply set aside. The right and duty of every citizen to know about our government, to engage is the civil process and to vote needs to be elevated again. Oh where are those 7th grade civics teachers of my youth?"

Polarization: Matt W, Yardley: "Our own culture of divisiveness is our biggest challenge. Tragically, this self-inflicted problem prevents us from dealing effectively with any of our other challenges (climate change, race relations, income inequality, Middle East Policy, declining infrastructure, underfunded basic science, etc., etc, etc.).

Nancy2431, Boomer, N.C.: "The biggest threat to the United States is "a house divided against itself cannot stand." The poisonous political state this country has seen develop over the past ten years or so has caused almost a standstill for economic and social growth. There are too many people with anti-attitudes about immigrants, social reforms, and economic disadvantages for the working class. People seem to be turning on each other instead of embracing what has made our country great over the centuries. We should be past the hate mongers, but we're far from it. In fact, it seems to be getting worse."

Alec MacLeod Oakland: "The greatest challenge that U.S. society faces is the loss of capacity for meaningful national dialogue. As greater numbers of citizens lose their trust not just in institutions from government health agencies to grounded journalism, we seem to become more focused on truthiness than on a skeptical relationship with reliable data. If we cannot even agree on basic facts and reasonable scientific hypotheses (such as climate change), finding ways to take meaningful action becomes increasingly difficult. As someone who grew up in a tiny politically conservative agricultural community who now lives in a politically liberal urban area, I have friends on varying sides of these epistemological divides. I experience ever widening gaps as I navigate these relationships.

Inequality, Sharmila Mukherjee: "The widening disparity between the rich and the poor, with the shrinking of the middle class is a challenge that might just tear into the democratic fabric of America. Historically, America has rarely been threatened by the specter of inequality of this magnitude. Donald Seekins, Waipahu, Hawaii: "The biggest challenge facing the United States in 2016 is social and economic inequality and how to narrow the gap between rich and poor. The way American institutions are performing now (for example, the education system from kindergarten to university, the tax system, the impoverished public sector, our social and religious values) we will soon arrive at a caste system in which reform will be impossible and America will become a very different country."

Kingfish52, Collbran, Colo.: "The biggest threat facing the United

States in 2016 is the same one that's faced us for almost four decades: Class warfare by the wealthy on the working class. Bernie Sanders understands this, while none of the other candidates do. We are watching the elimination of our middle class without a shot fired. We are on a steady march towards another era of the Robber Barons where there will be just two classes: rich and poor, and with the majority of Americans having less money, who will provide the fuel for our consumer-driven economy? And what will happen to our tax revenues? And then how will we service our debt to creditors like China and others? Most empires fail within before they fail to external enemies, and unless we reverse this war on the working class by our oligarchy, our empire will fail too." Though the concerns above came up frequently, they were far from the only ones readers mentioned. Below, a sampling of other readers' thoughts on the year ahead:

Joel, Miami Beach: "Reducing gun violence. About 90 Americans die every DAY from homicide, suicide, and accidents with guns. This dwarfs that of every other developed country. The proliferation of guns is a big reason for this (yes there are other factors too). Despite the fact that most Americans want sensible and enforceable gun laws, Congress refuses to act—because of the NRA and their ilk. This cannot be blamed on Citizens United, because it isn't the money—it's the political will of a determined few against the apathy of the many. Until Americans stand up (at the ballot box, statehouse, and Congress), they will continue to be injured and killed by guns at theaters, schools, their own homes, and virtually anywhere. We must care enough about our fellow Americans to stop this national suicide.

MIMA: "The biggest challenge America faces in 2016: getting people out to vote. We are faced with opportunities to make a difference in various aspects of making our votes count in 2016. The person who is elected to president will no doubt in their tenure have the responsibility to choose and appoint a Supreme Court Justice. There are many ramifications from this choice—women's reproductive rights, health care opportunities, just election rights, civil rights.

People, such as in Wisconsin, have been shown that elections have consequences. Our state was lax in voting. We have been left with government leaders who have taken away jurisdiction over open records, voting, court actions, environmental issues, health care benefits, educational opportunities, workplace statues—many aspects of our everyday living that used to be taken for granted. Perhaps through this turmoil, citizens will realize yes, their votes do make a difference—and even more, the lack of their votes makes a huge difference."

Rima Tututnji, Annapolis, Md.: "Racism, in all its aspects and manifestations. Implicit racism affects relationships and interactions among people and within communities. Although different ethnic groups experience the negative effects of racism in different degrees and intensities, whenever incidents occur that are horrific or even simply incompatible with what we consider to be commensurate with our American values, it plays a role in virtually every social conflict in the U.S. We need to confront racism openly, honestly and with as much integrity as we can muster. Maybe we can then deal with manifest discrimination."

William E. Dove, Lake Martin, Ala.: "A federal national debt of $20 trillion with no meaningful plan of repayment is a national disgrace. Both parties are to blame. As interest rate rise, the cost of this debt will further squeeze the federal budget for years to come. Just ridiculous. We must cut current spending or raise taxes and embark on a meaningful plan of repayment."

CW13, Blacksburg: "Our biggest challenge will be resisting the urge to panic. Terrorists will inevitably strike somewhere, sometime, more than once. We will require calm and resolve, not politicians who seek advantage by scaring us to death, nor public officials who, good intentions aside, cannot display empathy. Never have Franklin Roosevelt's words, "we have nothing to fear but fear itself," seemed wiser. We have, of course, much more to fear, but fear itself is likely to be the worst danger."

A. Stanton, Dallas, Tex.: "Overcoming the widespread ideas that rich people are the root of all evil and that more government is the answer to our problems would be at the top of my list." Bigsister, New York City:

"Right now the biggest challenge is to elect a president who can be trusted to lead this nation with competence—someone who is rational, sane, level-headed, open-minded—no cronyism, no ego trips."

Anne Russell, Wilmington, N.C.: "The greatest challenge is designing a work/home environment in which both mothers and fathers may earn a living and take care of their children and domestic life as a family. The old 40-hour work week model, in which fathers brought home the bacon while dependent-spouse mothers fried it up in a pan, is passé. Children need to be nurtured by both parents, and females as well as males need to earn our keep and use our talents and skills in the marketplace."

James J. Ritchie, Sandy Hook, Conn.: "In my view the biggest challenge that we face is restoration of our faith in the American way of life. We need to restore our pride in America and our can do ways. We need to restore our confidence in our ability to lead. We need to embrace our emerging diversity as a strength. We need to confidently look to the future and our place in that future. We need to reject talk of fear and rejoice in our ability to confront the overcome the challenges that we will face in the days ahead. As a country we are too good, too strong, too wise to give in to defeatism and negativity. As a country we have been blessed; let's use our blessing to return with strength and confidence to our place as a model for others to emulate." [End of Article]

As we can see from the above concerns, "we have really serious issues needing serious attention by a qualified leader," rather than, "someone who is seriously unfit with a platform geared towards accusations and name-calling, with obviously, "no viable or feasible plan for fixing anything!" Absolutely nothing! "But false promises to deceive and to control a racist populace of Americans resonating with his message of hatred of blacks and other people of color." Donald Trump will continue to generate strife, contention, and division in America "as he has shown himself as the voice for the KKK and other racist groups" who seek—taking America back and making it again—"as it was in the good old days."

18

Minds Resonating with Trump's Ideology

I SERIOUSLY CANNOT understand how any true Christian's mind could resonate with Donald Trump's mind that clearly has a mind full of bitter envy, self-seeking, showing clearly its earthly, sensual, demonic, boasts, and lies against the truth. Trump who calls everyone else a liar, is without doubt, the worse liar of all he's called liars; yes, by his own words, "he proven himself a most masterful deceiver and liar," of all others he has mustered in to support his racist agenda.

Trump will use people of any race and color in any position to remove any attention towards himself that he's racist. To Trump, people are merely peasants or as pawns on a chest board (i.e. the weakest; historically infantry, or more particularly, armed peasants or pikemen). Don't be deceived by Trump's cover; there's much more "going on inside that will soon be revealed." Just be patient and wait; "Exposure/disclosure is on the way!!!"

Because the Bible says: "Everyone proud in heart is an abomination to the LORD; Though they join forces, none will go unpunished (Prov. 16:5), I believe all who join forces with Trump—to mistreat blacks and other people of color—by willfully and intentionally perverting justice—so that white racists people can have an advantage—as they did in the good old days—will receive due vengeance from God. All who do not intend "ensuring justice for all" would be better off stepping down and removing themselves. Most of the people of America, in particularly, white America, is feed-up with this foolishness; yes, feed-up!

> [6] "Whoever causes one of these little ones who believe in Me to sin, it would be better for him if a millstone were hung around his neck, and he were drowned in the depth of the sea. [7] Woe to the world because of offenses! For offenses must come, but woe to that man by whom the offense comes! (Matt. 18:6-7)

> [8] "If your hand or foot causes you to sin, cut it off and cast it from you. It is better for you to enter into life lame or maimed, rather than having two hands or two feet, to be cast into the everlasting fire. [9] And if your eye causes you to sin, pluck it out and cast it from you. It is better for you to enter into life with one eye, rather than having two eyes, to be cast into hell fire. (Matt. 18:8-9)

Only with the proper fear, adoration, reverence, and awe of the Most High God can there exist in a person genuine joy in God's omnipotence, understanding without any doubt whatsoever, that He's in total control, even of those who choose not to acknowledge Him as God. We who are of the faith of God in Jesus Christ will trust Him through days of prosperity and days of adversity, knowing He has appointed the one as well as the other; and that He's in control of when one begins and the other one ends. Therefore, none of us should ever think more highly of ourselves than we ought to think; because He who has lifted us up can also bring us down, when, where, and how He so wills to do. This understanding should generate a state of humbleness.

We all are living houses of clay with our foundation in the dust from the earth; which clearly describes the mortality and fragility of our human existence. As such, being temporary houses of clay, we can perish at any time without anyone knowing exactly why. Since our bodies are fashioned from clay, God Almighty is the potter who fashioned these temporary houses of clay. Therefore, it would be wise and to our advantage to realize and understand, that God can easily turn us back to the dust from which we first came at His will; because He and He alone is the Creator. Therefore, we should all be thankful for each day He gives us life.

When we take time to contemplate (i.e. meditate on; look thoughtfully upon for a long time) the unique power and sovereign freedom of God, we should by no means be terrified; but rather, overwhelmed with joy knowing our care rests within Him. As such, we can be assured that He's not a capricious (i.e. volatile, unpredictable, temperamental) despot (i.e. a ruler who has total power and often uses that power in cruel and unfair ways). On the contrary, God is a God of unconditional love, understanding all our weaknesses and providing opportunities for all to come boldly to His throne of grace to obtain mercy and find grace to help in time of need.

God does no will that any of us should perish; but we all individually must make it our own personal will not to perish that his will be done in us as it is in heaven. Although the clouds, storms, winds, thunders, lightings, seas, and oceans all obey at His command; he chose to give humanity free-will in choosing whether or not to obey His commands. The two (2) greatest of all His commands are as follows:

> [36] *"Teacher, which is the great commandment in the law?"* [37] *Jesus said to him, "'You shall love the LORD your God with all your heart, with all your soul, and with all your mind.'* [38] *This is the first and great commandment.* [39] *And the second is like it: 'You shall love your neighbor as yourself.'* [40] *On these two commandments hang all the Law and the Prophets." (Matt. 22:36-40)*

> [12] *Therefore, whatever you want men to do to you, do also to them, for this is the Law and the Prophets. (Matt. 7:12)* [9] *"As*

the Father loved Me, I also have loved you; abide in My love. ¹⁰ If you keep My commandments, you will abide in My love, just as I have kept My Father's commandments and abide in His love. ¹¹ "These things I have spoken to you, that My joy may remain in you, and that your joy may be full. ¹² This is My commandment, that you love one another as I have loved you. (Jn. 15:9-12)

⁸ Owe no one anything except to love one another, for he who loves another has fulfilled the law. ⁹ For the commandments, "You shall not commit adultery," "You shall not murder," "You shall not steal," "You shall not bear false witness," "You shall not covet," and if there is any other commandment, are all summed up in this saying, namely, "You shall love your neighbor as yourself." ¹⁰ Love does no harm to a neighbor; therefore love is the fulfillment of the law. (Rom. 13:8-10)

America is a melting pot, where people from all over the world from different countries, races, and religions, COME hoping to find freedom, new opportunities, and a better way of life. No other country in the world has such diverse population as America, constituting a wave of immigrants bringing in their own cultures and traditions. Many immigrants have considered their passes to America as blessings for themselves and their families' children's children.

There's only one indigenous race (i.e. originating or occurring naturally; native) from America; that is, the Native Americans or American Indians; everyone else are immigrants. The only reason Native Americans are called Indians is because when Christopher Columbus discovered America in 1492, he thought he had discovered a western route to India, resulting in the name Indians. Therefore, the only race that can rightfully speak upon America being their country is the Native American Indians; everyone else are immigrants drafted in made a part of this great country.

Here in America, we have: 1) Africans, 2) Asians, 3) Arabians, 4)

Brazilians, 5) Chinese, 6) Danish, 7) Germans, 8) Hispanics/Latinos, 9) Indians, 10) Iranians, 11) Irish, 12) Italians, 13) Japanese, 14) Koreans, 15) Native Americans, 16) Norwegians, 17) Philippians, 18) Polish, 19) Scandinavians, 20) Scottish, 21) Vietnamese, 22) Welsh, and 23) British (i.e. Anglo-Saxons).

Therefore, here in America, it's this great diversity that makes America truly unique, and at the same time, creates the ongoing challenges she faces from day to day.

The British or Anglo-Saxons were the people who inhabited Great Britain from the 5th century. They comprised people from Germanic tribes who migrated to the island from continental Europe, their descendants, and indigenous British groups who adopted some aspects of Anglo-Saxon culture and language. The Anglo-Saxon period denotes the period of British history between about 450 and 1066, after their initial settlement and up to the Norman Conquest. Let it be resolved and clearly brought to light, that Anglo-Saxons (white people) are as much immigrants as all other immigrants in America.

The Anglo-Saxon settlement of Britain was the process, from the mid-5th to early 7th centuries, by which the coastal lowlands of Britain developed from a Romano-British to a Germanic culture following the Roman withdrawal in the early 5th century. The traditional view of the process has assumed an invasion of several Germanic peoples, later collectively referred to as Anglo-Saxons, from the western coasts of continental Europe, followed by the establishment of Anglo-Saxon kingdoms across most of what is now England and parts of lowland Scotland.

In America, our neighbor could be from any country, of any race, of any color, of any gender, of any religion or non-religion, of any sex, of any party or non-party. America's Declaration of Independence states: "We hold these truths to be self-evident, that all men are created equal, that they are endowed by their Creator with certain unalienable Rights, that among these are Life, Liberty and the pursuit of Happiness.—That to secure these rights, Governments are instituted among Men, deriving their just powers from the consent of the governed,—That whenever any Form of Government becomes destructive of these ends, it is the Right of the People to alter or to abolish it, and to institute new Government, laying its foundation on such principles and organizing its powers in such form, as to them shall seem most likely to effect their Safety and Happiness."

Regardless of who our neighbors may be, or what they believe and practice, it's immoral in the eyes of God to hate them; but rather, we are to love them and show them what we believe and practice through our daily life-styles. Surely, some of their life-styles are totally contrary to what we believe and practice and they feel the very same way about what they believe and practice. Nevertheless, the path we're to take is love and not hate; and if and when provided opportunity, we're to share with others our faith without forcing or coercing their attention.

Each and every person has to give an account to God for his or her doings; who is the Rightful Judge of all mankind. It's our personal responsibility to live peaceably with every person, if it be possible; however, some people are just unreasonable and wicked, which makes peaceable living an almost impossible, if not, an impossible task. Nevertheless, we're to make sure that where peaceable living can be accomplished, we're not the ones hindering this will of God from being accomplished.

Surely, we see life-styles that are ungodly according to our faith; and there are those who choose to force or coerce us who disagree with these life-styles to accept their behavior practices as normal and not sinful. Certainly, no true genuine Christian should ever compromise a known truth for the sake of friendship and/or relationship, which is, every person's personal right, which should also be accepted and respected. However, this difference has nothing to do with hate for the person; but rather, continued love for the person, but hate for the sin, just as God does Himself. God doesn't desire us to force or coerce His word upon anyone; but rather, give them opportunity to receive it of their own free-will.

Anyone who desires not hearing the word of God, his or her wish should be granted and respected; just if we desired not hearing someone else's doctrine and beliefs; we would desire our wish be granted and respected of them. This disagreement with each other shouldn't bring about strife, contentions, anger, hatred, or any other thing creating negativity; but rather, each person's desire or wish should just be honored and that particular subject left along unless one or the other chooses to engage in a peaceful manner. We all have moral standards we live by, even so, some people moral standards are immoral standards according to the word of God.

Racism is immoral; so immoral it dishonors and disrespects every commandment of God. From Native Americans (Indians called savages) to indenture servants (whites under contract to work for another person for a definite period of time, without pay, but in exchange for free passage to a new country; during the 17th century most of the white laborers in Maryland and Virginia came from England as indentured servants); to slaves (Africans captured and brought to America against their own free-will); to the Emancipation Proclamation (federal law freeing all slaves in 1863); to the Civil War (war initiated by the South to maintain slavery); to the KKK (a racist group founded in 1866 claiming white supremacy and terrorizing slaves; including murder, lynching, arson, rape, and bombing to oppose the granting of civil rights to African Americans).

Then to the Black Codes (laws passed by Southern states in 1865-1866 after the Civil War restricting African Americans' freedom, and of compelling them to work in a labor economy based on low wages or debt); to the Reconstruction Era (a period from 1865-1877 when the federal government made efforts to reconstruct the political, legal, and economic systems in the southern states that had seceded from the Union).

Though some legal protections for newly freed slaves were incorporated in the Constitution by the 13th, 14th, and 15th Amendments, conservative Southern Whites had reclaimed power and begun to disenfranchise blacks (deprive of their right to vote), with the help of President Andrew Johnson, who as governor, had championed his state's readmission to the Union under Lincoln's terms. As president,

Johnson revealed a hostility to the use of federal power to change the Southern way of life; in part, because he wanted to rebuild the Democratic Party and ensure his election in 1868.

Radical Republicans became incensed when Johnson issued a general pardon for most Confederates and then issued proclamations that permitted the Southern states to rejoin the Union after holding a constitutional convention and agreeing to three conditions: 1) repeal of the secession laws, 2) repudiation of the Confederate debt, and 3) the ratification of the 13th Amendment, which ended slavery in the United States. However, Johnson did not require the states to permit blacks to vote. In 1866, Southern Whites took back the reins of government and proceeded to pass Black Codes which restricted the freedoms of the newly freed slaves.

Racial Segregation was established, blacks were barred from serving on juries, and as appearing as witnesses, and unemployed blacks were arrested and then auctioned off to employers to pay their fines. Racist Southern Whites found ungodly ways to use or manipulate blacks for their own gain, wherein, paying them nothing while making themselves rich. Even when paying blacks a wage, racist whites paid to keep them poor and cheated them out of what little pay was to come to them many times.

This exploitation (i.e. taking advantage of blacks in adversity, stress, or unrest for personal gain; making the best for oneself out of others' bad situations) was an ongoing practice and has never ceased till this day. Racist Whites are still greedy and desire controlling all the money. Such greed as displayed in the actions of Donald Trump towards contractors he has refused to pay, and Trump University students he has refused to refund, and income tax returns believed to be shocking bombshells. Donald Trump has exploited whoever he can for his own profit.

The Jim Crow laws (were state and local laws enforcing racial segregation in the Southern United States; enacted after the Reconstruction period and continued in force until 1964). The Civil Rights Act 1964 (enacted July 2, 1964 is a landmark piece of civil rights legislation in the United States that outlawed discrimination based on race, color, religion, sex, or national origin) outlawed segregation in businesses such as theaters, restaurants, and hotels. President Lyndon Johnson signed this 1964 act into law.

The Voting Rights Act 1965 (enacted August 6, 1965 aimed to overcome legal barriers at the state and local levels that prevented African Americans from exercising their right to vote under the 15th Amendment) significantly widened the franchise and is considered among the most far-reaching pieces of legislation in U.S. history. President Lyndon Johnson signed this 1965 act into law.

Freedom fighters and civil rights activists have pursued since the Civil War to secure blacks and other people of color unalienable rights of life, liberty, and the pursuit of happiness through viable protest through governments empowered to secure these rights. Governments in many areas of our country have proven destructive of these ends, and people have gathered in protest for change in government or organizational structure to ensure that blacks and other people of color unalienable rights of life, liberty, and the pursuit of happiness are not by any means illegally interfered and prohibited.

Blacks and other people of color safety and happiness should not be minimized or under-prioritized in urgency and importance. The power and authority in the hands of our governments must be utilized to police and clean-up any corruption perverting equality and justice. All in upper positions of power and authority that are part of the problems and not part of the solutions in fixing our problems need to be declared unfit for duty and dismissed accordingly. This is not about anyone's tenure in holding a particular office or position, but rather, one's character and ability in ensuring equality and justice.

Racism cannot afford to be approached with mediocrity or ordinariness; but rather, it has to be approached seriously and aggressively, making everyone involved aware that this issue is extremely serious with serious consequences accompanying all choosing to practice it. Racism should have a zero (0) tolerance in every work location with supervisors, managers, and upper-managers, and executives held to the

Minds Resonating with Trump's Ideology

upper-most levels of responsibility ensuring its absence in the workplace. Change will come will those responsible and held accountable and disciplined and/or fired accordingly.

Arrogant people prate (talk foolishly or tediously) their knowledge with no fear of the living and true God. They have incompetent counsel and are forgers of lies, literally falsehood—plasterers (i.e. untruthful layers of lies; one lie after another); piously (hypocritically or holier-than-thou) accuse others of wrongs, wherein, smearing (messily or carelessly) their reputations with sham concoctions (bogus or phony fabrications) which they themselves are often guilty. Such persons strive desperately to keep accusations on others so that less attention is placed upon themselves. When they are held to the fire and made accountable for any specific or particular issue, they weaken as a baby in a fetal for fear of being exposed and are shocked they're actually held accountable, because, It should never have come to this (e.g. Trump University lawsuits and income tax returns).

Their interior strength is much weaker than what their exterior manifestations have reflected while boasting in their positions of power and authority and material possessions. But, when separated from these things and placed in a position of responsibility and accountability for a specific or particular issue, with no lead-way of swaying to the left or the right, but making them respond to the issue at hand, they feel very insecure and alone, as if someone is taking advantage of them or being unfair to them because they're incapable of handling the issue in fear of being exposed. There's no sympathy or empathy to be had for such persons because of their fear; because the same fear they used upon others is now rolling back upon themselves.

They're unable to call upon God in trouble because they don't truly believe that He is, and that He is a rewarder of those who diligently seek Him for help. Therefore, isolated in their pride, their hearts are incorrigibly (incurably or hopelessly) wicked; resulting in them not crying to God for help in so serious time of need. If when calling God because of being full of pride and devoid of pure motives, God does not answer and they're left without remedy. This is a terrible and horrible situation for anyone to be caught-up in and no true Christian would wish this upon anyone. Only God whose in control of days of prosperity and days of adversity can remove one or the other; only God!!!

> ¹³ Consider the work of God; For who can make straight what He has made crooked?
>
> ¹⁴ In the day of prosperity be joyful, But in the day of adversity consider: Surely God has appointed the one as well as the other, So that man can find out nothing that will come after him. (Eccles. 7:13-14)
>
> ⁷ Do not be deceived, God is not mocked; for whatever a man sows, that he will also reap. ⁸ For he who sows to his flesh will of the flesh reap corruption, but he who sows to the Spirit will of the Spirit reap everlasting life. (Gal. 6:7-8)
>
> ²³ And whatever you do, do it heartily, as to the Lord and not to men, ²⁴ knowing that from the Lord you will receive the reward of the inheritance; for you serve the Lord Christ. ²⁵ But he who does wrong will be repaid for what he has done, and there is no partiality. (Col. 3:23-25)
>
> ⁶ For whom the LORD loves He chastens, And scourges every son whom He receives." ⁷ If you endure chastening, God deals with you as with sons; for what son is there whom a father does not chasten? ⁸ But if you are without chastening, of which all have become partakers, then you are illegitimate and not sons. (Heb. 12:6-8)

Sin is called the works of the flesh, because the flesh, or corrupt nature, is the principle that moves and excites people to it. The works of the flesh are not only hurtful to people themselves, but tend to make them so to one another. We are to avoid and oppose sin and seek the utter ruin and destruction of it within ourselves. Sin affections and lusts are to be put to the same shameful and ignominious (deserving or causing public disgrace or shame) through lingering death, which our Lord underwent for our sakes. If we should approve ourselves to be Christ's, such as are united to Him and interested in Him, we must make it our constant care and business to crucify the flesh with its corrupt affections and lusts. Christ will never own those as His who yield themselves the servants of sin.

We are cautioned and exhorted to walk in the Spirit so that we will not fulfill the affections and lusts of the flesh. As members of the body of Christ, we are to love God especially and love one another for His sake. Children of God, the fruit of the Spirit (love, joy, peace, longsuffering, kindness, goodness, faithfulness, gentleness, and self-control) has no law against it to condemn and punish it. Concerning these things let us look into them as follows:

Joy (may be understood cheerfulness in conversation with our friends, or rather a constant delight in God); peace (with God and conscience, or a peaceable-ness of temper and behavior towards others); long-suffering (patience to defer anger, and a contentedness to bear injuries); gentleness (such a sweetness of temper, and especially towards our inferiors, as disposes us to be affable and courteous, and easy to be entreated when any have wronged us); goodness (kindness, beneficence), which shows itself in a readiness to do good to all as we have opportunity); faith, fidelity, justice, and honesty (in what we profess and promise to others); meekness (wherewith to govern our passions and resentments, so as not to be easily provoked, and, when we are so, to be soon pacified); and temperance (in meat and drink, and other enjoyments of life, so as not to be excessive and immoderate in the use of them).

As Christians, we're to cherish and cultivate our souls by being obedient and following promptings or guidance of the Holy Spirit so as to produce His fruits and not the works of the flesh. It's not enough that we just cease to do evil; but rather, we must learn to do well. Our Christianity obliges (morally bounds) us not only to die unto sin, but to live unto righteousness; not only to oppose the works of the flesh, but to bring forth the fruits of the Spirit as well. If therefore, we claim being Christ's, we are morally bound in making it our sincere care and endeavor to bring forth fruits of the Spirit.

Our character as Christians is supported by performing our duty in producing the fruits of the Spirit. Anyone professing to have received the Spirit of Christ, or being renewed in the Spirit of Christ should make it appear so by manifesting proper fruits of the Spirit in his or her life. Anyone professing being of this number and having obtained this privilege, it should be shown and confirmed a temper and behavior agreeable to Christianity. A proclamation of Christianity is insufficient; he or she must evidence good principles by good behavior practices. Such evidence is produced by mortifying the deeds of the flesh and walking in newness of life.

> *[19] Now the works of the flesh are evident, which are: adultery, fornication, uncleanness, lewdness, [20] idolatry, sorcery, hatred, contentions, jealousies, outbursts of wrath, selfish ambitions, dissensions, heresies, [21] envy, murders, drunkenness, revelries, and the like; of which I tell you beforehand, just as I also told you in time past, that those who practice such things will not inherit the kingdom of God. (Gal. 5:19-21)*

> *[22] But the fruit of the Spirit is love, joy, peace, longsuffering, kindness, goodness, faithfulness, [23] gentleness, self-control. Against such there is no law. [24] And those who are Christ's have crucified the flesh with its passions and desires. [25] If we live in the Spirit, let us also walk in the Spirit. [26] Let us not become conceited, provoking one another, envying one another. (Gal. 5:22-25)*

Trump has manifested works of the flesh as if he was target

practicing. He has thrown out hatred, outbursts of wrath, heresies, sown discord, created contentions, and dissensions as a direct result of his selfish ambitions and enviousness. The Bible says: "For where envy and self-seeking exist, confusion and every evil thing are there." (Ja. 3:15) Trump is profoundly desirous of vain-glory,—always exalting himself—and seeking undue regard to the approbation (approval, praise, respect, admiration) and applause of people. Trump has displayed a very nasty distasteful, haughty attitude towards everyone, in particularly, the elderly, the disabled, and family members of other good people—without a cause except his own cause.

As far as Trump's temper, he has remained ready to slight and despise those whom he look upon as inferior to himself; and to put out of humor if he is denied that respect, which he thinks is due to him from them. He's also apt to envy those whom his reputation is in any danger of being lessened, which has created his foundation for quarrels and contentions which are definitely inconsistent with that love which Christians ought to maintain towards one another; which is greatly prejudicial to the honor and interest of Christianity itself.

In Western culture today, there are many caricatures of evangelical Christians. For some, the term evangelical Christian is equivalent to "right-wing, fundamentalist Republican." For others, "evangelical Christian" is a title used to differentiate an individual from a Catholic Christian or an Orthodox Christian. Others use the term to indicate adherence to the fundamental doctrines of Christianity. In this sense, an evangelical Christian is a believer who holds to the inspiration, inerrancy, and authority of Scripture, the Trinity, the deity of Christ, and salvation by grace through faith alone. However, none of these definitions are inherent in the description "evangelical Christian."

It would be remiss of myself, a total lack of care and attention to my duty as a Christian and witness for Christ, if I do not inquire of the Evangelical communities, in particularly, "right-wing fundamentalists Republicans," as to why its members/followers are supporting Donald Trump—in spite of his immoral and despicable behavior practices before the world.

Regardless of whether you be a Democrat, Republican, Libertarian, or Green party member, your Christian values should supersede your political affiliation. I sincerely pray that not any of you suppress truth and submit your loyalty to the party rather than to God.

But his speech—the longest, at an hour and 15 minutes, since at least 1972—had relatively little new to offer women, Hispanics, blacks and others who have been turned off by Mr. Trump's incendiary brand of politics.—He did sound like a different sort of Republican at times, though, making no mention of abortion—a core issue for many Republicans—and saying of his support among evangelical voters,— "I'm not sure I totally deserve it." Even Trump himself "questioned whether he deserved support from evangelical voters."

Hillary Clinton is the most qualified in character, academically, and experience. When her resume is compared to Donald Trump's resume, there's absolutely a vast difference; in fact, "there's really no contest!" Trump is substantially below Hillary in every category of comparison; which will certainly, without question be revealed and confirmed further in the upcoming presidential debates.

Donald Trump's call on Russia to find Hillary Clinton's missing emails profoundly shows just how ignorant and totally unfit he is be president. The New York Times article entitled "Donald Trump Calls on Russia to Find Hillary Clinton's Missing Emails" July 27, 2016 by Ashley Parker and David E. Sanger states: "DORAL, Fla.—Donald J. Trump said on Wednesday that he hoped Russian intelligence services had successfully hacked Hillary Clinton's email, and encouraged them to publish whatever they may have stolen, essentially urging a foreign adversary to conduct cyberespionage against a former secretary of state.

"Russia, if you're listening, I hope you're able to find the 30,000 emails that are missing," Mr. Trump said during a news conference here in an apparent reference to Mrs. Clinton's deleted emails. "I think you will probably be rewarded mightily by our press." Mr. Trump's call was another bizarre moment in the mystery of whether Vladimir V. Putin's government has been seeking to influence the United States, presidential race. His comments came amid questions about the hacking of the Democratic National Committee's computer servers, which American intelligence agencies have told the White House they have "high confidence" was the work of the Russian government.

Mr. Trump later tried to modify his remarks about hacking Mrs. Clinton's emails, contending they represented an effort to get the Russians to turn over their trove to the F.B.I. Mr. Trump contended on Wednesday that the political uproar over whether Russia was meddling in the election—was a "total deflection" from the embarrassing content of the emails. Many Republicans, even some who say they do not support Mr. Trump, say they agree.

Almost as soon as Mr. Trump spoke, other Republicans raced in to try to reframe his remarks and argue that Russia should be punished. A spokesman for Speaker Paul D. Ryan termed Russia "a global menace led by a devious thug." The spokesman, Brendan Buck, added: "Putin should stay out of this election." Even Gov. Mike Pence of Indiana, Mr. Trump's running mate, issued a statement, saying that "if it is Russia and they are interfering in our elections, I can assure you both parties and the United States government will ensure there are serious consequences." Shortly after that Mr. Trump sent a message on Twitter declaring "If Russia or any other country or person has Hillary Clinton's 33,000 illegally deleted emails, perhaps they should share them with the FBI!"

The Clinton campaign, eager to turn the subject from the chaos caused by the email release to the question of Russian interference, accused Mr. Trump of encouraging Russian espionage. "This has to be the first time that a major presidential candidate has actively encouraged a foreign power to conduct espionage against his political opponent," said Jake Sullivan, Mrs. Clinton's chief foreign policy adviser, whose emails from when he was a State Department aide were among those that were hacked. "This has gone from being a matter of curiosity, and a matter of politics, to being a national security issue," he added.

For his part, Mr. Trump cast doubt on the conclusion that Russia was behind the hacking. "I have no idea," he said. He said the "sad thing" is that "with the genius we have in government,—we don't even know who took the Democratic National Committee emails." Mr. Trump then argued that if Russia, or any other foreign government, was behind the hacking, it showed just how little respect other nations had for the current administration. "President Trump would be so much better for U.S.-Russian relations" than a President Clinton, Mr. Trump said. "I don't think Putin has any respect whatsoever for Clinton." [End of excerpts from Article]

Donald Trump says he was only kidding when he appeared to encourage Russian intelligence agencies to find Hillary Clinton's thousands of deleted emails. "Of course I'm being sarcastic," Trump said in an interview on Fox News that aired Thursday morning. "You have 33,000 emails deleted, and the real problem is what was said on the emails from the Democratic National Convention."

Just hours after seemingly accepting Sen. Bernie Sanders' challenge for a debate, Donald Trump has already backed out, CBS News reports. On Thursday morning, Trump reportedly said he was just kidding when he agreed on Wednesday night's Jimmy Kimmel Live to face off against Sanders. Trump initially seemed keen on the idea because "it would have such high ratings," and he figured Sanders "would be easier to beat" than Hillary Clinton. Sanders had already agreed to the debate, tweeting he "look[s] forward to debating Donald Trump in California before the June 7 primary." (The Week May 6, 2016)

Donald Trump said in an interview that he was just joking when he made demeaning comments toward women in the past. Trump's comments—in which he degrades, ranks, and rates women—have been used against him by his opponents, even appearing in an attack ad from an anti-Trump super PAC. Trump has previously said he didn't recognize some of his own past comments and dismissed others as part of being in "show business." He told a local Wisconsin television station that he was just joking. Well, number one, I'm no different than anybody else, and people joke, and I joke," Trump said in a phone interview with Wisconsin local FOX 11. "And I never knew I was going to be running for office. And you joke, and you kid and say things, but you're not a politician so you never think anybody cares."

"All of a sudden you decide because the country's doing so badly that you're going to run for office, and then they take every single thing that you've ever said over a lifetime," he continued. "Much of that I said in jest, much of that I said—although with the Fox debate, I didn't say that in jest at all. I said that 100% because Megyn Kelly never treated me fairly and everybody knows it. But you say things, and I guarantee you I'm no different, if anything I'm far better than the people I'm running against." (End of BuzzFeedNews March 28, 2016)

Republican presidential candidate Donald Trump said Tuesday that he was just joking when he said he could shoot somebody and still not lose votes in the 2016 race. Trump told a crowd Saturday at a campaign rally in Iowa that it was "incredible" that he could "stand in the middle of 5th Avenue and shoot somebody and I wouldn't lose any voters." Fox Business Network host Maria Bartiromo asked Trump if he would say such a thing as President. "As President, I wouldn't," Trump said, adding that he has to be "a little bit verbose" because he's running against so many people for the GOP nomination.

"That comment was said with me laughing and thousands of other people laughing.—It was said as a joke—obviously it was a joke," Trump said. Even though the Fox Business host noted that there have been several mass shootings recently, Trump said he thought the comment was appropriate. (TPM January 26, 2016)

[18] Like a madman who throws firebrands, arrows, and death, [19] Is the man who deceives his neighbor, And says, "I was only joking!" (Prov. 26:18-19)

[3] But fornication and all uncleanness or covetousness, let it not even be named among you, as is fitting for saints; [4] neither filthiness, nor foolish talking, nor coarse jesting, which are not fitting, but rather giving of thanks. (Ephes. 5:3-4)

Coarse jesting or crude joking is simply turning a phrase smoothly to a witty or vulgar effect. A nimble-witted person is a versatile person capable of turning with ease one subject into another, being at home or comfortable in all of them. Such a person uses his or her versatile facility to suggest other nuances (subtle differences and/or shades of meaning, expression, or sound) manifested in facial expressions and body languages.

Some coarse jester or crude jokers are very capable of moving very easily into the mire of unbecoming expressions (i.e. a situation or state of difficulty, distress, or embarrassment from which it is hard to extricate oneself). Such persons seem to have a garbage-can type of mind, and every serious topic of conversation reminds them of an off-color jest or anecdote (an account or story regarded as unreliable or heresy).

Donald J. Trump, a coarse jester/crude joker, knew exactly what he said and said exactly what he meant. In every situation where he has placed himself in a state of difficulty, distress, or embarrassment, which he finds hard to extricate (free, disengage, or disentangle) himself, Trump said, "he was only joking;" well, the Bible says one thing and Trump says another thing;—"who are you going to believe?" Donald Trump is a miser (a person who hoards wealth and spends as little money as possible).

> *⁶ Do not eat the bread of a miser, Nor desire his delicacies; ⁷ For as he thinks in his heart, so is he. "Eat and drink!" he says to you, But his heart is not with you. ⁸ The morsel you have eaten, you will vomit up, And waste your pleasant words. (Prov. 23:6-8)*

> *¹⁶ A wise man fears and departs from evil, But a fool rages and is self-confident. ¹⁷ A quick-tempered man acts foolishly, And a man of wicked intentions is hated. (Prov. 14:16-17) ¹ A man who isolates himself seeks his own desire; He rages against all wise judgment. ² A fool has no delight in understanding, But*

in expressing his own heart. (Prov. 18:1-2) ⁹ *If a wise man contends with a foolish man, Whether the fool rages or laughs, there is no peace. (Prov. 29:9)*

WIRED Business article entitled "Buzzfeed Takes A Stand Against Trump, Rejects RNC Ads" June 6, 2016 states: "BUZZFEED CEO Jonah Peretti told employees Monday that the media giant is dropping the Republican National Committee as an advertiser, now that Donald Trump is the party's presumptive nominee. In an email to the staff, Peretti explained the decision, likening Trump ads to cigarette ads.— "We don't run cigarette ads because they are hazardous to our health," Peretti wrote, "and we won't accept Trump ads for the exact same reason."

Peretti took particular issue with Trump's proposed ban on Muslims, his approach to immigration, his comments about women, and his threats to limit the free press. "We certainly don't like to turn away revenue that funds all the important work we do across the company," the email reads. "However, in some cases we must make business exceptions."

Buzzfeed's decision to withdraw from the advertising deal illustrates just how thorny Trump's relationship with the media has become. As the candidate consistently bashes the press as "dishonest" and "disgusting," those same media outlets are struggling to remain unbiased, while also acknowledging that Trump's campaign—and many of its platforms—are anything but normal. Just as Trump is rewriting the rules around how politicians are supposed to behave, he's also rewriting the rules around how responsible journalists need to cover what is a historically incendiary and polarizing candidacy.

Peretti insisted that the advertising decision won't impact Buzzfeed's coverage of Trump, and yet, it's tough not to read this as, well, whatever the opposite of an endorsement is. Buzzfeed is not, however, the first media outlet to take such a public stand. The Huffington Post, which Peretti co-founded with Arianna Huffington, famously published all its early Trump coverage this election cycle under its Entertainment section. By December, it reversed that decision, but now ends its Trump coverage with a note that reads, "Note to our readers: Donald Trump is a serial liar, rampant xenophobe, racist, birther and bully who has repeatedly pledged to ban all Muslims—1.6 billion members of an entire religion—from entering the U.S."

Trump's campaign has also put new media sources, like Facebook, in a tricky position, as the company tries to balance its responsibility as a news source without appearing to back Trump's policies. Earlier this year, Facebook CEO Mark Zuckerberg, an immigration activist, appeared to criticize Trump's plans to build a wall on the Mexican border. Weeks later, when Facebook was accused of suppressing conservative content in its Trending Topics feature, that comment was considered by some to be evidence of Facebook's clear liberal bias.

In a typical election year, it's unlikely these public figures—particularly those in the journalism business—would feel so justified in speaking out against one candidate over another. But with Trump's historically low favorability ratings and his widespread rejection within the Republican Party, it's clear that this is no typical election year. To pretend that it is risks normalizing Trump's most radical ideas. [End of Article]

The year 2016 is absolutely no typical election year; but rather, an election year that Republicans allowed the most unqualified presumptive presidential nominee in U.S. history to become its Party's presidential nominee. The Seven (7) Core Social Values found in the National Republican Platform are: 1) Sanctity of human life (anti-abortion); 2) Protecting Traditional Marriage (anti-same-sex marriage); 3) Supporting the Right to Keep and to Bear Arms (2nd Amendment Rights); 4) Safeguarding Religious Liberties (1st Amendment Rights); 5) Ensuring Equal Treatment of All People (rejecting the forces of hatred and bigotry and in denouncing all who practice or promote racism, anti-Semitism, ethnic prejudice, or religious intolerance); 6) Freedom of Speech and of the Press (opposing any and all attempts to violate or weaken these rights, such as reinstatement of the so-called Fairness Doctrine); and 7) Protecting our National Symbols (the symbol of

America's unity is the flag to which we all pledge allegiance; Old Glory should be given legal protection against desecration; decisions by activist judges to deny children to say the Pledge of Allegiance in public schools is condemned).

Republicans have to be profoundly embarrassed with Trump as their Party's presidential nominee; and many aligning themselves with him are suppressing the truth to back him in efforts of saving the face of the Republican Party. Trump has not voiced and promoted Republican values; simply because he's no Republican, and certainly no conservative Republican. Donald J. Trump is a self-righteous greedy bigot promoting his own selfish values and agenda for his own personal gain. Trump does not care about America and its people; only himself! And that's a fact.

19
Trump's Black Soul

A BLACK SOUL describes an individual who lacks the capacity for empathy and compassion. Cold-heartedness describes being unsympathetic, unfelling, and sometimes even cruel in the process. Such a person disregards feelings of others and acts maliciously towards with behavior practices. A good or normal heart is associated with feelings of tenderness, compassion, and love, which most Americans, and especially Christians, operate their behavior practices from. Cold-heartedness is an abnormal heart condition unbecoming of most Americans, in particularly Christians, who are commanded to love one another and to witness the love of God unto every soul in the world.

The failure to witness the love of God through one's behavior practices is an explicit sign of hatred, which manifests ugliness and cruelty, unsympathetic-ness and insensitive-ness, a total incapableness of showing empathy towards others. There are both Christians and non-Christians with good or normal hearts that just generally treat others with dignity and respect because that's just the right thing to do. Various differences existing in religions and beliefs don't play a factor in treating one another with dignity and respect just as we would want others to treat us and our love ones. We as a people are to live peaceable with one another as much as possible; in order to do so, we all are to refrain from sowing discord that produces strife, contentions, and divisions.

The soul consists of the mind (which includes the conscience), the will and the emotions. The soul and the spirit are mysteriously tied together and make up what the Scriptures call the "heart." The soul and the spirit are the primary immaterial aspects of humanity; while the body is the container that holds them on this earth. These immaterial aspects (the spirit, soul, heart, conscience, mind and emotions) exist beyond the physical lifespan of the human body and are therefore eternal; meaning the soul/spirit will live eternally either in heaven with Jesus or in hell with Satan, the devil. Only the physical material body can be destroyed; however, it also will put on incorruption and immortality in the end. Therefore, understand this: "these immaterial aspects make up the whole personality of a person."

Human beings have a spirit, but we are not spirits; but rather, living souls. The spirit is the element in humanity which gives us the ability to have an intimate relationship with God. The spirit of man is that immaterial part of humanity that "connects" with God, who Himself is Spirit. Humanity is naturally evil and our souls are tainted because of the sin of Adam passed down to all generations. Because our spirits are tainted (contaminated or polluted) with sin, our souls have nothing to draw from our spirits but contaminations or pollutions that fall short of the glory of God.

The contamination or pollution of our spirits can only be cleared-up and healed for service to God by having them born-again of the Holy Spirit, who surgically removes all contaminations or pollutions of our spirits and replaces them with Himself, who is pure and perfect. Once this spiritual surgery has been performed by the Holy Spirit, our souls can then draw from the righteousness of God to perform what is that good and perfect and acceptable will of His. Any soul left without spiritual surgery by the Holy Spirit remains in a contaminated or polluted state; most susceptible and vulnerable to the influences of the devil and his demons.

Donald Trump, unfortunately, is operating from a very dark place. His arrogant-pride behavior has reached levels like none other in these modern times. He has taken mockery and scorning of others to heights that make him most despicable and actually hated by many. There is no such thing as toning it down in his persona (i.e. the aspect of his character that's presented to or perceived by other); simply because, he's too arrogant and overwhelmed with pride about himself. For him to say he's sorry and/or to admit he's made an error is below his character and would be exhibiting a weakness on his behalf that he chooses not doing at this time and may never choose to do so; he just that arrogant and it just doesn't matter to him what others thing.

Donald Trump has demonstrated over and over and again and again that he does have a black soul. Those of us who are Christians should feel very sorry for him, but in no way, should any true genuine Christian show support to him for enabling his cynical behavior practices. He has caused division in America amongst her people and has even caused division in the GOP Party that he represents as its 2016 Presidential Nominee. He has shown himself motivated by self-interest; concerned only with his own interests and typically disregarding accepted or appropriate standards in order to achieve his interests. He is unquestionable distrustful of human sincerity or integrity.

When asked by ABC host George Stephanopoulos about a particularly harsh line in a speech at the Democratic National Convention by Khizr Khan, the father of U.S. Captain Humayun Khan, a Muslim-American soldier who was killed in Iraq, Trump once again showed his arrogant-pride and inability to show empathy before the whole world.

Stephanopoulos said to Trump that Khizr Khan said you have sacrificed nothing and no one. Trump's first response was: "well, that sounds—who wrote that? Did Hillary (Clinton's) scriptwriters write?" Stephanopoulos then asked: "how would you answer that father? What sacrifices have you made for your country?" Trump's second response was: "I think I've made a lot of sacrifices. I work very, very hard. I've created thousands and thousands of jobs, tens of thousands of jobs, built great structures. I've done, I've had tremendous success. I think I've done a lot."

Stephanopoulos then asked: "Those are sacrifices? Trump's third response was: "Oh, sure. I think they're sacrifices. I think when I can employ thousands and thousands of people, take care of their education, take care of so many things, even in military. I mean, I was very responsible, along with a group of people, for getting the Vietnam Memorial built in downtown Manhattan, which to this day people thank me for."

All the things Trump boasts about concerning himself pertaining to his wealth and accomplishments are under MICROSCOPE because of lawsuits against Trump University and his relentless and profound reluctance to release his income tax returns. WE THE PEOPLE have developed an extremely high level of questionability of his honesty and integrity in business practices. Trump's response to our curiosity and right to know is that "his income tax returns are none of our business;" WE THE PEOPLE vehemently refuse accepting his response and demand his Trump University lawsuits be resolved and his income taxes be release immediately. These two (2) issues are vitally important to ensuring our country's security and credibility so that WE THE PEOPLE might avoid a possible catastrophic at Election Day.

WE THE PEOPLE must come together and hold Donald Trump and his Republican Party accountable in doing what is reasonable, sensible, and right for the citizens of America. This is not a matter of what Donald Trump wills to do; but rather, a matter of significant importance of what WE THE PEOPLE will him to do the 2016 Republican Presidential Nominee. WE THE PEOPLE have great need of these two (2) issues being resolved that will give light to his honesty, integrity, credibility, and fitness for the oval office; which Trump is terribly afraid of having either issue resolved because they overlap with one or the other exposing the other. Trump is extremely frightful and he and his Republican party will do all they can to stop the release of his income tax returns. The truth of how Trump has accumulated his wealth lies in his income tax returns. The truth is what Trump is very desperately seeking to hide from WE THE PEOPLE.

There is a story from the Bible that I would like to share with you about a certain rich man with arrogant-pride, who of course, thought more highly of himself than he should have thought; but obviously, being wise in his own eyes, also thought himself as being wiser than anyone else; so wise in himself, no one could tell him anything; his way was the only way. As such, for Trump and others like him (in wealth and/or just in mindset), we sincerely hope this warning will lead to repentance and a new way and outlook on life and those whom we interact with only a daily basis.

> [16] Then He spoke a parable to them, saying: "The ground of a certain rich man yielded plentifully. [17] And he thought within himself, saying, 'What shall I do, since I have no room to store my crops?' [18] So he said, 'I will do this: I will pull down my barns and build greater, and there I will store all my crops and my goods. [19] And I will say to my soul, "Soul, you have many goods laid up for many years; take your ease; eat, drink, and be merry."' [20] But God said to him, 'Fool! This night your soul will be required of you; then whose will those things be which you have provided?' [21] "So is he who lays up treasure for himself, and is not rich toward God." (Lu. 12:16-21)

> [26] For what profit is it to a man if he gains the whole world, and loses his own soul? Or what will a man give in exchange for his soul? (Matt. 16:26) [25] For what profit is it to a man if he gains the whole world, and is himself destroyed or lost? (Lu. 9:25)

> [4] "And I say to you, My friends, do not be afraid of those who kill the body, and after that have no more that they can do. [5] But I will show you whom you should fear: Fear Him who, after He has killed, has power to cast into hell; yes, I say to you, fear Him! (Lu. 12:4-5)

> [19] "Do not lay up for yourselves treasures on earth, where moth and rust destroy and where thieves break in and steal; [20] but lay up for yourselves treasures in heaven, where neither moth

nor rust destroys and where thieves do not break in and steal.
²¹ For where your treasure is, there your heart will be also. (Matt. 6:19-20)

I sincerely hope and pray that the above information, including Scriptural references provide an awakening and urgency for corrective action for those who are in need of guidance unto righteousness in the better interest of their souls. The Bible says: "Whoever loves instruction loves knowledge, But he who hates correction is stupid" (Prov. 12:1). Choosing to be stupid is folly and an unnecessary waste of time; don't let that be you! The soul as with the spirit is the center of many spiritual and emotional experiences.

There are certain ethical and moral core values that are vital to living well in our personal lives and to how we treat others in valuing them as human beings with feelings and emotions just as we have. As such, we serve others through these core values because our conscious convicts us that this is the right thing to do; and that such a thing is pleasing to God who created us all. As human beings, each of us is inherently valuable and deserving of respect. Dignity and humility are invaluable and essential components of acceptable ethical and moral values regardless of race, color, sex, gender, religion, nationality, political or non-political party. Human dignity lives by our ability to meet neighbors as equals irrespective of life circumstances, and the ability to accept the compassion of neighbors in times of need.

Personal core values are those to guide our behaviors and choices. Getting them right prepare us in being swift and focused in our decision-making with clear direction. On the other hand, getting them wrong or leaving them ambiguous causes us constant wonder as to how we got into certain messes. Although we do not have exactly the same core values, these values are the ones that either help or prevent us from determining our surrounding culture. Most of us consciously or unconsciously use our personal core values to select friendships, relationships, business partnerships, and in making other vitally important decisions, such as marriage and managing our personal resources such as time and money; and making our choices during elections.

For many, personal core values are decision guidelines that keep us true to ourselves and out of trouble. Some people are skilled liars. When people are not direct and honest in conversation, especially, when such persons have proven themselves being habitual liars, regardless of party affiliation and no matter how painful, there are certain personal core values that will not allow us to support such a person; in particularly, a person manifesting arrogant-pride and showing no remorsefulness when it's proven certain wrongfulness has occurred.

Diligence is a core value to ensure statements made are substantiated before speaking hastily with assumed absolutes without performing necessary homework or research and considering what's to be said so that it's done in a manner generally acceptable by the people. Since people pay attention to both things said and written, credibility is critical. Therefore, consistency in conversation (both orally and written) should be void of the deadly poison of hypocrisy which corrupts credibility and reputation. Anyone who uses their creativity to make their material compelling so that they can intrigue, entertain, and connect with people by speaking lies in hypocrisy to deceive and mislead should be withdrawn from, repudiated (refused to being accepted or being associated with).

Our core values remind us to disregard foolish and unprofitable things and people. Our brains challenge ridiculous and stupid things when it questions us saying, "Should I do that?" Each of us know personally whether we should or shouldn't, because some of our personally traits like passion, integrity, honesty, and energy don't agree with what we're being asked to do. Therefore, we are not to do something instinctively without due consideration, especially when it has been shown clearly that support for such a cause cannot be support with a clear conscious.

Everyone has to test his or her core values. If you can think of any

Trump's Black Soul

situation where following your core value hurts you rather than helps you; then you need to make adjustment to prevent yourself from being hurt. For example, you might think innovation sounds good until you realize that your life thrives on stability rather than constant change. You have to think it through very carefully. If you cannot identify a legitimate case where the value steers you wrong; you probably have a good core value in this matter. However, if it steers you wrong, your core value on this particular matter is bad; therefore, this should be considered as a fact.

This process in evaluating core values requires focused time and thought; which doesn't have to be done alone, but rather, with someone you trust in being truthful with you. Then, and only then will you get honest feedback and you can help each other in this process. It may require several discussions over a period of time; however, your values may adjust and develop over time just as we all do; so let us embrace the change if it be so necessary for the benefit of ourselves as well as others. As Mahatma Ghandi said, "Your beliefs become your thoughts. Your thoughts become your words. Your words become your actions. Your actions become your habits. Your habits become your values. Your values become your destiny."

The parents of a Muslim American soldier killed in Iraq said on Sunday Donald Trump was a "black soul" unfit for the White House, after he insulted them and suggested he had made sacrifices for the US comparable to their son's. Amid widespread astonishment at the conduct of the Republican presidential nominee, the family of the 27-year-old army captain Humayun Khan, who died in a suicide bombing in 2004, said Trump was morally deficient and incapable of empathy.—"He is totally unfit for the leadership of this beautiful country," said Khizr Khan, Humayun's father.

Khizr Khan told CNN's State of the Union Trump was "totally incapable of empathy", adding: "I want his family to counsel him. Teach him some empathy. He will be a better person, but he is a black soul." Reiterating his wife's explanation that she was too overcome by grief to say anything at the event as planned, Khizr Khan expressed disbelief that Trump still "had to take that shot at her". His wife also has high blood pressure and felt so unsteady she worried she might fall off-stage, he said.

"She said, 'You know my condition—when I see my son's picture I cannot hold myself together,'" said Khan, becoming tearful. "This country holds such a person in the highest regard, and he has no knowledge, no awareness. That is the height of his ignorance." In her article on Sunday, Ghazala Khan wrote: "I cannot walk into a room with pictures of Humayun ... Walking on to the convention stage, with a huge picture of my son behind me, I could hardly control myself." Khizr Khan said Trump lacked both the moral compass and sense of empathy necessary for any president. "This candidate is void of both traits that are necessary for the stewardship of this country," he said.

Trump was sharply criticized by Clinton; Tim Kaine, her running mate; and Bill Clinton, the 42nd US president. Bill Clinton said: "I cannot conceive how you can say that about a Gold Star mother," referring to the award given by the military to mark a death in combat. [End of Excerpts from [The Guardian August 1, 2016]

On Sunday at Imani Temple Ministries in Cleveland Heights, Clinton said: "[Khizr Khan] and his wife stood before our country to tell the story of their son, Capt Khan, who lost his life running toward danger to protect his soldiers. Mr Khan paid the ultimate sacrifice in his family, didn't he? "And what has he heard from Donald Trump? Nothing but insults, degrading comments about Muslims, a total misunderstanding of what made our country great: religious freedom and religious liberty.—It's enshrined in our constitution, as Mr Khan knows because he's actually read it."

Clinton added: "I don't begrudge anyone of any other faith or of no faith at all, but I do tremble before those who would scapegoat other Americans, who would insult people because of their religion, their ethnicity, their disability.—It's just not how I was raised. It's not how I was taught in my church." Later, on the campaign trail, she told reporters: "It's hard to imagine anyone who has ever run to be president of the United States saying any of what [Trump has] said. And the accumulation of it all is just beyond my comprehension." [End of Excerpts from [The Guardian August 1, 2016]

The New York Times article entitled "Donald Trump's Confrontation with Muslim Soldier's Parents Emerges as Unexpected Flash Point" July 31, 2016 states: "Donald J. Trump reeled on Sunday amid a sustained campaign of criticism by the parents of a Muslim American soldier killed by a suicide bomber in Iraq and a rising outcry within his own party over his rough and ethnically charged dismissal of the couple. The confrontation between the parents, Khizr and Ghazala Khan, and Mr. Trump has emerged as an unexpected and potentially pivotal flash point in the general election. Mr. Trump has plainly struggled to respond to the reproach of a military family who lost a son, and has answered their criticism derisively—first implying that Ms. Khan had been forbidden to speak at the Democratic National Convention, then declaring that Mr. Khan had "no right" to question Mr. Trump's familiarity with the Constitution.

And Mr. Trump's usual political tool kit has appeared to fail him. He earned no reprieve with his complaints that Mr. Khan had been unfair to him; on Sunday morning, he claimed on Twitter that Mr. Khan had "viciously attacked" him. Mr. Trump and his advisers tried repeatedly to change the subject to Islamic terrorism, to no avail. Instead, Mr. Trump appeared to be caught on Sunday in one of the biggest crises of his campaign, rivaling the uproar in June after he suggested a federal judge, Gonzalo P. Curiel, was biased because of his Mexican heritage. By going after a military family and trafficking in religious stereotypes, Mr. Trump once again breached multiple norms of American politics, redoubling pressure on his fellow Republicans to choose between defending his remarks or breaking publicly with their nominee.

Mr. Trump also risked reopening controversies related to religious tolerance and military service: His treatment of the Khans has brought on a new wave of criticism of his proposal to ban Muslim immigration, and of his mockery of Senator John McCain's time as a prisoner of war in Vietnam. Democratic leaders and candidates for Congress began over the weekend to call on Republicans to disavow Mr. Trump. And the top two Republicans in Congress, House Speaker Paul D. Ryan and Senator Mitch McConnell, the majority leader, signaled their strong disagreement with Mr. Trump, but stopped short of condemning him in blunt terms.

Hillary Clinton, the Democratic presidential nominee, sternly reprimanded Mr. Trump on Sunday morning, saying at a church in Cleveland that he had answered the Khan family's sacrifice with disrespect for them and for American traditions of religious tolerance. "Mr. Khan paid the ultimate sacrifice in his family, didn't he?" Mrs. Clinton said. "And what has he heard from Donald Trump?—Nothing but insults, degrading comments about Muslims,—a total misunderstanding of what made our country great."

Mrs. Clinton chastised Mr. Trump again on Sunday in Ashland, Ohio, calling his comments part of a disturbing pattern.—"He called Mexicans rapists and criminals," Mrs. Clinton said. "He said a federal judge was unqualified because he had Mexican heritage—someone born in the neighboring state of Indiana.—He's called women pigs.—He's mocked a reporter with a disability." Mr. and Ms. Khan stiffened their denunciation of Mr. Trump on Sunday, saying that he lacked the moral character and empathy to be president. Mr. Khan, who addressed the Democratic National Convention on Thursday, said on "Meet the Press" on NBC that Mr. Trump had shown disrespect to his wife, and he accused Mr. Trump of running a campaign "of hatred, of derision, of dividing us."

In a direct appeal to voters inclined to support Mr. Trump, Mr. Khan pleaded with them to reject his brand of politics. Addressing "patriotic Americans that would probably vote for Donald Trump," Mr. Khan said, "I appeal to them not to vote for hatred, not to vote for fearmongering.—Vote for unity. Vote for the goodness of this country."

And Ms. Khan, in an opinion article published in The Washington Post, rebuked Mr. Trump for suggesting earlier in the weekend that she had not been permitted to speak at the Democratic convention. Ms. Khan said she did not speak because she did not believe she could remain composed while talking about her son.—"All the world, all

America, felt my pain. I am a Gold Star mother. Whoever saw me felt me in their heart," Ms. Khan wrote, using the term for surviving family members of those killed in war. "Donald Trump has children whom he loves. Does he really need to wonder why I did not speak?"

Ms. Khan said Mr. Trump was "ignorant" of Islam and criticized him for offering his business career as evidence that he had sacrificed for his country. "Donald Trump said he has made a lot of sacrifices," Ms. Khan said. "He doesn't know what the word sacrifice means." It is too soon to say how severe the damage to Mr. Trump might be, but the clash has already entangled him in a self-destructive, days-long argument with sympathetic accusers who are portraying him as a person of unredeemable callousness. Still, he has proved remarkably resilient, getting past controversies that might have sunk other candidates.

Several prominent Republicans have condemned Mr. Trump's treatment of the Khans, calling his behavior outside the bounds of political discourse. But Republican congressional leaders responded cautiously to Mr. Trump. Mr. Ryan and Mr. McConnell released statements stressing their admiration for the Khan family; Mr. McConnell called Capt. Humayun Khan an "American hero." And both said they firmly opposed banning Muslim immigration, though neither mentioned Mr. Trump, whom they have endorsed, by name. "Many Muslim Americans have served valiantly in our military, and made the ultimate sacrifice. Captain Khan was one such brave example," Mr. Ryan said. "His sacrifice—and that of Khizr and Ghazala Khan—should always be honored. Period."

Mr. Trump's clash with the Khan family threatens to unwind any progress he may have made at moderating his campaign and rallying his party at the outset of the general election. He has sought to play down his proposal for banning Muslim immigration, focusing on blocking immigration from specific countries instead, but has never disavowed the idea of a religious test. And he has not apologized to the Khans for his comments about Ms. Khan. Those comments have deeply unsettled many leading Republicans. Jeb Bush, the former governor of Florida, and John Kasich, the governor of Ohio, have forcefully expressed disapproval. A spokesman for former President George W. Bush declined to comment directly on Mr. Trump's behavior, but suggested Mr. Bush takes a different view.

"President Bush remains deeply grateful for the sacrifice of all Gold Star families, as we all should be. He thinks about them and prays for them each and every day," said the spokesman, Freddy Ford. Other Republicans went even further in chiding Mr. Trump. Senator Kelly Ayotte of New Hampshire, who is seeking re-election, said the Khans deserved the utmost respect: "I am appalled that Donald Trump would disparage them and that he had the gall to compare his own sacrifices to those of a Gold Star family."

Senator Lindsey Graham, Republican of South Carolina, said on Sunday that Mr. Trump had crossed another inviolable line. Like his comments about Judge Curiel, Mr. Graham said, Mr. Trump's jabs at Mr. and Ms. Khan were unacceptable. — "This is going to a place where we've never gone before, to push back against the families of the fallen," he said. He added, "The problem is, 'unacceptable' doesn't even begin to describe it."

Representative Mike Coffman of Colorado, a Republican who served in combat as a Marine and now represents a crucial swing district in the Denver suburbs, said Mr. Trump had disrespected American troops. "Having served in Iraq, I'm deeply offended when Donald Trump fails to honor the sacrifices of all of our brave soldiers who were lost in that war," Mr. Coffman said. The pressure on Mr. Trump and other Republicans is unlikely to relent soon. But so far he has flailed and faltered in response.

He first criticized Ms. Khan for not speaking alongside her husband, implying that she had been prohibited from doing so. Facing mounting criticism from Democrats and Republicans, he released a follow-up statement on Saturday night, describing the Khans' deceased son as a hero, but insisting that Mr. Khan had "no right" to criticize him the way he did in Philadelphia. He made a third attempt to deflect the Khans' criticism on Sunday, writing on Twitter that the real issue at stake in the election was terrorism. The Republican vice-presidential nominee, Gov. Mike Pence of Indiana, appears to be in a particularly awkward position in the uproar. His son is a Marine, a fact he mentions frequently. Mr. Pence's ability to navigate a racially charged argument between Mr. Trump and a Gold Star family is emerging as his first difficult test as Mr. Trump's running mate.

For most of the weekend, Mr. Pence was silent. His aides referred inquiries to Mr. Trump's staff, and his lone public comment was a Twitter post about getting his hair cut in Indianapolis. Late Sunday, Mr. Pence issued a statement sidestepping Mr. Trump's criticism of the Khans. He expressed appreciation for the family's sacrifice and reiterated his support for blocking immigration "from countries that have been compromised by terrorism." [End of Article]

How long will some people, especially Christians, be caught between two (2) opinions: 1) one being support Trump, and 2) the other being not supporting Trump. It's clearly evident that Trump is operating from a very dark place; and as such, his operations are abominations to God and to mankind. Therefore, what God has created in His own image and likeness is not to be mistreated and scorned as if they're of a lesser or inferior creation; which is, supremacy or racist ideology. The following Scriptures are provided for examination and for consideration:

> [26] Then God said, "Let Us make man in Our image, according to Our likeness; let them have dominion over the fish of the sea, over the birds of the air, and over the cattle, over all the earth and over every creeping thing that creeps on the earth." [27] So God created man in His own image; in the image of God He created him; male and female He created them. (Gen. 1:26-27)

> [7] And the LORD God formed man of the dust of the ground, and breathed into his nostrils the breath of life; and man became a living being. (Gen. 2:7) [18] And the LORD God said, "It is not good that man should be alone; I will make him a helper comparable to him." (Gen. 2:18) [21] And the LORD God caused a deep

*sleep to fall on Adam, and he slept; and He took one of his ribs, and closed up the flesh in its place. ^{22} Then the rib which the L*ORD* God had taken from man He made into a woman, and He brought her to the man. ^{23} And Adam said: "This is now bone of my bones And flesh of my flesh; She shall be called Woman, because she was taken out of Man." ^{24} Therefore a man shall leave his father and mother and be joined to his wife, and they shall become one flesh. (Gen. 2:21-24)*

^{1}I beseech you therefore, brethren, by the mercies of God, that you present your bodies a living sacrifice, holy, acceptable to God, which is your reasonable service. ^{2} And do not be conformed to this world, but be transformed by the renewing of your mind, that you may prove what is that good and acceptable and perfect will of God. (Rom. 12:1-2)

^{18} Flee sexual immorality. Every sin that a man does is outside the body, but he who commits sexual immorality sins against his own body. ^{19} Or do you not know that your body is the temple of the Holy Spirit who is in you, whom you have from God, and you are not your own? ^{20} For you were bought at a price; therefore glorify God in your body and in your spirit, which are God's. (1 Cor. 6:18-20)

*^{23} Keep your heart with all diligence, For out of it spring the issues of life. ^{24} Put away from you a deceitful mouth, And put perverse lips far from you. (Prov. 4:23-24) ^{7} For as he thinks in his heart, so is he. "Eat and drink!" he says to you, But his heart is not with you. (Prov. 23:7) ^{9} "The heart is deceitful above all things, And desperately wicked; Who can know it? ^{10} I, the L*ORD*, search the heart, I test the mind, Even to give every man according to his ways, According to the fruit of his doings. (Jer. 17:9-10)*

¹² *Now we have received, not the spirit of the world, but the Spirit who is from God, that we might know the things that have been freely given to us by God. ¹³ These things we also speak, not in words which man's wisdom teaches but which the Holy Spirit teaches, comparing spiritual things with spiritual. ¹⁴ But the natural man does not receive the things of the Spirit of God, for they are foolishness to him; nor can he know them, because they are spiritually discerned. ¹⁵ But he who is spiritual judges all things, yet he himself is rightly judged by no one. ¹⁶ For "who has known the mind of the LORD that he may instruct Him?" But we have the mind of Christ. (1 Cor. 2:12-16)*

²⁰ *And the LORD spoke to Moses and Aaron, saying, ²¹ "Separate yourselves from among this congregation, that I may consume them in a moment." ²² Then they fell on their faces, and said, "O God, the God of the spirits of all flesh, shall one man sin, and You be angry with all the congregation?" ²³ So the LORD spoke to Moses, saying, ²⁴ "Speak to the congregation, saying, 'Get away from the tents of Korah, Dathan, and Abiram.'" ²⁵ Then Moses rose and went to Dathan and Abiram, and the elders of Israel followed him. ²⁶ And he spoke to the congregation, saying, "Depart now from the tents of these wicked men! Touch nothing of theirs, lest you be consumed in all their sins." (Num. 16:20-26)*

²⁷ *So they got away from around the tents of Korah, Dathan, and Abiram; and Dathan and Abiram came out and stood at the door of their tents, with their wives, their sons, and their little children. ²⁸ And Moses said: "By this you shall know that the LORD has sent me to do all these works, for I have not done them of my own will. ²⁹ If these men die naturally like all men, or if they are visited by the common fate of all men, then the LORD has not sent me. ³⁰ But if the LORD creates a new thing, and the earth opens its mouth and swallows them up with all*

that belongs to them, and they go down alive into the pit, then you will understand that these men have rejected the LORD." (Num. 16:27-30)

³¹ Now it came to pass, as he finished speaking all these words, that the ground split apart under them, ³² and the earth opened its mouth and swallowed them up, with their households and all the men with Korah, with all their goods. ³³ So they and all those with them went down alive into the pit; the earth closed over them, and they perished from among the assembly. ³⁴ Then all Israel who were around them fled at their cry, for they said, "Lest the earth swallow us up also!" ³⁵ And a fire came out from the LORD and consumed the two hundred and fifty men who were offering incense. (Num. 16:31-35)

1 Then Paul, looking earnestly at the council, said, "Men and brethren, I have lived in all good conscience before God until this day." (Acts 23:1) ⁴ God also bearing witness both with signs and wonders, with various miracles, and gifts of the Holy Spirit, according to His own will? (Heb. 2:4)

⁴ For whatever is born of God overcomes the world. And this is the victory that has overcome the world—our faith. ⁵ Who is he who overcomes the world, but he who believes that Jesus is the Son of God? ⁶ This is He who came by water and blood—Jesus Christ; not only by water, but by water and blood. And it is the Spirit who bears witness, because the Spirit is truth. ⁷ For there are three that bear witness in heaven: the Father, the Word, and the Holy Spirit; and these three are one. ⁸ And there are three that bear witness on earth: the Spirit, the water, and the blood; and these three agree as one. (1 Jn. 5:4-8)

⁹ If we receive the witness of men, the witness of God is greater;

for this is the witness of God which He has testified of His Son. ¹⁰ *He who believes in the Son of God has the witness in himself; he who does not believe God has made Him a liar, because he has not believed the testimony that God has given of His Son.* ¹¹ *And this is the testimony: that God has given us eternal life, and this life is in His Son.* ¹² *He who has the Son has life; he who does not have the Son of God does not have life. (1 Jn. 5:9-12)*

⁵ *Jesus answered, "Most assuredly, I say to you, unless one is born of water and the Spirit, he cannot enter the kingdom of God.* ⁶ *That which is born of the flesh is flesh, and that which is born of the Spirit is spirit.* ⁷ *Do not marvel that I said to you, 'You must be born again.'* ⁸ *The wind blows where it wishes, and you hear the sound of it, but cannot tell where it comes from and where it goes. So is everyone who is born of the Spirit." (Jn. 3:5-8)*

¹⁹ *The woman said to Him, "Sir, I perceive that You are a prophet.* ²⁰ *Our fathers worshiped on this mountain, and you Jews say that in Jerusalem is the place where one ought to worship."* ²¹ *Jesus said to her, "Woman, believe Me, the hour is coming when you will neither on this mountain, nor in Jerusalem, worship the Father.* ²² *You worship what you do not know; we know what we worship, for salvation is of the Jews.* ²³ *But the hour is coming, and now is, when the true worshipers will worship the Father in spirit and truth; for the Father is seeking such to worship Him.* ²⁴ *God is Spirit, and those who worship Him must worship in spirit and truth."* ²⁵ *The woman said to Him, "I know that Messiah is coming" (who is called Christ). "When He comes, He will tell us all things."* ²⁶ *Jesus said to her, "I who speak to you am He." (Jn. 4:19-26)*

¹⁸ *We know that whoever is born of God does not sin; but he*

> *who has been born of God keeps himself, and the wicked one does not touch him. [19] We know that we are of God, and the whole world lies under the sway of the wicked one. [20] And we know that the Son of God has come and has given us an understanding, that we may know Him who is true; and we are in Him who is true, in His Son Jesus Christ. This is the true God and eternal life. [21] Little children, keep yourselves from idols. Amen. (1 Jn. 5:18-21)*

The soul is the breath of God that makes the lifeless dust of the ground a living being or person. The soul is the immortal part of a man that lives on after physical death. A mortal person is a living soul rather than having a soul. As God is a tripartite (Father, Son, and Holy Spirit); so is man made in the image of God a tripartite (body, soul, and spirit). Every soul is precious and valuable in the eyes of God; if it was not so, He would not have given His only begotten Son Jesus Christ—to die on the Cross at Calvary for the sins of mankind. Therefore, we all should be careful in how we treat others whom God loves; advise worth heeding to!

Donald Trump is a black soul out of control; no doubt confused and having serious behavior issues detrimental to himself, his party, his supporter, and all who may be seriously seeking to help him in one way or another. However, supporting him wickedness is not what anyone who care for him and America as his or her country should consciously do before God.

20

Republicans Disavowing or Repudiating Donald Trump

KHAN ADDRESSED REPUBLICAN nominee Donald Trump directly in his speech, asking if he'd read the U.S. Constitution and telling him, forcefully, "You have sacrificed nothing and no one." In an interview with MSNBC, Khan implored Republican leaders to "repudiate Trump," specifically addressing Senate Majority Leader Mitch McConnell and House Speaker Paul Ryan. Khan said, "Isn't this time to repudiate Trump—what he has said, what he has threatened to do?" Khan further said, "This is a moral imperative for both leaders to say to him that, 'Enough. You are about to sink the ship of the patriot Republicans. Republicans are as patriotic as Democrats are. They are half of the goodness of this beautiful country, half of this political process that the rest of the world watches enviously, learns from it."

Media figures are criticizing Republican leaders, including House Speaker Paul Ryan (R-WI), Senate Majority Leader Mitch McConnell (R-KY), and Sen. John McCain (R-AZ), for refusing to rescind endorsing Republican presidential nominee Donald Trump while condemning his attacks on the Khans, an American Muslim family whose son was killed in action in Iraq in 2004. Media critics are calling the statements refusing to flat-out disavow Trump—"acts of cowardice,"—"less than worthless," and "empty words."

John McCain stated: "Arizona is watching. It is time for Donald Trump to set the example for our country and the future of the Republican Party. While our party has bestowed upon him the nomination, it is not accompanied by unfettered license to defame those who are the best among us." McConnell wrote: "All Americans should value the patriotic service of the patriots who volunteer to selflessly defend us in the armed services. And as I have long made clear, I agree with the Khans and families across the country that a travel ban on all members of a religion is simply contrary to American values. Ryan followed with a similar response saying: "America's greatness is built on the principles of liberty and preserved by the men and women who wear the uniform to defend it. As I have said on numerous occasions, a religious test for entering our country is not reflective of these fundamental values. I reject it."

Slate's Jamelle Bouie: Republican Leaders' Continued Endorsements of Trump Are "At Worst … Acts of Cowardice." Slate chief political correspondent Jamelle Bouie wrote that the statements had "no bite" because these Republican leaders were not "prepared to withdraw [their] endorsement[s] or add any conditions to [their] support." Bouie added that "At best, these half-measures are a failure of political imagination" and "At worst, they are acts of cowardice." Nevertheless, these Republican leaders refuse to disavow their presidential nominee.

The Republican Party is playing cowardly political gamesmanship when it disavows Trump's racist and destructive rhetoric, but willing to endorse him as the Republican nominee, but not disavow him for his racist, xenophobic (intense or irrational dislike or fear of people from other countries), and his inability to show empathy and the temperament to hold the highest office in the land. Maybe, just maybe, Trump is doing what he is doing because he is actually standing on a platform of hate that the Republican Party built for him, as pointed out by Senator Harry Reid.

The Republican Party has a long history of using race-based rhetoric and dog whistle politics to get votes and pander to the nativist and racist elements of its base. No, Donald Trump is not an isolated phenomenon; while extreme, Trump's platform of hate is neither new nor unprecedented. What has happened with Trump is that he is a run-away-train the GOP assumed it could control to get him in the oval office to accomplish their objectives; didn't work! The GOP experienced a similar situation or circumstance with its Tea Party, a new born baby that also acted like a run-away-train out of control rebelling against its own parent body, just as Donald Trump is currently doing.

The GOP or Republican Party is without question, confused and divided without any remedy for restoration in the near future. When Trump first proposed a ban on all Muslims entering the United States, his rivals and other Republican leaders were quick to denounce this plan. However, what they failed in doing was renouncing his candidacy for president. Speaker of the House Paul Ryan specifically said: "I'm going to support whoever the Republican nominee is and I'm going to stand up for what I believe in as I do that." Speaker Rayan was not alone; every Republican presidential contender remained true to the pledge they made this summer, under pressure from Republican National Committee Chair Reince Priebus, to support whoever ends up being the nominee. Senate Majority Leader Mitch McConnell criticized Trump's proposal but said nothing about his candidacy.

In the last few years, Republicans in Congress have refused to fix the Supreme Court's gutting of the Voting Rights Act and have blocked all attempts to pass comprehensive immigration reform. Trump's rivals for the 2016 Republican presidential nomination, Republicans in Congress, and Republican governors have all taken xenophobic stands against Muslim refugees fleeing horrific violence in the Middle East. These positions and policies are in line with the beliefs of many in the Republican Party's base. A recent Bloomberg poll found that 65% of likely Republican voters support Trump's plan to ban Muslims from entering the United States. Historic national polling data shows that people who identify as Republicans consistently hold more racist views about African-Americans than people who identify as Democrats.

WE THE PEOPLE are no longer blind of the facts and seek even more seriously than ever before no longer being deceived and discriminated against. The leaders of the Republican Party have a very important choice before them. They can pander (gratify or indulge) to their party's racist base and legitimize the politics of hate by failing to disavow or repudiate Trump's presidential nomination and show that their party is actually better than that; or they can continue showing their support and endorsement of Trump as it presidential nominee.

By doing the latter, the GOP is gratifying or indulging an immoral or distasteful desire, need, or habit, or a person with such a desire, in this case, Donald J. Trump. It is now encumbered upon the Republican Party to show WE THE PEOPLE that it's not a party of hate, as demonstrated by its presidential nominee, by withdrawing their individual pledges to support the Republican presidential nominee. It's time now to either put-up or shut-up; and the rest of the story we all will know for a fact.

Unease about Trump has already drawn a number of big names from Republican ranks to support Clinton. The Daily Beast offers this first definitive list of GOP bigwigs and former GOP officials, business leaders, thinkers and foreign policy analysts, some less well known than others, but indicative of what could be a stampede by November. Other informational sources have also provided GOP members disavowing or repudiating Trump as reflected as following:

Republican U.S. Sen. Mark Kirk said he "cannot and will not support" Donald Trump as the GOP's presidential nominee, citing Trump's "past attacks on Hispanics, women and the disabled like himself." Kirk further stated: "It is absolutely essential that we are guided by a commander in chief with a responsible and proper temperament, discretion and judgment. Our president must be fit to command the most powerful military the world has ever seen, including an arsenal of thousands of nuclear weapons." Sen. Mark Kirk who suffered a stroke in 2012, said finally; "After much consideration, he has concluded that Trump has not demonstrated the temperament necessary to assume the greatest office in the world."

No one has gone after Trump harder than Katie Packer, Mitt

Romney's 2012 deputy campaign manager and the co-founder of Burning Glass Consulting, a firm aimed at shedding the GOP's rep as the party of angry old white men. A proud #NeverTrump-er, Packer launched the anti-Trump Our Principles PAC back in January. Even now, her Twitter feed is awash in Trump-smacking commentary. When the Donald says something sexist or stupid, Packer is near the front of the line to kick him for it.

Packer stated: "My best hope is that the entire Republican Party is not tainted by his sexist, racist, irresponsible rhetoric. I hope that independent women and soft R and D women will see that there are Republicans who share their concerns about the dangers of Donald Trump. The party is divided. They aren't fooling anyone. I don't support Donald Trump. And I don't feel I'm obligated to do so. However, I will do everything I can to help down ballot candidates avoid being tainted by Trump. But I don't feel any obligation to support a candidate for president who I think is so dangerous for the country and the party."

Packer stated previously: "If we nominate Trump, [the party] is lost beyond this cycle. I think we lose women for a generation, in big numbers; says Packer, who has spent $10 million through Our Principles super PAC in an effort to stop Trump. "There's a feeling among Republican women that I talk to that the people who would nominate this guy don't have any real respect for us as women—especially professional women. They would rather see us in a "Mad Men" era, where women knew their place and catered to their husband, cooked dinner and met their sexual obligations and didn't have any other role in society. And there are other people who are supporting him because the guy's a blatant racist and they identify with that. "So there's a sense that, if this is who my party is, I don't really identify with it anymore."

According to The Resurgent, Packer's goal is now to make sure voters hear the insanity of Trump's own words: "Data has shown that when Trump is attacked, his voters just lock down harder for him. But when, instead of attacking Trump, voters just hear him in his own words directly contradicting everything he says, not only do some voters flee Trump, but undecided voters immediately decide against Trump."

Brent Scowcroft, foreign policy adviser to four GOP presidents, said that Clinton "has the wisdom and experience to lead our country at this critical time."

Henry Paulson Jr. former treasury secretary under President George W. Bush, said "Enough is enough. It's time to put country before party and say it together: Never Trump."

Richard Armitage, former deputy secretary of state to George W. Bush, told Politico, "If Donald Trump is the nominee, I would vote for Hillary Clinton."

Ken Adelman, U.S. Arms Control director under Ronald Reagan, said "Not only am I not voting for Donald Trump, but also I am not voting for any Republican who endorsed or supported Trump."

Dr. Patrick Cronin, senior official at USAID during the W. Bush administration, who said, "Only one candidate has thought through America's challenges… and is ready to be president, and I intend to vote for her—Hillary Clinton."

Philip Levy, member of President George W. Bush's Council of Economics Advisors, said, "Never Trump and I meant it. If Secretary Clinton is the only viable alternative, I would expect to support her."

Tony Fratto, W. Bush administration deputy press secretary said, "I'd prefer to have Hillary Clinton in the White House than Donald Trump."

Kori Schake, former George W. Bush National Security official, said she is voting for @HillaryClinton.

Jim Cicconi, former White House staffer under Presidents Reagan and H.W. Bush, said in a statement, "Hillary Clinton is experienced, qualified, and will make a fine president. The alternative, I fear, would set our nation on a very dark path."

Alan Steinberg, Bush administration regional EPA administrator, who worked with Clinton when she was New York senator, is voting for her and said, "She can work with people on the opposite side of the political aisle."

Doug Elmets, former Reagan White House staffer, who worked with conservative icons Lee Atwater and Ed Rollins, said, "I can live with four years of Hillary Clinton before I could ever live with one day of Donald Trump as president." This will be his first vote ever for a Democrat.

Max Boot, author and military historian, told Vox, "I am literally losing sleep over Donald Trump." A lifelong Republican, he said he would vote for Hillary Clinton.

Retired Army Col. Peter Mansoor, former aide to David Petraeus, now a professor of military history at Ohio State University, told The Washington Post he thinks Trump is too dangerous to be president, and that Clinton will be "the first Democratic presidential candidate I've voted for in my adult life."

Tom Nichols, Military College Professor and former GOP congressional staffer, @RadioFreeTom calls Clinton "a far more plausible Commander in Chief. And that's all that matters now."

Marc Andreesen, Silicon Valley venture capitalist and former Romney donor, said the idea of cutting off the flow of immigrants "makes me sick," tweeting "#imwithher."

Dan Akerson former General Motors CEO, says Clinton has "the experience and judgment to serve as an effective Commander in chief. In this election, I will cast my ballot for Secretary Clinton."

Hamid Moghadam, Prologis CEO and immigrant from post-revolutionary Iran, says America is about tolerance and inclusion "and that's why, as a lifelong Republican supporter, I endorse Hillary Clinton for president in this election."

Douglas Brand, professor of political science at the College of Holy Cross, wrote in Fortune Magazine, "To support Trump, we must sacrifice our principles and reconcile our minds to his. Better we should follow Hamilton's example and support an opposing party whose principles we reject—and remain a principles party of opposition."

Michael Vlock, Connecticut investor who has given nearly $5 million to Republicans in last two years, told The New York Times he won't donate to Trump because "he is too selfish, flawed and unpredictable to hold the power of the presidency."

William Oberndorf, California-based investor, who gave $3 million to Republicans in the last four years, told The New York Times that Trump is so unacceptable that he would vote for Clinton.

Mike Fernandez, a healthcare magnate and one of Jeb Bush's billionaires in Florida, told the Miami Herald if the choice is between Trump and Clinton, "I'm choosing Hillary."

Robert Smith, conservative former New York Supreme Court judge (and father of BuzzFeed editor-in-chief Ben Smith), says he's voting for a Democrat for president; it's "the first time I've done it in 36 years, and I think the decision is easy. Hillary Clinton is the only responsible choice."

Dan Webb, former U.S. attorney, told The Chicago Sun-Times that Trump is "not fit to be president" and he thinks "a huge volume of Republicans" are saying the same thing. He urged them to "get off the sidelines, give Hillary some money and support her because we can't afford to let him become president."

Larry Pressler, former South Dakota Republican senator, endorsed Clinton after the mass shooting in Orlando, citing her support for gun safety measures. "If someone had told me 10 years ago I would do this, I wouldn't have believed them," he told The Hill.

Arne Carlson, former Minnesota Republican governor, worked with Clinton when she was first lady and praised her for doing "something first ladies since Eleanor Roosevelt haven't done. And that was engage in public policy... She really drove the healthcare debate, and that was the first concerted effort to demonize her, orchestrated by the insurance companies."

Mark Salter, former top advisor to Sen. John McCain, told Real Clear Politics that Trump "possesses the emotional maturity of a 6-year-old," and that he "views the powers of the presidency as weapons to punish people who've been mean to him—reporters, rival candidates, critics."

Jamie Weinstein, Daily Caller editor, said that if it's Trump-Hillary with no serious third-party option, "there is just no question: I'd take a Tums and cast my ballot for Hillary."

Mike Treiser, former Romney staffer, wrote on Facebook, "In the face of bigotry, hatred, violence, and small-mindedness, this time, I'm with her."

Evan Siegfried, Republican strategist, told the New York Daily News, "I'm voting for GOP candidates in other races. But for the good of the country, I must do the unthinkable and say, I'm with her."

Mark Lenzi, former spokesman for the New Hampshire GOP, told Manchester television station WMUR that he "wrestled with the decision for a long time" but as a former U.S. Fulbright Scholar on NATO, he finds Trump's views toward Europe and our NATO allies dangerous. "There is a palpable fear in these countries about him becoming president."

Craig Snyder, Republican lobbyist with Ikon Public Affairs, wrote in an email to fellow former staffers of the late Pennsylvania Sen Arlen Specter, "I've been a Republican since high school and certainly never thought I would take any sort of public role in a Democratic presidential campaign, but I never imagined Donald Trump as the Republican nominee."

Rick Wilson, Republican operative: "I will never vote for Donald Trump, not even if he's the Republican nominee. I will never vote for Donald Trump, not even if Ronald Reagan and William F. Buckley rise from the grave and beg me to support him. I will never vote for Donald Trump, not even if it means he forms a third party and runs as the narcissist sociopath he truly is."

Former Sen. Mel Martinez (R-Fla.): "I would not vote for Trump, clearly" he said, according to reporting by the Wall Street Journal. "If there is any, any, any other choice, a living, breathing person with a pulse, I would be there."

Former Sen. Norm Coleman (R-M.N.), Congressional Leadership Fund chairman: In an op-ed for The Star Tribune called Trump a "misogynist," "bigot," "fraud" and a "bully" as he described why he would never vote for the real estate mogul. Who my choice may be, I know it will never be Donald Trump."

Former Rep. Ron Paul (R-TX): When asked on CNBC's Squawk Box if he would support Donald Trump if he were the Republican nominee, Paul chucked. "No, I wouldn't support him, at all," Paul said, calling Trump's populist-appealing, immigrant-blaming rhetoric "nonsense" and stating that while Trump's approach might be different, his policies mostly align with the establishment GOP policies Paul has eschewed. "In some places, he's worse than the establishment. He loves torture!" Paul said.

President Obama said that Republican presidential nominee Donald Trump is "unfit to serve as president." In a press conference with Singapore's prime minister, Obama added that Trump has shown he is not up to the task, in light of his handle on foreign affairs and his comments on military families. "The notion that he would attack a Gold Star family that made such extraordinary sacrifices on behalf of our country, the fact that he doesn't appear to have basic knowledge around critical issues in Europe, in the Middle East, in Asia means that he is woefully unprepared to do this job," the president said at the White House.

Western Journalism article entitled "Black Female Speaks Out about Working for Trump Family" May 3, 2016 states: "Lynne Patton had had enough, so she decided to lay out exactly what she thought about Republican presidential candidate Donald Trump. Patton, who is black, shared her judgments in a letter she read on a YouTube video, which has more than 127,000 views.

"I can no longer remain silent about the repeated and reprehensible attempts to align my boss and his family with racist hate-mongering groups, campaigns and messaging," wrote Patton, director of the Eric Trump Foundation and assistant to Eric Trump, Ivanka Trump and Donald Trump Jr. She said the video was not part of her employment but was triggered by the reaction Trump has received during his campaign.

"To the skeptics who will undoubtedly claim that I am doing this at the behest of the Trump family or with the promise of reward, I deliberately chose not to seek their approval nor council in advance to this video for fear that there would be more concern for me and its potential viral ramifications than they would be for themselves and the fact that quite simply this is the right thing to do," said Patton, who posted the video on YouTube and has been flooded with comments on Twitter.

"The Trump family that I know is, without question, one of the most generous, compassionate and philanthropic families I've ever had the privilege of knowing and the honor to call friends," she said. "They have been incredibly loyal to me and to the countless dedicated people they employ around the world—hiring more minority and female executives than any other company for which I've ever worked."

Patton defended Trump's policies for a temporary ban on Muslims entering the U.S. and the construction of a wall with Mexico. "To equate racism with my boss' call for a temporary moratorium on a flawed immigration system that radical Islamic terrorists continue to exploit, or the construction of an impassible wall to protect our borders from the influx of illegal drugs, is not only incendiary, it's wholly irresponsible and only serves to embolden the very hatred these draconian groups espouse," she wrote, later criticizing "paid protesters" who target Trump. [End of Letter]

21

Clinton's E-mail Server Issue Resolved

HILLARY CLINTON HAS been relentlessly loving, kind, and uncontroversial over her life-time. She has taken the core values instilled in her from her family and invested them as a public servant for more than four (4) decades. In the process she has made some mistakes in her efforts in service; but such mistakes have never been willfully and intentionally to the detriment of others. Her record as a public servant has proven her commitment, loyalty, honesty, and integrity in discharging her duties. The United States of America could not have been blessed more than having Hillary Clinton as one of her own.

Her personality traits personify her Christian status as she manifests behavior practices becoming of a moral, caring, and loving person. Regardless of her challenges over the years, she has remained sober, vigilant, steadfast and unmovable in her faith through her sufferings and adversities. But through it all, after suffering for a while, the God of all grace, who is able to do exceedingly abundantly above all any of us can ask or think, did as He promised in perfecting, establishing, strengthening, and settling her to get her where she is this day (the Democratic Presidential Nominee), according to His will and purpose for her and WE THE PEOPLE.

She has not been perfect in everything; just as none of us have

Clinton's E-mail Server Issue Resolved

been perfect in all that we do. But, perfection is always to be every Christian's goal; especially, making sure God's royal law of love is manifested to every person, regardless of race, color, gender, religion, political or non-political preference, national origin, or disability or non-disability; **simply because** that's what genuine love does, as Hillary Clinton has so graciously and patriotically demonstrated as an American public servant.

As such, in performing her duties as a public servant, she like many others in the process have made some mistakes, which she has admitted and has also been required to give an account before the United States Congress. Congressional inquiries are now over; and all investigations concerning issues of controversy by the Republican Party have been concluded and decisions have been rendered to close out any outstanding issues of concern entered by the Republican Party. Therefore, it's past time to let these issues rest in their resolved states and go forward with matters needing some current resolve.

The FBI's investigation of Secretary Clinton's use of a personal e-mail system during her time as Secretary of State was initiated by a referral from the Intelligence Community Inspector General; which focused on whether classified information was transmitted on that personal system. The FBI's investigation was performed to determine: 1) whether there is evidence classified information was improperly stored or transmitted on that personal system, 2) in violation of a federal statute making it a felony to mishandle classified information either intentionally or in a grossly negligent way, or 3) a second statute making it a misdemeanor to knowingly remove classified information from appropriate systems or storage facilities, and 4) whether there is evidence of computer intrusion in connection with the personal e-mail server by any foreign power, or other hostile actors.

FBI Director James B. Comey (a former Republican; now Libertarian) has stated the investigation was a painstaking undertaking requiring thousands of hours of effort. The FBI investigators read all of the approximately 30,000 e-mails provided by Secretary Clinton to the State Department in December 2014. The FBI also discovered several thousand work-related e-mails that were not in the group of 30,000 that were returned by Secretary Clinton to State in 2014. The FBI found "no evidence" that any of the additional work-related e-mails were intentionally deleted in an effort to conceal them.

The FBI also found that the lawyers doing the sorting for Secretary Clinton in 2014 did not individually read the content of all of her e-mails, as we did for those available to us; instead, they relied on header information and used search terms to try to find all work-related e-mails among the reportedly more than 60,000 total e-mails remaining on Secretary Clinton's personal system in 2014. The FBI also conducted interviews and done technical examination to attempt to understand how that sorting was done by her attorneys.

The FBI findings of fact are as follows: 1) With respect to potential computer intrusion by hostile actors, we did not find direct evidence that Secretary Clinton's personal e-mail domain, in its various configurations since 2009, was successfully hacked; 2) With respect to evidence of potential violations of the statutes regarding the handling of classified information, our judgment is that no reasonable prosecutor would bring such a case; 3) With respect to the mishandling or removal of classified information, no case could be found that would support bringing criminal charges on these facts.

FBI Director James B. Comey concluded that all cases prosecuted involved some combination of: 1) clearly intentional and willful mishandling of classified information; or 2) vast quantities of materials exposed in such a way as to support an inference of intentional misconduct; or 3) indications of disloyalty to the United States; or efforts to obstruct justice. None of these three (3) things were found in Hillary Clinton's case.

FBI Director James B. Comey also concluded that although there was evidence of potential violations of the statutes regarding the handling of classified information, our judgment is that no reasonable prosecutor would bring such a case. Prosecutors necessarily weigh a number of factors before bringing charges. There are obvious considerations, like the strength of the evidence, especially regarding intent.

Clinton's E-mail Server Issue Resolved

Responsible decisions also consider the context of a person's actions, and how similar situations have been handled in the past.

FBI Director James B. Comey finally concluded that the Department of Justice makes final decisions on matters like this, and that the FBI was expressing to Justice its view that no charges are appropriate in this case. Comey stated he knew there would be intense public debate in the wake of the FBI's decision, as there was throughout this investigation. He said, however, what he can assure the American people is that this investigation was done competently, honestly, and independently; no outside influence of any kind was brought to bear.

. What I can assure the American people is that this investigation was done competently, honestly, and independently. No outside influence of any kind was brought to bear.

Comey further concluded that he knew there were many opinions expressed by people who were not part of the investigation, including people in government, but none that mattered to the FBI. Opinions are irrelevant, and they were all uninformed by insight into our investigation, because we did the investigation the right way. Only facts matter and the FBI found them here in an entirely apolitical and professional way. I couldn't be prouder to be part of this organization."

The Republican Party has profoundly refused to accept the findings of this e-mail server investigation by the FBI and its recommendation to the Department of Justice and the Department of Justice's decision to adopt the FBI's recommendation and make it final. This means it's over! Finalized by procedure of law! She has been cleared and this matter is moot!

The problem with Republicans is their malicious refusal in accepting the findings of the FBI and the Department of Justice's final action; wherein, rebelling for the sake of rebellion because of their vehement objection to the outcome of the investigation. And no wonder; this same unbecoming attitude and behavior practice was manifested when President Abraham Lincoln signed Emancipation Proclamation on January 1, 1863 that declared "that all persons held as slaves" within the rebellious states "are, and henceforward shall be free."

Racist whites vehemently refused to accept and abide by this 1863 federal order from the President of the United States of America. Racist whites had already individually declared their secession from the U.S. and formed the Confederate States of America. The Civil War broke out in April 1861 and ended in 1865; leaving some 620,000 to 750,000 soldiers dead and millions more injured; in an effort by racist whites to keep blacks enslaved and under their power and control. And of course, we all know that racist whites' aggression and cruelty towards blacks didn't stop at the end of the Civil War. These racist people couldn't get it out of their system in having to let blacks go free; regardless of what the law had declared. These racist whites have continued in their rebellion until this very day.

Although the FBI found some deficiencies or discrepancies in Secretary Clinton's use of a personal e-mail system during her time as Secretary of State, the FBI concluded there was evidence that Clinton and her staff were extremely careless in their handling of very sensitive, highly classified information. The FBI also developed evidence that the security culture of the State Department in general, and with respect to use of unclassified e-mail systems in particular, was generally lacking in the kind of care for classified information found elsewhere in the government; mandating the FBI to make recommendations for improvements in the process, as most every investigation does regardless of investigators.

It should be noted: the slightest handling of any very sensitive highly classified information would be rated extremely carless, even if "it was only 1 email out of 50,000 emails that was rated very sensitive highly classified information; which would have equated to .002% of a 50,000 emails handled. The FBI's extremely careless rating is not to be over-emphasized.

WE THE PEOPLE should access a reasonable judgment on this matter through understanding the amount of responsibility as Secretary of State, and the amount of error she implemented as opposed to her accomplishments for our country as Secretary of State. And furthermore, the bottom line is that she jeopardized our country and its people in any manner. Fortunately, what might have possibly happen if this or that had happened didn't happen; and that's the bottom line; case closed! WE THE PEOPLE accept the facts and are now ready to move on from this e-mail issue!

Forward Progressives article entitled "In Brilliant Letter, Lifelong Republican Resigns from Position after Donald Trump Nomination" June 23, 2016 by Allen Clifton states: "Donald Trump's rise from a joke candidate to the Republican party's presidential nominee has been one of the most "interesting" processes we've seen in modern political history. On one hand, he set a record for the number of votes received by any Republican candidate in history. On the other hand, more people actually voted against him than for him, and he's pushed the GOP to the verge of total collapse.

It really has been rather remarkable to see someone become a presidential nominee while simultaneously being the most popular *and* hated candidate in the party. While the Republican Party itself will obviously back him and claim that they hope he becomes our next president—we all know that's not really true. It's actually been kind of funny to sit back and watch Republicans force themselves to act as if they're glad Donald Trump is the party's candidate. However, beyond the thinly veiled "party unity," some Republicans have flat-out refused to endorse Trump—while others have actually *left* the party altogether.

Take for instance lifelong Republican Chris Ladd who resigned from his position as a precinct committeeman for the York Township Republican Organization in a brilliant letter where he absolutely trashed what the GOP has become. Normally this wouldn't be something I'd write about considering this is just one random Republican resigning from a conservative organization most people have probably never heard of. However, this letter is absolutely amazing. Here are a few excerpts:

"We come together in political parties to magnify our influence. An organized representative institution can give weight to our will in ways we could not accomplish on our own. Working with others gives us power, but at the cost of constant, calculated compromise. No two people will agree on everything. There is no moral purity in politics. At the national level, the delusions necessary to sustain our Cold War coalition were becoming dangerous long before Donald Trump arrived. From tax policy to climate change, we have found ourselves less at odds with philosophical rivals than with the fundamentals of math, science and objective reality.

The Iraq War, the financial meltdown, the utter failure of supply-side theory, climate denial, and our strange pursuit of theocratic legislation have all been troubling. Yet it seemed that America's party of commerce, trade, and pragmatism might still have time to sober up. Remaining engaged in the party implied a contribution to that renaissance, an investment in hope. Donald Trump has put an end to that hope. From his fairy-tale wall to his schoolyard bullying and his flirtation with violent racists, Donald Trump offers America a singular narrative—a tale of cowards. Fearful people, convinced of our inadequacy, trembling before a world alight with imaginary threats, crave a demagogue. Neither party has ever elevated to this level a more toxic figure, one that calls forth the darkest elements of our national character.

Trump is not merely a poor candidate, but an indictment of our character. Preserving a party is not a morally defensible goal if that party has lost its legitimacy. Our leaders' compromise preserves their personal capital at our collective cost. Their refusal to dissent robs all Republicans of moral cover. Evasion and cowardice has prevailed over conscience. We are now, and shall indefinitely remain, the Party of Donald Trump. I will not contribute my name, my work, or my character to an utterly indefensible cause. No sensible adult demands moral purity from a political party, but conscience is meaningless without constraints. A party willing to lend its collective capital to Donald Trump has entered a compromise beyond any credible threshold of legitimacy. There is no redemption in being one of the "good Nazis.""[End of Letter]

I've seen a lot of people write things about the GOP, Donald Trump and how the Republican Party is essentially "dead;" and this is probably one of the best summaries of the entire Trump situation and what it means for the party. Reading Ladd's words, you could feel the frustration, anger and disgust that's clearly been building inside of him for decades as he's witnessed his party transform into essentially nothing more than a hate group. [End of Article]

WE THE PEOPLE truly thank Mr. Lade for sharing his heart with us, and we sincerely hope that this very valuable information he has shared be utilized by WE THE PEOPLE of the United States of America in making our choices in November 2016 in selecting our next President and congressional members and other officials on the city, state, and federal levels. WE THE PEOPLE cannot and must not have a demagogue (a political leader who seeks support by appealing to popular desires and prejudices rather than by using rational argument) for any office, especially, for the office of President of the United States of America.

WE THE PEOPLE must do what required of every patriotic American citizen having knowledge of the facts; that which Trump's own Republican leadership has unpatriotically refused to do; that which Khizi Khan, the father of U.S. Captain Humayun Khan, a Muslim-American soldier who was killed in Iraq asked Republican leaders, in particularly, House Speaker Paul D. Ryan and Majority Leader Mitch McConnell to do; WE THE PEOPLE must disavow or repudiate Donald Trump with the power of our votes in November 2016; and furthermore, WE THE PEOPLE must ensure anyone who supports Donald Trump is repudiated or disavowed.

In November 2106, WE THE PEOPLE of the United States, in Order to form a more perfect Union, establish Justice, insure domestic Tranquility, provide for the common defence, promote the general Welfare, and secure the Blessings of Liberty to ourselves and our Posterity, must vote Hillary Clinton for the 45th President of the United States of America.

22

Clinton's Benghazi Issue Resolved

CNN POLITICS, JUNE 28, 2016 article entitled Benghazi panel caps 2-year probe: No bombshell, faults administration by states: "Washington (CNN) House Republicans capped a partisan, two-year investigation of the Benghazi terror attacks Tuesday with a report that faults the Obama administration for security lapses that led to the deaths of four Americans but contains no revelations likely to further damage Hillary Clinton.

The more than 800-page report paints a picture of a perfect storm of bureaucratic inertia, rapidly worsening security in Libya and inadequate resources in the months that led up to the killings of Ambassador Chris Stevens and three colleagues on September 11, 2012. The administration initially claimed the attack was carried out by an angry mob responding to a video made in the U.S. mocking Islam and the Prophet Mohammed. But the assault was later determined to be a terrorist attack—a finding Republicans accused the White House of covering up to protect President Barack Obama's re-election prospects.

The House Benghazi Committee report doesn't directly blame Clinton, who was secretary of state at the time and is now the presumptive Democratic presidential nominee, for the attacks. But it does suggest she and other administration officials did not adequately address the risks involved. It also suggests Stevens himself bore responsibility for securing his post. When it comes to Clinton, the report stresses that intelligence was available suggesting an attack was possible and she and a top aide, Patrick Kennedy, should have realized the risks posed to the Benghazi mission by extremist groups.

"It is not clear what additional intelligence would have satisfied either Kennedy or the Secretary in understanding the Benghazi mission compound was at risk—short of an attack," the report says. Clinton told the House Benghazi Committee last year that she was aware of the dangers in Libya but "there was no actionable intelligence" indicating a planned attack. On Tuesday, she reacted to the report by saying that after two years, the committee had found "nothing, nothing" to contradict an independent Accountability Review Board she commissioned herself while Secretary of State. "I'll leave it to others to characterize the report but I think it's pretty clear it's time to move on," Clinton said at a campaign event in Denver.

Presumptive Republican presidential nominee Donald Trump tweeted his reaction later Tuesday, saying: "Benghazi is just another Hillary Clinton failure. It just never seems to work the way it's supposed to with Clinton. Hillary Clinton's Presidency would be catastrophic for the future of our country. She is ill-fit with bad judgment." The report reveals that Stevens and senior department officials were apparently keen to set up a permanent consulate in Benghazi ahead of a planned visit to the city by Clinton in October 2012. But the difficulty finding a suitable secure facility prompted officials to exclude the Benghazi compound from official department rules and standards that would have otherwise been more stringent.

"If you are in a non-diplomatic facility, there are no security standards. They don't exist," one unnamed diplomatic security agent told the committee. Conservative members of the panel released a more political analysis of the attack Tuesday that's far more critical of Clinton and the Obama administration. That study, authored by GOP Reps. Mike Pompeo of Kansas and Jim Jordan of Ohio, blames the attack on a "tragic failure of leadership."

Their decision to release an addendum to the main report appears to suggest that Pompeo and Jordan believe the committee report does not go far enough in criticizing Clinton and the administration. "The overall report, it's about the facts, what happened," Jordan told Chris Cuomo Tuesday on CNN's "New Day." "But Mr. Pompeo and I thought it was important to ask the questions. Why were we still in Benghazi when almost every other country had left? Why did we stay in Benghazi when the security situation was so terrible, so dangerous? And why did the administration mislead us?"

Democrats preemptively rebutted the findings Monday by releasing their own dissenting report. They accused Gowdy and the committee of flagrant political bias while arguing the investigation wasted taxpayer money to try to damage Clinton ahead of the November election. State Department spokesman Mark Toner said "the official facts surrounding the 2012 attacks in Benghazi have been known for some time." He cited "great progress towards making our posts safer since 2012" and said "our priority continues to be carrying out our national security mission while mitigating the risks to our employees." Rep. Elijah Cummings, the panel's top Democrat, blasted partisanship on the committee.

"Democrats offered to work with Chairman Gowdy on a joint report, and we even offered to give him a draft of our report ahead of time," Cummings said. "Instead, he mocked our idea and decided to go it alone right before the presidential conventions. We can't comment on his partisan report because we haven't read it, and we haven't read it because Republicans didn't want us to check it against the evidence we obtained." White House press secretary Josh Earnest said the report was evidence of the GOP's intent on damaging Clinton.

"There seems to be only one remaining question," Earnest said. "It's simply this. Is the RNC going to disclose the in-kind contribution they received from House Republicans today?" South Carolina Republican Rep. Trey Gowdy, the committee chairman, defended his committee's work, insisting the panel uncovered valuable new evidence that should change how the events in Benghazi are viewed. "The seven of us believed that there were more questions to ask, that there were more answers to acquire, more witnesses to interview, more documents to access," Gowdy said. "And this report validates that belief."

Tuesday's report includes testimony from senior State Department and intelligence officials along with lower-ranking diplomats and diplomatic security agents. It adds color and texture to the public record of the attacks already unveiled by multiple congressional and independent investigations.

It shows that the State Department assessment of the situation in Benghazi in 2011 and 2012 noted rising crime levels, rampant firearm ownership, and a high risk of militia violence in the security vacuum left by the toppling of Libyan dictator Moammar Gaddafi. The precarious security situation, according to the report, was exacerbated by inadequate security at the Benghazi outpost, which was plagued by equipment failures, a lack of manpower and relied on an often-disorganized local militia for protection.

The report says requests for more security in Benghazi repeatedly met no response or were refused by senior officials in Washington, though the parts of the report seen by CNN do not directly lay the fault at Clinton's door. The full details surrounding the attack may never be fully understood, the report says. The panel blames Clinton and the State Department for failing to turn over all emails from her private server—an omission it describes as "shameful."

But Mark Toner, the State Department spokesman, said officials went out of their way to cooperate. 'When combined with the seven previous Congressional inquiries, the Department has participated at least in 15 hearings, 64 briefings, 72 interviews, and has provided 100,000 pages of documents," Toner said, adding that the panel requested huge volumes of information over a long period of years that was not relevant to the Benghazi tragedy.

The report reveals the determination of Stevens to keep the post open in Benghazi—"Chris had, I think a different tolerance of risk than I did," said Joan Polaschik, former U.S. deputy chief of mission in Libya. After the fall of the Gadhaffi regime in 2011, one of Clinton's top State

Department aides, Jake Sullivan, asked a colleague what it would take to get a team back to the Libyan capital of Tripoli to re-open the U.S. embassy.—"An ambassador to Libya who actually wants to go. Locking Pat Kennedy (then Under Secretary for Management) in a closet for long enough to actually take some real risks," the colleage emailed back.

In testimony to the committee, Charlene Lamb, formerly a senior State Department official, said that Stevens was ultimately responsible for security at his post. "It is very unfortunate and sad at this point that Ambassador Stevens was a victim, but that is where ultimate responsibility lies." Throughout late 2011 and through 2012, security became perilous in Benghazi and there were at least two attacks on the compound and on diplomats and other international facilities.

A diplomatic security agent in the city in November 2011 told the committee that security was "woefully inadequate" with no perimeter security, low walls and no lighting. The report said the Benghazi mission made repeated requests for new agents in late 2011 and early 2012. After a series of attacks on international targets in the city, more requests were made. But "no additional resources were provided by Washington D.C. to fortify the compound after the first two attacks. No additional personnel were sent to secure the facility, despite repeated requests for security experts on the ground."

At one point, then-State Department spokeswoman Victoria Nuland emailed Stevens to ask how to publicly describe the security incidents in 2012: "Washington D.C. dismissed Stevens' multiple requests for additional security personnel while also asking for help in messaging the very violence he was seeking security from," the report said. The report, citing a cable from the U.S. embassy in Tripoli, suggests there simply were not sufficient resources in the unstable nation to send to properly protect Benghazi. In early August 2012, there were only 34 security staff at the embassy. By the end of the month there were only six. Such shortages might explain the overreliance on the February 17 local militia in Benghazi to help secure the outpost—but a diplomatic security agent quoted in the report said the group was "undisciplined and unskilled."

In 2011 and early 2012, security sometimes became so difficult in Benghazi that staff were unable to do their jobs reaching out Libyans to report back to Washington on the restive political situation in the city. But the report says that in February 2012, the lead diplomatic security agent at the Tripoli Embassy told the post that "substantive reporting" was not its job anyway. "Unfortunately, nobody has advised the (principal diplomatic officer) that Benghazi is there to support [redacted] operations, not conduct substantive reporting," the agent wrote, in a possible sign that the primary purpose of the mission was in fact to support the CIA.

The report also finds that the military did not carry out then-Defense Secretary Leon Panetta's order to deploy U.S. forces to help rescue Americans under fire in Benghazi. "What was disturbing from the evidence the Committee found was that at the time of the final lethal attack at the Annex, no asset ordered deployed by the Secretary had even left the ground," the report says. The panel also argues that initial administration talking points framing the attack as the result of an angry protest over an anti-Muslim video released in the U.S. were drawn up by administration officials and did not include accounts from eyewitnesses or the Americans under attack.

The report quotes an agent at the Benghazi compound as hearing chanting before a full-on attack begins, including explosions and gunfire and "70 people rushing into the compound with an assortment of "AK-47s, grenades, RPG's ... a couple of different assault rifles." Another security officer described the assault as "a full on attack against our compound." Asked if he had seen a protest before the attacks, the officer said: "zip, nothing, nada."

The U.S. House of Representatives (The Select Committee on Benghazi), Trey Gowdy Republican), Chairman, after more than two (2) years of investigating, including interviewing, released an 800 page Report that ripped the Obama administration's handling of the 2012 terrorist attack that Democratic Presidential Nominee Hillary Clinton and her campaign has consistently slammed the probe as a political vendetta; dismissing the findings as discredited conspiracy theories by

Republicans seeking primarily to damage Mrs. Clinton's character and reputation before the November 2016 election.

The Benghazi Committee's Investigative Report has proven to be an accumulation of partisan data by Republicans to accomplish its chief or primary objective in damaging Mrs. Clinton's character and reputation before the November 2016 election. This report did not name Mrs. Clinton directly for being responsible for the 2012 terrorist attack, but rather, the entire Obama administration, which Mrs. Clinton served in the capacity as Secretary of State. This partisan Republican move was a very desperate attempt to deceive WE THE PEOPLE.

Democrats went out of their way to cooperate with this partisan Republican committee, and in return were mocked and scorned. This Committee conducted 7 Congressional inquiries, and subjected the State Department's participation in some 15 hearings, 64 briefings, 72 interviews, and required provision of some 100,000 pages of documents; even some huge volumes of information over a long period of years that was not even relevant to the Benghazi tragedy.

There's no doubt that the 2012 Benghazi attack took place on the evening of September 11, 2012, when Islamic militants attacked the American diplomatic compound in Benghazi, Libya, killing U.S. Ambassador J. Christopher Stevens and U.S. Foreign Service Information Management Officer Sean Smith; and a second assault several hours later targeting a different compound about a mile away, killing CIA contractors Tyrone S. Woods and Glen Doherty, and injuring ten (1) others <u>were both tragedies occurring under the Obama administration</u>.

The 1983 Beirut barracks bombings were terrorist attacks that occurred on October 23, 1983, in Beirut, Lebanon, during the Lebanese Civil War when two truck bombs struck separate buildings housing United States and French military forces—members of the Multinational Force in Lebanon (MNF)—killing 241 U.S. and 58 French servicemen, six (6) civilians, and the two (2) suicide bombers. An obscure group calling itself 'Islamic Jihad' claimed responsibility for the bombings and that the bombings were aimed to get the MNF out of Lebanon.

Two (2) suicide bombers detonated each of the truck bombs. In the attack on the building serving as a barracks for the 1st Battalion 8th Marines (Battalion Landing Team-BLT 1/8), the death toll were 220 Marines, 18 sailors, and 3 soldiers, making this incident the deadliest single-day death toll for the United States Marine Corps since World War II's Battle of Iwo Jima, the deadliest single-day death toll for the United States Armed Forces since the first day of the Vietnam War's Tet Offensive, the deadliest single terrorist attack on American citizens in general prior to the September 11 attacks, and the deadliest single terrorist attack on American citizens overseas.

Another 128 Americans were wounded in the blast. Thirteen (13) later died of their injuries, and they are numbered among the total number who died. An elderly Lebanese man, a custodian/vendor who was known to work and sleep in his concession stand next to the building, was also killed in the first blast. The explosives used were later estimated to be equivalent to as much as 9,525 kg (21,000 pounds) of TNT. Beirut experienced a second (2nd) attack on September 20, 1984. This time a truck bomb killed 24 people, including two (2) Americans and injured an additional 21. These attacks prompted the United States to take a new perspective regarding the protection of diplomatic premises.

The 1983 and 1984 Beirut terrorist attacks <u>occurred under the Ronald Reagan administration with George P. Shultz serving as Secretary of State.</u> There's no doubt that these Beirut terrorist attacks were even a greater tragedies than the tragedies occurring in Benghazi when death tolls are compared. The Democrats in 1983 and 1984 did not take negative courses of action against the Reagan administration and its Secretary of State George P. Shultz as the Republicans pursued taking in 2012 until this very date.

At the time of the bombing, an obscure group called the "Islamic Jihad" claimed responsibility for the attack. There were many in the U.S. government, such as Vice President Bush, Secretary of State George Shultz, and National Security Adviser Robert McFarlane (who was formerly Reagan's Mideast envoy), who believed Iran and/or Syria were/was responsible for the bombings. After some years of investigation, the U.S. government now believes that elements of what would eventually become Hezbollah, backed by Iran and Syria, were responsible for these bombings as well as the bombing of the U.S. Embassy in Beirut earlier in April.

It is believed that Hezbollah used the name "Islamic Jihad" to remain anonymous. Hezbollah eventually announced its existence in 1985. To date, Hezbollah, Iran and Syria have continued to deny any involvement in any of the bombings; even though, in 2004, the Iranian government erected a monument in Tehran to commemorate the 1983 bombings and its "martyrs."

Two (2) years after the bombing, a U.S. grand jury secretly indicted Imad Mughniyah for his terrorist activities. Mughniyah was never captured, but he was killed by a car bomb in Syria on February 12, 2008. Commentators argue that the lack of a response by the Americans emboldened terrorist organizations to conduct further attacks against U.S. targets. Along with the U.S. embassy bombing, the barracks bombing prompted the Inman Report, a review of the security of U.S. facilities overseas for the U.S. State Department.

The Inman Report, formally known as the Report of the Secretary of State's Advisory Panel on Overseas Security, was a report released in June 1985 in response to the Marine barracks bombing and the April 1983 US Embassy bombing in Beirut, Lebanon. The report is usually known by the name of its Chairman, Admiral Bobby Ray Inman, USN (Ret.)

The report recommended a range of security improvements, including increased setback between embassies and public streets. It also recommended a major building program to improve security in existing embassies, and build new embassies to replace those that could not meet security standards. A direct result from the Report was the creation of the Bureau of Diplomatic Security and the Diplomatic Security Service within the U.S. State Department.

Pursuant to Title III of the Omnibus Diplomatic and Antiterrorism Act of 1986, 22 U.S.C. § 4831 et seq., (the "Act"), Secretary of State

Hillary Rodham Clinton convened an Accountability Review Board (ARB) for Benghazi to examine the facts and circumstances surrounding the September 11-12, 2012, killings of four U.S. government personnel, including the U.S. Ambassador to Libya, John Christopher Stevens, in Benghazi, Libya. As required by law, Clinton convened and appointed the bipartisan Accountability Review Board for Benghazi. Thomas R. Pickering, George H.W. Bush's United Nations ambassador, was chairman. Another board member was Catherine Bertini, who served in the Reagan and Bush administrations.

In a report released December 18, 2012, the independent board said responsibility for the attack rests "solely and completely with the terrorists." However, it also said "systemic failures and leadership and management deficiencies at senior levels within two bureaus of the State Department (the "Department") resulted in a Special Mission security posture that was inadequate for Benghazi and grossly inadequate to deal with the attack that took place." In particular, the report said the "perimeter and interior security" at the temporary diplomatic facility was inadequate and its security equipment was "severely under-resourced."

Partisan Republicans vehemently refused to accept the findings and recommendations of the Accountability Review Board (ARB) for Benghazi and the *U.S. House of Representatives (The Select Committee on Benghazi), Trey Gowdy Republican), Chairman, created its own committee, which the Benghazi Research Center has declared that the Benghazi Committee's Investigation is one of the longest investigations in U.S. history. This Committee was granted an unlimited budget to perform its investigation. There were 10 Congressional committees that participated. There were approximately 252 witnesses called. There were 13 reports published. There were 62 hours spent in publicly available hearings. There were 3, 194 questions asked in public hearings. There were 33 Congressional investigations held. There were 1,192 pages in published reports.*

The number of questions posed by Republican Committee members to Sidney Bulmenthal during his 9 hour disposition was 20 out of more than 550 or about 3.6 %. The number of questions posed by Republican Committee members to Hillary Clinton in a letter to her was 8 out of 136 or about 5.9 %. The number of public hearing held by the Benghazi Committee was 4. The approximately total salary expenditures in 2015 for Select Committee Staff on Benghazi were approximately 3.29 million. The number of witnesses brought in for interviews was 107.

The approximate number of pages of Secretary Clinton's emails provided to the Committee was 900. The approximate number of pages of Secretary Clinton's related to Benghazi and provided to the Committee was 300. The number of pages of documents provided by the State Department and other agencies to the Committee was 100,000 plus. The number of professional staff members who have worked on the Committee was 46.

Former Secretary of State Hillary Clinton, now, Democratic Presidential Nominee Hillary Clinton has followed the rules, taken responsibility, and partisan Republicans continuously refuse to leave it along. In interviews, testimony and in her book, former Secretary Clinton has taken responsibility repeatedly. She was determined to leave the State Department and our country safer, stronger, and more secure, which she worked in doing until the end of her appointment.

Former Secretary of State Hillary Clinton, now, Democratic Presidential Nominee Hillary Clinton has taken required action as appropriate that WE THE PEOPLE might know the truth; but partisan Republicans refuse to leave it along. As previously mentioned, she appointed a non-partisan independent Accountability Review Board to review what happened and began the process of implementing the 29 recommendations put forth by the ARB before leaving the State Department. She took these steps in order to ensure a tragedy like this might never happens again.

She has made every possible effort to be fully transparent; and regardless of her serious efforts, partisan Republicans still refuse to leave it along. She fully and publicly answered questions before Congress; and the report of the Accountability Review Board is just the second (2nd) to be made public, making it one of the most transparent internal reviews in State Department history. The investigations have included ten (10) different congressional committees and over 30 hearings dealing with the tragedy, more than 50 senior level staff briefings, more than 20 transcribed interviews, multiple independent/bipartisan reports and the disclosure of at least 100,000 pages of documents.

Past investigations of the tragedy have cost taxpayers millions of dollars and thousands of man-hours. The newest committee has already cost taxpayers more than $6.8 million to date, at a rate of 8,000 per day, while the committee chairman presents false information to the press. This Committee was created by partisan Republicans not to gather any additional facts, but rather, to destroy Hillary Clinton; all at the expense of the taxpayers.

Trey Gowdy and his Select Committee on Benghazi have received increased scrutiny after the not-so-shocking admissions by Republican Reps. McCarthy and Hanna of its blatantly political motivations. It's often forgotten that Gowdy's committee is the 8th congressional investigation into the tragedy that took the lives of 4 brave Americans. In the course of those previous investigations, all of the questions have been asked and answered, and recommendations were made as to how to prevent another tragedy from happening again. However, preventing another tragedy has never been the focus of Gowdy's committee.

Take a look at the sheer number and size of the investigations thus far, as well as Gowdy's committee's deranged obsession with former Secretary Clinton and her emails, and it's clear that this committee was formed with no other purpose other than to destroy Hillary Clinton.

Number of days (1,335) since the beginning of the ongoing investigations into the tragedy in Benghazi, and there is no end yet in sight. [As of 5/8/16] The minimum total cost to the taxpayers of congressional investigations into Benghaz is $23 million plus.

The State Department has spent more than $14 million responding to congressional investigations into Benghazi. "During yesterday's meeting, the State Department reported that it has now spent more than $14 million responding to the eight congressional investigations of the Benghazi attacks, turning over tens of thousands of pages of documents, and making dozens of witnesses available for scores of hearings, interviews, and briefings." [Benghazi Committee Democrats press release, 10/10/15] **"The Benghazi Committee's investigation has cost more than $7.1 million.** [Benghazi Investigation: The Cost to Taxpayers, accessed 6/27/2016].

The Pentagon said multiple investigations into Benghazi had cost the Department of Defense "millions of dollars ($2 million plus)." "The Pentagon said Tuesday that its work to comply with the six congressional investigations into the September 2012 attack in Benghazi, Libya, has cost the military millions of dollars and thousands of man hours. The Pentagon said in a letter to Rep. Adam Smith (Wash.), the top Democrat on the House Armed services Committee that Defense Department officials have participated in 50 congressional hearings, briefings and interviews about the attack." [The Hill, 3/22/14]

Partisan Republicans have clearly shown that they do not have the best interests of our country and its people at heart; showing clearly a waste and mismanagement of governmental funds in an attempt to accomplish a devious end, rather than, to ensure the safety our marines, sailors, soldiers, civilians, ambassadors, and others at oversea locations. There nothing worse than taking a tragic event as an opportunity to accomplish a selfish objective, rather personally and/or collectively, as Donald Trump and his partisan Republican Party have done.

WE THE PEOPLE owe it to ourselves and all who have paid the ultimate price in sacrificing their lives for our country not to be deceived and led astray from the truth by anyone lying to deceive us in order to accomplish his or her own selfish desires and/or the selfish desires of a particular party. As such, we all have a shared responsibility to ensure our country is safe by ensuring that we all personally utilize our vote to elect the best possible candidate for public office on all levels of government (city, state, and federal); especially, to the oval office for the President of the United States of America.

Hillary Clinton is no doubt the candidate of choice for WE THE

PEOPLE. First Lady Michelle Obama criticized the "hateful language in the presidential campaign from the mouth of Donald Trump; and said the lesion she and President Obama have taught their children is, "When they go low, we go high." Mrs. Obama also praised Mrs. Clinton's "guts" and "grace." As secretary of state, she said, "there were plenty of moments when Hillary could have decided that this world was too hard ... that she was tired of being picked apart for how she looks or how she talks or how she laughs." But, Mrs. Obama added, "she never buckles under pressure, she never takes the easy way out. And Hillary Clinton has never quit on anything in her life."

Mrs. Obama drew a direct line between her husband, the first black president, and Mrs. Clinton, who would be the first woman to hold that position. "I wake up every morning in a house that was built by slaves. And I watch my daughters—two beautiful, intelligent black young women—playing with their dogs on the White House lawn; and because of Hillary Clinton, my daughters and all our sons and daughters now take for granted that a woman can be president of the United States;" she said.

Mrs. Obama is one of a kind just is President Obama; and Hillary Clinton is one of a kind, just is former President Bill Clinton. All who spoke about Mrs. Clinton, including her daughter, Chelsea Clinton Mezinsky spoke wonderfully and their kind and heart-felt words were moving and touching to our souls; mostly because such words graciously spoken referenced a real person worthy of their humble praises unto her; unlike those spoken by Republicans about Donald Trump, whose words falsely referenced not the real Donald Trump.

Donald Trump's history shows he has left a trail of broken-hearted people deceived by his lies and games to produce unjust and wicked prosperity for himself and his family. Trump's legacy has thus far been characterized as a liar and cheat who needs to pay-up, shut-up, and be locked-up, just as Bernard Lawrence "Bernie Madoff, a former stockbroker, investment advisor, and financier convicted of fraud. Madoff was the former non-executive chairman of the NASDAQ stock market, and the admitted operator of a Ponzi scheme that is considered the largest financial fraud in U.S. history. Trump University and NASDAQ stock market appear being similar type schemes constituting the willfully and intentionally rip-off defenseless people.

Hillary Clinton has a marvelous legacy that she continues to build upon. WE THE PEOPLE to be blessed with the opportunity of having her to VOTE FOR as President of the U.S. of America is praiseworthy unto God for providing us with this choice; and indeed, we are thankful and grateful.

23

Trump's Audacity to Question Clinton's Faith

DONALD TRUMP HAS argued that the American public knows very little about Hillary Clinton's religion, raising questions about how her faith will impact her leadership should she become president. Trump said: "We don't know anything about Hillary in terms of religion," speaking to a group of Christian leaders in New York. "Now, she's been in the public eye for years and years, and yet there's no—there's nothing out there. There's like nothing out there. It's going to be an extension of Obama but it's going to be worse, because with Obama you had your guard up. With Hillary you don't, and it's going to be worse."

Trump was addressing a small group of high-profile evangelicals ahead of speaking before a larger group of religious leaders at a gathering hosted by the Christian group, United in Purpose. E.W. Jackson, who tweeted video of Trump's remarks, said the comment came while Trump was trying to say that conservatives tend to get questioned more about their faith than liberals. Jackson told CNN, "I think everybody in there knows Hillary Clinton is a Methodist and by definition a Christian."—"He was saying for those of us who are students of the Christian faith—for evangelicals that can mean everything is thoroughly examined, like what do you believe about marriage? What do you believe about abortion?"

Jackson, who ran as the 2013 Republican nominee for lieutenant governor in Virginia, said he was "accused of believing all kinds of crazy things" when he was a politician. "All (Trump) was saying was she hasn't had that same examination, so we don't really know what she believes," he added. Ken Blackwell, a Family Research Council fellow and Ohio politician, praised Trump's comments about "protecting religious liberty and speech, because I know this administration—and given that the Hillary administration will be a third term of Barack Obama, she would be a third term in her attack on religious liberty in general."

"I have no reason to attack her faith, I just question her ability to defend my right, my family's right, my church's right to practice our faith in the public square," Blackwell said. Marjorie Dannenfelser, the president of the Susan B. Anthony List, said there's been "very little public conversation about (Clinton's) faith."—"I think it would be very helpful to hear what her faith is, what the core of her belief is," she said. (Excerpts from CNN politics June 22, 2016]

Donald Trump faith certainly isn't Christian, as he has clearly shown orally and written. Just how any true Christian follower can support him should be beyond all true Christian followers' comprehension. There's just no way unless racism if factored in that anyone claiming Christianity, within his or her right mind could consciously support Trump without being convicted of his or her unrighteousness.

WE THE PEOPLE believe it's time, past time, for Donald Trump to reveal his tax returns immediately, so that WE THE PEOPLE will have an opportunity to evaluate for ourselves whether or not he's con-man and a thief as many of us believe he is. The Trump University income from students will reflect on those tax returns, as well as all the expenditures related to running TU. If these incomes from TU were obtained in a deceiving and illegal manner, then, Donald Trump is a thief and a liar and should be disavowed or repudiated as the Republican Presidential Nominee 2106.

The Bible teaches us that we should not defraud anyone (illegally obtain money from anyone by deception); yet Donald Trump has the audacity to question Hillary Clinton's faith as to how it would impact her leadership ability. The Bible teaches us that we shouldn't hate, lie, sow discord, have arrogant-pride, be wise in one's own eyes, call people ugly or degrading names and any other thing ungodly; yet Donald Trump has the audacity to question Hillary Clinton's faith as to how it would impact her leadership ability. Hillary Clinton has revealed her tax returns for decades; and it is past time for Donald Trump to do the same if he wishes as the Republican Presidential Nominee to be vote for on November 8, 2016.

CNN Political article entitled "Fareed's Take: Why I called Trump a BS artist" August 5, 2016 states: Fareed Zakaria says he wasn't using the label "bullsh** artist" lightly when he used it to describe Donald Trump. Zakaria, host of GPS on CNN, received both flak and praise earlier in the week when he said Trump continuously tries to clarify his positions with "a tweet or a statement... it's sort of amusing to watch—how's he going to pull it off this time? What is he going to argue? Usually he adds that the press hates him. But there's a term for this kind of thing. This is the mode of a bullsh** artist," Zakaria told Wolf Blitzer.

Zakaria took to his show to explain why he decided to use this term to describe the Republican presidential nominee. "He boasts and boasts and boasts about his business, his buildings, his books, his wives; much of it is a concoction of hyperbole and falsehood. And, when he is found out, he's like that guy we have all met making wild claims at the bar, who when confronted by the truth quickly responds, 'I knew that.'" Zakaria said.

One of the examples Zakaria points to is the "non-relationship" between Donald Trump and Russian President Vladimir Putin. At the National Press Club in May 2014, Trump said he spoke to Putin, who "could not have been nicer." During the Fox Business and Wall Street Journal debate in November 2015, Trump said he got to know Putin "very well." "Did Trump really believe that you can say something like that on live TV and no one would check? Did he think that no one would notice that the '60 Minutes' show consisted of two separate prerecorded interviews with Putin in Moscow, and Trump in New York? By that logic I've gotten to know Franklin Roosevelt very well because I've run some clips of him on my television show. In fact, it was just BS." Zakaria quips.

Another issue that Zakaria brings up is the one that fueled Trump's political rise: President Barack Obama "birtherism" conspiracy theories. In 2011, Trump said that he had sent investigators to Hawaii and "they cannot believe what they're finding." "For weeks, Trump continued to imply that there were huge findings to be released soon.... That was five (5) years, in April 2011. Nothing happened. It appears highly unlikely that Trump sent investigators to Hawaii in the first place," Zakaria says.

"As the crazy talk continues, standard rules of fact, truth, and reality have disappeared in this campaign. Donald Trump has piled such vast quantities of his trademark product into the political arena that the stench is now overwhelming and unbearable," Zakaria says.

The fact is Donald Trump's fake cover has been blown through the words and the works of Donald Trump himself. He has been so wise in his own eyes that he actually believed himself as being someone untouchable that can do anything he wants to do without having to suffer any repercussions ; simply because, he has only himself that he's answerable to; and with that being the case, he's always right and never wrong. Trump has prepared himself for one of the greatest falls in the history of mankind; and he will be able to add this to all the other "I dids" that he has done.

> [1]*My son, if you have put up security for your neighbor, if you have shaken hands in pledge for a stranger, [2] you have been trapped by what you said, ensnared by the words of your mouth. (Prov. 6:1-2) [12] A troublemaker and a villain, who goes about with a corrupt mouth, [13] who winks maliciously with his eye, signals with his feet and motions with his fingers,[14] who plots evil with deceit in his heart—he always stirs up conflict. [15] Therefore disaster will overtake him in an instant; he will suddenly be destroyed—without remedy. (Prov. 6:13-15)*

¹² Therefore, whatever you want men to do to you, do also to them, for this is the Law and the Prophets. (Matt. 7:12) ²⁰ Therefore by their fruits you will know them. (Matt. 7:20) ²³ And then I will declare to them, 'I never knew you; depart from Me, you who practice lawlessness!' (Matt. 7:23)

³⁴For out of the abundance of the heart the mouth speaks. ³⁵ A good man out of the good treasure of his heart brings forth good things, and an evil man out of the evil treasure brings forth evil things. ³⁶ But I say to you that for every idle word men may speak, they will give account of it in the day of judgment. ³⁷ For by your words you will be justified, and by your words you will be condemned." (Matt. 12:34-37)

¹Therefore, since we have this ministry, as we have received mercy, we do not lose heart. ² But we have renounced the hidden things of shame, not walking in craftiness nor handling the word of God deceitfully, but by manifestation of the truth commending ourselves to every man's conscience in the sight of God. (2 Cor. 4:1-2)

24

The Ban on Assault Weapons

ON MAY 19, 1986, the Firearms Owners' Protection Act (FOPA) was signed into law. The first comprehensive redraft of the federal firearm laws since 1968, FOPA was predictably lauded as "necessary to restore fundamental fairness and clarity to our Nation's firearms laws" and damned as an "almost monstrous idea" and a "national disgrace." The controversy was not limited to the rhetorical. Seven years passed between FOPA's introduction and its Senate vote; the House vote required passage of a discharge petition—only the eighth to succeed in the last twenty-six years. The controversy surrounding FOPA's genesis is commensurate to the legal impact of its provisions. FOPA effectively overrules six decisions of the United States Supreme Court, (pg.586) moots what would have become a seventh, and negates perhaps one-third of the total case law construing the Gun Control (pg.587) Act of 1968.

FOPA's impact, however, is not limited to the Gun Control Act, nor even to federal statutes. By expressly exempting interstate transportation of firearms from the reach of many state firearm laws, it affects state proceedings as well. A detailed comprehension of FOPA is thus essential to an understanding of both federal and state firearm laws. (pg.588) Unfortunately, such a comprehension is not easily achieved. FOPA reflects not a simple, single legislative decision, but a complex series of compromises, many of which are only partially reflected in the record. Even where the record is complete, it is rarely clear. The House bill that ultimately became FOPA is supported by a report, but the report explains not why FOPA should have been adopted, but rather, why it ought to have been rejected.

The House bill's predecessor and Senate counterpart, S. 49, was never referred to committee and went instead to the floor with no report whatsoever. S. 49's ancestors were the subject of two reports which, unfortunately, are in hopeless conflict in certain aspects. To add to its original complexity, FOPA was, prior to its effective date, amended by a second enactment which was in turn modified by a concurrent resolution. The need for a comprehensive review of this (pg.589) controversial and convoluted legislation is thus clear. The statute's core can be found in the real consistencies obscured by seeming chaos.

The purpose of this Article is to examine the Firearms Owners' Protection Act in both historic and legal perspectives. Accordingly, the Article first examines the framework of federal firearm legislation as it evolved prior to FOPA. Then, the seven-year evolution of FOPA itself is analyzed. Finally, this Article evaluates the nature of the more significant changes embodied in this controversial enactment.

FOPA's amendment of the Gun Control Act is both deep and wide-ranging. Congress clearly accepted that the alterations would be dramatic. Its deliberations extensively reflect judgments that repudiated either the Gun Control Act in toot or its administration as a traditional regulatory system. FOPA will require greatly increased sensitivity, efficiency and coordination on the part of the administering agency. Delays may run afoul of FOPA's various limitation periods; unjustified administrative inspections may clash with its restrictions on searches; a failure to coordinate with litigation teams may result in criminal adjudications that bar the agency from undertaking forfeiture or revocation; and unfounded actions, civil or criminal, may risk liability for the citizen's attorneys' fees.

Conversely, FOPA confers both substantive and procedural rights upon citizens accused of Gun Control Act violations. Scienter requirements limit application of most of the Act's sanctions to willful violators; a citizen who wins a criminal acquittal need not face civil sanctions based on the same allegation; the length of time seized property may be held without hearing is strictly limited; and the unprecedented availability of attorneys' fees awards ensures that the financial risks of a meritorious defense may well be shifted to the prosecuting agency. FOPA's safeguards are entirely innovative, and largely (pg.682) unique. If they prove able to withstand the passage of time and experience, they may well merit extension to proceedings under other criminal and civil penalty systems.

On April 9, 1986, the battle began on the House floor. When the dust had settled, Rep. Volker's bill had been passed, and Chairman Rodina's defeated. Rodina amendments that would have diluted FOPA's provisions on intent and broadened its definition of who must have a dealer's license were turned back. One anti-gun amendment offered by Rep. William Hughes, D-N.J.—a provision that limited civilian sale of fully automatic firearms to those already existing and in lawful ownership—did pass on a highly questionable voice vote.

The Hughes amendment created a dilemma. Investigation showed there was little chance of rescinding it. This was 1986, not 2011. Many House members were already being attacked as tools of the demonic "gun lobby," and already feared they had stuck their necks out too far. To rouse them on behalf of fully automatic firearms was hopeless. The amendment could not be removed. The choice was to accept the bill as a package, or to kill it as a package. Rep. Volker has described FOPA as the measure that saved gun ownership as we know it. There is much to be said for this appraisal.

In 2011, we seem to be at the beginning of a new stage in the American gun culture. Firearm sales are at record levels, many anti-gun politicians fear to touch the issue and the courts are recognizing the constitutional right of gun ownership. Would we have survived this far if, for the last 25 years, gun dealers had been subject to arrest on paperwork errors and their entire inventories confiscated even if they were found not guilty; and gun shows had regularly seen half a dozen honest collectors hauled away in handcuffs? It's safe to say that the entire picture of gun ownership would be different. 1986 was the last, best shot at getting these protections. To kill the bill, lose seven years of development and alienate the majority of representatives who had rebelled against their leadership by signing the discharge petition would have ended hopes for stopping the many abuses.

In 1986, the gun rights movement really came into its own when it established its power to win on the offensive—even with one house of Congress under anti-gun leadership and the mass media in fervent support. When the fight began with David Moorhead's testimony six years earlier, NRA-ILA and other pro-gun groups were in their infancy. When President Reagan signed the bill into law on May 19, 1986, they had earned their spurs.

Finally, if the collector or dealer won the case, the government would have to pay the owner's attorneys' fees. (The bill's opponents protested, correctly, that gun owners would have protections that no one else had in forfeiture proceedings!)

Confiscations and license revocations despite acquittal: Without FOPA, prosecuting agencies had forfeited collections and revoked licenses despite the gun owner being found not guilty in criminal proceedings. FOPA provided that seized guns must be returned upon their owner's winning acquittal or dismissal of charges, and that license revocations could not be based on such charges, either.

Prohibited possessor" reforms: Under the Gun Control Act, conviction for a felon in possession of a firearm could be obtained even if the possessor had received a pardon, had the conviction set aside or had his civil rights restored. Under FOPA, winning any of these remedies would restore gun rights, unless the order expressly provided to the contrary.

Dealer records: The Gun Control Act allowed unlimited repetitive search of dealers' records and inventory, which had been used as a tool for harassment. FOPA allowed one annual inspection, plus inquiries to trace a specific gun or to carry out a criminal investigation of someone other than the dealer. If records are taken, the dealer must be given a copy so he can continue his business.

Gun shows: The Gun Control Act only allowed licensees to transfer guns at their licensed premises. FOPA allowed dealers to conduct business at events sponsored by groups "devoted to the collection, competitive use, or other sporting use of firearms"—making possible gun shows as we know them today.

Transportation of firearms: Under FOPA, notwithstanding any state or local law, a person is entitled to transport a firearm from any place where he or she may lawfully possess such firearm to any other place where he or she may lawfully possess it, if the firearm is unloaded and locked out of reach.

Politick Virginia In Partnership with Richmond Times-Dispatch presented an article February 4, 2016 entitled "Lopez says Reagan banned machine guns, backed assault weapons band," which states: "Private citizens remain free to buy and transfer machine guns that were registered prior to May 20, 1986—provided they pass a background check, receive signed approval from their local police chief or sheriff and pay a $200 federal tax. There are 512,790 registered machine guns in the United States, according to a 2014 report by the Bureau of Alcohol, Tobacco, Firearms and Explosives. Virginia was home to 31,825 of them, more than any state.

Now, let's move to the assertion that Reagan also backed a ban on assault weapons, which are often described as semi-automatic firearms with detachable magazines and pistol grips. They are capable of firing many rounds without reloading, but the trigger has to be pulled for each shot. Lopez referred us to a May 1994 signed by Reagan and former Presidents Gerald Ford and Jimmy Carter urging members of the U.S. House of Representatives to support a pending bill banning assault weapons. They wrote, "While we recognize that assault weapon legislation will not stop all assault weapon crime, statistics prove that we can dry up the supply of these guns, making them less accessible to criminals. We urge you to listen to the American public and to the law enforcement community and support a ban on the further manufacture of these weapons."

Reagan also sent a personal note that month to one of the fence sitters on ban: Rep. Scott Klug, R-WI. "I know there is heavy pressure on you to go the other way, but I strongly urge you to join me in supporting this bill," he wrote. It must be passed." The measure cleared Congress, with Klug's support, and was signed by then-President. Bill Clinton. The assault weapons ban expired in 2004 when Congress refused to extend it. We should note that since Lopez's speech, the General Assembly has killed a number of gun control bills, including by Lopez that would legislation have restricted the sale and ownership of high-capacity firearm magazines. [End of this portion of article]

Common sense would resolve as President Ragan in 1986 of machine guns (i.e. automatic guns that fires bullets in rapid succession for as long as the trigger is pressed), he also supported the assaults weapons' ban. The 1986 law barred the private sale and ownership of machine guns that were not already registered on the day Regan signed the bill. Therefore, there was no need of gun manufactures to manufacture machine guns because it was illegal to purchase and own them. This measure prohibited, but did not necessarily stop machine guns from entering the private market; those already existing in the private market were legal. [My analogy]

Regan did, in 1994 after his presidency, sign a letter along with former Presidents Gerald Ford and Jimmy Carter urging the House of Representatives to pass an "assault weapons ban." By definition "an assault weapon is a semi-automatic firearm with a detachable magazine and a pistol grip, and sometimes other features such as a flash suppressor or barrel shroud."

An assault rifle uses small caliber rifle ammunition in a select fire weapon system. Calibers such as 5.56mm NATO, and 7.62x39 are common assault rifle calibers. Semi-automatic and full-auto (select fire) are requirements of an assault rifle. They typically incorporate a detachable box magazine. No weapons systems, labeled as such by the government are in fact assault rifles, because they do not have select fire capability. An M4 carbine, firing a 5.56 mm round is an example of an assault rifle.

A submachine gun uses pistol caliber ammunition in a select fire capability (or full auto only), often keeping the entire weapons package very small with a short barrel, and collapsible stock. An UZI firing a 9mm pistol cartridge is an example of a submachinegun.

Another class of weapons that many people leave out are battle rifles. Battle rifles fire full size rifle cartridges such as the 7.62 NATO, or 30-06 Rifle Cartridges. They may or may not be select fire, and they may or may not have detachable magazines. An M14 is a battle rifle, as is the M1A SOCOM II, both fire 7.62mm NATO.

The DRS Precision DRS 50 Sniper Rifle is the most dangerous rifle of the world and has 7.62x51mm and 660 mm NATO caliber. The Thompson M1921 Submachine Gun is the 2nd most dangerous rifle of the world. This is very effective and amazing gun that is utilized by a good number of officials, soldiers, cops, agencies etc. regularly. It is even utilized by many criminals all over the world just as of its astonishing shoot rounds as well as an accurate target.

The Uzi Submachine Gun is the 3rd most dangerous rifle of the world. This Gun was planned in Israel by Uzi Gal. this gun is measured as the small but useful package for the expert shooters. It is very easy to use as well as successfully hit the object so the army officials and individuals use to have this for their safety. The XM307 ACSW Advanced Heavy Machine Gun is the 4th most dangerous rifle of the world. This Gun was planned by the American army that is activated by two people. It shoots approximately 260 rounds in a single minute with preciseness and accuracy.

The MG3 Machine Gun is the 5th most dangerous rifle of the world. This gun was lengthily utilized in the 2nd World War because of its unbelievable speed. The F-2000 Assault Rifle is the 6th most dangerous rifle of the world. Produced by FN Herschel the Belgium Company, this damaging weapon was initiated for the initial time in the Abu Dhabi in the year 2001. This deadly weapon has NATO caliber of 5.56x45m that makes this very powerful. The Thompson M192 Machine Gun is the 7th most dangerous rifle of the world. It has the skill to shoot six hundred rounds in just a minute that is very amazing; this excellence put this gun into the group of semi machine. It is best for security reasons.

The Ban on Assault Weapons

The Heckler and Koch HK416 Assault Rifle is the 8th most dangerous rifle of the world. This is the greatest rifle planned by the famous Heckler and Koch. It is even measured as the updated edition of American M4. The Heckler Koch HK MG4 MG43 Machine Gun is the 9th most dangerous rifle of the world. The Kalashnikov AK-47 is the 10th most dangerous rifle of the world. This powerful gun is important to compare to other guns from several decades; it was initially planned by the USSR for the current warfare. It has the skill to shoot 580 rounds in just a minute and because of this feature, it is still utilized by several security agencies at the present time.

Not any one of these most dangerous weapons or anyone of their kind or similarity has any place on the private market for purchase considering the serious and deadly harm they present to society as a whole. It's just common sense that these types of weapons should be banned; gun rights and profits from gun sales are way less important than loos of human lives. This issue should have nothing at all to do with politics; it's a moral and ethical issue of health and safety. However, GREED and RACISM entered as a factors reflect the moral decay of our nation. [End of My analogy]

Alfonso Lopez, a Democrat, as served in the House of Delegates since 2012, representing portions of Arlington and Fairfax Counties. He received a B.A. degree from Vassar College in 1992 and a J.D. from the Tulane University School of Law in 1995. Lopez served as Gov. Tim Caine's director of the Virginia Liaison Office in Washington, where he directed congressional and federal relations for Virginia. He also served as Caine's representative to the National Governors Association, the Democratic Governors Association and the Southern Governors Association.

An article in the Washington Post entitled House Democrats are staging a very rare sit-in to protest guns, June 22, 2016 states: "As the House of Representatives was about to take a break for the afternoon on Wednesday, Democrats did something that has only been done twice before since the 1970s: seize the floor to demand a vote, specifically on gun control measures. "Sometimes you have to do something out of the ordinary," said Rep. John Lewis (D-Ga.), a civil-rights icon, who led his own sit-ins at segregated lunch counters in Tennessee decades ago. "Sometimes you have to make a way out of no way."

Right now, anyone on the FBI's various terrorist watch lists can legally buy a gun. Senate Republicans and Democrats both agree that suspected terrorists shouldn't be able to do that, but they're split on whether to let the attorney general ban people from buying guns before or after the courts have a chance to weigh in.

To state the obvious, what fails in the Senate is almost certainly doomed in the House. The composition of the House is much more conservative than the Senate: Republicans have their largest majority since World War II in the lower chamber, while Senate Republicans have only a slight majority. And sit-ins have happened before to little effect. According to Matt Green, a political scientist at Catholic University who's written a book about House minority party tactics, Democrats have even been on the receiving end of the sit-in.

In 1995, House Democrats spent a few hours on the floor in protest of a budget that House Republicans passed. In 2008, House Republicans seized the floor in August for the entire recess to demand Democrats let them vote on oil drilling to lower $4-a-gallon gas prices. They ended up getting a vote, but more because Democrats feared the sit-in would endanger Barack Obama's presidential campaign.

This time around, House Democrats' hopes of turning their sit-in into any kind of legislative victory would seem to rest on the sliver of compromise introduced Tuesday by Sen Susan Collins (R-Maine). Collins wants to let the attorney general stop people on two of the FBI's most serious terrorist watch lists from being able to buy guns. That amounts to about 2,700 Americans.

Like we said, it's a narrow window of compromise. And like any good compromise, there are some Republicans who support it, and some Democrats who support it. But no one's really enthusiastic about it. A lack of enthusiasm is exactly what House Democrats are up against, and exactly why they're staging this sit-in. If a majority of Congress isn't particularly gung-ho about the one piece of legislation that could actually pass the Senate, House Republicans have absolutely no incentive to bring it up for a vote. Why would Speaker Paul Ryan risk taking a politically divisive vote on guns when he's not getting pressure from his party to take it? He's got enough problems to deal with.

Indeed, Ryan indicated as much when he told reporters Wednesday he probably wouldn't bring this compromise up for a vote unless it did really, really well in the Senate. And as The Post's Karun Emirian reports, we don't know if the Collins compromise can even pass the Senate, let alone fly through it. So we're back to where we started. No big breakthrough in the gun debate after Orlando. No enthusiasm for the one compromise on gun control in Congress. And no real viable political path to passing any gun control measures in this Congress—sit-in or not.

Our nation is in its most critical and final stages of destruction before the Rapture and the Second Coming of Christ. Our people, politicians and leaders "are more politically driven than God driven," and as a result, "we will suffer the impending consequences of our character as a nation."

WE THE PEOPLE have prioritized party affiliation and other things as a premium above God and what he requires of us. We as a people have listen to unholy cries with loud voices and demands, and given in to their cries and demands, which are against the will of God. We as a people have placed God out of everything possible to satisfy ungodly cries and demands, so that their ungodly cries and demands are not infringed upon (violated or broken), while allowing our own godly rights infringed upon. We as a people have allowed ungodly cultural demands to become acceptable ways of live, knowing such behavior practices are abominable to the LORD.

Popular demand, regardless of its ungodliness, motivates and drives the minds of those in positions of power and authority against what's in the best interests of the people as a whole, knowing that ungodliness is unprofitable; but insisting on tempting God nevertheless. WE THE PEOPLE, must humble ourselves and pray, and seek God's face, and turn from our wicked ways; then and then only, will God hear from heaven, forgive us our sins, and heal our land (nation). (2 Chron. 7:14)

The United States suffered the worst mass shooting in its modern history when 50 people were killed and 53 injured in Orlando, Fla., after a gunman stormed into a packed gay nightclub. Yet, there are those who proclaim that the 1986 Machine Gun Ban, or otherwise known as Hughes Amendment, was incorporated at the very last minute into the FOPA as a poison bill to basically screw over gun owners. Such persons feel disgusted and profoundly frustrated living without the right to purchase and have machine guns, and being limited to what they can and cannot do by the ATF and the federal government, in particularly, "not being able to possess a machine gun manufactured after May 19, 1986."

Those arguing this matter state that this ban is a most blatant infringement on their Second Amendment rights, and they're waited too long, while the prices have climbed sky high, that ordinary citizens cannot afford to own a full size automatic weapon; in that, such weapons are simply out of reach of common folk, which is where the word "unavailability" becomes synonymous to the word "illegal." NRA's Wayne LA Pierre stated that the entire organization would have the repealing of this ban on its top priorities of things to do to have this law proven unconstitutional once and for all.

Any law abiding citizen who wishes to use a machine gun for lawful purposes should not be denied liberal access to these weapons by the federal government. In other countries, they take the machine guns away, then they come after the semi-automatics, and pretty soon, everyone's down to single shotguns. Many of the gun grabbers have been weakened, and it is now necessary to go even further when they're even more vulnerable. Therefore, as argued, it's time for the NRA and the armed citizens of the USA to prove a point, by getting out there and getting our rights back and keeping them.

The Federal Assault Weapons Ban (AWB)—officially, the Public Safety and Recreational Firearms Use Protection Act—is a subsection of the Violent Crime Control and Law Enforcement Act of 1994, a United States federal law that included a prohibition on the manufacture for civilian use of certain semi-automatic firearms it defined as assault weapons, as well as certain ammunition magazines it defined as "large capacity"

The ten (10)-year ban was passed by the U.S. Congress on September 13, 1994, following a close 52-48 vote in the Senate, and signed into law by then President Bill Clinton the same day. The ban only applied to weapons manufactured after the date of the ban's enactment, and it expired on September 13, 2004, in accordance with its sunset provision. In public policy, a sunset provision or clause is a measure within a statue, regulation, or other law that provides that the law shall cease to have effect after a specific date, unless further legislative action is taken to extend the law. Most laws do not have sunset clauses and therefore remain in force indefinitely, except under systems in which desuetude applies. Several constitutional challenges were filed against provisions of the ban, but all were rejected by reviewing courts. There were multiple attempts to renew the ban, but none succeeded.

Since the September 13, 2004 expiration on the ban, the following tragedies have happened in the USA that might have been avoided if legislative action had been taken on September 13, 2004 to extend the law on the ban.

Blacksburg, VA, 2007, 32 killed and 17 injured; Fort Hood, TX, 2009, 13 killed, 32 injured; Binghamton, NY, 2009, 13 killed, 4 injured; Aurora, CO, 2012, 12 killed, 58 injured; Newtown, CN, 2012, 27 killed, 1 injured; San Bernardino, CA, 2015, 14 killed, 21 injured, and Orlando, FL, 2016, 50 killed, 53 injured. Prior to the extended ban in 1994, San Sedro, CA, 1984, 14 killed, 6 injured; Edmond OK, 1986, 14 killed, 6 injured; Killeen, TX, 1991, 22 killed, 20 injured. These are the ten (10) most-deadest mass shootings in U.S. history. Do we or do we not need "a ban on machine guns and other assault weapons" to help ensure the safety and welfare of our people; looking at this from a common sense perspective.

The United States Senate defied the will of a large majority of Americans by failing to pass common-sense gun reforms in the wake of the deadliest mass shooting in American history. The chamber voted on four (4) pieces of gun-related legislation, two (2) of which would have strengthened gun laws and saved lives. The first, an amendment introduced by Senator Dianne Feinstein (D-CA), would have allowed the U.S. Attorney General to prohibit those suspected of terrorist activity from purchasing firearms, while allowing for due process. The second, by Senator Chris Murphy (D-CT)—who led an emotional 15-hour filibuster on calling for the votes—would have required universal background checks on all gun sales, while exempting gifts between immediate family members. Unfortunately, the Feinstein and Murphy amendments were defeated by votes of 53 to 47 and 56 to 44, respectively. All four (4) proposals needed 60 votes to advance.

According to national polls, both reforms are widely supported by the American people. A CNN/ORC poll release found that 92% of American voters support "a background check on anyone attempting to purchase a gun," with only 8% opposing. The same poll found that 85% of American voters supported "preventing people on the U.S. Government's Terrorist Watch list or no-fly list from owning guns," with only 14% in opposition.

Two (2) substitute amendments introduced by Republicans were also voted down, one by Senator John Corny (R-TX) and the other by Senator Chuck Grassley (R-IA). Both would have weakened federal gun laws, as opposed to strengthening them. "We will not be deterred by this Congress's continued fealty to the National Rifle Association," said Coalition to Stop Gun Violence Virginia State Director Lori Haas. "The 'Terror Gap' and universal background check reforms are incredibly popular reforms and there is a growing national movement coalescing around them. We will push these bills, and others, during the remaining days of this Congress and demand new votes until the House and Senate do their jobs."

"Eventually, the senators who voted against the Feinstein and Murphy amendments—or for the weak substitute amendments offered by Republicans—are going to have to answer to their constituents for their inaction," stated CSGV Executive Director Josh Horwitz. "Americans are sick and tired of watching this Congress sit on their hands and do nothing, tragedy after tragedy. It is clear—we must change this Congress in November—in order to save lives and preserve our most basic freedoms." The Coalition to Stop Gun Violence seeks to secure freedom from gun violence through research, strategic engagement and effective policy advocacy.

It's a shame and a disgrace, but very obvious, that there're U.S. Republican Senators who value selfish desires of the NRA and its members over and above injuries and deaths of the American people caused primarily by guns in the hands of those that should not have them in the first place. Additionally, there are guns manufactured for warfare that civilians have no business at all in their possession. These are weapons of war and should be restricted for that purpose and that purpose only. Certain Types of guns just shouldn't be available to civilians.

Murphy, one of the most persistent gun control advocates in Congress since the 2012 massacre at Sandy Hook Elementary School, said he felt that the mood of some Republican lawmakers is changing. "Clearly, there are a lot of Republicans who are trying to get better on this issue, and I think in a sincere way. I don't mean that in a snarky way," Murphy said. "I think the electorate is changing."

25

Trump's Idiocy is Endless

DONALD TRUMP HAS continuously shown that he is extremely stupid or foolish through his idiotic actions or statements. The volume of his idiocy continues to reach level highs than any other presidential nominee in U.S. History. His idiotic or stupid comments continue to cause ruin to himself and to the Republican Party which he has took hostage and converted into the Trump Party. Everyone who supports him will pay the cost for tens of years to come. Trump is not by any means a person to be identified and/or associated with if you're a politician seeking a successful political career.

> [9] If a wise man contends with a foolish man, whether the fool rages or laughs, there is no peace. [10] The bloodthirsty hate the blameless, But the upright seek his well-being. [11] A fool vents all his feelings, but a wise man holds them back. [12] If a ruler pays attention to lies, all his servants become wicked. (Prov. 29:9-12)

> [16] When the wicked are multiplied, transgression increases; But the righteous will see their fall. (Prov. 29:16) [20] Do you see a man hasty in his words? There is more hope for a fool than for him. (Prov. 29:20) [22] an angry man stirs up strife, and a furious

> man abounds in transgression. ²³ A man's pride will bring him low, but the humble in spirit will retain honor. ²⁴ Whoever is a partner with a thief hates his own life; He swears to tell the truth, but reveals nothing. (Prov. 29:22-24)

> ²⁵ But Jesus knew their thoughts, and said to them: "Every kingdom divided against itself is brought to desolation, and every city or house divided against itself will not stand. ²⁶ If Satan casts out Satan, he is divided against himself. How then will his kingdom stand? ²⁷ And if I cast out demons by Beelzebub, by whom do your sons cast them out? Therefore they shall be your judges. ²⁸ But if I cast out demons by the Spirit of God, surely the kingdom of God has come upon you. ²⁹ Or how can one enter a strong man's house and plunder his goods, unless he first binds the strong man? And then he will plunder his house. ³⁰ He who is not with me is against me, and he who does not gather with me scatters abroad. (Matt. 12:25-30)

Donald Trump causes strife and contentions and creates confusion that has divided his own Republican Party as well as the American people. He has no problem at all with division as long as it helps him in accomplishing his own selfish objectives. He is a habitual liar and everyone who attempts to explain his idiotic comments are just as much a lair and the Republican Presidential Nominee they are defending and supporting. Those who are defending his idiotic comments look and sound just as idiotic as Trump does. Idiocy or foolishness can never be explained in a manner of acceptance to sensible and reasonable people, which most Americans are a part. Such foolishness only appeals to a very limited population with warped or distorted minds.

> ³ In the mouth of a fool is a rod of pride, but the lips of the wise will preserve them. (Prov. 14:3) ⁵ A faithful witness does not lie, but a false witness will utter lies. ⁶ A scoffer seeks wisdom

and does not find it, but knowledge is easy to him who understands. ⁷ Go from the presence of a foolish man, when you do not perceive in him the lips of knowledge. ⁸ The wisdom of the prudent is to understand his way, but the folly of fools is deceit. (Prov. 14:5-8)

Everyone who partners with Trump after all that's been clearly revealed about him has no excuse and will suffer the consequences of their partnership. It's one thing being wrong every now and then, than being wrong consistently, and at that, un-apologetically and proudly showing un-remorsefulness. There's absolutely no excuse for backing and supporting Donald Trump nor anyone supporting Trump's unacceptable behavior practices; absolutely no excuse; none at all. His behavior practices are abominations to mankind and unto God; absolutely no excuse; none at all.

¹⁸ "If the world hates you, you know that it hated me before it hated you. ¹⁹ If you were of the world, the world would love its own. Yet because you are not of the world, but I chose you out of the world, therefore the world hates you. ²⁰ Remember the word that I said to you, 'A servant is not greater than his master.' If they persecuted me, they will also persecute you. If they kept my word, they will keep yours also. ²¹ But all these things they will do to you for my name's sake, because they do not know Him who sent me. (Jn. 15:18-21)

²² If I had not come and spoken to them, they would have no sin, but now they have no excuse for their sin. ²³ He who hates me hates My Father also. ²⁴ If I had not done among them the works which no one else did, they would have no sin; but now they have seen and also hated both me and My Father. ²⁵ But this happened that the word might be fulfilled which is written in their law, 'They hated me without a cause.' (Jn. 15:22-25)

Trump is a hater because that's his true nature; and his true nature is exactly what's being manifested which the Republican Party has unsuccessfully been unable to get him to decrease his xenophobic (fear of people from other countries) expressions.

Trump is a psychopath appearing normal, even charming to those he deceives. Underneath, he lacks conscience and empathy, making him manipulative, volatile and often (but by no means always) criminal. Trump appears to be living his life with a clarity and moral courage that many find exhilarating. He boasts intellectually and appears physically adventurous. However, he has a very troubling pattern of leaving people broken-hearted and financially exhausted while bragging about the wealth he has accumulated.

Trump is an opportunist (i.e. one who takes advantage of any opportunity to achieve an end, often with no regard for principles or consequences. He controls or plays upon others by artful, unfair, or insidious means to his own advantages. He's a parasite that takes something from someone or someone else and does not do anything to earn or deserve it. He seeks to exhaust other people resources from them just because he can without caring what financial troubles they might experience afterwards. He has absolutely no empathy for others at all.

Tech guru John McAfee spent a lot of time bragging about hoaxes he'd pulled off, gleefully styling himself as a "BS" artist. Sometimes McAfee just lied for fun, like when he told a reporter that his tattoo was a Maori design he'd gotten in New Zealand, a country he's never actually been to. Sometimes he lied strategically, like the Facebook posting he put up about how he'd just bought a house in Honduras. At the time, McAfee was facing a raft of lawsuits. McAfee said: "The judge in one case couldn't understand why I would put incorrect information about myself on the web; I said, I thought that if somebody wanted to serve me papers, it would be more enjoyable for everyone involved if they tried to serve those papers to me in Honduras."

After an unflattering article was written about McAfee, a number of people from McAfee's past reached out and provided even more troubling stories. It became apparent that McAfee was not merely a disingenuous person but a true psychopath. Schouten says that we shouldn't be surprised to find psychopaths among the ranks of successful entrepreneurs like McAfee. Indeed, he emphasizes that psychopathic traits can be positively helpful. Schouten states: "psychopathy could confer a competitive advantage, at least over the short term; grandiosity and over-the-top confidence, as well as skill at conning and manipulating can go a long way toward convincing investors of one's vision."

Trump throws anything that comes on his mind out to the media because he knows it's going to get attention and that attention will be directly upon him; and he loves it with a passion; because he get to embellish the subject matter he created with more interesting or entertaining by adding extra details, especially ones that are not true. This is exactly why today there are a number of Trump supporters time and time again speaking a damage control mode attempting to clarify and explain exactly what Trump meant when he said what he said. It's just totally insane and ridiculous that just about everything Trump says has to be clarified as to what he actually meant.

We would think that anyone who has been selected as the Republican Presidential Nominee should be able to speak clearly and precisely upon issues of concern without having to have interpreters to explain what he actually meant as if he was speaking some foreign language incomprehensible to the American people. The fact is, Trump is not speaking some foreign language incomprehensible to the American people, but speaking exactly what he feels and desires saying that ruining his chance of becoming President elect and the Republican Party as a whole. He's not only taking himself down; he's taking the entire Republican Party down with him.

Donald Trump threatened to stop raising money for Republicans after party leaders were urged to give up on his presidential campaign and focus on preserving their majorities in the House and Senate. More than 70 Republicans asked Republican National Committee Chairman Reince Priebus in a letter to stop giving money to Trump's candidacy.

Trump responded by saying that if the party gives up on him, he would stop raising money for the party.

"If it is true, that's OK too," Trump said on Fox News' "The O'Reilly Factor." "... All I have to do is stop funding the Republican Party." In July, the Trump campaign reported an $80-million haul, with $64 million coming from joint efforts with the RNC. As of Aug. 3, the campaign reported $37 million on hand and another $37 million in the hands of the joint fundraising committees. "I'm raising a lot of money for the Republican Party," Trump said, adding that the people who signed the letter are not those he wants supporting him anyway. The letter, first reported by Politico, included signatures from former Rep. Chris Shays (R-Conn.), former Sen. Gordon Humphrey (R-N.H.) and former Rep. Tom Coleman (R-Mo.) as well as from several former RNC staffers.

The letter's signatories include a handful of Republicans who have already pronounced themselves as never backing Mr. Trump—and some, like former Connecticut Rep. Chris Shays, who have endorsed Democratic nominee Hillary Clinton. "Every dollar spent by the RNC on Donald Trump's campaign is a dollar of donor money wasted on the losing effort of a candidate who has actively undermined the GOP at every turn," the letter reads. "Rather than throwing good money after bad, the RNC should shift its strategy and its resources to convince voters not to give Hillary Clinton the 'blank check' of a Democrat-controlled Congress to advance her big government agenda."

The vast majority of signatories to the letter are former Republican staffers, including 15 who worked for the RNC. Others signing include Bruce Bartlett, who was an economic policy adviser to President George W. Bush, Rory Cooper, who was communications director for then-House Majority Leader Eric Cantor, and Sharon Castillo, who worked for the 2004 Bush-Cheney campaign and the RNC. "Signing an appeal such as this is not easy for any of us," the letter reads. "But in our view, Trump's divisive and dangerous actions are not only a threat to our other candidates, but to our Party and the nation.

Only swift and decisive action can save the Republican Party and protect the hundreds of other GOP candidates running for office.

We urge the RNC to immediately halt all support for Donald Trump and invest its resources in a real and winnable campaign to save the Republican Senate and House." The letter, which is being organized by former Newt Gingrich aide Andrew Weinstein, comes as the RNC is handling an unprecedented amount of campaign operations typically handled by the party's presidential nominee.

Donald Trump's mouth cannot cease from pouring out foolishness. His tongue is a huge river filled with darkened and clouded water unsuitable for living creatures. Everything coming off his tongue creates controversy that has no real or true value to humanity; on the other hand, what comes from his tongue clearly reveals his soul and who he really is as a human being; from this perspective or viewpoint, the foolishness coming from his mouth has valuable meaning to all who are willing to use it as a tool in determining who he is as a human being and his fitness to be president of our country.

Just recently at a rally in Wilmington, NC, he set off a fierce new controversy with remarks about the right to bear arms that was interpreted by many as a threat of violence against Democratic Presidential Nominee Hillary Clinton. Trump said: "Hillary wants to abolish—essentially abolish the Second Amendment. By the way, if she gets to pick, if she gets to pick her judges, nothing you can do, folks. Although the Second (2nd) Amendment people, maybe there is, I don't know. But I tell you what, that will be a horrible day, if Hillary gets to put her judges in, right now we're tired."

Trump's ambiguous comments alarmed some political observers as to whether he was threatening her life or calling for increased political activity. Robby Mooch, Clinton's campaign manager, issued a two-sentence statement in response to Trump. Mooch said: "This is simple—what Trump is saying is dangerous. A person seeking to be the president of the United States should not suggest violence in any way."

The former head of the CIA, retired Gen. Michael Hayden, told CNN's Jake Tapper: "If someone else had said that said outside the hall, he'd be in the back of a police wagon now with the Secret Service questioning him. You're not just responsible for what you say. You are responsible for what people hear. That was more than a speed bump. That is actually a very arresting comment. It suggests either a very bad taste with reference to political assassination and an attempt at humor or an incredible insensitivity—it maybe the latter—an incredible insensitivity to the prevalence of political assassination inside of American history. That is a topic that we don't ever come close to even when we think we are trying to be lighthearted."

Trump defended his comments, insisting that he was telling his supporters to use the power of their vote to stop Clinton from appointing justices who could restrict their Second Amendment rights. Trump said to Fox News' Sean Hannity: "This is a political movement. This is a strong political movement, the Second Amendment, and there can be no other interpretation. Even reporters have told me. I mean, give me a break."

However, we must carefully observe the time which Trump was referring; which was a time after Clinton would have been elected President and appointing Supreme Court judges (meaning Election Day would have come and been long gone). There's no other way than through the process of deductive argument for this matter to be concluded. When we carefully examine or scrutinize whether the conclusions of CIA, retired Gen. Michael Hayden and Robby Mooch, Clinton's campaign manager indeed necessarily follow from the premises of what Trump actually said, rather than, what he and others insisted he said, since the premises are true or acceptable, the conclusion must also be true and acceptable.

The logical relationship between the premises and the conclusions is 100% supporting, which invalidates other arguments, such as from Trump and Jason Miller, Trump's senior communications adviser who said: "It's called the power of unification—2nd Amendment people have amazing spirit and are tremendously unified, which gives them great political power. And this year, they will be voting in record numbers, and it won't be for Hillary Clinton, it will be for Donald Trump."

Miller was suggesting that Trump was merely talking about Second

Amendment supporters large influence as a group, which is not worthy of any credence whatsoever; but can clearly been seen as just another attempt to clean-up the garbage coming from Trump's mouth.

US Secret Service communications director Cathy Mollohan told CNN the agency "is aware of Mr. Trump's comments." Sen. Chris Murphy, D-Connecticut, who supports increased gun control measures, tweeted: "Don't treat this as a political misstep. It's an assassination threat, seriously upping the possibility of a national tragedy & crisis."

Trump's running mate, Indiana Gov. Mike Pence, told WCAU TV in Philadelphia that "Donald Trump was very clear. Hillary Clinton has made it very clear that she wants to see changes in the right of law-abiding citizens to keep and bear arms. What Donald Trump is clearly saying is that people who cherish that right, who believe that firearms in the hands of law-abiding citizens makes our communities more-safe, not less safe, should be involved in the political process and let their voice be heard."

Former New York City mayor Rudy Giuliani, campaigning with Trump in Fayetteville, North Carolina, slammed the media and the Clinton campaign. Giuliani said: "They spin out that what he meant by that was that it was a joke; and that what he meant by that was that they would kill her," Giuliani said as the crowd dropped to a deafening silence, before erupting in boos. "Now, OK, to buy that you have to be corrupt because if you sent that to me I would say to you are you out of your mind? I saw it, I heard it, and I know what it meant." Giuliani insisted Trump told voters "you have the power to do something about it," meaning that his supporters "have the power to vote against" and "campaign against" Clinton. Even Giuliani's response to this issue sounds ridiculous and confusing, as he struggled extremely hard to look and sound sensibly, but unsuccessfully.

Clinton surrogate Christine Quinn, a former New York City Council speaker, said on New Day: "To think that joking about any kind of violence could be funny ... simply reflects a disregard for the impact of violence. To think that joking about any kind of violence could be funny ... simply reflects a disregard for the impact of violence." Former

Michigan Gov. Jennifer Granholm agreed, telling Cuomo that joking about assassinating a candidate is not presidential. "It is, in fact, dangerous for the country," she said. Bernice King, the daughter of civil rights leader Martin Luther King Jr., took to twitter to voice her concerns. "As the daughter of a leader who was assassinated, I find #Trump's comments distasteful, disturbing, dangerous," she tweeted.

And former CBS Evening News anchor Dan Rather posted on Facebook that Trump "crossed a line with dangerous potential. By any objective analysis, this is a new low and unprecedented in the history of American presidential politics. This is no longer about policy, civility, decency or even temperament. This is a direct threat of violence against a political rival. It is not just against the norms of American politics, it raises a serious question of whether it is against the law."

Green Party candidate Jill Stein also weighed in, calling for Trump to be disarmed. Dr. Jill Stein @Brillstein "Gun violence is no laughing matter, we need a President who understands it's not funny to call on people to shoot opponents. Disarm Trump." And the daughter of Sandy Hook School Principal Dawn Hoch sprung, who died in the school shooting there along with 20 children and five (5) other staffers, sent a message to Trump via Twitter. Erica L. Smegielski @EricaSmegs @realDonaldTrump "you think gun violence is a joke? Would love to tell you about Mom's life and gruesome MURDER."

A US Secret Service official confirms to CNN that the USSS has spoken to the Trump campaign regarding his Second Amendment comments. "There has been more than one conversation" on the topic, the official told CNN. But it's unclear at what level in the campaign structure the conversations occurred. The campaign told the USSS that Donald Trump did not intend to incite violence, according to the official. "No such meeting or conversation ever happened," Trump tweeted in response to CNN's report.

Just recently also at a rally in Florida, he set off another fierce new controversy with remarks about President Obama being the founder of ISIS and Democratic Presidential Nominee Hillary Clinton being the co-founder of ISIS. Donald Trump said that he meant exactly what he said when he called President Barack Obama the "founder of ISIS" and objected when a conservative radio show host tried to clarify the GOP nominee's position.

Trump was asked by host Hugh Hewitt about the comments Trump made in Florida, and Hewitt said he understood Trump to mean "that he (Obama) created the vacuum, he lost the peace." Trump objected and said: "I meant he's the founder of ISIS, I do. He was the most valuable player. I give him the most valuable player award. I give her, too, by the way, Hillary Clinton." Hewitt pushed back again, saying that Obama is "not sympathetic' to ISIS and "hates" and is "trying to kill them." Trump then said: "I don't care, according to a show transcript he was the founder. His, the way he got out of Iraq was that that was the founding of ISIS, okay?"

Hewitt and Trump went back and forth after that, with Hewitt warning Trump that his critics would seize on his use of "founder" as more example of Trump being loose with words. Clinton later hit back on Twitter, saying it was Trump who was unfit to be president. Clinton tweeted: "It can be difficult to muster outrage as frequently as Donald Trump should cause it, but his smear against President Obama requires it. No, Barack Obama is not the founder of ISIS. ... Anyone willing to sink so low, so often should never be allowed to serve as our Commander-in-Chief."

Sen. Susan Collins of Maine, one of the most senior Republicans to oppose Trump, said her decision came down to Trump making the world a "more dangerous" place, in her estimation. While Trump remains around 40% in national polling, Obama's approval rating was at 54% after the Democratic convention, according to CNN polling. But Trump remained steadfast, saying it was "no mistake" what he said, standing by his labeling of the Democratic opponent as a "co-founder of ISIS." Trump asked Hewitt: "Do you not like that?" Hewitt said: "I think I would say they created, they lost the peace. They created the Libyan vacuum, they created the vacuum into which ISIS came, but they didn't create ISIS. That's what I would say." Trump replied: "well, I disagree."

Trump's Idiocy is Endless

Donald Trump, although being under near-constant scrutiny for his discussions of sensitive world events, with his opponents using favorable comments he has made toward Vladimir Putin and other dictators as evidence of his misplaced priorities has chosen not to back off what he says, not to apologize for what he says, not to have any empathy towards anyone he might have offended, and to continuously be accusatory towards Barrack Obama, Hillary Clinton, and anyone else he chooses without any valid or concrete evidence of his allegations.

Trump's mouth has proven again and again to be a river of water contaminated with poisonous rhetoric and propaganda unprofitable for humankind. He has proven being a habitual liar tending to attract attention of a select population, mainly racist, because of his exuberance, selfish confidence, and stylishness. He has absolutely nothing, absolutely zero, to offer America as a whole in terms of political, economic, judicial, educational, spiritual, peaceful, and caring advancement. He all about himself and a very, very, select few that continue supporting and defending him regardless of what he does or what lines he cross with his inappropriate and insensitive behavior practices. There's absolutely no doubt; some are with him all the way!!!

RNC Chairman Reince Priebus turned-up and spoke-out at the Donald Trump rally in Erie, Pennsylvania. When Reince started talking about Hillary Clinton's many lies the crowd started shouting, "Lock her up!" Reince responded that Trump will defeat her instead! This came right after The Politico reported that 70 GOP turncoats signed a letter to tell Reince to stop funding Trump. It also came after Trump had made his most recent most foolish comments about the 2nd Amendment and ISIS. Yet RNC Chairman Reince Priebus remains with Trump all the way, in spite of Trump's historically unacceptable behavior practices that have profoundly turned-off most sensible and reasonable people regardless of party affiliation.

RNC Chairman Reince Priebus made a surprise appearance at the Trump rally in Pennsylvania, pushing back against reports about a rift in the GOP and enthusiastically backing Trump. Preibus said: "Don't believe the garbage you read; let me tell you something, Donald Trump, the Republican Party, all of you—we're going to put him in the White House and save this country together." Although his appearance and words ignited excitement and enthusiasm amongst GOP based Republicans, Priebus himself was not truthful to Trump supporters, because the GOP is divided and in a mess. He most likely came and said what he said hoping it would not become more divided with long-time GOP faithful's getting off board who are displeased with Trump.

Priebus whipped or stirred-up the massive crowd by touting the integrity of Trump and his running mate Pence, which he said was the major difference with Democratic Presidential Nominee Hillary Clinton. He said: "Here's the difference. Donald Trump and Mike Pence will tell the truth. They'll protect your Second Amendment rights; they'll protect the southern boarder; they'll protect the sovereignty of the United States—our great country." As we can see here, Priebus did not offer any apologies for Trump's foolishness; as a matter of fact, Priebus shows support for Trump will enables him to continue the same foolishness he'd been showing throughout his campaign.

Those Republicans who have chosen to get off-board this wrecked ship; have wisely chosen not to sink on this severely damaged ship with Trump as its captain. RNC Chairman Reince Priebus, House Speaker Paul Ryan, and Senate Majority Leader Mitch McConnell had the opportunities and should have disavowed or repudiated Trump actually before he became the Republican Presidential 2016 Nominee. To make matters worse, after Trump became the GOP 2016 Nominee, there were many occasions when they could have disavowed or repudiated Trump and allowed its party to have a more credible and respectable candidate for its party members to support and vote for in this November 2016 presidential election. However, this they failed to do; and this will place a dark cloud on their party for years and years to come.

There are good people in every party and all good people should not be deprived of good leadership within their respective parties to make decisions in critical times of what's best for its party respectfully. The Republican leadership has failed grossly in providing leadership for its members at a most critical time; a failure done willfully and intentionally with arrogance and malice. Acting as such, Republican leadership has not acted in the best interest of our country and should be remembered for such conduct of gross negligence and voted out of the senate and house as our consciences are guided to the rightness or wrongness of one's behavior practices.

All who fear the Lord have knowledge and wisdom and know that the knowledge of the Holy One is understanding (Prov. 1:7; 9:10); and in all our getting we're to get understanding (Prov. 4:7). The Lord gives wisdom; From His mouth come knowledge and understanding (Prov. 2:6). Know this: God says exactly what He means and means exactly what He says.

> [10] *"For as the rain comes down, and the snow from heaven, And do not return there, But water the earth, And make it bring forth and bud, That it may give seed to the sower And bread to the eater,* [11] *So shall My word be that goes forth from My mouth; It shall not return to Me void, But it shall accomplish what I please, And it shall prosper in the thing for which I sent it. (Isa. 55:10-11)*

> [21] *Though they join forces, the wicked will not go unpunished; But the posterity of the righteous will be delivered (Prov. 11:21)* [5] *Everyone proud in heart is an abomination to the* LORD; *Though they join forces, none will go unpunished. (Prov. 16:5)* [8] *Better is a little with righteousness, Than vast revenues without justice. (Prov. 16:8)* [18] *Pride goes before destruction, And a haughty spirit before a fall. (Prov. 16:18)* [6] *But He gives more grace. Therefore He says: "God resists the proud, But gives grace to the humble." (Ja. 4:6)*

> *⁷ Do not be deceived, God is not mocked; for whatever a man sows, that he will also reap. ⁸ For he who sows to his flesh will of the flesh reap corruption, but he who sows to the Spirit will of the Spirit reap everlasting life. ⁹ And let us not grow weary while doing good, for in due season we shall reap if we do not lose heart. ¹⁰ Therefore, as we have opportunity, let us do good to all, especially to those who are of the household of faith. (Gal. 6:7-10)*

When God's word says it will not return to Him void, but shall accomplish what He pleases, and shall prosper in the thing He sent it to do, He means exactly what He says. When His word says it will punish, or He resists, or He gives, or whatever a man sows that he will also reap, He means exactly what He says. When He says pride is before destruction, and a haughty spirit before a fall, He means exactly what He says, and we can count on it happening just as He has said it would. He did not tell us that better is a little with righteousness than vast revenues without justice or unrighteousness without a cause; He means exactly what He says and it's wise if we take heed to all He has said that it might be well with us as we live out this life on earth.

Those who do not fear the Lord have no respect for His word as seen in many people, which we interact with on a daily basis either directly and/or indirectly. Nevertheless, God's word is of no less effect; whatever He has said applies to those who does not acknowledge Him as Creator and Lord as well; we're all under His sovereign control and our lives and every breathe we take are subject to His mercy and grace. Those who are wise in their own eyes and/or hasty in their words provide for themselves enmity between themselves and God which is not wise. Let us separate ourselves as necessary from Trump and others like him that do not love and hold the people whom God loves in their best interest; they are worthless and unprofitable.

Finally, but surely not the end of Trump's idiocy, wherein, his foolishness continues to escalate to unprecedented highs that confirms without question that he indeed is the "most unfit presidential nominee ever;" Donald Trump held a rally in Altoona, Pa., during which he told the audience that the only way Hillary Clinton could win the state was if "in certain sections of the state they cheat."

The "certain sections of the state" to which Trump is referring is almost certainly are a reference to a long-standing conspiracy theory involving the results in Philadelphia in 2012, where, in some places Mitt Romney got zero votes. Trump ally Sean Hannity raised it during a dispute with CNN's Brian Stelter. Seann Hannity @seanhannity: Calling us unpatriotic? 59 districts not one Romney vote. So you are voting for the liar HRC. Did DNC hurt Bernie? This matter raised by Sean Hannity had been previously and adequately addressed by the Philadelphia Inquirer.

The Philadelphia Inquirer wrote about the absence of Romney votes after the election, but included a key phrase: "The unanimous support for [President] Obama in these Philadelphia neighborhoods—clustered in almost exclusively black sections of West and North Philadelphia—fertilizes fears of fraud, despite little hard evidence." Little hard evidence—and the voting was clustered in areas with a high percentage of black voters. Obama won 93% of the black vote in 2012.

Sean Hannity's twit was also replied to by Ryan Godfrey@ rgodfrey: "I'm an inspector of elections for a Philly voting division. Independent but was a Republican as recently as June. Claim that 59 divisions in Philadelphia engaged in electoral fraud in 2012 because no votes for Romney is absurd & personally insulting. First, there's absolutely no way to erase votes from the machines we use in this city. ... Next, we get a paper tally at the end of the night that we match against physical count of voters who used machines (like an odometer). We match that against the count of the individual names of voters who have signed our rolls (and whose names we also recorded in books). ... So, # of votes corresponds with # of voters, & can't be tampered with after fact, but what about having machines change R votes to D? ... Why would they ever change *ALL* R votes to D votes, when anybody who voted R could easily refute the results just by saying they had?

Godfrey continues—but that last point is key, and he reiterates it: Let's move to the bigger picture. In July 2012, the state stipulated that there had been no in-person voter fraud in the state. There have been instances of other types of fraud, as Godfrey notes, including an incident in which election workers in Philadelphia tampered with voting machines to add six votes. There have also been many instances in which voter rolls in different counties had two people that appeared to be identical, like Mr. Cheeseboro; but few instances in which both of those people have cast ballots and raised concerns.

Usually, such dual ballots "melt down to one or two if any at all," a researcher from MIT told the Pittsburgh Tribune-Review. Why, in part because they are usually data errors or people with similar names. But also because there are a lot of protections, as Godfrey outlines. (Those protections, in fact, made it hard for Trump to vote in 2004). What's above is a tally of *rare incidents*. In 2012, 5.5 million presidential ballots were cast in Pennsylvania. There's no evidence that thousands of fraudulent votes were cast—or hundreds, or dozen, or even a handful.

Perhaps more importantly, Trump is also *already* losing Pennsylvania. The RealClearPolitics polling average in the state shows Clinton with a lead of more than nine (9) points. This, of course, doesn't include Trump's alleged, unproven voter fraud. It's an average of a number of polls in the state. (Trump has claimed that polls underrepresent his support; there's no evidence of that).

Trump is convinced that he will win Pennsylvania; it seems, because of the support he sees in the state. Fair enough. But thousands of people at a rally doesn't compare to millions of voters. Why is Trump likely to lose Pennsylvania? Half the state thinks Obama is doing a good job. Thirteen percent (13%) of the electorate in 2012 was black; 93% of those voters supported Obama. In a new NBC/Marist poll, Clinton gets 94% of the black vote. Clinton and Trump are tied among white voters, thanks to Clinton winning women by 25 points. Obama won them in 2012 by 13.

What's more disconcerting than Trump's baseless assertion that Clinton can only win by cheating is his suggestion that his supporters—and law enforcement—police the polls. Even the Inquirer, which raised the question in 2012, notes that voter ID laws wouldn't somehow erase votes for Romney. What Trump is encouraging is vigilante citizens harassing voters at polling places, asking that they prove they are who they say they are. He's asking for intimidation, explicitly: Challenge suspect voters. This is a recipe for tension, if not violence—and the lack of voter fraud incidents reveals that there's no purpose to it.

Political campaigns often have staffers at polling places track who has voted for turnout efforts. Trump, ironically, has no real get-out-the-vote effort, which could help him police this imaginary threat. So he suggests he will turn to untrained supporters. American politics succeeds because the transfer of power is gracious. Trump's comments once again seem to anticipate that his response to what increasingly looks like it will be a loss will not fall into that category. [End of Article]

Why then would Republican presidential nominee Donald Trump tell supporters at a campaign rally in Columbus, Ohio, August 1, 2016 that he worries the November 8, 2016 Election is going to be rigged; simple because he's stupid and takes idiocy to an all new high. The most annoying thing about Trump is that he, being the Republican 2016 presidential nominee has forced the American people to devote much of their time to a man who is a liar and fundamentally a bore; especially, once sound people come to the understanding he's a habitual liar and trouble-maker who talks endlessly about himself and his accomplishments; a true bore.

Occasionally Trump tries to impersonate being a devote churchgoer, or an antiabortion activist, or an NRA believer, but usually botches the role because he has prepared; and the reason he hasn't prepared is because he's not really interested in what anyone else believes—not gun enthusiasts (NRA members), not Christians, not antiabortion activists, or anyone else; he only has one interest, and that's his own, an extreme self-regard that makes him totally unfit to be president.

The true trademark of the insufferable bore is the conviction that he is doing us a great favor by spending time with us. He brings this to his campaign every day—his conviction that he doing the entire country a great favor by taking time out of his life to serve as our president is an enormous sacrifice. As a matter of fact, he says: "I could be having a very nice life right now." And if he loses, he says: "that's ok too; I'm going to have a very, very, nice long vacation." However, Trump's very, very, nice long vacation could very well not be very, very, nice at all; his Trump University lawsuits could land him in a very, very, bad place; prison!

Not the Republican base, but rather, the majority of Americans is convinced that Trump is a raging fool and dangerously unstable that no sensible and God fearing American would want as President of the United States of America; even many inside the Republican base have come to this very conclusion.

Among the conservative talking points that refuse to die is the idea that there is widespread voter fraud in America. The most recent warning about the scourge of illegal voting came from Texas Gov. Greg Abbott, who recently claimed "the fact is voter fraud is rampant." That's simply not true, as many new outlets reported. According to Politifact, there were just 85 prosecutions for voter fraud in Texas from 2002 to 2015, and not all of them led to convictions. That's a paltry number considering that more than 42 million ballots were cast in the state's general elections from 2002 to 2014.

The reality is that voter fraud—which includes a range of offenses from impersonating another voter to casting more than one vote—is extraordinarily rare. And the tsunami of voter ID laws, address requirements, and sloppy purges of voter rolls has made it much harder for Americans—particularly minorities and poor voters—to cast their ballots. The scoop straight from Mother Jones of some selections from reporting on the voter fraud myth and the impact of ant-voter-fraud laws is as follows:

- The rate of fraud in US elections is close to zero.
- UFO sightings are more common than voter fraud.
- So is getting struck by lightning.
- Florida's aggressive efforts to root out voter fraud before the

2000 election erroneously purged 12,000 names from the voter rolls—of the 12,000, 44 percent, more than 4,700 voters—were African American. That was more than enough votes to change the outcome of that year's presidential election.
- Native Americans are fighting a slew of high-stakes legal battles over voting rights; many of the lawsuits are linked to rules that were designed to prevent voting fraud.
- Voter ID laws are among a host of hurdles that minorities face when they cast a ballot.
- A national voter ID card could end the debate on voter fraud, but both parties hate that idea.
- GOP presidential contender Ted Cruz's Iowa chairman spent $250,000 to stop people from voting.
- Interestingly, a conservative activist inadvertently demonstrated how hard it is to commit voter fraud.

In the state of Texas as reflected above during a 14 years period with more than 42 million ballots cast, there were just 85 persecutions of voter fraud. Those who are able to perform simple math calculation know that if we take 42 million ballots and divide that by 14 years it would equate to an estimated average 3 million ballots per year cast. And if we were to apply the same math and divide 85 persecutions by 14 years it would equate to and estimated average of 6 voter fraud cases per year. As we can clearly see, our election process system across our country is secure, and equipped to pick-up and to have those persecute those who commit voter fraud. As Mother Jones has said, the rate of fraud in US elections is close to zero.

Voter ID laws are becoming increasingly common across the country. Today, 30 states require voters to present identification to vote in federal, state and local elections, although some laws passed during the 2011 legislative session have not yet gone into effect. In 15 of those states, voters must present a photo ID—that in many states must be government-issued—in order to cast a ballot.

Many Americans do not have the necessary identification that these laws require, and face barriers to voting as a result. Research shows, for example, that more than 21 million Americans do not have government-issued photo identification; a disproportionate number of these Americans are low-income, racial and ethnic minorities, and elderly.

Voter ID laws have the potential to deny the right to vote to thousands of registered voters who do not have, and, in many instances, cannot obtain the limited identification states accept for voting. Many of these Americans cannot afford to pay for the required documents needed to secure a government-issued photo ID. As such, these laws impede access to the polls and are at odds with the fundamental right to vote.

The Republican Voter ID legislation is not premised on the ground for ensuring valid voting in the election process, but rather, premised on the ground for disenfranchising blacks and other people of color of their right to vote. This Voter ID law is a wolf in sheep's clothing that appears to be doing something for the good, but inwardly, it's devious and immoral; nothing but an evil and underhanded practice to deprive blacks and other people of color of their right to vote, which WE THE PEOPLE should not allow to happen; and we should hold each and every person supporting such a devious enactment accountable. Voter fraud is not an easy thing to pull off and the possibility of it happening in next to zero; such a law is disrespectful and ungodly.

CBS's Sopan Deb transcribed Trump's comments as follows: "We're gonna watch Pennsylvania. Go down to certain areas and watch and study and make sure other people don't come in and vote five times. ... The only way we can lose, in my opinion—and I really mean this, Pennsylvania—is if cheating goes on. I really believe it. Because I looked at Erie and it was the same thing as this. ...

[L]et me just tell you, I looked over Pennsylvania. And I'm studying it. And we have some great people here. Some great leaders here of the Republican Party, and they're very concerned about that. And that's the way we can lose the state. And we have to call up law enforcement. And we have to have the sheriffs and the police chiefs and everybody watching. Because if we get cheated out of this election, if we get cheated out of a win in Pennsylvania, which is such a vital state, especially when I know what's happening here, folks. I know. She can't beat what's happening here.

The only way they can beat it in my opinion—and I mean this 100 percent—if in certain sections of the state they cheat, OK? So I hope you people can sort of not just vote on the 8th, go around and look and watch other polling places and make sure that it's 100 percent fine, because without voter identification—which is shocking, shocking that you don't have it." [End of Transcript]

Pennsylvania is a keystone state that has participated in all 57 presidential elections through 2012. This state is generally considered a battleground state, although, it should be noted that it has voted Democratic in the last six (6) elections or last 24 years. In 2012, Barack Obama won over Mitt Romney by about five percent (5%). This is the state in which our U.S. Constitution was written and was the second (2nd) state admitted to the union, officially becoming a state in December 1787.

While still an important prize, with 20 electoral votes, Pennsylvania, like many industrial northern states, has seen population migrate away in recent decades. Peaking at 38 electoral votes in the 1910s and 1920s (second (2nd) only to New York), the state has lost 45% of its electoral clout in 80 years. These 20 electoral votes are vitally important, especially, to the Republican Presidential Nominee Donald Trump.

However, how is that he expects to win in a state where Republicans haven't won in 24 years, and then have the audacity to publically state before the world: "Because if we get cheated out of this election, if we get cheated out of a win in Pennsylvania, which is such a vital state, especially when I know what's happening here, folks. I know. She can't beat what's happening here. The only way they can beat it in my opinion—and I mean this 100 percent—if in certain sections of the state they cheat, OK? So I hope you people can sort of not just vote on the 8th, go around and look and watch other polling places and make sure that it's 100 percent fine, because without voter identification—which is shocking, shocking that you don't have it."

Trump does not realize and is too stupid to understand that a lot of people do not like him like most racists love him; in fact, he's hated by many, simply because, he's not a likeable person to most Americans. Trump's mouth has ruin him as well as the Republican Party as a whole; however, the Republican Party as a whole has ruin itself by not disavowing or repudiating Trump and transferring its support to a more credible and fit person. For this, they have themselves to blame, in particularly, its leaders who gave up the party to come on board with Trump.

Now in a serious attempt to save the face of the party, rather than disavowing or repudiating Trump, which would have been the right and appropriate thing to do, Republican leadership choose to support and defend Trump; and in doing so, take the party down as Trump goes down; truly selfish and unpatriotic, showing no love for the country, but rather, only manifesting selfish-ambitions like the man it supports.

It's much, much, too late for Trump and the Republican Party. Maybe, just maybe, Trump and the Republican Party will seize this time as an opportunity to examine and test themselves, especially, those claiming to be of the household of faith, to see if in fact, if Jesus Christ are in them; unless indeed, they are disqualified. Nevertheless, godly sorrow leads to repentance which provides opportunity for one or some to change their ways of life to the way required of them by God.

> [12] *Sow for yourselves righteousness; Reap in mercy; Break up your fallow ground, For it is time to seek the* LORD, *Till He comes and rains righteousness on you.* [13] *You have plowed wickedness; You have reaped iniquity. You have eaten the fruit of lies, Because you trusted in your own way, In the multitude of your mighty men. (Hosea 10:12-13)*

> [6] *But we are all like an unclean thing, And all our righteousnesses are like filthy rags; We all fade as a leaf, And our iniquities, like the wind, Have taken us away.* [7] *And there is no one who*

calls on Your name, Who stirs himself up to take hold of You; For You have hidden Your face from us, And have consumed us because of our iniquities. (Isa. 64:6-7) **¹⁸** *If I regard iniquity in my heart, The Lord will not hear. (Psa. 66:18)*

⁷ *But if we walk in the light as He is in the light, we have fellowship with one another, and the blood of Jesus Christ His Son cleanses us from all sin.* **⁸** *If we say that we have no sin, we deceive ourselves, and the truth is not in us.* **⁹** *If we confess our sins, He is faithful and just to forgive us our sins and to cleanse us from all unrighteousness.* **¹⁰** *If we say that we have not sinned, we make Him a liar, and His word is not in us. (1 Jn. 1:7-10)*

¹⁶ *But now you boast in your arrogance. All such boasting is evil.* **¹⁷** *Therefore, to him who knows to do good and does not do it, to him it is sin. (Ja. 4:16-17)*

Author's Closing Comments

I've worked continuously, very hard, and with a very serious sense of urgency to get this book completed and available to the general public prior to this November 8, 2016 election day. I thank God for His grace, knowledge, wisdom, and understanding He has provided in my efforts to accomplish this task for the benefit of His human creation (the saved and the unsaved). It's only through His grace and mercy are we all able to have opportunities granted unto us daily to make our lives, as well as the lives of others better through His only begotten Son Jesus Christ.

We're all under God's control, whether all acknowledge that or not. The very air we breathe and every breath we take from one faction of a second to the next is under His control. It is a very wise thing to grasp an understanding in all things, in particular, the hands of the One in whom our very existence lies. It's His will that none of us perish, however, it's entirely left up to every person to make it his or her own personal will that he or she doesn't perish because of failing to accept God's gift of salvation by grace through faith alone in Jesus Christ. There's no greater joy than knowing you have eternal security from the wrath of God to come forever and ever.

However, while we continue living in this world that continues getting worse and worse, we will continue having the responsibility to make important choices or decisions that affect us directly and/or indirectly. Therefore it's good to have knowledge on situations or circumstances we're involved directly and/or indirectly so that we might make the best choices or decisions possible. Quality and reliable information from reliable sources are of great value and this is exactly where I'm providing this work through this book as guidance to helping make a good choices or decisions, not only during this November 2016 election, but beyond for many voting elections to come on the city, state, and federal levels.

The vote is a very powerful tool, and like anything else, when used or applied in the wrong manner, our vote can cause unnecessary sorrows and pains. Remember, a no vote is a vote for what you are in need; and also a no vote does not give honor to the freedom fighter, civil rights activists, and other who shed their blood and lost their lives so that we might have the right to vote and make a difference in matters or issues affecting us directly and/or indirectly. God has informed us through His word that His people are destroyed for lack of knowledge. It's up to all of us within our God-given abilities or gifts to share our knowledge, wisdom, and understanding with one another for each other's profit.

I sincerely pray that each of you grow and develop unto spiritual maturity, having not only your best interests at heart, but also the best interests of others. Always know and remember that God is able to do exceedingly abundantly above all we can ever ask and think; and that His eyes go to and fro throughout the earth to show Himself strong on behalf of all whose heart is loyal to Him. Stay focus on God and His Son Jesus Christ and they will through the Holy Spirit guide you in all truth and tell you things to come, just as He has promised. Seeking firstly the kingdom and God and His righteousness is the key for having all our needs supplied or provided unto us. The Bible says: *[19] And my God shall supply all your need according to His riches in glory by Christ Jesus. [20] Now to our God and Father be glory forever and ever. Amen.* (Phil. 4:19-20)

www.ingramcontent.com/pod-product-compliance
Lightning Source LLC
Chambersburg PA
CBHW020730160426
43192CB00006B/169